Virginia M. Williams
1931

# BY ARTHUR TRAIN

PURITAN'S PROGRESS

## NOVELS

PAPER PROFITS
ILLUSION
AMBITION
HIGH WINDS
THE BLIND GODDESS
THE NEEDLE'S EYE
HIS CHILDREN'S CHILDREN
THE GOLDFISH
THE EARTHQUAKE
THE WORLD AND THOMAS KELLY
THE CONFESSIONS OF ARTEMAS QUIBBLE
"C. Q."—IN THE WIRELESS HOUSE
THE BUTLER'S STORY

## STORIES

THE LOST GOSPEL
AS IT WAS IN THE BEGINNING
TRUE STORIES OF CRIME
McALLISTER AND HIS DOUBLE
MORTMAIN
THE HORNS OF RAMADAN

## ABOUT MR. TUTT

THE ADVENTURES OF EPHRAIM TUTT
WHEN TUTT MEETS TUTT
PAGE MR. TUTT
TUT, TUT! MR. TUTT
TUTT AND MR. TUTT
BY ADVICE OF COUNSEL
THE HERMIT OF TURKEY HOLLOW

## ABOUT LAW AND LAWYERS

THE PRISONER AT THE BAR
ON THE TRAIL OF THE BAD MEN
COURTS, CRIMINALS, AND THE CAMORRA

# PURITAN'S PROGRESS

# Puritan's Progress

## AN INFORMAL ACCOUNT:

Of certain *PURITANS* & their descendants from the *AMERICAN REVOLUTION* to the present time, their manners & customs, their virtues & vices.

### TOGETHER,

With some possibly forgotten episodes in the development of *AMERICAN* social & economic life during the last one hundred & fifty years.

## By
## Arthur Train

"Say not thou, What is the cause that the former days were better than these? For thou dost not inquire wisely concerning this."
—ECCL. 7: 10.

New York · Charles Scribner's Sons
1931

TO

<small>MY SON</small>

JOHN TRAIN

<small>BORN 1928</small>

# Acknowledgment

FOR most of my data and many of my citations I am indebted to the works of others, whom I have freely quoted or, on occasion, paraphrased. To have acknowledged the source in each instance would have necessitated distracting the eye of the reader and destroying the symmetry of the pages by crowding them with footnotes, in which the same names would have appeared over and over again, and, since I make no pretense that this is anything more than a compilation so far as its historical aspect is concerned, I have decided to omit footnotes altogether and make instead a general acknowledgment of my obligations, once and for all, here at the beginning.

The books to which I am chiefly indebted are:

"The Stammering Century," by Gilbert Seldes.
"The Sabbath in Puritan New England" and "School Days in Old New England," by Alice Morse Earle.
"The Old Farmer and His Almanach," by George Lyman Kittridge.
"History of the United States from the Compromise of 1850," by John Ford Rhodes.
"History of the People of the United States," by John Bach McMaster.
"History of the United States of America under the Constitution," by James Schouler.
"History of the United States," by Edward Channing.
"The Expansion of New England," by Lois Kimball Mathews.
"The Diary of Philip Hone," edited by Bayard Tuckerman.
"Puritanism a Literary Force," by H. L. Mencken.
"Our Times," by Mark Sullivan.
"Valentines Manual" (1920–1929), edited and largely written by Henry Collins Brown.
"Prosperity—Fact or Myth," by Stuart Chase.

Other works from which citations and a certain amount of data have been taken are:

"Social and Industrial Conditions in the North During the Civil War," by David Emerson Fite.

"The Adams Family" and "Our Business Civilization," by James Truslow Adams.

"Not Quite Puritans," by Henry W. Lawrence.

"Puritan Nomenclature," by C. W. Bardsley.

"Quakers and Puritans," by Henry Seidel Canby.

"Social History of the American Family," by Arthur W. Calhoun.

"American Social History as Recorded by British Travellers," edited by Allan Nevins.

"Stelligeri; and other Essays Concerning America," by Barrett Wendell.

"Puritan Principles and American Ideals," by Henry Hallam Saunderson.

"Romantic Days in the Early Republic," by Mary Caroline Crawford.

"Middletown," by Robert S. and Helen Merrell Lynd.

"Forty Years of American Life," by Dr. T. L. Nichols.

"The Fabulous Forties," by Meade Minnigerode.

"Commodore Vanderbilt," by A. D. H. Smith.

"Adventurous America," by Edwin Mims.

"Anthony Comstock, Roundsman of the Lord," by Margaret Leech and Heywood Broun.

"Puritanism and Prosperity," by Reinhold Niebuhr.

"Our Standards of Living Viewed as Going Higher," by W. F. Ogburn.

"Queen Victoria," by Lytton Strachey.

"History of Massachusetts," by William Barry.

"History of Framingham," by J. H. Temple.

"History of Weston," by Daniel S. Lamson.

"The Cheney Genealogy," by Charles Henry Pope.

Authors directly quoted are credited in the text.

                    A. T.

# Contents

# PURITAN'S PROGRESS

# PURITAN'S PROGRESS

## CHAPTER I

## An Author in Search of a Grandfather

### (New York—1930)

THE searchlight raking the sky caught the wing-tip of the night mail for Chicago droning west 3,000 feet over our heads; thirty stories below us darted schools of black shining minnows released by the traffic towers' automatic signals; a powdery haze of parti-colored light dimmed that of the moon looking down upon the proud, preposterous, incredible city with its blazing caldrons of tinted fire; while high over all the white beam wavered anxiously up and down, slanting hither and yon, searching the stars—for what?

"Amazing!" remarked my friend.

"Magnificent—and terrifying!" I replied.

We turned from the penthouse balcony and stepped inside his apartment. He paused by a sideboard.

"Scotch?"

I nodded.

"Who would have thought when I used to kick you around at school that you'd ever be making three hundred thousand dollars a year!" I said, looking at the prints and tapestries which covered the walls.

"That's not so much! There are two hundred and eighty-three men in the United States with an annual income of over a million. By the way"—he stepped to a screen—"the Great Northern has just opened its new tunnel through the Cascade Range. There's a nation-wide hook-up—Schumann-Heink is going to sing 'The Star-Spangled Banner' from San Francisco after the train goes through, and Hoover's going to make the dedication speech from Washington. We might listen in." He snapped on the radio.

Distinct, as if from just beside us, came the voice of the announcer.

"There she comes, folks! You can hear her whistle. First train through the tunnel. James J. Hill's dream of a lifetime realized!—There she blows again! She's coming on fast now. I'll swing aboard as she flies by, and talk to you from Scenic, at the other end. So long, then for a few minutes!"

From our hanging garden in the modern Babylon we listened to the great train in the bowels of the mountain 3,000 miles away shrieking nearer and nearer until it thundered past the microphone.

"Hoover won't begin his spiel for another twenty minutes. Let's try Havana," said my friend. "There's a band concert down there in the Piazza."

Instantly from over the moonlit waves of the Caribbean came to us the tantalizing syncopations of the tarantella.

"I'll try Washington now!"

"Er—er—" rasped an oracular voice—not that of the President. "Beyond question the world has made greater progress in the last seventy-five years than during the entire span of human life before the Civil War. Think of it, folks— the telephone, the automobile, the radio, the submarine, the aeroplane! The North Pole and the Antarctic both conquered. Comfort and luxury in every home. Imagine how surprised one of the old Puritans would be if he——"

My friend shut him off abruptly.

"That's enough of that!"

"Hold on!" I protested. "I'd have liked to hear what that chap was going to say. I'm not sure, when you come right down to it, whether all these things are so conclusive as to progress."

He regarded me humorously.

"Did you read how the New York *Times* the other evening radioed 13,000 miles to Byrd in the Antarctic, to ask him to radio 13,000 miles back to Astoria, only three miles away, in order to ask their operator to hang up his receiver so they could speak to him—and got him in two minutes?— 'Byrd says you want to talk to me'!—Or, for that matter, just look out the window!"

"I don't want to look out of the window! That fellow down in the Department of Commerce, or wherever he was, started to ask if one of the Puritans happened to turn up on Broadway what he'd think of it. That's easy. It would knock him flat! What I'd like to know is whether he'd find he got any more out of life now than he did a century ago. Maybe you didn't know it, but I'm a Puritan myself."

"You look it!" He glanced at the glass in my hand.

"I am—by inheritance, at least," I retorted with a sudden resolve. "I've an idea. To-morrow's Sunday. I'll motor up to Massachusetts and give the old town my people came from the once-over. I haven't been there since I was a kid. It'll be a pleasant run. I'd just like to see. Want to come?"

He shook his head.

"No, thanks. Motoring bores me. I'd rather sit here and listen in on a good prize fight," he admitted frankly.

That is how the Puritan came to revisit the home of his ancestors the following afternoon. More especially he was looking for his grandfather's meeting-house,—the white, wooden, "Wrenn" meeting-house with narrow green blinds and tall thin spire, set in the grove of maples, where his grandfather had preached more than a century ago. He had seen the old church once before, when he was a little boy, on a visit to Framingham with his father in 1881, and the impression made upon his childish mind by its serenity and grace had never faded.

There had been other churches in his life,—the massive

stone Doric temple, with its high-backed pews and sour-smelling green cushions, on Tremont Street in Boston which he had attended as a child, the baroque Romanesque structure of fireproof brick and porphyry on Madison Avenue in New York City in which he had been married, and divers other rococo ecclesiastical edifices in the various localities where his children had been baptized. Yet, save for the Cathedrals of Chartres and Rheims, no temple built by human hands had ever so touched his spiritual emotions as the simple neo-classic country meeting-house from whose pulpit his grandfather had preached, and to which, according to veridical tradition, Phillips Brooks had made an annual pilgrimage throughout his lifetime to refresh his soul with the sight of its pure beauty.

Our Puritan was on a not dissimilar errand. That casual conversation the evening before had fired his mind with a curiosity, tinged with a shadow of misgiving, to find out if he could, just what that so-called "progress" had meant to him and to his. So, despite his family's original hereditary inhibition against Sunday travel, he had set forth by motor at nine o'clock next morning to make in six hours a journey which would have taken his grandfather at least six days, had lunched comfortably at Springfield, and now at four o'clock in the late spring afternoon was, for the moment, lost. Characteristic of his era he had run clean past what he was looking for! That he should not have recognized the abiding place of his forefathers might be regarded as excusable since it was forty-five years since he had been there, and travelling at fifty miles an hour one tended to miss things,—even meeting-houses with white steeples. Mere speed, it appeared, might actually be on occasion a disadvantage.

He had vaguely recalled the town as a cluster of low wooden and red-brick buildings,—a blacksmith shop, a tavern, a few high-stooped stores and a bank,—at the turn of a narrow, dusty road beside an embowered "common," the tops of whose fanlike elms were pierced by several spires. To his

memory it had been as sleepy as "Sleepy Hollow" itself.
Now, in place of the winding uneven country road, there
lay a smooth ribbon of level concrete over which motors
were humming in continuous streams in both directions.

A signpost showed that he had overrun his destination
by six miles, so he waited for a hiatus in the line of whizzing
cars and turned back. A few minutes later and, beyond a
curve in the highway, the strident blues and scarlets of a
cluster of filling stations caught his eye.

Could this be Framingham? This busy square with its
traffic cop, its garages, its raucous radio, lunch counters, barber, cigar and candy shops? Where were the tavern and the
brick bank? Where the old harness shop over which had
hung the sign of Hollis Hastings, harness maker, who had
advertised "Carryalls, Riding Saddles, Circyngles, Bridles,
and Martingals, Pew Cushions on hand or made to order at
short notice"? There was nothing recognizable left of the old
town! The glacier of time had ruthlessly ground it all away.
Yet, like the Nantucket skipper in James T. Field's poem,
who, when asked to "taste the lead" which one of the crew
had covertly rubbed over the earth in a box of parsnips standing on deck, instantly exclaimed: "Nantucket's sunk! And
here we are, right over old Ma'am Hackett's garden!" so
the Puritan sniffed the air and sensed that he was upon
or near the spot where his ancestors had dwelt. Something
in his subconscious mind responded to things of which his
senses were wholly unaware. Was there some subtle kinship
between himself and these tanned youths who manned the
gasoline pumps or those other swarthier ones who were vend-
ing "eats" to the waiting motorists,—doughnuts, ginger ale,
"hot franks," cider and "Eskimo pie"? No, these last at any
rate were not natives of Framingham, but of Italy or of
Poland.

"Can you tell me if there's an old church,—a Baptist
meeting-house,—around here?" he asked of a natty motor-
cycle cop in khaki who was ordering the traffic.

"Better ask one of them fellers!" The officer waved

towards the filling station.—"I'm from Worcester."

The uniformed attendant at the nearest red sentinel jerked his thumb down the road.

"Church?—Sure! Go along and you'll see it all right. The common'll be down to your left. No, I don't belong here. I just run the station. I come from Woonsocket."

The Puritan left him making change for a man with a car bearing a Florida license and containing a woman, three children, an Airedale terrier, and a complete camping outfit.

"Why, it'll be a cinch to make Portsmouth to-night! Only eighty miles, ain't it?" the driver was saying. "Sure, I come from Florida,—Miami. Say, brother, that's the only place to live! If you want to make a wad of money——"

The clang of an over-laden trolley, to whose running boards and steps a holiday-making crowd of mill hands was clinging like a swarm of bees, drowned the conclusion of his panegyric.

The gorge of the Puritan—transplanted offshoot of the parent stem, as he was,—rose in his throat! Inured to the bedlam of Times Square he had still cherished inviolate his ideal of the New England Sabbath. However hectic his career in New York he had always comforted himself with the thought that in his native state of Massachusetts he could find, far from the madding crowd's ignoble strife, an asylum for his declining years,—"Sabine Farm" stuff.

Nothing had so shaken his ostrich-like concept of modernity as this unexpected experience. As a pseudo-Brahmin he had always secretly condescended to the tinsel glitter of the Metropolis;—there was a God's country elsewhere, albeit a slightly chilly one. Even Henry Adams was like that, and every man born within fifty miles of the Bulfinch Front of the Boston State House is a potential Henry Adams. The very fact that the Puritan was not a genuine Brahmin (his mother had been apologetically born in South Boston) had given him a "defense complex" which made him all the more superior. How could he longer imitate the Adams tone of arrogant humility which affected homespun before duch-

esses and patronized Boston from Quincy? He had lost part
of his stock in trade. This home of his ancestors—this peaceful New England village on that Sunday afternoon,—was as
like to the Atlantic City Turnpike as two peas, and its denizens were listening in to the same sacred concert broadcast
from WEAF. The universe had become standardized with
a vengeance! Tranquillity was an unknown commodity, unat-
tainable, this side of the Glassy Sea, where perhaps cherubim
and seraphim were even now casting down their golden harps
in favor of a celestial radio.

Nursing his distemper the Puritan followed the procession of motors until, inadvertently raising his eyes, he caught
the gleam of a white fane above the elm tops. An old-fashioned meeting-house! Could it be—? He turned off the
highway and stopped the car beside the little tree-covered
knoll. He had found it—his grandfather's church! Unmindful of the hurly-burly of the square it stood there calm and
unperturbed—a white evangel—pointing the eternal way to
Heaven.

The foliage splintered the sun's last rays which dappled
the old church with gold. The caw of a crow in the near-by
branches belittled the honk of the motors beyond the turn.
On the farther side of the knoll the ancient horse-sheds still
offered an unaccepted and unnecessary hospitality. He
climbed out of the car, stepped across the young grass to the
porch, and entered. The inside was almost chill in contrast to
the warmth of the afternoon outside, faintly sweet with the
odor of dried timber, empty, save for the shadowy presences
who seemed to throng the aisles and fill the pews about him.
His eyes ran over the long rows to the pulpit where his
grandfather had preached from 1811 to 1839, and the uncle,
for whom he had been named, from 1866 to 1872.

Good old church! For over a century its clanging bell had
summoned its congregation to Sunday worship or tolled for
the passing of the village fathers,—from the days of John
Quincy Adams to those of Herbert Hoover. What incredible changes it had witnessed: from the stage coach to the

motor car, the aeroplane and the submarine; from the daguerreotype to the talking motion picture and television; from the flint-lock musket to monster guns that could hurl shells forty miles and gas bullets that could be fired around corners; from the handloom to the automatic repairing machine for silk stockings!

Suppose his grandfather should come back and find himself face to face with all these things, what a bewildered old gentleman he would be! What would he think of yonder village square with its bizarre activities on this Sabbath afternoon? Would he stride down there in his wrath and scourge the money changers from about the portals of the temple? Lucky for him perhaps that he could not come back, and thus escape being committed to an observation ward,—lucky at least that he had lived when he had, in an era when there was time to live!

It is, I believe, customary for writers of similar memoirs who return to the ancestral shades, to indulge at some such point as this in a dream or vision of the past, thus conveniently enabling them to contrast for the benefit of their readers the scene as it then was with the present. I have debated this method, but convinced as I am that truth is not only stranger than fiction, but vastly more entertaining and instructive, I have resolved it in favor of my conscience. I might have resorted to the excusable, if somewhat fanciful, expedient of imagining myself suddenly reincarnated in the body of my grandfather, and conducting the simple service of over a century ago. But this was rendered difficult. if not impossible, by my lack of knowledge of him.

As I sat in that old church a strange sensation—such as in my childhood I had been wont to call "a life-and-death feeling"—encompassed me. I felt not only a tremendous nearness to the past, but as if I were actually touching it. In that very pulpit my grandfather had faced his congregation. These very walls had echoed to his voice. His hand had swept the rail where mine now rested. And yet for all his nearness—a nearness that was almost contact—he was almost as mythical a personage, as far as I was concerned, as Prester John or the Wandering Jew. I knew little about him beyond the bare facts that he was the son of a farmer in Weston, had worked his way through Harvard College with the intention of becoming a lawyer but, having "experienced religion," had determined to study for the ministry and, after having been graduated in 1805, had six years later become preacher of the "Baptist Church in Weston and Framingham."

There is a portrait of him in the Framingham Public Library showing an intellectual-looking man of early middle age, in a black stock, although otherwise his clothes do not appear so very different from those of to-day. The face is austere but kindly, yet it tells nothing else, and the meagre records of his life are insufficient to piece out the man beyond establishing that he had unusual ability, as well as a sweetness of character, which led the townsfolk to call him "Father Train." He must have been held generally in high regard since (as was not uncommon for a clergyman in an era when he was expected to act as the political as well as the spiritual adviser of his flock) he was chosen as a representative to the State Legislature for seven years in succession from 1822 to 1829,—with the exception of the year 1827, when apparently he was not returned because of two rather vehement sermons which he preached upon the subject of temperance. My grandfather was ahead of his time. In those days people liked their toddy. I could not but wonder what his attitude towards prohibition would be were he still alive.

Well, here I was, over a hundred years later, sitting in the very church from whose pulpit he had preached. Had he not seen almost as many startling changes before he died in 1849 as the old church had witnessed since then? Certainly he must have thought that the climax of scientific ingenuity had been achieved when he heard that one could travel from New York to Albany in a boat propelled by steam. I could imagine how thrilled he must have been at seeing his first velocipede in a museum in 1816, his first gas light in 1822, his first coal fire in 1824; his excitement on taking his first ride behind a locomotive ten years later! But "progress"? Had I learned anything about that?

It was growing dark and I tip-toed out of the old church and crossed to where my car was standing. The stream of motors was still flowing by and I joined it, thinking of my grandfather's life as compared with mine;—of his early years of teaching school, living at the houses of his pupils and walking for miles each way in the rain and snow over roads that were little more than sloughs; of his cold, carpetless room, his scanty food, his patched clothes of homespun, his lack of books, of any amusement in the modern sense of the word; then of the period during which he started out upon his ministry,—the ascetic young clergyman who had heard the call to labor in the vineyard and who, having answered it, had remained loyal to his flock until, to the knell from his own spire, he had been buried in the little graveyard hard by the church to which he had dedicated his career. What would he think of me, his grandson, in my "plus fours" and high-powered car, motoring in a single day—and that a Sunday! —from New York to Boston? Would he regard me as a waster, a sybarite and a Sabbath breaker? A doer of iniquity with my novels and stories? I remembered that one of my recent works—"High Winds"—had been banned in Boston. A good title, I reflected,—"Banned in Boston"! Yet I kept insisting to myself that my grandfather would undoubtedly, had he lived, have been a liberal-minded and progressive old man.

I pressed the accelerator and my car, with a soft whirr, leaped ahead towards the distant lights. The countryside was a spider's web of electricity, all its filaments converging towards Boston. And like a luminous spider I seemed to be sliding towards it down my own particular thread. Triumph of scientific ingenuity, that motor car. And yet it was nothing like as wonderful as a spider! Moreover, had it seen fit to stop I should probably have been helpless to make it go. I did not understand its machinery. I had merely bought it. I had accepted motors, along with aeroplanes and radios, just as I had accepted horse cars in my childhood. Somebody had invented them and they were convenient things to ride in. Most convenient! We needed them. But who had got the more out of life,—my grandfather or I?

## CHAPTER II

# Hands Across the Sea of Time

### (1783–1931)

THE first result of my visit to Framingham was the sense of nearness to the past already referred to, the second an acute realization of my ignorance of my immediate ancestors and the circumstances under which they had lived. My grandfather had been born, as I have stated, in 1783; my father, in 1817. Thus our three lives spanned nearly a century and a half of the most thrilling period of American history. We three Trains between us had seen greater changes than any three men in any other like period of time since the creation of the world.

My grandfather had been born before the United States came into being and through him I was in practical contact with the critical (or post-revolutionary) period of American life. As its influences had moulded him, so through him they had moulded me and would, to some extent at least, continue to mould my son. There was probably a lot of my grandfather in my bones, and a lot of his ideas in my head. Yet what had this man been like, who begat the man who in turn begat me? How did he live? Was he radically different from, or essentially like, my father and myself? Was he better or worse off than I am? Had I profited by what he learned while on this earth? And was the earth a pleasanter and better place to live in now than in his time?

So far as I could I determined to find out,—to take a little stock of the world before I was quit of it. Obviously the first thing I must do was not to remedy the aching void of my ignorance but to sweep my mind clean of error. I had said that I was a Puritan, but what had I meant by it? Frankly, I did not know. Even now as I pen the word there rises against the background of my mind a tall, sour-visaged individual in a long cloak and conical hat, with a blunderbuss over his shoulder and an apprehensive lady in a bonnet clinging to his arm, on his way to church. Obviously there are Indians, or at very least wolves, lurking hard by. The original of this cheerful picture was on a calendar I had as a child,—probably a reproduction of some well-known painting. For me Puritans will always be tall, wear conical hats, and carry blunderbusses; they can never be short and fat, wearing straw headgear and carrying fishing rods. Imagine a Puritan carrying a fishing rod! This same gaunt spectre stalks across the cartoons of our daily papers and before the footlights of our musical shows. O yes! We all know what a Puritan must have been like!

Ideas casually conceived have a horrible persistence. There used to be a wood cut of an armadillo, with an embroidery of tropical flora and fauna, in my geography opposite the short paragraph devoted to Brazil. To-day I am convinced that the swamps, pampas and forests of that country are alive with anteaters, with perhaps a few Indians peeping through giant banana leaves. Nothing will ever obliterate that belief. I cannot efface it. I can only fight it, and in fighting it I give it new vitality. My imagination is stronger than my will, since, being primarily located in my subconsciousness, I do not control it. Hence for me the map of Brazil will forever be spotted with armadillos, and an armadillo will always merge into a pink-and-yellow map of Brazil. One vivid picture is worth a page of statistics in fostering an impression.

Were I attempting to write history, I would sweep away with one magnificent gesture every generality regarding times and peoples penned by historians since the Fall of Constantinople. I am willing to hazard that there is more of inaccuracy than of truth in all unqualified statements and that it is more dangerous to generalize about periods and nations than about individuals, which, Heaven knows, is bad enough.

Were the French at any period in history "a frivolous

nation addicted to dancing and light wines"? They were not.
A more deadly serious nation never lived. Yet shall we ever
outgrow that belief engendered in us as children by our
school geographies?

Carry it farther. Were the inhabitants of Paris merely, at
any period, frivolous and addicted to dancing and light
wines? They were not. Most of them drank wine rather than
water, it is true, but the last thing they were addicted to was
frivolity. Our well-meaning geographer, with his recollection playing upon the court life of Versailles and his subconsciousness swarming with pictures of the French dancing
masters and hairdressers of grand opera, imagines the entire forty million inhabitants of France pirouetting through
the Palais Royal or capering around the Place Vendome.
And, no doubt, his unconsidered casual statement has cost
the French nation billions of francs and thousands of lives!
Yet this is only another way of saying that until the rise of
the common man (or the decline of the uncommon man) history was made by courts, kings, emperors and popes and no
one else mattered,—just as to-day the same thing is more or
less true of movie-actors, famous criminals, athletes, and
prize fighters. The King of Swat is our hero, instead of Le
Grand Monarque.

We are apt to think of the events of a couple of centuries
or even of a single century ago as almost obliterated by time,
and of the people who took part in them as wholly different
from ourselves. Our tendency is to belittle and even deride
the intellectual equipment and opinions of those who have
lived before, because they did not know the extraordinary things with which we are so familiar, as well as because
they wore such preposterous clothes. Anybody attired in wire
bustles, hoop skirts, knee breeches or high boots must have
been, we feel, in the very nature of things more or less sim-
ple-minded and just the least little bit ridiculous.

Yet many of them are almost our contemporaries. There
are men still alive to-day who could have talked with survivors of the siege of Louisburg, of "Braddock's Defeat," and

of "The Old French and Indian War," to say nothing of those who marched to Lexington and Concord and Bunker Hill more than a quarter century thereafter. I am myself a great-great-half-uncle at the age of fifty-five, while my own great-grandfather Samuel Train took an after part in the battle of Lexington. According to the Government reports for 1926 there were five mothers of soldiers who had fought for the Union during the Civil War still on the pension rolls, together with forty-one widows of veterans of the war with England of 1812. Hands across the sea of time!

Have not I talked with a lady whose husband knew Louis XV, who died in 1794? I have, although at first this may seem rather preposterous. The explanation, however, is simple enough. Her husband, who was born in 1760, had been a page of Louis' at Versailles and, having lived until after 1850, married for his second wife a comparatively young girl. When I knew her in 1895 she was just over sixty, hale and hearty, and it is quite possible that she is still alive. That brings Louis XV easily within the span of two lives, and anyone who is now ninety-five or over and who, when a child, talked with anyone then as old as he himself is to-day, could easily have received first-hand information as to events which occurred in the middle of the eighteenth century. The only reason that the survival of such persons is not brought more often to our attention is, I suppose, that, although there would be quite a chorus if they could be got together, they are now so few and scattered and their voices so thin, high and quavering that they are not heard.

Even more apparently surprising is the fact that my friend, Mr. Richard Hale of Boston, once sat on the lap of a man, who in turn had sat on the lap of a man, who had attended the funeral of one of the passengers on the *Mayflower*. In other words, a man living to-day has seen a man, who saw another man, who in his turn saw one of the Pilgrim Fathers—or more properly, perhaps, one of the Pilgrim children! Yet this on analysis proves no more astonish-

ing than the previous story. Peregrine White was born on the
*Mayflower* in Cape Cod Harbor, Massachusetts, Nov. 20,
1620. Even if he cannot be rated strictly as a passenger, he
was at least "a stowaway." He was the first white child born
in New England, and lived until 1704. The person who
went to his funeral, the celebrated Deacon Cobb,—born before 1700 and living until after 1800,—was known as "The
man who lived in three centuries." Deacon Cobb in 1804
took upon his knee William Thomas, later the great-uncle
of Mr. Hale, saying to him: "Remember my child that you
have sat upon the lap of a man who went to the funeral
of someone who came over upon the *Mayflower*." Some
seventy years later, Mr. Thomas, who lived until about
1890, lifting in turn the youthful Richard upon his knee, enjoined him to remember that he had sat on the lap of a man,
who had sat on the lap of a man, who had gone to Peregrine
White's funeral. Two laps, so to speak, from Peregrine White
to Richard Hale! I trust the latter will in the fullness of
years duly perform a similar ceremony with, or upon, my
own son John.

No, the Puritans did not live so very long ago, after all.
And unless there is, so to speak, a Statute of Limitations of
some sort applying to inheritance, a lot of us are Puritans
yet. It is true that we do not think of ourselves as such, and
at worst prefer the adjective "Puritanical" to the noun itself;
but if I am not a Puritan, when, may I ask, did I or my
father or his father cease to be one? At what point did a
Puritan stop being a Puritan? When he abandoned the blunderbuss for the flintlock musket, or the conical hat for the
squirrel cap with ear-tabs, or breeches for pantaloons, or the
surtout for the Tuxedo? Or was it when he gave up singing
through his nose or followed the bass viol? Or dipped fur-
tively for the first time into Shakespeare? Or went to the
lodge of a Saturday night? Or stealthily bought a ticket to
"The Black Crook," or maybe—fifty years later—to Earl
Carroll's Vanities?

The truth is, I fancy, that, just as there were Puritans and

Puritans, so some of the real ones were still born while others are with us yet. The same generation of the same family will produce priests and pickpockets, drunkards and divines. No doubt while the Puritan in the picture of my childhood was tempting the wolves on his way to meeting, his brother,—or shall we say, his step-brother?—who had in all probability been baptized "Praise-God-and-fear-not" or "Remember-Thy-Creator-in-the-days-of-Thy-Youth," was lying stewed to the gills in a haymow, was carrying on most shamefully with some Indian jade, or was challenging the Calvinistic doctrine of infant damnation over a glass of toddy in some nearby kitchen. No general statements can be accurate concerning either Puritan times or our own. Communities differed, like individuals. What was true north of the Chesapeake was untrue south of it. City and rural life differed utterly everywhere. And one city differed from another, and one town from another, vastly more than they do now when life has become standardized. Everything, moreover, was constantly changing, politically, socially, economically.

One could find enough material upon almost any subject connected with American life which, while true of the precise time and place to which it related, would, if made the basis of general inference, create a totally false picture of any era. Every lawyer knows that he can find plenty of decisions in the law books to support practically any proposition no matter how fanciful; and the Bible is an unfailing source of authority for the most diversified of religious tenets. Puritans did not all wear tall hats and carry blunderbusses, any more than all United States Senators wear frock coats. But of course, if historians did not generalize, their tasks would never be finished and they would be noting exceptions and qualifications on their death beds to all that they had written throughout life.

Moreover most history has been written either to satisfy the patriotic or religious cravings of the reader or in such a grand manner as to be utterly inhuman. Our generals and statesmen have stalked through the pages of our school books uttering patriotic claptrap of a kind to make any child above the primary grade squirm with self-consciousness. To question the sincerity, sobriety, and general godliness of our forefathers was an impiety savoring of slandering a deceased prelate or a breach of taste like washing the family's dirty linen in public.

Yet how are we to know whether or not we have progressed unless we know what manner of folk our ancestors really were? If, as we have been often told, they were all sturdy, courageous, upright men and patient, sweet-souled, self-sacrificing women there's an end on't! Our question is answered. The present-day Americans are not all that—even in New England.

After all, the "debunkers" have served a purpose. I remember when I took Professor Channing's course in American History at Harvard in 1892 he commented on the fact that at the Battle of Monmouth the Father of His Country swore "till the leaves shook on the trees, charming, delightful." Some of those present quite disapproved of what they regarded as Professor Channing's sensationalism. Yet I have thought more highly of George Washington ever since. The trouble with most "debunkers" is that they are such poor historians.

Strachy left Victoria every inch a queen. The same thing has happened in most similar instances. The faults in our heroes pointed out by their detractors have only served to emphasize their virtues and the men themselves, heretofore half-mythical characters in whom we did not quite believe, have stood forth greater than ever.

So now having disposed in a few paragraphs of the myths of heroic utterances, death-bed and execution scenes, and traditional historic pageantry in general, let us cast a hard-boiled eye in the direction of the probable truth. It is a mistake to emphasize the political and military aspects of history at the expense of the social and economic. The latter are not only more important, but essential to a correct interpretation and understanding of the former. The printing press,

the steam engine, the telephone, the bicycle and the automobile, have affected history more than all the conquests of
Alexander, many of whose victories no doubt turned on the
efficiency of his digestive process.

Consider the bristle tooth brush for a moment. I can find
no mention of this modest instrument until after 1800. To
its absence may be attributed in large measure the premature
decay of American teeth during the first two centuries of our
history and the general use of false ones among those who
could afford to pay for them. Washington's were famous.
In one of his letters from Valley Forge, I am informed, he
lays stress on having a special screw driver sent to him immediately wherewith to tighten the plate. The loss of that
celebrated set, a bad adjustment, or a jabbing toothache during the preliminaries to the crossing of the Delaware, might
have resulted in our still being loyal subjects of King
George.

If the stamp tax had not led to the famous Tea Party on
Long Wharf, most of us would not know from reading the
histories whether the Bostonians drank tea or not. Yet it is
enormously important, if you want to find out what people
were like at any given time, to know what they drank, how
they drank, and when they drank it. Bismarck saw the Prus-
sian army "grow groggy on its legs." A judge's "hang-over"
has sent many a poor fellow to the gallows. Liquor has
played its part in most famous events, whether strategic, fo-
rensic, artistic, or amorous. Even smaller influences than intoxication or sobriety may have far-reaching consequences.
What effect did Napoleon's hemorrhoids have on the result
of the Battle of Waterloo or his subsequent decision to throw
himself on the mercy of the British? Probably none, but I
mention them as a possible example, since on the excellence
of a man's physical condition depend the accuracy of his
judgments, his courage, his ability to inspire others, and most
of all his élan.

To understand history it is more important to know what
people ate and what diseases they had, than what kings or

generals the rabble cheered for, or what alliances and treaties
their rulers made. One would gain the impression from reading most books about the revolutionary period that the American farmers and tradesmen spent most of their time thinking
about the tyranny of England, the greatness of George
Washington and Samuel Adams, and the horrors of hell. I
doubt it. I think they would have preferred, most of them, to
remain comfortably under English rule, to doff their caps to
a lord, and that, in their heart of hearts, hell probably bored
them to death. I wonder how much my great-grandfather
Samuel, when he marched to Lexington, knew what it was all
about. How far he thought of himself as striking a blow for
liberty rather than as grabbing the chance to take a pot shot
with his squirrel rifle at a red coat. I wonder if his conscience
smote him when from behind the security of a stone wall he
plugged one of the retreating Britishers in the back. I wonder
if he had a conscience. I wonder if he really knew or cared
anything about taxation without representation or merely
took things as they came and asked the squire or the minister
how he should vote.

I wonder what he thought of Washington anyway, how
seriously he took the Calvinistic doctrines he was compelled
to listen to, and whether he had any faith in those new-
fangled French imports labelled "natural rights" and "liberties." Even if he was my honored, and perhaps sainted,
ancestor I wonder if he pulled any longer face or thought
any more about politics and religion than I do. I fancy
he was more interested in getting in his crops and perhaps
buying a new pair of boots than he was in whether the
British stayed in Boston or got out of it. People are chiefly
concerned with their own private affairs. I suppose that a
couple of centuries from now unregenerate historians will
try to induce their readers to believe that the ordinary inhabitants of the United States had daily emotional spasms
over Farm Relief, the Dawes Plan, the Federal Reserve
Bank, the Tariff, or the League of Nations, whereas there is
not one voter in a hundred who could give an intelligent

account of any one of them, or of what sort of representation the United States has at the World Court, and how said representative or representatives are chosen.

Now I knew no more about the "Boys of Seventy-six" than I did about the "Pilgrim Fathers." Just as my idea of a Puritan was based on my recollection of the cadaverous Sabbatarian with his blunderbuss and conical hat, so my mental picture of the men of the revolutionary epoch derived from another—the advertisement of a life insurance company—in which if I remember correctly, a drummer boy was portrayed as blithely accompanying to certain death a silvery-haired fifer and a bandaged patriot bearing the Stars and Stripes, presumably at Bunker Hill. I had never thought of them out of their uniforms.

I had no pride of race such as might lead me to wish to visualize my ancestors either as stern men of God or as picturesque patriots. I wanted to know them as they were in the common clay. To form some idea, if I could, as to whether their lives contrasted on the whole favorably or unfavorably with those of the men and women of my own time. Were they healthier, happier and generally more useful than ours? Or, were we really any better off for what the voice on the radio from the Department of Commerce had called "progress"?

I knew comparatively little of American history, for whatever I had learned at school and college—little enough at best—I had practically forgotten. What I wanted was the truth not about kings and captains, but about the plain people, who with their hands and heads had made the nation what it had ultimately become. I knew that I could get a better idea of my ancestors and how they lived from a few basic, homely facts than from a whole library of histories of the old-fashioned type, for circumstantial evidence, if true, is the best of all evidence since it does not depend for its validity upon the memory, the sincerity, or the temperament of any individual narrator.

In my inquiry I had recourse to town records, old newspapers, bills, letters, sermons, time tables, almanacs, books on etiquette,—all the rubbish of daily existence. I also engaged in a considerable amount of desultory reading in the course of which I stumbled upon a number of facts which, while no doubt familiar to the historian, were startling to me as a layman. How many people, for example, knew that Massachusetts after the Revolution harbored a distinctly "red" faction or constantly threatened to secede from the Union in the early part of the nineteenth century; that matches were not invented until 1827, that, except for stages, wheeled vehicles were a rarity in 1800, or that at Harvard and Yale students were not listed alphabetically but in accordance with the social rank of their families? Surely such things would be of interest to everybody were they known, yet they were usually buried in a mass of dry and repellent matter, illumined neither by a ray of light nor of humor, where the vast majority of the reading public would never take the trouble to look for them. If only those who write serious history were not so fearful of the suspicion of light-mindedness, many of their volumes would be avidly read by old and young instead of gathering dust upon the shelves of reference libraries.

Familiarity with these more weighty works led to the disclosure that there were numbers of pseudo-historians who made a living by palming off the work of others as their own. The laborious research of a few thorough students had been seized upon by a shoal of plagiarists, literary freebooters and Jeremy Diddlers, engaged in serving it up in palatable form to a public who preferred a light book to a heavy one and instinctively avoided the label of history. These light-fingered gentry, desirous of reaping where they had not sown, and finding in Channing, McMaster, Adams or Rhodes something that pleased their fancy or—what was far more to the point—which might please the fancy of their lady readers, would bodily lift it from its context, change a "but" to a "yet," a transitive verb to an intransitive, put in a qualifying adjective much as a government agent might put poison in good liquor, and pass it off as their own without a "by your leave" or "thank you," thus creating an impression that it was the result of prodigious labor upon their part amid the monuments of the past.

O, I have caught you, you pretentious historical pick-pockets with your heavy paper and double gilt and reproductions of ancient prints, for in a swift coursing through many volumes for mere pleasure I have recognized over and over again not only what you have stolen from the great but from each other!

Mayhap I am not without sin in this respect myself. Having read so much that was informative and entertaining in a number of works of history and near-history regarding the manners, customs and mode of life of the American people during the last century and a half, and being desirous to give those who may peruse this volume the benefit of it, I wish it plainly understood that there is no original material in this book except family documents and letters. I make no claim whatever to research, unless the digging up of a few old newspapers and obsolete books be rated as such. All else is the result of the labor of other and better men and women most of whose names appear in the front matter. No, this is a synthetic product, written as I wanted to write it, and to please myself.

# CHAPTER III

# A Puritan Patriarch

## (Newbury—1635)

I MAKE no overstatement when I claim to be a Puritan, for on both sides I come of authentic Puritan lineage for three hundred years. No one could deny that I am of original Puritan stock, whatever I may have since become. John Train, the founder of my family upon the paternal side, (the name being then also spelled Trayne, Traine, or Tran) came to America in *The Susan & Ellyn* in 1635 and settled in Watertown, Massachusetts, where he built a mill and sold rum to the Indians,—a business which was in those days, perhaps, the moral equivalent of bootlegging. There is a vague and unconvincing tradition that he was a valet, or servant, to some aristocrat with whom he crossed the ocean and that he married Margaret Dix, a lady's maid, also on the same passenger-list, but so far as I am aware there is nothing to substantiate this in the records, and I am now inclined to believe that I fabricated the story to annoy certain of my more snobbish family connections. All I know about John Train is that he probably came from the town of Irvine, then an important Scottish seaport, about thirty miles south of Glasgow, in Ayreshire, where the family (who figure in the records as Tran) were substantial burgesses.

On the distaff side I am somewhat better documented. John Cheney, my maternal ancestor, may well have come over to America on the same vessel with John Train, for the

Reverend John Eliot, that remarkable "Apostle of the Indians," made entry in his own hand in the records of the Church of Roxbury, Massachusetts, of which he was the pastor, that "John Cheney he came into the Land in the year 1635. He brought four children, Mary, Martha, John, Daniel. Sarah his 5t child was born in the last month of the same year 1635, cald February. He removed from Or church to Newbury the end of the next suer 1635."

Both Johns were fruitful and multiplied exceedingly, their descendants seeming for the most part to have remained in Massachusetts in and about the localities first occupied by their forebears.

This John Cheney, a farmer and shoemaker, proved himself a stout burgher, actively interested in the affairs of Newbury. He took great interest in Winthrop's campaign for the governorship against Sir Harry Vane, and on May 17, 1637, walked with nine others forty miles afoot from Newbury to Cambridge to take the "freeman's oath" and qualify himself to vote in the election. It was by such strenuous and prompt efforts that Governor Winthrop was elected and the conservative party triumphed. John Cheney was several times elected to the board of select men, and died in 1666.

In his will he provided for Martha, his wife, by leaving her "the libertie of dwelling in the house her lifetime" and enjoined his eldest son Daniel "to maintain her comfortably with meat and drink, linen and wollen and other necessaries as her adg shall requier during the term of her naturall life" or, if she preferred to live elsewhere, "ten pound by the year to be paied out of my living in good merchantable wheat, barley and Indian in equal proportions."

After devising lands to his son John, he then proceeds:

"Also I doe give unto my Son John my wearing Apparel, namely one Coate, one cloke, one cloth suit; one serge suit; one lethen suit; two shirts; two paiers of stokins and my hoes and my best Hatt, also my matchlock musket; and the shortest Croscutt sawe, also I doe give him one 3 year old

haifer caled brendle. . . . Also I do give unto the said John
after my wife's decease the great brass kettel and one new
pewter dish marked with I C; and one white bed Rugg.
Also I doe give unto the sayd John: six boshels of Apples
out of the Orchard yearly for Seven years after my
decease.

"Next I do give unto my son Nathaniel Cheney my four
oxen with their yoaks and chaine also I doe give unto him
Two Cowes with their Calves the one Caled old Line; the
other Caled Pie and one thre year old hayfer with the Calf
and a yearling Colte, also I doe give unto the sayd Nathaniel
one yearling hayfer caled Kurle, also I doe give unto him his
Armes compleat, and one broad howe and one Axe and his
Sithe and sickle.

"Also I doe give unto him one half headed bedsted with
the bed and one bolster and one pillow and one paier of
shetes and a Cotton yellow Rug: and I doe give unto Nathaniel the great yarn pott and the lesser posnit; . . . also
I doe give unto Nathaniel the best Chest and my Bible, and
one pewter platter after my wive's decease, and I doe give
unto the sayd Nathaniel six boshels of Aples a year for 7
years.

"And as Concerning my Grandchild Abiel Sadler, his father deceasing, before he was borne I was by the honnord
Hampton Coarte Intrusted to take Care of him as Gardian,
And the Honnored Coart Ordered him to have Ten poundes
out of his ffathers esstatt; at the adge of one and twentye for
p formance of whereof I stand engaged. And I do also ad
unto the same five poundes to be payed; the whol fivten
pound unto the sayd Abiel at the Adge of one and twentye by
my Executor. Also I doe give unto the sayde Abiel Sadler My
lastes and Toles belonging to my Trade. Thear is also a great
bosed bible and a pewter bason apertayning to him of his fathers which I enioyne my Executor to deliver to him when
he cometh to adge.

"And I doe Ordayne and appoynt my Son Daniel Cheney
to be my Soall and Alone Executor to this my last will and

Testament in witnes whearof I have set to my hand and Seale: The 5th day of the 4th Month: 1666

Sighned & Sealed         John Cheney    Sonior
in the presence of
us underwritten
     Richard Dole
     William Ilslie."

The inventory of his estate contains among other items the following:

Item    One house, barne and twelve agres of plowground, 40 Acres of marsh and medow with the orchard with 20 acres of pasture   £350

Item    17 neat Catell   £60

Item    the wearinge clothes   £12

Item    a parcell of Books   £1

Item    two spinning wheles   8s

Item    working Tooles 42 lastes   10s

Item    9 aule haftes with 13 aule blades   4s

Item    two payr of pinchers & 8 tackes & one punch 3 knives & two dressers two krissing wedges one holowing sticke one stoping sticke one cutting knife and paturing one Shoomakers hamer   1s

Item    one piece of bakon   £1

Item    one warming pane & a Bras Skimer   8s

Item    one baster   3s

Item    3 porengers & one pint pot   6s

Item    2 puter Chamber potts   6s

Item    one great Iron pott   16s

Item    one leser Iron pott   14s

Item    two tramels in the chimny   8s

Item    one payer of beloows   3s

Item    one silver spoone   5s

Item    one Chist and box   12s

Item    one hour glass   1s

Item   3 chayers & two cushins  4s
Item   trayes & dishes & trenchers  6s
Item   one gune & sword & bandiliers  £1.10
Item   one old musket  5s
Item   one Iron postell  1s
Item   one sadle & pilion & bridle  £1.6
Item   a parcell of flaxe  10s
Item   3 rakes  1s
Item   one hide att the taners  10s

This will and inventory are all that is necessary to reconstruct a complete picture of John Cheney, his household, their manner of life, the economic conditions under which they lived, their pronunciation of English (note the phonetic spelling of the words "stokins," "hayfer" and "haifer," "chist," "cushins," etc.) with some indication of the amount of their education and culture. "A parcell of books" worth £1 was something of a library for a farmer-shoemaker. They lived off their own land, spun their own flax, had their own wheat and barley ground at the mills, kept horses, oxen, cows, swine, and probably sheep, and made their shoes and clothes out of leather and wool from their own animals. They told the time outdoors by the sun and indoors by the glass, used sheets and pillow cases, and on occasion napkins and table cloths. They had "one silver spoone," and much brass, warmed their beds, used "cushins" in their "chayers," ate hugely of cheese, bacon, Indian corn products (chiefly, I suppose, "porridge" and "fried mush"), eggs, chickens, and a prodigious number of apples. A simple, industrious, but solid and comfortable existence, without radio, telephone, flivver, movies or bridge. The women were chaste and so, as a rule, at least after marriage, were the men. They read and believed their Bible, spoke the truth, forgave their debtors (in their wills), and consumed large quantities of hard cider, gin and rum, as antidotes to exposure from weather and disease. Many of them lived to an astonishingly great "adge." In those days it was not uncommon to find persons of over a hundred years travelling on horseback and taking care of their steeds.

Now my people have been all humble folk, tillers of the soil, hewers of wood and distillers of rum, numbering so far as I am aware not one "gentleman" among them. Yet I rejoice in John Cheney. There was a man, if not a gentleman! A Puritan of the Puritans was he, with his Bible and his "lethen suit," his matchlock musket, "armes compleat," his "great yarn pot" and "lesser posnit," his cow "caled old Line" and the other "caled Pie." This old John was a patriarch, a man of dignity and solid worth, one who, standing engaged as guardian of his grandchild Abiel Sadler to pay him "Ten poundes out of his ffather's esstatt at the adg of one and twentye," could have been relied on by the "Honnered Hampton Coart" to meet his engagement if it took his last cent. I do not know how old either John Train or John Cheney was when he died, but from those two Johns I am in the eighth generation of lineal descent on both the paternal and maternal side. It is worth noting that three centuries will iron out all irregularities due to the variation in births, marriages and deaths so that at the end of that time the generations march evenly together again.

The descendants of John Cheney of Newbury are as the sands of the sea in number, and among them are rich men, poor men, beggars and thieves. I know little or nothing of my forebears on that side of the family until I come to my maternal grandfather, a resident of South Boston, Massachusetts, a ship owner of sorts engaged in the West India trade and vaguely referred to by my mother as an "importer." She never explained the nature of the merchandise he imported, but it may be guessed from the fact that he took his own life on May 20, 1860, in order, I would fain believe, to prevent being hanged as a pirate under the laws of the United States for slave running.

From John the Patriarch to Jonathan the Slave Trader is something of a step down. There is little evidence of progress one might think, although it is quite probable that in the eyes of the original John Cheney of Newbury slavery was an institution ordained of God. On the other hand, rather paradoxically, my paternal grandfather Charles, who was descended from John Train of Waltham, the bootlegger, became a Baptist clergyman and died in the odor of sanctity in 1849, which inclines one to the suspicion that upon the genealogical tree, if nowhere else, one may gather grapes from thorns and figs from thistles.

# CHAPTER IV

## "Boys of Seventy-Six"

THE Train family is as good a breed by which to test the revolutionary tradition as another, since my great-great-uncle Joshua Train (born in 1718) took part in the siege and capture of Louisburg, losing his health owing to the hardships he underwent in Canada, my great-great-grandfather, Samuel Train, Sr., was an "Alarm Man" of Middlesex, while his son, my great-grandfather Samuel Train, Jr., was one of the "Minute Men" who chased the British back from Lexington and Concord. Since we have got to begin somewhere let us discard the hero of Louisburg and start with my great-great-grandfather, Samuel Train, Senior, who, born in 1711, did not die until 1806 and who lived to attend the graduation at Harvard College in 1805, of his grandson, my grandfather, Charles Train. This old boy, whose life spanned practically the entire eighteenth century, is worth something more than passing attention.

Samuel Train, Senior, was born before the treaty with "the eastern Indians at Portsmouth," the suppression of the buccaneers in the West Indies and the overthrow of proprietary government in Carolina; he had been nine years old when the first "trading-house" was erected at Oswego and negotiations had with the Six Nations at Albany; he was eleven during the war with the Abinakis and the burning of Norridgewock; he was twenty-one at the time of the settlement of Georgia, the last of the thirteen Colonies, under James Oglethorp; he was still a young man during "King George's War," a part of the Austrian Succession; he was thirty-four at the time of the Louisburg Expedition in 1745 in which his brother took part as a volunteer, lived not only through "The Old French and Indian War" (1755–1763),

33

but throughout the entire Revolutionary period, and survived to see Thomas Jefferson re-elected to his second term as President of the United States. It was a long stretch, and since he lived until my great-grandfather was sixty-one, and my grandfather twenty-three, they both must have heard a great deal from him at first hand about what had gone on in the early part of the century. How far he conformed to either the traditional type of psalm-singing deacon or heroic drummer boy can best be inferred from the records.

Weston, although but twelve miles from Boston, was, down nearly until Revolutionary times, in effect a frontier town, surrounded by forest and occasionally menaced by hostile Indians. Those twelve miles, which if the speed cop be inadvertent may now be covered by motor in twenty minutes, constituted for the native farmer a long and difficult journey not lightly or often undertaken in the eighteenth century. Weston is adjacent to Watertown where the first John Train built his mill and sold his rum to the Indians, and the region thereabout was the ancestral stamping ground of the Train family. Although there are none of them there now, "Train's Hill" in Weston still perpetuates the name.

One of the oldest houses mentioned in the existing town records is that of "John and Samuel Train" built in 1738, from which it would appear that great-great-grandfather Samuel shared his own father's house in conformity with the custom of the period whereby the eldest (or at any rate one of the sons) carried on the farm and brought up his own family under his father's roof. The Middlesex farm house in those early days was usually a very crude affair often of only one story and perhaps of but two rooms. Yet it was apt to hold not only two families, but various decrepit aunts, uncles, great-aunts and great-uncles, widows and spinsters, for there were no old folks' homes and every man had to look after his own relatives. Life was laborious, incredibly frugal, and in most respects probably not unlike that of the Kentucky mountaineer to-day.

Weston was a typical Puritan town founded for religious

reasons and its inhabitants and their descendants were typical Puritans. The church was the centre not only of the spiritual but of the social and the political life as well, and the townsmen rotated in public office much as they do now in the rural districts of Maine and Massachusetts, where the theory obtains that every voter ought to have his whack at the taxes. The Trains of the Revolutionary period present a normal example of a Yankee family who were both patriots and to a slight degree profiteers. All were assiduous job hunters,— part of the local "ring," if the universally followed system deserves to be dignified as such. They also earned bounties of a few shillings by shooting blackbirds and squirrels, whose multitudes at that time resembled the plagues of Egypt.

As an office-holder Samuel Train, Sr., seems to have been a sort of hardy perennial, for he was in turn surveyor, fence-viewer, "wardin," constable, and selectman, and as soon as one term ended he started in on another. His favorite office was that of constable, but although his salary as such amounted to only 20 shillings per annum, he made a fairly good thing out of his perquisites and fees for "warning town meetings" at 4 shillings each, "making rates" (usually spelled "rats") and "carrying" paupers "out of town."

He, like the other townsfolk, boarded the poor for hire. In 1757 he was voted £1 1s. 1d. for "keeping Thos. Partridge's wife 3 weeks," and later in the same year, the Partridges evidently not proving properly grateful, received 4 shillings "for Carrying Thos. Partridge & Family out of Town." In 1763, being now over fifty years of age, this local Poobah achieved the position of selectman as well as that of Surveyor of Highways, so that he was paid for "prambelating the Town lines." He seems also to have been a constable at the same time, for the record in that year says "there Remains In the hand of Samuel Train Late Constable 12/11/0/3" and "In the hand of Samuel Train Present Constable 119/15/8/0," and he was also being constantly hired as a substitute constable for others. Can it be that I inherited my predilection for the pursuit of crime, if not of public office, from this ancestor who fed so continuously out of the public crib?

That the family by mid-century was an influential one is shown, not only by the fact that Samuel Train held three salaried offices at once, but that he was able to persuade his fellow citizens to accept responsibility for the path that led from the highway to his house in the woods, for "it was Put to vote to know the minds of the town Whether they Would Except of a Bridle Way for Samuel Train, and it Passed in the afermetive as followeth: viz: from Samuel Train Dwelling hous as it is Now trod by John Joneses and so on by his barn to the town Way Leeding to the Contrey Road: Nesesary gates being hange$^d$ and Cept in Repare at the Charge of Samuel Train and Abr$^m$ Jones," from which it would appear that to reach the family mansion in those days from the "country" or county road, one would first turn down some sort of a town way until one reached John Jones' barn, when one cut across lots past the latter's "hous" and so on thence to "Samuel Train Dwelling hous."

While no doubt this may have been a meritorious and much-needed public improvement—for surely a constable-selectman-surveyor ought to be accessible to the tax payers —it committed the town to the ownership and upkeep of a bridle path, or "way," leading apparently only to the Train house. Promptly the very next year (1766) Samuel Train offered a "Petision . . . to Know the minds of the town Whether the Gramer School Shall be Kept in the four Quarters of the town only" and if so "to make all Nesesary Provision therefor" (Heed this well!) and *also to ask that the town open the way from Mr. Samuel Train's Dwelling hous by Lewt. Abram Jones to the County Road Where it was formerly Voted a bridel way.*" There was method in all this, as we shall see.

The town said "No" to his school "Petision," but voted to "Open the gate Way from Mr. Samuel Train's Dwelling hous by Lewt. Abr$^m$ Jones$^s$ Dwelling hous to the County road" and granted the sum of two hundred and five Pounds old ten

(tender) to Enabel the Parties Concerned to Do it: viz: To
Mr. Samuel train one Hundred & Sixty Pounds old ten to
Mr. John hastings ten Pounds old ten to Abr^m Jones thirty
five Pounds old ten." All of which is no more reminiscent of
Colonial times than of what goes on in some country towns
to-day.

Well, great-great-gran'ther Train, having lost out on
the schools, took his £160 "old ten" and went on collecting
his "rats" and fees for one thing or another, boarding paupers and running them out of town, until, in 1768, he accomplished that which on its face even a Tammany alderman would regard as a miracle.

"Pd. Mr. Samuel Train in full for his Supporting Thos.
Train In his Lifetime and for the Costs of his funeral at
his Death £22-13-4."

I have often pondered upon who this "Thos. Train"
might have been. Was he a pauper on standing order, so to
speak? A relative? Was the name merely a coincidence? Did
charity begin at home and by some Yankee hocus pocus
help to keep the family pot a-boil? Or was there some hidden mystery concerning his birth or begetting? I fear that I
shall never know.

In 1769 Samuel Train, the elder, was a "fence viewer,"
later a "wardin," always a constable, but never so far as I am
aware a "hog reeve" or a "scalor of Leathers." Yet he could
not get away with everything, for in 1770 it was "put to vote
to know the minds of the town whether they would abate to
Sam^ll Train What he is in arrears in his Collections and it
Passed in the Negative." His influence, however, was only
temporarily in abeyance, and he had a trick or two still up his
sleeve as we shall see.

In this same year of 1769 for the first time the name of
his son, my great-grandfather, Samuel Train, Jr., makes
its appearance in the town records. They had a "pew auction"
in Weston and "the first Pew set up Was that Mr. Williams
formerly Set in at the East End of the Meeting house Next
the Door and it was struck off to Samuel Train jun^r he being

the Highest Bider for the Sume of £-22-0-0-0 By the Vandoemaster."

Samuel the First was now fifty-nine years old; Samuel the Second (or Jun^r) was twenty-five. In 1770 Samuel Junior begins to follow his father's example of public service by becoming a "surveyor and Collector of Highways" and also a "Field Driver." Coincidently the Elder Samuel had the satisfaction of seeing his constant hammering for schools begin to have its effect, for the Town voted £60 "to Support Schooling" and "to Have 5 Reading & wrighting Schools in the winter Season."

Great-great-gran'ther Train may have had no personal ax to grind, for the glaring need for "Reading and wrighting" schools is obvious from the following contemporaneous masterpiece of original orthography.

"At a Publick meeting of the freeholders and other Inhabitence of the town of Weston Quallified according to the Royal Charter to Vote in the Cheoyce of a Reprsentetive at the Publick Meeting-haus in Said town on Monday twentieth Day of May Ad 1765 at two of the Klock afternoon: the mager Pat of the Elictors then Present Did In the Presence of the Selectmen Make Cheoyce of M^r Abraham Bigelow to Serve for and Represent then In a Great an Geniral Court to be Convend Cept and held at the Courthaus In boston."

To continue our study of this shrewd Puritan, in 1772 Samuel Senior, now sixty-three years old, is back as a "Survayer & Collector," "preambelating" the town lines, and two years later is petitioning for schools again. And here I will pause long enough to let out what I fancy was the cat in the bag. Great-great-gran'ther Train wanted to sell wood to the schools! Perhaps I am quite unjust to my husky old progenitor. It may never have occurred to his simple mind. But one thing is certain. No sooner had the schools been started than he began to supply them with wood! Had he not already induced the town to open up a way from his home lot to the main road?

The Revolution was now imminent, yet the atmosphere of those stirring times is little reflected in the dry leaves of the Weston town records. One has to listen between the lines to catch the gallop of hoofs and the beat of the drums. In 1773 there were 218 voters and 16 slaves in Weston. Of the former a good many were Tories whose lives were doubtless made miserable by the constant surveillance of their fellow townsmen, but both Whigs and Tories looked upon themselves as Englishmen and were equally proud of it, and the determination to resist unjust measures and laws was not at first associated with any idea of a separation from the mother country. Indeed, until after Bunker Hill any such struggle by force of arms would have been thought impracticable, in view of the fact that in April, 1775, there was only one-half a pound of gunpowder to each man under arms in Massachusetts.

Samuel Train, Jr., my great-grandfather, belonged to one of the militia regiments known as "train bands," one-third of whose members were "alarm men," holding themselves ready at an instant's notice to repel any Indian or other attack. They were a sort of "home guard" who, in return for their supposedly unceasing vigilance, enjoyed the privilege of never being sent away. After the Indians ceased to be a menace their activities were largely confined to training day festivities. Local taxpayers complained that they wasted powder and ball in hunting and turkey matches. This was probably so, but shooting at turkeys was an excellent training for shooting at the white of an Englishman's eye. "It was considered an impropriety to shoot a squirrel or turkey anywhere except in the head." Yet in the war of 1861 it was found that a large percentage of the agricultural contingents were utterly ignorant of the first principles of loading and firing a gun! Towards the Revolutionary period the 'alarm men" became known as "minute men." Samuel Train, Jr., was a "minute man" in 1775.

General Gage in Boston had planned originally to march via the highway leading through Weston to Worcester and

seize the continental stores deposited there, but being informed that, owing to the preparedness of the country folk
and the unfitness of the roads for artillery, it was unlikely
that he would ever reach his destination he changed his objective to Concord. The news that the British were coming
flashed from town to town with amazing speed and Captain
Lamson's company of Weston "Minute Men," numbering
one hundred men and three officers, hurriedly assembled.
Parson Woodward drove his cow into the woods and ordered
his family after it, then grabbed his gun, ran to Lamson's
house, delivered a prayer and fell into line beside Samuel
Train. Next minute they were tramping over the hill towards Concord but, hearing that the British were in retreat,
they cut across through the woods to the Lexington road
where they struck the British and followed them to Charlestown. It was here that their turkey matches showed good results.

Great-grandfather Samuel was one of the few men from
the town of Weston forming a part of the forces "sent to
Canada" in 1777 to meet the British on their march south
from Quebec under Burgoyne towards Albany to effect a
juncture with Howe, which resulted in the surrender of the
British and the "Saratoga Convention." For this he was paid
£6. 6s. 8d. by the town, in addition to the bounty granted by
the General Court.

The following items appear in the account of the "Toun
Treasurer" March 2, 1776–March 1, 1777:

"Pd. Benj$^a$ Hurd for one gun   0-18-0-0 (the last 0 rep-
resents farthings)

Pd. John Lawson for one Gun and Boyonet   2-8-0-0

Pd. Tho$^s$ Rand for Supporting the Poor & Numbering
ye People   1-15-0-0

Pd. Jon$^a$ Underwood for Clothing for the W-d-o Partridge   3-0-9-0

Pd. Christ° Capron for keeping Wid° Partridge from
Nov$^m$. 5th, 1775 to March 5th 1776   1-14-0-0

Pd. Sam^el Train **Jr.** for keeping W^m Partridge 2 weeks
0-10-0-0"

How history repeats itself; Here are the Partridges back
again! Was it not in 1758 that Samuel the Elder collected
£1-1-1 "for keeping Thos. Partridge's wife 3 weeks" and
four shillings more for "carrying Thomas Partridge and
family out of town"? Perhaps it was not one of the same
covey of Partridges that his son Samuel Junior harbored at
5 shillings per week eighteen years later, but something tells
me that it probably was.

In 1778 we flush the Partridges again. This time

"Pd. Henry Coggen for Bording & Clothing William
   Partridge 67 & ½ weeks   21-0-0-0
Pd. Christopher Capron for bording Widow Partridge and
   her son W^m 13 weeks   5-17-8-0
Pd. Chris^to Capron for Bording & Clothing y^e Wid° Par-
   tridge and her Son W^m 18 weeks   10-16-0-0"

Apparently the good burghers of Weston had ever the
Partridges with them for they cost the town over £70 in
1779, while in 1780 Jonas Harrington boarded the "Wid°
Partridge & her son" to the tune of £162 and, for "Clothing and Beding her," received £43 more.

It is at this point in the record (1780) that the deprecia-
tion of the Continental Currency becomes evident, for the
"toun" votes £50,000 for raising men, in addition to its previous commitments, although the war was practically over,
and pays Isaac Flagg £1200 for "a Horse for the Publick
Service," while the "Wid° Partridge's bord" with the "Wid°
Willington" suddenly jumps to the unheard-of proportions
of £2420; James Smith receives £90 "for 1½ Coard of
wood for the NW School" and, not to lose a chance, Great-
great-grandfather Samuel, Sr., now in his seventy-first year,
collects £195 for the same service. The men who served in
the army get as high as £2263 each paid by the "toun,"

and Dr. Saml Woodward receives £680 for keeping school two months and "Bording him Self."

Sam Fisk, Toun Treasurer, credits himself

"To Counterfiet money upon my hands   £102

To loss sustained by receiving Bills of the New Emmission & Paying them out at four for one   £847-10

To Ballence Due to the Toun in Old Continental Curriancy which I have given Credit for in Silver   £1445-4-3"

So far as these earlier Trains are concerned the record is fragmentary, but it at least shows them to have been much the same sort of folk as are to be found throughout New England to-day—sturdy, patriotic, and penny wise.

My great-great-grandfather Samuel Train, Sr., born in 1711, died in 1806 at the age of ninety-five. My great-grandfather Samuel Train, Jr., "The Minute Man," born in 1745, died in 1839 at the age of ninety-four. Charles Train, my grandfather, was born on January 7, 1783.

# CHAPTER V

## "In Those Days"

### (1783)

ENOUGH of ancient history. Let what has gone before serve merely as an introduction to the bustling, modern, fin de siecle life of 1783 and after, which is where our study of progress properly begins.

This year of 1783 in which my grandfather Charles Train chose to be born was a vital moment in American history. The Revolution was just over. The preliminary articles of peace had been signed but two months previous, the Continental Army had not been disbanded and actual hostilities had not yet ceased: the British, indeed, did not sail down the Narrows until nearly a year later. It was six years before George Washington became president, six before the storming of the Bastile, ten before Louis XVI and Marie Antoinette lost their heads upon the guillotine.

It was exactly one hundred and forty-eight years after my grandfather's original ancestor John Train had arrived in America in *The Susan & Ellyn* in 1635; and exactly one hundred and forty-eight years before the publication of this book. Hence his birth not only bisects our family history, but practically that of the United States.

He lived through the period of the French Revolution and the Napoleonic Era, was already twenty years old at the time of the Louisiana purchase, attained maturity before Aaron Burr shot Alexander Hamilton, and was graduated from college the year of Nelson's Victory at Trafalgar, the Battle of Austerlitz, and the re-election of Thomas Jefferson as president.

Politically it was the beginning of a new national existence, a date so important that John Bach McMaster commences his monumental History of the People of the United States

43

with the year 1784. Economically the changes wrought during my grandfather's lifetime were no less revolutionary, although the most significant of them did not occur until half a century later.

At this time the United States had a population of less than a million adult males; the country, except for a few miles inland along the coast, was covered with forest; the interior was a wilderness; coal was unknown as fuel; the sulphur match had not been invented, and candles were lit with flint and steel; there were no stoves, furnaces, soil pipes, bathtubs, toilet paper, tooth brushes, or overshoes; there were no postmen, no pencils in common use, no newspapers as we know them; there were no iron-wheeled ploughs, no drills, no potato diggers, no reapers and binders, no hay rakes or corn cutters; there was no telephone or telegraph, no steamboat or locomotive, and, apart from the stage coaches, there were few wheeled vehicles; all clothes including shirts, stockings and straw hats were made at home; there was no national coinage for there was as yet no nation and accounts were kept in pounds, shillings and pence, French crowns, English guineas, "Spanish milled dollars," "half-joes" and pistareens, but the currency was so mutilated that it not only varied greatly in different localities but had to be scrutinized with as much care as any doubtful merchandise. I still have my grandfather's money scales with their thin circular brass disks, like watch crystals, suspended by silken threads, with its accompanying tiny weights, all folding into a faded shagreen case not much larger than one now used for spectacles.

The "Old Farmer's Almanack" for 1797 contained the following:

"The Value of the several Pieces of Silver Coin now in Circulation in the United States, in Federal Currency

|  | CENTS. | MILLS. |
|---|---|---|
| One fourth of a Pistareen or half dime.... | 5 | 0 |
| Four pence halfpenny................ | 6 | 2½ |

|  | CENTS. | MILLS. |
|---|---|---|
| Half Pistareen, or Dime............... | 10 | 0 |
| Nine pence piece, or ⅛ of a Dollar....... | 12 | 5 |
| Pistareen or two Dimes................. | 25 | 0 |
| Quarter of a Dollar.................... | 25 | 0 |
| Half a Dollar........................ | 50 | 0 |
| Dollar ............................. | 100 | 0 |
| Half a Crown, French................. | 55 | 0 |
| Half a Crown, English................ | 55 | 5 |
| Crown, French ...................... | 110 | 0 |
| Crown, English ...................... | 111 | 0 |

| 10 Mills are | 1 Cent. |
|---|---|
| 10 Cents— | 1 Dime, or Disme. |
| 10 Dimes— | 1 Dollar. |
| 10 Dollars— | 1 Eagle." |

Wrote Lieutenant John Harriott in 1807:

"The various currencies of money, in the different states, are troublesome and harassing even to the natives of the United States, and still more so to strangers. A dollar, in sterling money, is four shillings and six pence; but, in the New-England states, the currency is six shillings to a dollar; in New-York, eight shillings; in New-Jersey, Pennsylvania, and Maryland, seven shillings and six pence; in Virginia, six shillings; in North Carolina, eight shillings; and, in South Carolina and Georgia, four shillings and eight pence. All agree that the evil is great and wants to be remedied; but they say, such is the prejudice of the country-people in the different states in favour of the currency they have always been accustomed to, that it is feared, were an act of congress passed to enforce a general uniform currency, the country-people would consider it as bad as they formerly did the stamp-act."

The first entry in the Weston town records substituting dollars and cents for pounds, shillings and pence was in 1796.

In those days nightgowns (or dressing gowns) were worn often in bed outside the underclothing, while owing to the coldness of the sleeping rooms many people did not undress at all; everybody wore a nightcap; the hour glass was still in general use; land in what is now Maine and Vermont sold for ten cents an acre; astrology had a wide vogue and sea captains and owners, especially of slavers, customarily employed an astrologer to cast a horoscope in order to determine the best day and hour for sailing; even in courts of law as well as among the people many notions persisted akin to folk lore and magic, such as, for example, that the corpse of a murdered man would bleed if touched by his assassin; there were no public libraries, and few books; people made their own ink; it took twenty days for a letter to go by express rider from Maine to Georgia, four from Boston to New York, two from New York to Philadelphia, and the postage was from six to twenty-five cents per written sheet depending upon the distance it was to be sent; there was no postmaster in Weston and up to 1783 the mail was brought but once a week from Boston by a rider who collected and took back what was to be sent.

The question of what postage to put on a letter gives little trouble to-day, but in old times it often required considerable figuring. In 1793 the table of rates was as follows:

"Rate of POSTAGE of every single Letter by land.

|  | MILES. | CENTS. |
|---|---|---|
|  | 30 | 6 |
|  | 60 | 8 |
|  | 100 | 10 |
| For every single letter | 150 | 12½ |
|  | 200 | 15 |
|  | 250 | 17 |
|  | 350 | 20 |
|  | 450 | 22 |
| For more than | 450 | 25 |

"No allowance is to be made for intermediate miles. Every double letter is to pay double the said rates; every triple letter, triple; every packet weighing one ounce, at the rate of four single letters for each ounce."

In 1783 people stopped where they were and did no gadding. Few owned other than cart horses, fewer still had anything to travel in, and journeys were usually taken on horseback, even after the stage lines had become numerous. A private "chaise" was tantamount to a Rolls-Royce to-day, and a town which could boast as many as two pointed to them with pride.

In 1834 the local historian of Ipswich wrote "about thirty-five years ago, horse wagons began to be employed. Gradually increasing, they have almost altogether superceded riding on horseback among our farmers. . . . They have prevented the method of going in a cart, as often practised before they were invented, by social parties, when wishing to make a visit of several miles."

But mostly people walked, and on other than mail days, if a man had an important letter destined for a distant point and requiring haste, he would often trudge the whole twelve miles to Boston in order to post it. Frederick Manson of Framingham, aged seventy-seven, one of my great grand-father's friends, who in his youth had also been a "Minute Man" and had fought at Bunker Hill, having an errand to perform in Cambridge seventeen miles distant, walked there, transacted his business, turned around and walked back again without having sat down.

If a man wanted to go to Hartford, instead of as now buying a seat in the Pullman and burying his nose in a magazine for a couple of hours, he might follow on foot the Indian trail, known as the "Old Connecticutt Path," by which a sturdy tramper could walk through the woods to the settlements on that river in ten days or two weeks.

It was in 1783, the year of my grandfather's birth, that the first systematic stage route went into operation between Boston and New York. The usual run was about thirty miles a day, but even the forty miles journey to Providence was broken by a stop over night. The trip took from eight to ten days and cost between $20 to $25; while if one went by stage to Providence and thence by sailing sloop through Long Island Sound considerably more time was required, although the cost was reduced thereby a third.

Thomas Twinning, an Englishman, described an American stage as "a long car with four benches. Three of these in the interior held nine passengers, and a tenth passenger was seated by the side of the driver on the front bench. A light roof was supported by eight slender pillars, four on each side. Three large leather curtains suspended to the roof, one at each side and the third behind, were rolled up or lowered at the pleasure of the passengers. There was no space nor place for luggage, each person being expected to stow his things as he could under his seat or legs. The entrance was in front, over the driver's bench. Of course the three passengers on the back seat were obliged to crawl across all the other benches to get to their places. There were no *backs* to the benches to support and relieve us during a rough and fatiguing journey over a newly and ill-made road. It would be unreasonable to expect perfection in the arrangements of a new country; but . . . a mere strap behind the seats would have been a great comfort, and the ponderous leather curtains, which extended the whole length of the wagon, would have been much more convenient *divided* into two or three parts, and with a glass, however small, in each division to give light to the passengers in bad weather, and enable them to have a glimpse of the country. The disposal of the luggage also was extremely incommodious, not only to the owner, but to his neighbors. We were quite full, having ten passengers besides the driver."

To the east a single stage ran once a week to Portsmouth. There were but three wagon roads across the mountains to the west, and the heavy coaches floundered along through bogs and forests at an average rate of four miles an hour. The best thoroughfare in the county ran through Weston from Boston to Worcester, but distances that can now be covered by motor in fifteen minutes were viewed ordinarily as prohibitive, so that members of the same families living but ten miles apart sometimes did not see each other oftener than once a year, and then usually at Thanksgiving.

Travel when possible was by water which was hardly more hazardous than by land. There were no steamers, and no one went to Europe. Under these circumstances news travelled but slowly.

Even in the last century the habit of "staying put" was firmly riveted in the New Englander. My former law partner, Mr. Charles Albert Perkins, told me that his grandmother, who lived at a distance of only eight miles, visited her family but once a year in Topsfield, Mass.; and my friend, Mr. Joseph Warren, contributes the statement that his two great-aunts who lived at Jamaica Plain, three miles from Boston, usually visited town only twice a twelvemonth. This difficulty of communication is perhaps the most important single fact to be considered in connection with the development of social and economic life in America in the early nineteenth century.

Finally, but not least in importance, there were in 1783 no hospitals, clinics, pharmacies, trained nurses, or alms houses, no anæsthetics and no vaccination against smallpox, which ravaged the land.

While there were substitutes for tooth brushes few people made use of them and the teeth were systematically neglected. People knew "why they were shunned" in those days, so that when they laughed ladies covered their mouths with their fans, while gentlemen did so with their handkerchiefs. Perfume was a necessity.

The use of gunpowder, applied to the teeth by means of a butcher's skewer, was recommended as a dentifrice in the New York *Gazette and General Advertiser* for August 12, 1799:

"Rules for the Prefervation of the Teeth and Gums.

"The teeth therefore are to be cleaned; but with great precaution, for if you wear the enamel off fafter, by cleanfing the out-fide, than nature fupplies it with, your teeth will fuffer more by this method, than perhaps by a total neglect. A butcher's fkewer or the wood with which they are made, muft be bruised and bit at the end, till with a little ufe it will become the fofteft and beft brufh for this purpofe; and, underftand, you muft clean your teeth with this brufh alone, without any powder whatever; and once in a forthnight, not oftner, dip your fkewer brufh into a few grains of gunpowder, breaking them firft with the brufh, and this will remove every fpot and blemifh and give your teeth an inconceivable whitenefs. It is almoft needlefs to fay that the mouth muft be well wafhed after this operation; for befides the neceffity of fo doing, the falt petre &c ufed in the compofition of gunpowder would if it remained be injurious to the gums &c but has not, nor can it have any bad effect in fo fhort a time. I have conftantly practifed this method for twenty-five years and am thoroughly convinced it is fafe and effectual."

Paul Revere, always "Johnny on the Spot," advertised in the *Boston News Letter* of August 25, 1768:

"PAUL REVERE—Whereas many Persons are so unfortunate as to lose their fore Teeth by accident, and otherwise, to their great Detriment, not only in looks, but speaking both in Public and Private:

"This is to inform all such, that they may have them replaced with false ones, that look as well as the Natural, and answer the End of Speaking to all intents by PAUL REVERE, Goldsmith, near the head of Dr. Clark's Wharf, Boston,—

"All Persons who have had false Teeth fixt by Mr. John Baker, Surgeon-Dentist, and they have got loose (as they will in Time) may have them fastened by the above, who learnt the Method of fixing them from Mr. Baker."

In weighing these numerous "had nots" and attempting to evaluate the life of our ancestors it should be borne in mind as mitigating the at least external poverty of their existence, that there were no crowds, no subway crushes, no stock market crashes, no telephones, no "loud-speakers," no Sunday newspapers, no advertisements in the landscape, no motor accidents, no prohibition, and that since there was no plumbing there were, at least, no plumbers.

The bathtub is neither an unmixed blessing nor conclusive evidence as to progress. The first of these interesting contrivances to be built and connected up in America (outside the bathing houses erected on certain southern estates) was, I am informed, made of mahogany and lined with sheet lead, and exhibited by its proud owner at a Christmas party in Cincinnati in 1842. Next day it was denounced by the newspapers as a sybaritic luxury and anathematized by the local medicos as a menace to health,—as perhaps it was. In Virginia bathtubs were taxed thirty dollars per year and the first one to be installed in the White House was under President Fillmore in 1852. The Saturday night bath was a universal institution down to 1900—"women and children first." It is still the subject of jest. And there is a recorded instance of a purchaser of a tub ordered in August, who refused to take delivery of it in October on the ground that, time being of the essence of the contract, he no longer had any use for the article "since the bathing season was over." Recently I was told of an elderly lady who attributed a temporary ailment to the fact that she had taken "her bath" too early in the spring. Can progress be measured by hot-water piping and is the bathtub one of its mile stones? If so, have we progressed beyond the age of Caracala? Indeed it might be argued that the boasted bathtub, that emblem and sign manual of civilization, has done little more than to decrease our powers of resistance.

Passing now from the social-economic to the political aspect of the year of my grandfather's advent into the world, it should be noted that in 1783 the United States was not even a "noble experiment." Nobody knew whether or not there would ever be a "United States," for the states were anything but united, and many people looked forward to a constitutional monarchy under George Washington as King.

*The Pennsylvania Gazette* of November 25, 1789, carried the following item:

"Extract of a letter from Boſton, dated October 28.

" 'This day, at eleven o'clock, the Preſident was conveyed in the Admiral's barge on board the Admiral's ſhip—the Major of the fleet ſteered, the Midſhipmen rowed, all dreſſed in red—when the Preſident arrived he was received on board, after the ſame ſtile they receive their Kings, viz. The officers took off their ſhoes—and the crew all appeared with their legs naked.' "

It was a pessimistic era. Everything was in confusion; everybody was poor—at least in the rural districts—and everybody was depressed. The discharged soldiers from the Continental Army were drifting home, complaining of their treatment, their food, most of all their pay, and being swindled by land grabbers out of their grants in Maine for a few cents per acre. There is to-day a township in Maine officially known as "Revolutionary Soldiers."

In 1783 Noah Webster published his famous spelling-book and a medical department was first added to Harvard College; and in 1784 the first law school in America was established at Litchfield, Connecticut.

Divorce was practically unknown; the whipping-post, pillory and stocks were still in active use; people were jailed for debts of less than a shilling, and the tything man—a sort of "moral policeman"—made his rounds on Sundays to see that everybody was properly at church and that other decencies were observed.

George Washington was 51 years of age, Aaron Burr 27, John Adams 48, Thomas Jefferson 40, James Madison 32, J. Q. Adams 16, Andrew Jackson 16.

This in brief was my grandfather's world—a Puritan world, to be sure, but very different from what a Puritan world had once been. There was, doubtless, almost as much divergence between the point of view of the original John Train and his great-great-great-grandson Charles, as between that of the latter and myself.

The town of Weston had changed little during the revolutionary period, and although the forest had been steadily driven back (owing in part perhaps to Great-great-gran'ther Train's wood-selling activities) and the original rude farmhouses had been replaced by more ambitious dwellings, it still exhibited many of the characteristics of a frontier town. It was true that Boston was only twelve miles away across the Charles River, but there was no bridge and the road was abominable. The extreme difference between city and country life, owing to the rudimentary facilities of transportation at this period, cannot be overemphasized. Thus, while there was a comparatively elegant society in Tory Boston, existence became cruder and cruder inversely to the square of the distance to Worcester and Springfield.

In winter-time, during the occupation of Boston by the British, the officers had driven out on sleighing parties and got drunk at the Weston taverns and, after the Red Coats had sailed away, occasional young blades still imitated their example; but, for the most part, the only strangers who passed through the town were travellers bound for the West, wood sellers, or drovers, convoying herds of sheep and cattle to the Boston market, for Weston enjoyed the advantage of being situated both on the Worcester turnpike, which was the highway to New York, and upon the freight haul to the coast from Vermont and the Connecticut Valley. As a result, it early developed a trade of its own from the hinterland and neighboring countryside, since in order to save the extra twelve miles farmers and their wives, who had come long distances, would stop and do their trading there without going on to Boston. Thus it acquired an individual importance with nothing of a suburban flavor. Ecclesiastically and politically it was well organized. It had several stores and at least two taverns; and enjoyed the æsthetic distinction of being the place where "rusticated" (or suspended) Harvard students were sent to study during a probationary period and to repent them of their former sins.

There were few houses in Weston of any importance that

had not first or last served as taverns. It was the most profitable business of all country towns along the main arteries of
travel, and it was not unusual for fifty or one hundred teams
to put up over night at a single inn. My great-uncle Isaac
Train kept one of these.

In spite of tavern roysterers, life in Weston was still a
serious and rather sombre business, the Devil a familiar personality, Hell ever imminent, and Sunday a "field day for
the discussion of obscure points of theology, in which the
young, who had taken down the heads of the sermon in
their little notebooks, were expected to show an active interest." The Puritan spirit still dominated the community, and
although card games, dancing and the playing of musical
instruments were no longer universally regarded in the light
of abominations as in early Colonial days, the dour attitude
of Calvinism, which held laughter unseemly, had led to the
smileless humor commonly known as "dry." Theatrical performances were unlawful in Boston even as late as 1797, and
in rural districts the ownership of a set of Shakespeare was
ground for the suspicion of secret immorality.

Even so, there were plenty who welcomed diversion of
any sort when they could get it, and then, as now, some laws
were "liberally enforced." In lieu of the footlights, there
were circuses, fireworks, and animal exhibitions, such as a
very famous elephant (almost as celebrated as the later
"Jumbo"), a "tyger," a cassowary, "a Fine Large White
Bear" advertised as "a Sight far preferable to the Lion in
the judgement of all Persons who have seen them," and a
"Sapient Dog" who lit lamps and fired off cannon. And all
for the small sum of one pistareen!

A law prohibiting stage plays was passed by the Massachusetts General Court in 1750. This resulted in clandestine
performances, and there were repeated but unsuccessful efforts to have the law repealed. For over half a century theatrical performances were camouflaged under the name of
"exhibitions." In December, 1792, the "New Exhibition
Room" in Boston was raided by the sheriff, armed with a

warrant for the arrest of the actors. This so incensed the audience that it became riotous and tore down the arms of the State, together with a portrait of Governor Hancock, and trampled them underfoot. I have not been able to find out what happened to the actors. Governor Hancock was a bitter opponent of the theatre, and during his lifetime the law was enforced; but after his death in 1797 the law became a dead letter and was finally repealed.

The absence of entertainment, no less than the coldness of the houses, made drinking a popular form of amusement, the place of water, which was regarded as hardly potable, being taken by rum and cider. The usual weekly per capita allowance in the average family was two quarts of rum and a pint of molasses. This was in addition to the "flip," or home-made beer of hops. The best rum sold for thirty-seven cents per gallon. The prejudice against water postponed the advent of the great American drink, ice-water, until well into the nineteenth century. Ice, in fact, was almost, if not quite, unused. On the other hand every adult had his noon toddy, and great numbers of otherwise respectable men spent their lives in a chronic state of saturation. Indeed, it was not unheard of for a clergyman to exhibit signs of an unnatural stimulation in the pulpit. There was at least one out and out drunkard in almost every family.

Professor Channing tells how in 1787 Nathan Dane lodged in New York City with Elbridge Gerry and Rufus King and after two weeks' stay paid for, on behalf of all three, six gallons of Madeira, three dozen bottles of porter, four gallons of spirits, and five dozen bottles of claret; and how Jefferson during his presidency spent over $10,000 for wines and liquors at a time when his salary was but $25,000 per year. The "general store" was in effect a local bar. But already Dr. Benjamin Rush and others were active in urging reform.

Wages and salaries were ridiculously low judged by modern standards. Carpenters received 80 cents per day, hired help was paid at the rate of $40 per year, the salary of the

Chief Justice of the United States was $4,000, and that of the Associate Justices and the Secretaries of State and the Treasury was $3,500 each.

*The Pennsylvania Packet* of September 23, 1780, contained the following:

"Wanted at a Seat about half a day's journey from Philadelphia, on which are good improvements and domestics, A single Woman of unsullied Reputation, an affable, cheerful, active and amiable Disposition; cleanly, industrious, perfectly qualified to direct and manage the female Concerns of country business, as raising small stock, dairying, marketing, combing, carding, spinning, knitting, sewing, pickling, preserving, etc., and occasionally to instruct two young Ladies in those Branches of Occonomy, who, with their father, compose the Family. Such a person will be treated with respect and esteem, and meet with every encouragement due to such a character."

Such a paragon, if found, would have received at best £50 per annum. To-day she could command her own terms, even unto the name and half the earthly goods of her employer.

It is not easy to form an opinion as to the sexual morality of these earlier descendants of the Puritans.

Much has been made of the fact that in Colonial days kissing in public was regarded as an abomination, and that kissing, even by husband and wife, upon the Sabbath, was a criminal offense. The classic example is that of Captain Kemble, who, returning home after a long voyage, kissed his wife on the front steps of their house in Boston and was promptly lodged in the stocks. Anyhow, he seems to have "cut up considerable," as they used to say. And, after all, it was a unique case. I wager that a husband and wife of the present day could get themselves arrested without much difficulty for kissing on Fifth Avenue, and, what is more, be fined in due course for disorderly conduct; just as modern young people would be arrested for "petting" if they were caught "petting" hard enough,—certainly for "immoderate great petting," as the Puritans might have called it.

Youth will be served and human nature does not greatly change. An early Massachusetts statute declared "it is a common practice in diverse places for young men irregularly and disorderly to watch all advantages for their evil purposes, to insinuate into the affections of young maidens, by coming to them in places and seasons unknown to their parents for such ends, whereby much evil hath grown amongst us, to the dishonor of God and damage of parties."

The evidence seems to indicate that even in very early days unchastity was common, and, from the number of sermons among my reverend grandfather's papers directed against the sin of fornication, it seems likely that it was fairly prevalent around Boston.

My friend, Mr. Charles Cushing, who lives in Bath, Maine, recently unearthed in his attic a mildewed diary which had been kept by his great-uncles in the early part of the last century. That the town was a Puritan town seems to be established by the fact that, as late as 1880, his sister was refused membership in the local Presbyterian Church because she declined to give up dancing. Now this diary, kept by two boys of Puritan descent in a blue Puritan town, is written partly in cipher, and since the winter evenings are long and cold in that part of the country my friend amused himself in trying to decode it,—a not over-difficult task. The cryptic portions when deciphered shed an entirely new light upon so-called Puritan life in New England, especially the morals of the youth of that day, and from the record it might have been fairly inferred that Casanova would have found himself as at home there as in Bologna or Milan. Yet this same town had tythingmen until 1840!

"Necking" and "petting" are nothing new, and in my grandfather's time took the form of "bundling," a practice said in fact still to exist in certain parts of the Northwest today. This was the seemingly grotesque custom of allowing a courting, or even merely friendly, couple to get into bed with their clothes on, ostensibly to keep warm during an evening call. It gradually died out as a result of general ridicule,—

a consummation accelerated by a famous ballad published in an almanac about 1785, entitled

A New

## BUNDLING SONG:

OR A REPROOF TO THOSE YOUNG COUNTRY WOMEN, WHO
FOLLOW THAT REPROACHFUL PRACTICE, AND TO THEIR
MOTHERS FOR UPHOLDING THEM THEREIN.

> Since bundling very much abounds,
> In many parts in country towns,
> No doubt but some will spurn my song,
> And say I'd better hold my tongue;
> But none I'm sure will take offence;
> Or deem my song impertinence,
> But only those who guilty be,
> And plainly here their pictures see,
> And let it be in common fame,
> Held up to view a noted shame.
> Young miss if this your practice be,
> I'll teach you now yourself to see:
> You plead you're honest, modest too,
> But such a plea will never do;
> For how can modesty consist,
> With shameful practice such as this?

"Parties of men and girls spend the night together at inns both sexes sleeping together," writes a contemporary. "Such great control have the females acquired, that several who have bundled for years, it is said, have never permitted any improper liberties. Indeed, it is considered as not in the least indelicate."

Mr. H. R. Stites, who wrote a book on the subject, refers to it as "that ridiculous and pernicious custom which prevailed among the young to a degree which we can scarcely credit—sapped the foundation of morality and tarnished the escutcheons of thousands of families."

Even in those old days it was not unknown for young gentlemen and ladies to form an acquaintance without a formal introduction. Indeed "The New Academy of Compliments" published in 1795 expressly prescribes how it must be done, by approaching, bowing ceremoniously and making use of one of the following modes of address:

"Pardon my rashness if I presume so far as to proffer my services unto you; your beauty hath so far prevailed over me that I have long desired to attain to the honour of speaking to you," or, "Though I have not yet been so happy as to be known to you by any service, yet the zeal I bear to your obedience hath obliged me to come and salute you."

§

The newspapers or "gazettes," as they were generally called, consisted of but a couple of sheets printed on the roughest sort of paper such as would now be used for wrapping butcher's meat. The Revolution caused a rag famine during which most of them suspended and it became a patriotic duty to save every scrap of rag and sent it to the nearest paper mill. In every household the rag bag became as familiar as the Bible. The *Norwich* Courier of May 27, 1797, in the first recorded "slogan" upon the subject, besought every loyal citizen to say to his wife: "Molly, make a rag bag and hang it under the shelf where the big Bible lies," and the Boston *Gazette* urged its readers to teach every child its "rag lesson," just as during the World War we were told to "eat less flour, sugar," etc. The shortage continued until well into the next century. Many of us remember the family rag bag, but few, I imagine, realize what started it.

The "news" itself consisted merely of a hodgepodge of clippings from other papers, letters on politics, anecdotes, and notes of European events brought by sailing vessels and already months old, moralistic essays alongside dirty poetry and coarse stories, appeals from the printer for payment from his delinquent subscribers, and notices offering rewards of a few dollars for the return of runaway slaves and stray animals. One gains the impression that the items were set up in the order received without regard to date or even of importance.

Thus it is impossible to construct from the newspaper press of the last quarter of the eighteenth century any chronology of the War of the Revolution. The newspapers gave only scattered and meagre accounts of the struggle, made up chiefly of letters from distant correspondents and of stray items brought to the printer by post riders. There was no "spot news," no "bulletin," no "flash" in the modern sense. War news was submerged beneath advertisements of patent medicines "to cure scurvy," sales of farm lands, and advertisements of wet nurses possessed of "full breasts of milk" with which to "suckle the young."

To illustrate, the New York *Gazette* and *The Weekly Mercury* of July 8, 1776, published the following item on page three:

"Philadelphia, June 3

"Yeſterday the Congress unanimouſly Reſolved to declare the United Colonies FREE and INDEPENDENT STATES,"

while page one contained a lengthy report of proceedings of the House of Lords, dated *March 5*.

The first Presidential election was reported in the New York *Packet* of April 7, 1789, on page two, column four, thus:

"New York, April 7

"Yeſterday the Hon. the Congreſs of the United States met in Federal Hall, when the ballots for Preſident and Vice-Preſident being canvaſſed, it appeared that his Excellency GEORGE WASHINGTON is chosen President, and his Excellency John Adams, Vice-President. We learn that diſpatches are to be sent to each of these gentlemen THIS DAY, and their arrival here may soon be expected."

Page one of this issue contains War Department notices, advertisements of land sales, pills, etc. The New York *Morning Post and Daily Advertiser* of the same date, April 7, 1789, contained nothing on this subject.

*The Pennsylvania Gazette* of September 2, 1789, carried the following notice:

"Philadelphia, September 2.

"Extract of a letter from Frederickſburg, dated August 25, 1789. 'Mrs. Waſhington, the mother of our Preſident, died this afternoon'."

Washington himself died between ten and eleven o'clock on the night of December 14, 1799. We can imagine how that impressive intelligence would have been handled by the press of to-day, yet the first newspaper announcement of his death was made by *The Times* of Alexandria, Virginia, on December 16. It said:

"It is our mournful duty firſt to announce to our country and to the world the death of GENERAL GEORGE WASHINGTON. This mournful event occurred on Saturday evening about 11 o'clock. On the preceding night he was attacked with a violent inflammatory affection of the throat, which, in leſs than twenty-four hours, put a period to his life."

This item was picked up two days later by *The Gazette of the United States and Philadelphia Daily Advertiser*, and was published on page three, column four, followed by a brief announcement that the House and Senate had adjourned that morning out of respect, and a letter from "A Customer," written from Alexandria, December 15, which gave a few additional details of the death.

Yet a study of these old yellow sheets reveals the germ of every aspect of the most modern journalism. Thus in *The Continental Journal and Weekly Advertiser* for December 25, 1783, appears the following which might be regarded as "sex stuff":

"The people of the western part of the State who style themselves Shaking Quakers, and who suppose they and they only have discovered the true mode of worship, have of late ('tis said) utterly disclaimed the use of any garments when engaged in their religious exercises; presenting themselves unpolluted by the vain and unChristian articles of dress, and performing all their dancings, turnings, jumpings, tumblings, twistings, wrigglings in that condition."

Accidents, calamities and crimes were reported with little or nothing in the way of what we would call a "head-line" to-day, the traditional newspaper "lead" was unknown, and editorial comment was frequent. The following are general news items taken from the Boston *Weekly Magazine* of November 6 and 13, 1802.

"On Thursday, the 7th ult. a son of Mr. Simon Griggs, of Colwell's Manor (Vermont) about 6 years of age, having found a rope, in a playful mood, put one end around his body, and the other on a cow's tale. The lad then struck her with a stick, which occasioned her to run, dragging him after her. She made for the lake and in her course struck his head against a log. Mrs. Griggs, observing the dreadful situation of her son, ran into the water, caught the cow, from which she extricated her son by cutting the rope—but alas! It was too late, her son having already expired.

"On the 6th Ult. Mr. Levi Marston, of North Yarmouth, N.H. was at work in a well, a stone weighing about 20 pounds, fell directly on his head and threw him to the bottom, in which were seven feet of water. After three attempts he was brought out of the well apparently dead. He was in the water about two minutes, but no water issued from his mouth or nose, after he was taken out; he was considerably bruised, but is on the recovery.—Instances like this,—peculiarly call for a grateful acknowledgement to an overruling Providence.

"Some time in July last, Mr. William Warner (says the Ohio *Gazette* of Oct. 4) was lost in the woods between the Scioto salt works and the head waters of leading creek, for twenty-four days.—During which he subsisted on pole cat and wood turtle. For twenty-two days he saw no human being. One of his feet was bit by a snake, which occasioned him to go on his hands and knees for several days. He was quite deranged when taken up."

Nor were the precursors of "Beatrice Fairfax" and "Dorothy Dix" absent.

In the Boston *Weekly Magazine* there was a first-page column signed "The Gossip" who, whatever his (or her) original intention, speedily became an adviser to bewildered young females. Already in 1802 we find "Almira" and "Isabella" pouring out their innocent hearts in the search for guidance.

There were also many letters bewailing the depravity of the young. In the Boston *Weekly Magazine* for May 21, 1803, an elderly man writes as follows:

"Do, sir, say a word or two on this subject, and don't forget to mention the idle expensive and profligate manners of our young men; how boys of sixteen will boast of their amours; spend their money in gaming, and their time in drinking; how they put more on their back at one time; than would have served their grand-fathers for Sunday suits a whole life-time; I mean in regard to expense—how they saunter away their time—read novels, plot mischief, and talk nonsense and impiety. . . . This was not the method those brave men were brought up, who gave liberty to America, and much I fear, does this pernicious system continue, a very short period must make the race of men extinct from us, who will, neither feel the inclination nor possess the power to preserve that liberty sacred as it was transmitted to them."

Many of the advertisements of the period are classic for the realism of their descriptions and their naïve humor. What could surpass the following from *The New England Chronicle or The Essex Gazette,* issue of Thursday, November 9, to Thursday, November 16, 1775, while the British were bottled up in Boston and the Colonial troops were encamped on Arlington Heights?

"Deserted from Col. Brewer's regiment—Capt. Harvey's

Company, one Simeon Smith of Greenfield, a joiner by trade, a thin spar'd fellow about 5 feet 4 inches high, had on blue coat and black vest, a metall button on his hat, black long hair, black eyes, his voice in the hermaphrodite fashion, the masculine rather predominant; Likewise one Matthias Smith, a small smart fellow, a sadler by trade, grey headed, has a younger look in his face, is apt to say I swear! I swear! and between his words will spit smart; had on a green coat, and an old red great coat; he is a right gamster although he wears something of a sober look; Likewise one John Daby, a long hump-shouldered fellow, a shoemaker by trade, drawls his words and for comfortable says comfable, had a green coat, thick leather breeches, slim legs, lost some of his fore teeth; Also one John Guilson, a man well known in Sunderland, wears a watch, midling stature, a cooper by trade, has a black beard, wears a light colour'd coat and jacket and has a surly look; Likewise his brother in law Gideon Graves, about a midling stature, somewhat stocky, his looks, gestures and words generally crabbed, had a sad red coat, a pale blue vest, dark brown thickset breeches, and had a large cutlas. They have been apt to make excuses for their running away, and intimate they took a dislike to one Eliphalet Hastings who was put in ensign over them, and found much fault with the Continental allowance. Whoever will take up said deserters and secure or bring them into camp, shall have two dollars reward for each and all necessary charges paid by me.          Moses Harvey Capt.

Prospect Hill, Nov. 8, 1775.
P.S. Said deserters have been gone some time, and because I have expected they would return I have omitted advertising them."

It is worthy of note that in most of the newspapers published on December 25, 1783, there is not the slightest mention of Christmas.

§

Although the Trains owned no slaves there were plenty of them in the neighborhood, and it never occurred to my great-grandfather that there was the slightest inconsistency between owning a negro and the ideal of religious and political freedom which had animated the early Colonists or led to their revolt against England. The first statute legalizing slavery in Massachusetts, adopted in 1641, was still the law. It read:

"There shall never be any bond slaverie, villinage or captivities amongst us unless it be lawfull captives taken in just warres, and such strangers as willingly selle themselves or are sold to us. And these shall have all the liberties and Christian usages which the law of God established in Israell concerning such persons doeth morally require. This exempt none from servitude who shall be judged thereto by Authoritie."

This statute was never repealed. For "an absolute recognition of slavery as a legitimate status, and of the right of one man to sell himself as well as that of another man to buy him," it has no parallel in the contemporary codes of any of the other New England colonies or, indeed, anywhere else.

In view of the romantic attachment of Massachusetts for the negro cause in 1861, when Robert Gould Shaw died leading his colored troops and was "buried with his niggers," it is interesting to recall that Massachusetts sea captains for years were among the most active of slave traders and that the wealth of many of our so-called "best" American families is directly traceable to the barter in human beings. This continued down to the Civil War, and as I have already said, my own maternal grandfather was hard at it in 1860 when he cut his throat to cheat the sheriff.

At the time of the Revolution negro slaves were in general use in Boston, and throughout the rural districts they played the part of unpaid "help," often entrusted with much responsibility in farm management. There had been, how-

ever, considerable protest against slavery and the slave trade
and when the Colonies revolted the inconsistency of a
struggle for liberty which at the same time perpetuated
slavery became obvious.

The Massachusetts State Constitution of 1780 contained
the phrase in the first article of its Declaration of Rights, "all
men are born free and equal," but in point of fact no act of
abolition was ever passed and it seems plain from contemporary evidence that abolition was not intended.

Slavery, for climatic reasons, never really flourished in the
North and there was more effort to get rid of black babies on
account of their being a nuisance than to breed them. An advertisement from *The Continental Journal* of March 15,
1781, reads:

"To be SOLD, an extraordinarily likely Negro Wench,
17 years old, she can be warranted to be strong, healthy and
good natured, has no sense of Freedome, has been always
used to a farmer's kitchen and dairy, and is not known to
have any failing, but being with child, which is the only
cause of her being sold."

Note that the date of this advertisement is 1781. In the
year after my grandfather's birth the State census showed
a population of 4,377 blacks. What their exact situation was
is an interesting subject for speculation.

The courts soon began to reflect anti-slavery sentiment,
and in 1783 a judgment of the Supreme Judicial Court in
the County of Worcester virtually effected the abolition of
slavery in Massachusetts, prompting large numbers of negroes to leave their masters although others were deterred
"on account of their age and infirmities, or because they did
not know how to provide for themselves, or for some pecuniary consideration." Gradually the custom of owning slaves
died out, like the custom of purchasing the time of redemp-
tioners, or binding out apprentices. Most Boston people do
not know that slavery ever existed there.

There was, however, another form of slavery in Massachusetts far more detrimental to the happiness of the com-

munity. In those days husbands and wives were legally one person, and as has been said "the husband was that person."

The worst feature of the situation was that, as a practical matter, there was no way for a woman to get rid of a worthless husband, for while the civil authorities could grant divorces they rarely did so. Under these circumstances persons unhappily mated frequently, as they do now, settled the matter for themselves and in addition invited the public to share in their relief and joy.

Thus the long suffering Josiah Woodbury, having been deserted by his spouse, advertised in the Essex *Gazette,* September 17, 1771:

"Ran away from Josiah Woodbury, Cooper, his houſe Plague for seven long yⁿars, Maſury Old Moll, Alias Trial of Vengeance. He that ᷾ft will never ſeek her; he that ſhall keep her, I will give two Buſhal of Beans. I forewarn all perſons in Town and Country from truſting ſaid Trial of Venegance. I have hove all the old shoes I can find for joy; and all my neighbors rejoice with me. A good Riddance of Bad Ware. Amen.

Joſiah Woodbury."

Similarly Mrs. Susannah Randall in the Salem *Mercury,* July 1, 1785:

"Ran away from the ſubſcriber, on the 13th of May, one Joseph Randall, a tall, trim-built fellow: Had on, when he went away, a blue coat, velvet waiſtcoat and breeches, mixt coloured ſtockings, and wore away two felt hats; he rode away a black horſe, and led a ſorrel horſe; he is ſuppoſed to be lurking in the ſouth part of Scantick after a ſtrumpet that he has ſpent the moſt of his time with for three years paſt. Whoever will take up ſaid Randall and return him to me, ſhall have three coppers reward; but whoever will take the trouble to keep him away ſhall have ten dollars reward, and all neceſſary charges paid by me.

Susannah Randall.

N. B. All perſons are forbid harbouring him, for I am determined to maintain him no longer."

It is encouraging to know that things were not bad enough
to destroy all sense of humor in the parties involved.

§

It was in many respects a cruel age, when men based their
treatment of one another on the recorded acts of the vengeful
deity of the ancient Hebrews. A mere painless death was regarded as far too merciful a punishment for major crimes,
and burning at the stake, hanging in chains over a slow fire,
cutting off ears and other members, and branding with red
hot irons as entirely proper and wholly Christian.

No thought was given to the pathologic aspects of crime,
the economic or social conditions which produce it, or its
prevention, and both criminals and insane as well were
treated with an inhumanity which extended to all those,
whether criminals or not, who found themselves in gaol even
for debt. The "crime as a disease" theory had not been
promulgated.

Many felonies were punishable by death, save where the
defendant could plead "benefit of clergy," and all sentences
were for a fixed and definite term, unalterable save by pardon from the supreme executive. The ducking stool, the pillory, the whipping post and stocks were all actively in use in
America during my grandfather's early manhood. I have no
knowledge of a ducking stool used in the neighborhood of
Weston or Framingham but, as late as 1824, a Philadelphia
scold was sentenced by the Court of Sessions to be ducked.
Perhaps Massachusetts women were not as shrewish as those
farther south.

The Boston *Evening Post* of Sept. 22, 1755, contains this
item:

"Thursday last, in the Afternoon, *Mark*, a Negro Man,
and Phillis, a Negro Woman, both Servants to the late Captain *John Cadna*, of *Charlestown*, were executed at *Cambridge*, for poisoning their said Master . . . The Fellow
was hanged, and the Woman burned at the Stake about Ten
Yards distant from the Gallows."

The first time my grandfather was taken as a small boy to Boston, in August, 1789, one of his chief thrills was derived from seeing eleven culprits receive what was called "the discipline of the post." Samuel Breck, writing in 1771, said:

"The large whipping post painted red stood conspicuously and prominently in the most public street in the town. It was placed in State Street directly under the window of a great writing school which I frequented, and from there the scholars were indulged in the spectacle of all kinds of punishment suited to harden their hearts and brutalize their feelings. Here women were taken in a huge cage in which they were dragged on wheels from prison, and tied to the post with bare backs on which thirty or forty lashes were bestowed among the screams of the culprit and the uproar of the mob."

The pillory like the whipping post also stood on State Street and was in use as late as 1803. "On Sept. 9, 1787, in one Boston court one burglar was sentenced to be hanged, five thieves to be whipped, two greater thieves to be set on the gallows, and one counterfeiter set on the pillory."

Whipping at the cart's tail and riding the wooden horse were also not uncommon as forms of punishment. On January 15, 1801, during my grandfather's freshman year at Harvard, a certain Hawkins, for the crime of forgery, stood for an hour in the Salem pillory, and had his ears cropped.

The greatest curse of the poor lay in the ability of their creditors under the law to throw them into prison for the smallest debts. Says McMaster:

"One hundred years ago the laborer who fell from a scaffold or lay sick of a fever was sure to be seized by the sheriff the moment he recovered, and be carried to jail for the bill of a few dollars which had been run up during his illness at the huckster's or the tavern . . . the face of the land was dotted with prisons where deeds of cruelty were done, in comparison with which the foulest acts committed in the hulks sink to a contemptible insignificance. . . .

"At Northampton the cells were scarce four feet high, and filled with the noxious gases of the privy-vaults through which they were supposed to be ventilated. Light came in from two chinks in the wall. At the Worcester prison were a number of like cells, four feet high by eleven long, without a window or a chimney, or even a hole in the wall. Not a ray of light ever penetrated them. In other jails in Massachusetts the cells were so small that the prisoners were lodged in hammocks swung one over the other.

"Into such pits and dungeons all classes of offenders of both sexes were indiscriminately thrust. It is therefore not at all surprising that they became seminaries of every conceivable form of vice, and centres of the most disgusting diseases. Prostitutes plied their calling openly in the presence of men and women of decent station, and guilty of no crime but an inability to pay their debts."

The approved method of dealing with the insane was to string them up by the thumbs and beat them until their ravings ceased.

It has been estimated that 75,000 persons were annually incarcerated for debt in the United States. In 1829 in Philadelphia alone eighty jailed debtors owed less than one dollar each. Only two States abolished imprisonment for debt—Ohio and Kentucky—before 1830. Southern States imprisoned debtors until the Civil War; but in the North it had been practically abolished by 1840.

§

They were parlous times into which little Charles Train had been born. Every family in the town was suffering as a result of the war. Every able-bodied man had seen service, and his pay, including his bonus, was hardly more than a scrap of paper. There was no hard money and the currency was so depreciated that it was practically valueless. Flour where obtainable cost $500 per barrel.

The State debt was enormous and the people were saddled with taxes beyond endurance, particularly the farming class who had nothing wherewith to pay them. The Massachusetts federal debt was £1,500,000 with private debts computed at but little less. Mortgages were being foreclosed on all sides. From 1784–1786 every fourth, if not every third, man was subjected to one or more executions for debt, and in the year 1784 over 2,000 executions were entered at the court at Worcester. The sheriff could levy on cattle and personal property so that the debtor was at the mercy of the creditor.

On the one hand was the urban creditor capitalist class, with whom the clergy and lawyers tended to ally themselves, constituting a sort of merchant aristocracy distinctly Tory in sympathy. On the other was the agrarian debtor class, stimulated by the revolutionary spirit which had thrown off the yoke of England, demanding the separation of Church and State and the abolishment of capitalistic domination in politics. Their dislike and distrust of the Boston burgesses was much the same as that of the "Farm Bloc" for "Wall Street." They wanted to be rid not only of the fetters imposed by British rule, but of those of every other kind—religious, social, intellectual. Essentially it was the same old struggle between the "haves" and the "have-nots."

It came to a head over the adoption of the Massachusetts Convention of 1780 with the Baptists leading the fight for religious and political liberty. They were beaten, the property qualification for the suffrage was doubled, and the dominies, the doctors, the lawyers and the merchants remained the dominant class.

There was nothing left for the bankrupt farmers but revolt. In May, 1783, when my grandfather was but a few months old, occurred "Shays's Rebellion" in which a pitched battle took place between State troops and a new variety of "embattled farmers" for possession of the Springfield arsenal. Weston, midway between Boston and Worcester, where the malcontents had mobbed the courts in an effort to prevent the issuance of executions for debt, was in the thick of the mêlée. The militia en route to Springfield bivouacked there and picked up a local doctor as a volunteer surgeon.

Naturally the forces of "law and order" including those of "privilege and conservatism" won, and "mob rule" and "liberty" both received a severe temporary set-back.

With the restoration of domestic quiet a curiosity of political psychology manifested itself. The general objection to distant government, which had been hitherto directed against England, did not abate but shifted towards the Federal Government; and from 1803 to 1814 Massachusetts leaders constantly threatened secession from the Union, alleging that the conditions were just as intolerable as those existing when they were colonists under the British crown. The menace of Jeffersonian radicalism set the powdered wigs wagging in Tory Boston and drew the upper classes together in a bitter antagonism to national control.

Said Fisher Ames in 1800: "Our country is too big for union, too sordid for patriotism, too democratic for liberty. What is to become of it, he who made it best knows." "A democracy cannot last. Its nature ordains that its next change shall be into a military despotism,— of all known governments perhaps the most prone to shift its head, and the slowest to mend its vices."

In 1809 the Massachusetts Legislature passed a resolution to the effect that the men of Massachusetts would have to choose "between the condition of citizens of a free state, possessing its equal weight and influence in the national government; or that of a colony, free in name, but in fact enslaved by sister states," and in February, 1811, during a Congressional debate over the admission of Louisiana as a State, Josiah Quincy declared: "If this bill passes, it is my deliberate opinion that it is virtually a dissolution of this union; that it will free the States from their moral obligation, and, as it will be the right of all, so it will be the duty of some, definitely to prepare for a separation,—amicably if they can, violently if they must."

This, later, did yeoman's service in the mouths of the orators of the South.

In point of fact, the State of Massachusetts supported

a violent radical minority during my grandfather's early childhood, and was openly secessionist until he was over thirty. But once the forces of conservatism had prevailed, they remained steadily in control until well into the next century. It was not until 1820 that the religious test for office was abolished, along with the property qualification for the suffrage; and, although for many years it had been virtually a dead letter, the clause in The Declaration of Rights compelling church attendance was annulled only in 1832.

§

My great-grandfather, Samuel Train, Jr., although a discharged soldier, a farmer and no doubt a debtor as well, did not take down his squirrel rifle and join Shays's malcontents. Instead he showed his resentment against the established order by becoming a Baptist. He and three others got together and undertook to build a meeting-house. While small —but thirty-one feet square—it was ample to hold all the Baptists at that time in Weston and who numbered only sixteen in 1789.

Calvinism with its doctrine of "the elect," a theocratic aristocracy under an imperialist God, was distinctly sympathetic to a Tory viewpoint, and throughout the Colonial and pre-Revolutionary period we find the clergy as a class aligned with the established order. The aristocratic tradition, according to which the "people" meant the "best people," was not dispossessed from the White House until Andrew Jackson. George Washington and John Adams were democrats neither by nature nor by doctrine, and even Jefferson was a democrat in mind rather than body. As is natural considering our conception of God as an Absolute Monarch, the democratic idea was even slower in gaining a foothold in religion than in politics, and the intolerance of the Puritans towards those who differed from them in belief died hard. In fact the "religious freedom" originally sought by them signified the privilege of subjecting to the most cruel punishment all Quakers, papists, and other "heretics," and of harrying them from the land.

The word "Puritan" in the title of this book is not to be taken in its primary or theologic sense. I have concerned myself not with the original Puritans, but with their descendants irrespective of creed. The dogma of Calvinism no longer interests most people, but its influence upon the national character still persists both for good and ill, and will undoubtedly continue to do so for a long time to come. The Puritans came direct from England after a tempestuous struggle for their rights as Englishmen under Magna Carta. They believed that the Church of England, in spite of its independence of Rome, was relapsing into superstition and were determined that nothing of the sort should occur in their churches here. This was the reason for their antipathy to the reading of Common Prayer, and the celebration of Christmas, Easter, Saints' days and other ecclesiastical feasts.

Naturally "the best people" in any Puritan community were those whom God had predestined to dwell with him in glory in the hereafter. Hence church membership and strict adherence to the tenets of Calvinism were originally essential to social position. A man's belief in hell—a hell, moreover, of a particular sort, description and temperature—determined whether or not he should be invited to dinner. In a word, the Puritans were conservatives in religion and government, and continued to be so throughout revolutionary times. The liberals, the reformers, the forward lookers were usually, at least from the point of view of their contemporaries, spiritual outcasts. Thus in my grandfather's time a sharp line of a social, as well as of a religious, character divided the members of the established or congregational church, which was supported by state taxes, from the newer and more liberal societies, and, as usual, the "Right" represented the ruling order. The spread of Unitarianism, especially in Boston, eventually destroyed not only Calvinism but its value as a social asset, and democracy made itself felt in religion as in politics.

The Baptists—or Anabaptists as they were first called—had always been a thorn in the side of the Massachusetts civil authority. At the time of the Protestant Reformation there was much disputation over points, some of which would not be regarded as particularly important to-day, but were at that time exalted into dominant principles. The original contention of the Anabaptists that the civil law must not be enforced against Christian believers had led to a terrible massacre at Munster about a century before the founding of Boston. Regarded as anarchists they were nearly exterminated, and when the movement revived in the following century there was a coincident return of the old prejudices against what had been regarded as an anarchistic sect. "Against Anabaptists we have a severe law," said Edward Winslow, and no great wonder, since they still held themselves as free from interference by the civil authorities, and believed, not only in the complete separation of church and state, but held sharply antagonistic views to those of the founders of the colony regarding infant baptism.

The Puritans believed that baptism was a means of regeneration; the Baptists claimed that the only true baptism was that of adults who signified their profession of faith. Some went so far as to claim that the Baptists, being the only true Christians, were the only persons entitled to the suffrage and that the Puritans, who were not Christians at all, since they had been baptized in infancy, should be disfranchised. Firmly established by 1665, these vigorous sectarians endeavored to enforce their views on their Puritan neighbors so aggressively that they became excessively unpopular. Under Governor Bellingham the Baptists were severely persecuted, but after his death the laws against them were not generally enforced. Nevertheless a mild taint of anarchism adhered to the sect and, beyond the violence of their religiosity, they were chiefly objected to as a menace to existing institutions. At the time of my grandfather's birth the Baptists were the extreme liberals in politics and association with them stamped one as a malcontent, if not a "red."

The organization of a new religious society in any Massachusetts town in those days carried with it not only a social but a financial risk, for the support of the Congregationalist church was compulsory under the law, and, unless there were at least sixty parishioners of any other sect, their taxes went to support the "established church." My great-grandfather and his associates attempted to "sign off," as it was called, from the Congregationalist church in 1788 by praying "to be excused from paying tax to the other religious society, as they bear their part in supporting the gospel with the Baptist Society," and protesting against being compelled to pay taxes for the salary of the minister and repairs of the town church as being against "the Bill of Rights" and illegal. It does not appear from the records that the rest of the taxpayers paid any attention to their application. Owing possibly in part to this double taxation the Baptist Society in Weston had no settled minister until twenty-three years later in 1811, at which time my grandfather Charles Train was ordained pastor, and a branch was also organized in Framingham.

Throughout the revolutionary period, due to French influence and to Thomas Paine's "Age of Reason," which had had a large circulation, there had been a widespread tendency towards atheism. This tendency increased after the war to such an extent that according to M. R. Werner "students at Yale College boasted of their infidelity and went about calling themselves Diderot, D'Alembert, Voltaire, Rousseau, Robespierre and Danton instead of by their own names. At Bowdoin College during this period only one student had the courage to admit that he was a Christian in the technical sense of the term. It was the common belief in the intellectual circles of the time that Christianity, so-called, would not survive two generations."

By 1783, when my grandfather was born, while the tythingman still summoned the townfolk to meeting and sat watchful that no one slept during the sermon, only the shell of religious orthodoxy remained and people were becoming restive under its discipline. Of course this was far truer of the urban population than that of the country, which was less open to outside influence and temptation. But even in Weston there was a marked "post-war" reaction. The young were beginning to ask questions which their elders found difficulty in answering. The old conservative respect for religion, government, age, education and experience was going fast. The Rev. Dr. Kendall still read his interminable theological dissertations on "predestination" and "original sin," and thundered against the evils of Sabbath breaking, play-going and fornication, but the congregation in practice exercised a liberal private discretion.

We hear a great deal about card playing and gambling being held in abhorrence by the New England Puritans, yet gambling, particularly at cards, was, both before and after the Revolution, a common pastime among old and young, rich and poor alike. No one thought it wrong to stake money or valuables upon the result of games of chance of any sort. In fact no games were played without a stake, however small. Lotteries prevailed everywhere. In 1791 Thomas Hancock advertised State lottery tickets for sale, in "halves, quarters, and eighths" for a prize of $10,000. The anti-card playing and gambling crusade did not get under way until after 1825.

The habit was so general that Joel Smith, who besides being a "Minute Man" ran a tavern not far from the Train homestead and directly opposite one of the churches, kept a concealed room in the tavern attic in which was a table covered with a green baize cloth, and where even on Sunday many Revolutionary heroes, and later their sons, gathered to deal the devil's cards, drowning in free potations of rum and sugar not only the voice of their own consciences but that of the Rev. Kendall across the way. It is perhaps invidious to record that many of these Sabbath breakers were both then and later overtaken with great worldly prosperity.

## CHAPTER VI

# A Grandfather Discovered

MY grandfather made his entrance into the post-Revolutionary world without medical assistance, for the ministrations of doctors on such occasions were very generally in those days considered both unnecessary and indelicate,—the latter, unless the patient were entirely covered by a sheet and the doctor consented to perform his task by sense of touch only. No suave high-priced obstetrician—but an old woman from the village, a "practical nurse" as we would say—slapped Charles Train on his little back in the freezing upstairs bedroom in which my great-grandmother, Deborah Savage, was lying, wrapped him in a blanket, carried him down to the kitchen, soused him in a tub in front of the fireplace and tucked him away in the trundle bed in the ingle nook, which on similar occasions had previously held his elder brothers Arthur and Isaac, now nine and four respectively, and later on his younger brother and sister, Samuel and Betsy.

While one, at least, of the Weston doctors was above the average, neither was as efficient in domestic emergencies as old Hepzibah Allen, the midwife, who in order to be ready when wanted came several days in advance and helped with the housework. Otherwise my great-grandfather might have had to get up in the night, light his lantern, and fetch the doctor on snow-shoes, with a fair chance that both he and the medico might lose themselves in a snow drift and fail to arrive until everything was over.

The very next Sunday the three-day-old infant was taken out of bed, bundled up and carried half a mile to the unheated meeting-house where, after the Rev. Kendall had cracked the ice in the font, he was duly baptized. This experience, a rigid church requirement at the time, might easily have finished him had he come of a less hardy race. Little attention to such hazards was paid in a community where it was generally believed that nothing could save a child foredoomed to Hell and that the best he could do in this world was to make an effort to find out in advance what his fate in the Hereafter was to be. Any baby who escaped the dangers of sepsis at birth from the dirty fingers of the *sage femme,* or of pneumonia at the hands of the clergyman the Sunday after, had a fair chance to survive the epidemics that inevitably followed.

Nowhere did the evolutionary doctrine of the survival of the fittest as applied to human beings have fairer play than in Colonial and Revolutionary New England, and any child that succeeded in running the gauntlet of tuberculosis, scarlet and yellow fever, dysentery, smallpox and the rest proved himself a good risk. In point of fact the mortality of children was almost beyond belief. Few families reached maturity entire and frequently less than half survived the ordeal of baptism, contagion, and sitting for hours on end in ice-cold churches every Sunday. In this respect conditions had improved little, if any, since Colonial times, when but two of Judge Sewell's children lived out of fourteen and of Cotton Mather's but three out of fifteen. In the early nineteenth century, irrespective of the season of the year, half the deaths in certain years in New York and Philadelphia were of children under ten, of which the chief cause outside epidemics was tuberculosis, the yearly average in Boston being from 20 per cent to 25 per cent of the total.

Only the toughest survived, and these, once their health was established, were apt to live to great age. My great-great-grandfather's ninety-five years, and my great-grandfather's ninety-four, might be instanced in support of this; but, lest it should appear that the Train family had a monopoly of longevity, I may quote Professor Channing to the effect that "in Salem, Massachusetts, in 1811, on one street within a distance of 350 feet, there were 13 persons whose aggregate years numbered 1,012, the youngest being 70 and the oldest 95."

Large families were an economic necessity. It was a good old Puritan tradition to fill one's quiver and keep it filled. Women often married at from fourteen to sixteen years of age. One of my great-great-aunts is said to have been a widow at thirteen. But the widows never remained single,— that is, hardly ever. Excessive childbearing was the curse of New England womanhood. Most wives died young, and "solitary indeed was the old Puritan who did not have at least two wives lying beside him in the churchyard." The average family was over nine persons. Some women had twenty children or more. One child followed another until the exhausted wife surrendered her functions to her successor.

In my grandfather's day there was a recognized form of primo-geniture (without the "primo," as it were), and the son, not necessarily the eldest, who showed most interest in agriculture inherited the farm and lived with his parents— the rest gradually drifting away to other occupations. The unmarried women, since they had nowhere to go, remained at home until they died, or until, like the "Wid° Partridge" they became public charges.

And now while the newly born Charles is lying in his trundle bed or shivering beside the baptismal font, or being toted between the two,—whichever it may be,—this is as good a time as another to comment upon the medicine and the doctors of those first years of our national existence.

It has already been noted that until the year of my grandfather's birth in 1783 Harvard offered no medical instruction whatever. The only way for a young man to become a doctor was to pick up what knowledge he could by serving as an apprentice to some older practitioner, sweeping out his office, mixing his pills and holding the basin when he "bled" or "cupped" his patients, a recognized cure for everything.

Having learned how to grind a powder, put on a plaster, and bind up a wound, the medical tyro returned to the town whence he had come and started in to "cup" and "bleed" his former schoolmates and their parents. The commonest remedies of to-day were entirely unknown. He had no knowledge of sanitation, personal hygiene, or of micro-organisms and their effect. He knew nothing of anæsthetics, antiseptics, vaccines, or serums. He pounded his own drugs and put up his own prescriptions, carrying his pharmacopœia, his balances, and his mortar in his saddle bags. The doctors went around dosing sick and well alike, "purifying the blood," "purging the bowels," "exciting the kidneys," cleansing the system with sulphur and molasses,—a practice still prevalent in rural New England,—"removing the bile" and—charging well for their nostrums.

Since it was not until 1798 that vaccination was discovered by Jenner, it was the accepted practice (although one held by many to be attended with divine punishment) to inoculate perfectly well people with genuine smallpox in order to prevent a subsequent and more virulent attack.

As an example of that interesting and usually painful experience let us take that of Mr. Thomas, the editor of "The Old Farmer's Almanack," in 1792. Smallpox had broken out in Boston and he decided to go to Worcester for inoculation. The treatment lasted for five weeks. His account, given in his autobiography, is probably typical of what hundreds of sensible people underwent. "I flattered myself," he writes, "and was flattered by the doctor, of being a good subject, and would have the disease light, *having never exposed myself to heat and cold nor excessive labor, and had ever been temperate*; but it turned out quite otherwise. I had the disease very severely. For many days my life was despaired of; and, in fact, it was, I afterwards learned, currently reported in the neighboring towns that I was dead. After I returned home I was weak and feeble for some months; after which I enjoyed good health and, in general, have to this day, though advanced in life."

Just as a successful practitioner had to be a nurse, druggist, surgeon, dentist, and veterinary; so the grocer, the barber, and the *sage femme* trespassed on his preserves and compounded drugs, let blood and advised young ladies who did not know what to do. Many people primarily engaged in other occupations practised medicine as a side line.

The rarity of trained physicians, their high charges, and their insistence upon the use of the lancet and the purge, resulted in a rage for patent medicines, which were widely advertised in the newspapers and by handbill, including all sorts of "elixirs," "restoratives," "drops," "teas," and "pills." There was Daffy's Elixir Salutis, Stoughton's Elixir, Turlington's Original Balsam of Life, Bateman's Pectoral Drops, Betton's True and Genuine British Oil, Anderson's Scotch Pills, Hooper's Female Pills, Godfrey's General Cordial, Walker's Jesuits' Drops, Golden's Spirits of Scurvy Grass, and Swinisen's Electuary. And even then, no less than now did the beautiful and good give testimony to their virtue! So great a luminary as the Hon. Luther Martin, attorney general of Maryland, stated over his signature in print that Doctor Hamilton's Elixir had cured him of "a painful and troublesome aflection of the breast, accompanied with soreness and obstructed and difficult breathing." "Oil of Earthworms" and "Emulsion of Dried Rattlesnake" (suggesting the "powdered lizard" of the Chinese pharmacopœia) were popular for consumption, and other remedies no less bizarre found universal favor. The American people is still addicted to the patent medicine. It has been the basis of many a Puritan fortune.

In spite of being dosed with noxious concoctions, the virtue of which was held to be in direct ratio to their loathsomeness, eating indigestible and badly cooked food, sleeping in a room with sealed windows which had no warmth even in winter, save what percolated through the boards of the floor from the fireplace below, little Charles Train managed to survive. Betsy, his sister, died at the age of ten. He had practically no toys, being given "stints" of various sorts to do in lieu of them, such as braiding straw. Much of his childhood he passed indoors where his mother could keep an eye on him while doing her work, and his eyes smarted constantly from the smoke of the open fireplace where she was cooking. He adored his mother, but he was terribly afraid of his father, a bearded man of gruff manners who smelt of liquor and called him "boy."

The God of the Puritans was a harsh and jealous God who visited the sins of the fathers upon the children, and it would have been sacrilege then to claim that a harsh and jealous father, who used the birch and paddled his children's little backsides with a shingle, was an ungodly man. On the contrary, the more he paddled them the more godlike he was. The parental attitude, therefore, being modelled on that of the Hebrew Jehovah was severe and arbitrary. Children were taught that their father was their master. Their mothers were taught the same about their husbands. As late as 1884 my own mother never called my father in my hearing by any name more tender than "Mister Train."

His grandfather Charles liked better, for the old man, although grim and thin lipped, told him stories of the French and Indian War and made him whistles out of straw. But they all, including his mother, gave him to understand that somehow he had already managed to offend God deeply, perhaps merely by being born,—that they all had in fact, although he was never very much convinced of it so far as the rest of the family were concerned. This sense of guilt was omnipresent. He was sure that God, who had some sort of secret understanding with his parents about the matter, was always watching to see if he were not going to commit some other abomination in addition to whatever it was he had done already. Watching him also was his father, who would certainly tell God about it if he caught him, besides birching him severely. So was the minister. So in a lesser degree was his grandfather. And so was his mother—only maybe she wouldn't tell.

He naturally was unaware of the fact that this quasi-identification of God with his parents, and the awe in which he held his father, was a remnant of a primordial nightmare which made the young prehistoric male tremble at the fierce looks of the "Old Man" of the tribe and try to hide at his approach. He feared the wrath of God, as whose agent his father was obviously acting, because he was constantly assured that he was the object of it.

> "No pity on thee can I show,
> Thou hast thy God offended so.
> Thy soul and body I'll divide,
> Thy body in the grave I'll hide,
> And thy dear soul in hell must lie
> With devils to Eternity."

The first book placed in his childish hands—"The New England Primer"—rubbed this in deeply, declaring that

> "In Adam's fall
> We sinnèd all."

Most children in America who learned to read up to 1800 did so out of this book. So did some children in 1875, including myself. The picture that gave me delicious shivers— not always delicious, if I had been a bad little boy— was that of the Reverend John Rogers being burned at the stake surrounded by his admiring family. The caption read:

"Mr. John Rogers, Minister of the Gospel in London, was the first Martyr in Queen Mary's Reign and was burnt at Smithfield, Feb. 14, 1554. His wife with nine small Children, and one at her Breast, following him to the Stake; with which sorrowful Sight he was not in the least daunted, but with wonderful Patience died courageously for the Gospel of Jesus Christ."

As the text was beyond me as well as being slightly ambiguous, and because the smoke in the wood cut appeared to embrace the entire family, I always assumed that the children were included in the martyrdom. That, I suppose, is what gave me the shivers. I thought they were being burned because they had been bad.

At first Charles was sent to a "dame school' in the village

kept by an old woman, who for a mere pittance took care of both boys and girls, largely to relieve their mothers during the day. Later on he was sent to one of the regular public, or district, schools for two months every winter where he was prepared for college and to which girls were not eligible. Girls, in fact, were hardly considered worth educating in those days. In Boston public schools they were not admitted at all until 1789, but occasionally in the country the schools for economic reasons were opened to the girls for part of the year after the regular term was over. Thus the records of Weston show that, as early as 1768, the town (doubtless under pressure from great-great-gran'ther Samuel Train), "voted to have five women's schools kept three months in the next season and to Begin Aboute the middle of May next"— when the boys would be busy on the farms. But two years later the question came up again "to know the minds of the town whether they will have five women schools in the summer *and it passed in the negative.*"

The district school was a small wooden box and bitterly cold, except when some of the Train logs were blazing in the fireplace. Then it became stifling. Practically none of the children wore shoes except in winter, and many had to stay away in cold weather for lack of them. "Old enough to go to meeting barefoot" was a perfectly serious New England standard of age.

A contemporary of my grandfather wrote of this period: "Old men had a great coat and a pair of boots. The boots generally lasted for life. . . . Shoes and stockings were not worn by the young men, and by but few men in farming business. Young women in summer, when engaged in ordinary work, did not wear stockings and shoes."

The school itself would to-day hardly be regarded as deserving of the name. There were no maps, globes, blackboards, slates or pencils until after 1800 (although pencils with India rubbers had been offered for sale in Boston as early as 1740), practically no books or paper. Instead of a pencil my grandfather used a goose quill with ink which he

made from powder and carried in a leathern ink bottle. Some
children made ink by steeping the bark of swamp maple in
water, boiling the decoction till thick, and diluting it with
copperas. They made their own copy-books out of foolscap
stitched together and ruled with lead plummets which were
run into moulds. Quill pens were in general use for writing
until about 1835, when steel pens took their place to some
extent. There was no blotting paper. Black sand was used for
drying the ink on freshly written letters or ordinary writing,
except in books when writers either waited for the ink to dry
or used China paper, taken from the inside of tea chests.

The teacher, usually a young divinity student of seventeen, walked around among his pupils giving each in turn a
few words of instruction. Spelling and arithmetic lessons
were chanted aloud, as the Arabs do to-day, and exercises in
rhyme were common, such as

> "A gentleman a chaise did buy,
>   A horse and harness, too;
> They cost the sum of three score pounds,
>   Upon my word 'tis true.
> The harness came to half the horse,
>   The horse to twice the chaise,
> And if you find the price of them,
>   Take them and go your ways."

The "Tutor's Guide" in 1801 had

> "When first the Marriage Knot was tied
>   Between my Wife and Me
> My age did hers as far exceed
>   As three times three does three.
> But when Ten years and half ten Years
>   We man and wife had been
> Her age came up as near to mine
>   As eight is to sixteen.
> Now tell me I pray
>   What were our Ages on our Wedding Day?

This rather curiously recalls the "How Old Is Ann?" problem that racked the United States a century later.

The Bible was the chief text-book. Next in importance came arithmetic. As one of the old villagers said: "The Bible and figgers is all I want my boys to know." Spelling was just becoming unified under the influence of Noah Webster, whose blue-backed "Spelling Book" and "American Preceptor" my grandfather learned by heart. He also used "Bingham's Child's Companion," "Morse's Geography" and "Pike's Arithmetic," which had 360 rules without a word of explanation. One of these read illuminatingly:

"Deduct the Tare and Trett. Divide the Suttle by Amount given; the Quotient will be the Cloff which subtract from the Suttle the Remainder will be the Neat."

The geography had a map of the United States a few inches square, on which all the land west of the Mississippi was called "Louisiana" and most of that north of the Ohio the "Northwestern Territory." It was highly refined and contained many improving dialogues between teacher and pupil, such as:

"I am very thankful, sir, for your entertaining instruction, and I shall never forget what you have been telling me.

"I long, sir, for to-morrow to come that I may hear more of your information.

"I am truly delighted, sir, with the account you have given me of my country. I wish, sir, it may be agreeable to you to give me a more particular description of the United States.

"I hope, sir, I have a due sense of your goodness to me. I have, sir, very cheerfully, and I trust very profitably, attended your instructions."

Pattillo's "Geographical Catechism" published in 1796 gave this explanation of comets:

"Their uses are mere conjecture. Some judge them the seats of punishment where sinners suffer the extremes of heat and cold. Mr. Whiston says a comet approaching the sun brushed the earth with its tail and caused the deluge, and that another will cause the conflagration."

The teacher stood over the children like a slave driver while they feverishly sought to escape the rod by memorizing that which meant nothing to them whatever, but where ten words would have made everything plain. One scholar of the period spent three weeks in a hopeless attempt to solve a simple example in division. Charles learned long chapters from the Bible by heart and countless hymns by Doctor Watts, as well as making a digest of the sermon every Sunday.

The teacher "boarded 'round," often walking five miles or more to the school in the depth of winter, usually on snow shoes. He taught little more than the "Three R's"—enough to make change, write a simple letter and keep family accounts. Usually as did my grandfather in later years, he met his future wife under circumstances where he could be fairly certain of her ability as a housewife.

In 1782 the Rev. John Eliot wrote from Boston to Jeremy Belknap, then minister at Dover, N. H.:

"We don't pretend to teach yᵉ female part of yᵉ town anything more than dancing, or a little music perhaps, (and these accomplishmᵗ· must necessarily be confined to a very few,) except yᵉ private schools for writing, which enables them to write a copy, sign their name, &c., which they might not be able to do without such a privilege, & with it I will venture to say that a lady is a rarity among us who can write a page of commonplace sentiment, the words being well spelt, & yᵉ style & language kept up with purity & elegance."

There were private schools for girls in Boston, but the instruction at best was negligible, and painfully polite. Arithmetic was considered "an almost useless subject for women to understand." Letter writing was an art in those days and writing was often taught in special schools, as was sewing, patchwork, sampler making and embroidery. Not until 1828, two centuries after the first public schools were opened, were girls admitted with full equality in Massachusetts.

The question of proper books for the young presented no difficulty in the eighteenth century.

Cox & Berry, the Boston booksellers, advertised in the Boston *Gazette and Country Journal*,

"The following Little Books for the Instruction and Amusement of all good Boys and Girls:

The Brother Gift or the Naughty Girl Reformed.
The Sister Gift or the Naughty Boy Reformed.
Hobby Horse or Christian Companion.
Robin Good-Fellow, a Fairy Tale.
Puzzling Cap, a Collection of Riddles.
The Cries of London as exhibited in the Streets.
Royal Guide or Early Instruction in Reading English.
Mr. Winlove's Collection of Moral Tales."

The best sellers of the post-Revolutionary period were "Sanford & Merton" (1783), by Thomas Day; "The History of the Fairchild Family" (1788), by Mrs. Sherwood; "The Parent's Assistant" (1796), by Maria Edgeworth, and "Evenings at Home" (1792), by Dr. Aiken and Mrs. Barbauld.

To-day they would turn a child's stomach or make him scream with laughter.

The "Fairchild Family," which was generally considered a charming book for little children, revelled in sin and punishment. Mr. Fairchild, in order to show his little ones "something which I think they will remember as long as they live, that they may love each other with perfect and heavenly love," takes them to see a corpse hung in chains from a gibbet. "The horror of the Progress through the gloomy wood to this revolting sight, the father's unsparing comments, the hideous account of the *thing*, rattling, swinging, turning its horrible countenance while Mr. Fairchild described and explained and gloated over it, and finally kneeled and prayed—all this through several pages," as Alice Morse Earle points out, "no carefully reared child to-day would be permitted to read. . . . The children recite verses and quote Bible texts to prove that all mankind have bad hearts, and Lucy commits to memory a prayer, a portion of which runs thus:

" 'My heart is so exceedingly wicked, so vile, so full of sin, that even when I appear to be tolerably good, even then I am sinning. When I am praying, or reading the Bible, or hearing other people read the Bible, even then I sin. When I speak, I sin; when I am silent, I sin.' "

No wonder that the infant Charles began life with an overwhelming consciousness of guilt. In other respects my grandfather's childhood did not differ markedly from that of a small boy brought up in Maine or Vermont to-day. The only noticeable difference probably would be the presence of the telephone, the radio, the movie, and the flivver. Country children did in the 1780's about what they do now. They played the same games,—tag, blind man's bluff, and hunt the slipper or, there being usually no slippers, hunt the something else,—they went berrying and fished for minnows, and were given rides on the farm horses, pitched coppers and horseshoes, but they probably had much less time for pleasure.

Instead of being well dressed, well fed, comfortably housed, and allowed plenty of time for play and exercise, my grandfather and his brothers and sisters were told that they should be grateful for brown bread and milk for breakfast and supper the year round. The family had no coffee on the breakfast table. Tea was kept for sickness or special occasions. When the minister called, a jug of rum and a bottle of brandy were brought out, or, if he was not very thirsty, he was offered a glass of currant, elderberry, or noyan wine.

As a boy my grandfather when on dress parade wore leather breeches which came to his knees, being met there by a pair of long, blue woollen stockings; his feet were encased in a pair of well-greased cowhide shoes; he wore a shirt of blue homespun, on Sunday covered with a false bosom which was taken off and carefully folded away on his return from meeting.

It was his task to kindle the kitchen fire, and it required no little moral courage on his part on a winter's morning, with the thermometer below zero and his breeches frozen stiff, to get into them, feel his way shivering down the stairs in the dark, shovel out the snow that had fallen down the chimney during the night and, with tinder box and flint, struggle to start a blaze.

The family ate their meals in the kitchen in front of the huge fireplace that sent half the smoke into the room and half the heat up the chimney. The dishes were cheap and coarse, and so was the food. Beef, pork, salt fish, dried apples, and vegetables was the bill of fare the year round. The bread was of rye or Indian meal. White bread was a delicacy—accounting for the famous brown bread and baked beans sacred to New England. The forks had but two prongs wide apart and were inconvenient as carriers of food. In fact peas absolutely refused to stay on them as they would on the broad, sticky back of the knife. As a result the knife was popular as a food shovel. Since there were no table luxuries there was little temptation to masticate properly which was almost impossible under the most favorable conditions in view of the condition of the teeth. Hence food was gulped and helped down by heavy swigs of rum and cider.

Table manners were far worse than those of a present-day lumber camp. Spitting was already a popular pastime and, while the fire was considered the more desirable target, it was perfectly proper, according to the "School of Manners," a contemporary handbook, to "spit in the corner" so long as you did not fail to "rub it in with your foot," somewhat as a cleanly dog performs a similar ceremony. Later on "The Juvenile Guide" cautioned its young readers to use "the spit box" instead. I suppose the universal predilection of children for spitting was in imitation of their elders, a gesture of maturity. Handkerchiefs, as very generally to-day in all but the higher circles, were used for the wipe after the blow, which was accomplished with the fingers, but one should not forget that this was also the habit of Cleopatra, Catherine de Medici, Isabella D'Este, and Mary Queen of Scots.

Investigation as to the toilet facilities in the Palace of Versailles at the time of the French Revolution leads to some almost unbelievable, and quite unprintable, results although it fully explains the great demand for heavy perfumes in the court circle.

Here are a few excerpts from the "Manual of Good Manners" published over sixty years later in 1844. For example:

"Never be squinting and scowling and examining the victuals, to see if you can discover a coal or a speck or a hair; if you find one, take it out decently, and not make a great ado about it. For your honour's sake never make a mountain out of a mole-hill.

"Eat what you need before you rise from the table; and not be picking and eating afterwards. Never pocket victuals at the table, it denotes a thievish disposition.

"When you have done eating, clean your plate, knife and fork, lay the bones you have picked in a snug heap by the side of your plate, scrape up your crumbs, and cross your knife and fork on your plate.

"Scratching the head, or any part of the body, picking the nose or ears, belching, snuffing the nose, smacking the lips, picking the teeth, etc., are accounted awkward habits, and should not be practiced by anyone who desires to be agreeable and honorable.

"Speak not at table. Laugh not at table; it shows unthankfulness.

"Put not your hand to any part of the body not ordinarily discovered in company.

"The mouth and teeth should be scoured out once each day with cole dust, which is not only good to cleanse the teeth, but is also an excellent preservative to them.

"Always wash your ears, neck and feet as often as once a week; and the washing of the whole body will not be neglected by cleanly persons, and in warm weather, if engaged in dirty work, it should be done weekly."

I give the Train family the credit for acting 100 per cent up to these comparatively modern—and as it may well have seemed to some of their generation—rather finicky conventions.

Coarseness was not confined, however, to personal habits.

The newspapers teemed with vulgarity and obscenities. Smutty doggerel appeared in every "Poet's Corner," and words at which the most abandoned flapper of to-day would blush to the ears were used in every-day conversation with entire unconsciousness by all.

The children stood apart until told to sit down and did not speak unless spoken to. They were ordered, not asked, to do things. "Hon'd or Hond Parent" was the customary form of epistolary address.

There were no carpets, curtains, or pictures. Over the fireplace in my great-grandfather's kitchen hung the flint-lock rifle he had carried to Lexington—the only ornament, save for a few odd pieces of pewter. There were practically no books in the Train house, or any other house for that matter. In fact there were only three or four libraries in the entire country. The dearth of text-books in colleges, as in schools, was pathetic. From 1780 to 1784 no books were advertised in the Boston *Evening Post,* except one colonial library which was offered for sale at auction.

My great-grandfather disapproved of novels and never allowed his children to look into those of Richardson, Fielding, Smollett, or Sterne—never into Shakespeare which had not yet been "Bowdlerized." Instead he borrowed for their perusal from Dr. Kendall "The Conquest of Canaan" by Mr. Dwight of New Haven, Mr. Trumbull's "McFingal," Joel Barlow's "Vision of Columbus," "Pilgrim's Progess," "The Lives of the Martyrs," "Young's Night Thoughts," and "Watt's Improvement of the Mind," from which they very likely sought relief in "Rollins' Ancient History," "The Federalist," "The Letters of Junius," the "Spectator," and possibly Spencer, Pope, and Dryden.

There was nothing worthy of the name of "American letters." Up to 1800 no novelist, no historian, no playwright, or poet of the first rank had appeared in print.

Washington Irving was born in 1783 in the same year as my grandfather, Cooper six years later in 1789, Bryant in 1794, Prescott in 1796, and Bancroft, Emerson, Willis,

Longfellow, Whittier, Holmes, Hawthorne, and Poe in the decade between 1800 and 1810. The only books I know definitely to have belonged to my grandfather during the period of his boyhood are a couple of odd volumes of "The Rambler," a 16mo edition of Dr. Samuel Johnson's "Rasselas," and a well-thumbed copy of "Sanford & Merton," published in the year of his birth, in which the two small heroes are depicted in top hats and pantalets.

§

Charles Train was a boy of unusual intelligence as well as sweetness of disposition. He was naturally serious, a quality intensified both by the death of his younger sister Betsy at the early age of ten and the intense religiosity of his father, who was now a deacon of the little Baptist society of which he had been one of the organizers. Charles led his classes at the district school and showed so much promise that the Rev. Samuel Kendall, the pastor of the regular Congregationalist society, told his father that he ought to send the lad to college and offered to prepare him for it. This from the head of a rival denomination was in itself a high compliment. The boy of course was all in favor of it.

He was good at his studies, quick at argument and a persuasive talker. Going to Harvard would mean the opportunity of escape from the drudgery of farm life, admission to the aristocracy of lawyers and clergymen, and a chance to win fame and perhaps fortune in Boston. On the other hand, he was needed on the farm and to send him to college would entail serious financial sacrifices. Dr. Kendall's offer naturally became the subject of exhaustive family discussion in which the minister took frequent part. Charles' father shared in the general post-Revolutionary prejudice against lawyers and wanted him, if he went at all, to become a clergyman. The boy, however, had ambitions toward the bar. From a worldly point of view unquestionably he was right. The way to preferment throughout the nineteenth century lay in the law and, had my grandfather adhered to it, he might well have looked forward to high place in the Commonwealth. Most of the Presidents of the United States have been lawyers, and no other single fact has exercised a greater influence upon American politics.

But the two Samuels were both "sot agin' " Charles being a "l'yer"; if he wanted to become a preacher there "might be some sinse in more book larnin'." The minister occupied the highest social position in any rural community, and while local government was in the hands of "select men," the clergyman exercised an authority equal to that of the magistrate, who inevitably gave ear to his recommendations. The open disapproval of the local representative of the established church was not only equivalent to excommunication but to outlawry. In the eyes of most of the men, and all the women, the minister was the oracle of God, and whoso would not listen to him justly deserved to be damned. He was a man of great authority, both in things spiritual and things temporal as well, a political leader whose opinion was often asked on matters of importance and who requently represented the community in the state legislature.

But there was one thought in the back of all their minds— a thought probably not expressed in words—that, while it was one thing to be a minister of the established church supported by taxes and with a large and flourishing congregation, it was quite another to be a Baptist preacher in a town like Weston, or Framingham, with a congregation of from only ten to forty members. It ended by Charles taking a term at the Framingham Academy and being fitted by the Rev. Kendall for Harvard without any final decision as to his future having been reached. We can imagine him a slender, grave lad of eighteen, slightly stooping from the plough, dressed in homespun breeches and three-cornered hat, waiting with his bundle on the highway in the early dawn for the stage from Worcester that was to take him to Cambridge.

The "student" of the present day at Harvard may well ponder his opportunities as contrasted with those of the Harvard of 1801. The academic department at that time contained about two hundred students, and the entire teaching staff consisted of seven persons,—the President, the three professors (theology, Hebrew, and mathematics), and four tutors. In general the same conditions existed as had obtained there for more than forty years. The requirements for entrance were a strict examination in Dalzel's "Collectanea Græca Minora," the Greek Testament, Virgil, Sallust and Cicero's Select Orations; a thorough acquaintance with the Greek and Latin grammars, including prosody; also an ability to translate those languages correctly, and a knowledge of geography and of arithmetic to the rule of three.

President Willard, who received a salary of $1,400 per annum, wore a large full-bottomed wig and beaver cocked hat, and the students uniforms of black with ornaments called "frogs" or "crows-feet" worked on their sleeve-cuffs to distinguish the classes, which were almost strangers to one another. No social connection existed between the students and the inhabitants of Cambridge.

Judge Story writing of Harvard at the end of the eighteenth century (1789) said: "The intercourse between us and foreign countries was infrequent, and except to English literature and science, I might almost say, we had no means of access. Even in respect to them we had little more than a semi-annual importation of the most common works. Two ships only plied as regular packets between Boston and London, one in the spring and the other in the autumn, and their arrival was an era in our college life. They brought books and periodicals from England. The English periodicals were then few in number and I do not remember any one read by the students except the monthly magazine."

Life was hard, the students arising in the morning at six for chapel and retiring with the curfew at nine. They all lodged in the dormitories and ate at commons the food of which would have made the present menu at Dannemora look like the Ritz. Breakfast consisted of a tin cup of unsettled coffee, a "size" of biscuit, and a "size" of butter weighing about an ounce. Supper was of bread and milk. The big feed came in the middle of the day when each student received a pound of meat, which, being boiled on Mondays and Thursdays, caused them to be known under the festival nickname of "Boiling Days." There was a ration of two potatoes with each pound of meat. Pewter cans containing cider, which was supplanting the "small beer" of earlier days, were passed around like loving cups, until they had to be refilled.

"The students who boarded in Commons," wrote Sidney Willard of the Class of 1798, "were obliged to go to the kitchen door with their bowls or pitchers for their suppers, where they received their modicum of milk or chocolate in their vessel, held in one hand, and their piece of bread in the other, and repaired to their rooms to take their solitary repast. They were suspicious at times that the milk was diluted by a mixture of a very common tasteless fluid, which led a sagacious Yankee student to put the matter to the test by asking the simple carrier-boy why his mother did not mix the milk with warm water instead of cold. 'She does,' replied the honest youth."

The Harvard Commons, notoriously bad at all times, was the cause of a series of historic rebellions, strikes and "walk outs" on the part of the students, of which perhaps the "Great Butter Rebellion" in 1766 and the "Rotten Cabbage Rebellion" in 1807 are the most celebrated.

Dr. Peabody thus describes a student's room:

"The feather bed—mattresses not having come into general use—was regarded as a valuable chattel, but ten dollars would have been a fair auction price for all the other contents of the average room, which were a pine bedstead, washstand, table and desk, a cheap rocking chair and from two to four other chairs. I doubt whether any fellow student of mine owned a carpet. A second hand furniture dealer had a few defaced and threadbare carpets which he leased to certain Southerners, members of the senior class, at an extravagant price. Coal (this was 1830) was just coming into use and hardly found its way into the college. The students' rooms and several of the recitation halls were heated by open wood fires. Almost every room had a cannon ball which on very cold days was heated to a red heat, and placed as a calorific radiant on a skillet or some other extemporized metallic stand; while at other seasons it was often utilized by being rolled down stairs at such times as might most nearly bisect a proctor's night-sleep."

The four years were spent, according to an eminent authority, "in the acquisition of Latin and Greek, a smattering of mathematics, enough of logic to distinguish barbara from celarent, enough of rhetoric to know climax from metonymy, and as much of metaphysics as would enable one to talk learnedly about a subject he did not understand."

Among the books recommended to the students, who like my grandfather were interested in theology, were Butler's "Analogy of Religion to the Constitution and Course of Nature," Paley's "View of the Evidences of Christianity," Abernethy's "Discourses on the Being and Perfections of God," Leland's "Advantage and Necessity of the Christian Religion," and his "View of the Principal Deistical Writers of England."

Sidney Willard the president's son, who became librarian of Harvard College in his twentieth year, wrote, "the Bible was our text-book, and primary, daily study, in which everything centred."

Palæontology, according to McMaster, was so little understood that the bones of a mastodon which had been dug up near the Hudson seventy-two years before were still supposed to be those of a giant and the indicia of the Glacial Age were cited as conclusive evidence of the Story of the Flood.

The custom of fining students for misconduct was universal in early days, and a sidelight is thrown on the Puritan attitude of the first half of the eighteenth century by those inflicted at Harvard for infractions of its moral code.

|  | s.d. |
|---|---|
| Profanation of Lord's Day, not exceeding | 3.0 |
| Frequenting taverns | 1.6 |
| Profane cursing | 2.6 |

|                                          | s.d. |
|------------------------------------------|------|
| Graduates playing cards                  | 5.0  |
| Undergraduates playing cards             | 2.6  |
| Lying                                    | 1.6  |
| Drunkenness                              | 1.6  |
| Tumultuous noises                        | 1.6  |
| Tumultuous noises, second offense        | 3.0  |
| Keeping guns, and going on skating       | 1.0  |
| Fighting, or hurting persons             | 1.6  |

From which it will be observed, as G. Birkbeck Hill acutely points out, that graduate card-playing (a purely secular offense) was held twice as bad as profane cursing, and over three times as bad as lying or getting drunk on the part of an undergraduate, who in turn was almost as wicked if he went skating as if he got tight or lied, and nearly twice as much so if he played cards as if he did either.

Card-playing was still, like any form of dancing, anathema to the devout long into the last century. If possible, it was regarded as even worse,—for it was indissolubly associated with gaming, tavern life, and all sorts of debauchery. While it remained undeniable that Solomon had said "There is a time to dance" and that David had "danced before the Lord," the Puritan theologians made it clear, to themselves at least if not to their congregations, that reference to the original Hebrew showed that David did not really dance after all; for "he took no steps"; all he did was to "jump up and down." And they also proved satisfactorily that "what time for dancing Solomon might have had in mind it is unnecessary to inquire, for he cannot have referred to any moment of the time allotted to men on earth."

The life of the student was circumscribed in every minor detail. According to the laws of Harvard in 1790, and in the early decades of the nineteenth century, the students' Sabbath began at sunset on Saturday night, at which time they were supposed to "lay aside all diversions" and retire to their chambers. Walking or visiting on the Sabbath was forbidden. All had to attend chapel daily, morning and evening, or be fined, perhaps expelled. All were supposed to remain in their chambers and diligently follow their studies, except half an hour after breakfast, from twelve to two, and after evening prayers until nine o'clock, under penalty of fine. Tutors snooped around to see if the boys stayed where they belonged.

The Harvard man of 1800 was forbidden to go beyond the college yard without coat, cloak or gown, hat or covering allowed by the authorities of the college, to buy, sell or barter among themselves books, apparel, or any other thing above twelve shillings in value; and he was especially forbidden to "presume to be an actor in, or spectator at, or in any way concerned in, stage plays, interludes or theatrical entertainments in the town of Cambridge."

Studying was made neither easy, comfortable nor in any way attractive. There was a library, of course, but the students were greatly restricted in its use. The laws provided that the college library should be well aired one day in a week—if the weather permitted—that it should be swept and dusted once a month. Between the first of November and the first of May a fire was to be built in the library once a week only. No candles or lamps were allowed.

The lack of proper heating, the severity of the rules and the absence of athletics were probably responsible for the numerous riots and the excessive amount of drunkenness among the students. During the first quarter of the last century the annual Harvard Commencement was a drunken debauch, during which the rum bottle might aptly have replaced the cod fish as the state emblem of Massachusetts, and the word "Veritas" upon the college seal suggested that the preceding "In vino," of the ancient Latin motto, had been accidentally omitted.

Professor Peabody says: "The entire Common, then an unenclosed dust-plain, was completely covered on Commencement Day, and the night preceding and following it, with drinking-stands, dancing-booths, mountebank shows, and gambling tables; and I have never heard such a horrid din, tumult, and jargon of oath, shout, scream, fiddle, quar-relling, and drunkenness as on those two nights. . . . Pious citizens of Boston used to send their slaves to Commence-ment for their religious instruction and edification and it came to be the great gala day of the year for the coloured people in and about Boston, who were, by no means, such quiet and orderly citizens as their representatives now are."

Josiah Quincy relates how on July 7, 1820, he paraded with the Harvard Washington Corps Band on which occa-sion he "drank an enormous quantity (of "Black Strap," compounded of rum and molasses) to say nothing of what I eat." This organization was composed of seniors and juniors, to be an officer was held a great distinction, and the uniform required all officers to appear in tights. "How is he off for a leg?" was the first question regarding any candidate for promotion. "How is he off for a stomach?" would have been even more pertinent.

There were also in that period what were known as "Blow-ing Clubs" in connection with which drunkenness was ex-hibited with a publicity that would not now be tolerated. "One of these societies was wont to have a dinner on exhibi-tion days. After the exercises in the chapel, the brethren would march to Porter's tavern, preceded by a full band; and the attempt was made to return in the same way. First would come the band, the only steady part of the show, whose music attracted a crowd of lookers-on. Then came, reeling and swaying from side to side, a mass of bacchanals, in all stages of intoxication. That this disgraceful sight should have been tolerated by the college authorities will seem surprising to those who fail to realize the radical and beneficent change in public sentiment which has taken place."

It is significant that in 1836 the Rev. John Pierce recorded in his diary: "Be it noted that this is the first commencement I ever attended in Cambridge in which I saw not a single per-son drunk in the hall or out of it."

In spite of the multitude of "laws" there was very little discipline; on the other hand there were plenty of students, like my grandfather, who had come to college with an earnest purpose of acquiring knowledge and fitting themselves for a profession. From the Calvinistic viewpoint it was a period of startling liberalism among the institutions of higher learning. Willard, in his "Memories of Youth and Manhood," says: "Traditionary, dogmatic theology had begun to be suspected. Still there was a feeling of timidity which sought relief rather by a modification than a denial of some of the doctrines as they were commonly received. It was not until several years afterwards that an irreparable breach was made in our Congregational Churches, which charity in its full perfection, that beareth, believeth, hopeth, endureth all things could not heal. Yet we found there were among the reputed Orthodox clergy those who were less startled at doubts concerning the letter of some of the generally received doctrines, or a departure from them, than we had been accustomed to expect. . . . I well remember, that, in the course of my studies in the New Testament doctrines, I opened with some hesitation my difficulties concerning the Trinity to my father. He was not shocked at the disclosure, nor inclined to offer illustrations of what he deemed to be mysterious; and he left on my mind the impression, that he was willing to trust me to the unbiased results of my own investigation in the matter, whatever might have been his own views concerning it."

That there was plenty of independent thinking inside the meeting-house walls, coupled with an equal readiness to dispute doctrinal points even with the clergyman, is demonstrated by the following letter written at Hopkinton, Massachusetts, in 1802 by Dr. Jeremy Stimson to his brother-in-law Dr. Howe, and which I am enabled to print through the generous courtesy of my friend Hon. F. J. Stimson.

"Mr. Howe                              "Hopkinton, May 3d, 1802

Did I understand you rightly in your discourses of last Sabbath—& Sabbath before—If I did, you attempted to establish the following doctrines from Scripture, viz.—that Deity ever since the transgression of Adam to the present time has been using the most powerful means with sinners of the human race, in order to convince, convert and save them —But all those means have proved abortive—have never answered the designs of Deity—nor ever will, & all the hope you now have that any will be saved is—that God is possessed of *almighty* power, has the hearts of all men in his hand & it is possible he may save some. If I did not mistake, nor misunderstand you, this is the doctrine—that Deity has been using the most powerful means with sinners is granted—But that those means have ever proved effectual is denied—What should we say of an earthly Monarch who continued to use the most favourable means in his power for a great number of years with his rebellious subjects, just in order to conceive, reclaim, & make them return to their allegiance—when he knew at the same time that the means he made use of (although the best in his power) would never answer his purpose. Should not we say he was a fool, & incapable of governing his subjects if they were to return to their Allegiance? It might indeed be urged in favour of an Earthly Monarch, that the means he used were well calculated to answer his purpose—& therefore, if he continued to use them, they might take effect some time or other, but this will not apply to Deity—If your doctrine be true—he knew when he adopted the means, they would never answer his purpose— & He never intended they should. Deity never intended to save one of the human race—by the use of means—He determined to save the few He had *elected* by an act of Sovereignty, that is, in plain, English, He determined to force them into Heaven Neck and Heels by an almighty arm of power—If you think this is preaching the Gospel, I pity you —I make no doubt but there are Millions now in Heaven Blessing God for the means He used with them while in this world, to convince, and convert & save them—& that they are now reaping the blessed fruit of those means—You express great surprise (that) there is no greater Engagedness in Religion—& that there are so few applicants for admission into the church—But why should you be surprised at this? If people believe your Doctrine—that means answer no purpose except it be to plunge them in deeper in guilt, why attend to any? I take it to be the natural fruits of your preaching—& am far from being surprised at it—I have known & can well remember most of the inhabitants of the town for more than forty years—& I never knew them so wicked—Vile & quarrelsome as they have been for two years past—& I don't hesitate to give it as my opinion that it is in a great measure owing to your preaching—whether it be good or bad I do not make these objurations out of any personal disrespect to you—but the reverse, for as a Man, I both esteem & love you—But such preaching as I have heard the two last Sabbaths I abhor & condemn & I think it is my duty not only to tell you so, but to use all the means in my power to prevent my Friends—but especially my Family— from believing it—

"The foregoing observations are made under the full belief that I did not mistake your meaning in the discourses referred to. It is possible however the case may be otherwise —if it is, I shall be happy to be set right—I remain with great sincerity your Friend and very humble servant

Jeremy Stimson."

It is certainly of significance that in 1805, the year of my grandfather's graduation, a Unitarian was elected to the Hollis Professorship of Divinity at Harvard.

The Rev. Henry Ware of Hingham having been nominated for that chair, objection was made as to the soundness and orthodoxy of his Calvinism, which was successfully met by the argument that "a categorical examination into the creed of a candidate was a barbarous relic of Inquisitorial power, alien alike from the genius of our government and the spirit of the people;—that the college had been dedicated to Christ and not to Calvin;—to Christianity and not to Sectarianism—and that Hollis by his statutes, prescribed the Scriptures of the Old and New Testament as the rule of his Professor's faith, and not the assembly's Catechism."

My grandfather had worked hard at college and what he had seen of drinking had made him an ardent supporter of temperance. He could be ill spared from the farm and throughout his course he was constantly called home to help with the plowing and getting in of the crops. During his junior year he had a genuine religious "experience" at a Baptist "revival" to which he had been taken by his father in Boston. Thereafter he had no doubt of his "call" to the ministry and abandoned all leanings towards the law.

This in itself was no small sacrifice, but it was an even greater one for him to enter the ministry in a denomination then so greatly depressed as scarcely to offer a decent support to its preachers. Nevertheless, having made up his mind, he did not look back. Thereafter he devoted himself to theology, distinguished himself as a student, as he had at school, and at his graduation was awarded "a Hebrew oration." For two years more he continued his theological studies, teaching meanwhile at the Framingham Academy as "preceptor" where he received a shilling per week for each pupil and an allowance of fifty cents per week towards his board. Here he made his first attempt at preaching.

There were but five professing Baptists in the town and the total sum that could be raised by these towards church expenses amounted to only sixty dollars. This, at four dollars a week, the agreed salary, would pay him for but fifteen weeks. The meeting-house had been built nearly a century before in the days of Whitefield by those known as "New Lights." In its pristine state it had been little more than a windowless shanty, and once the "New Light" had failed, it had led a literally abandoned existence, been taken down, moved around, and used variously as a House for the Lord and a depository for hay and grain. In 1780 it had been bought by the Baptists and,—small as it was already,—had been taken apart, reduced in size, and now, sadly dilapidated, stood perched on a ledge of rock, wholly inaccessible to any except pedestrians.

This was the vineyard in which my grandfather at twenty-four years of age, and as yet unordained, believed himself called to labor. He patched the roof and the windows, shovelled away the snow, built the fires, led the singing and preached the sermons. Gradually the size of the congregation increased. Two years later in 1809 he gave up his position with the Academy, and in 1811 was ordained in Framingham, administering the sacrament on that occasion to eighteen members, of whom six came from Weston. These now voted to unite both societies under the name of "The Baptist Church in Weston and Framingham" and for the next fifteen years he preached in the two towns on alternate Sundays until 1826, when the connection between the two societies was dissolved by mutual consent, after which he confined himself to the church in Framingham where he preached until 1839.

During the thirty-two years of his ministry the number of professing members increased from five to one hundred and thirty and he became a man of wide influence, affectionately known among the townspeople as "Father Train." He died in 1849, outliving his father (Samuel Train, the "Minute Man") by only ten years. He married twice, first Elizabeth Harrington of Weston, by whom he had one son, Arthur, for whom I was named, and second Hepzibah, her sister, my father's mother. The records of the period disclose that the English prejudice against marrying a deceased wife's sister did not obtain in New England, it being, quite to the contrary, a common practice.

His life would have seemed to us incredibly frugal. When in 1811 he began to preach his salary was fixed at $200 for the first year and, although it was gradually increased during his twenty-eight years of service, it never exceeded $500 and was no doubt, at least in the earlier days, paid partly in corn, beans and bacon. Yet he was unquestionably among the well-to-do, and, in spite of his meager salary, managed to maintain a comfortable home, send both my father and his elder brother, Arthur, to college, and give his three daughters a first-class education. He led an austere and frugal life, his clothes were often patched, his meals scanty, but he had his reward in the love and respect of his fellow men and the consciousness of being, not only a theologian, but a practical and authoritative power for good in the community.

The precise form of my grandfather's religious faith is of no importance. It may or may not have concerned itself with the dogmas of total depravity, or of foreordination and election. Yet there is no doubt that he "believed" in the fiery hell and personal devil of the earlier Calvinism.

The Puritan theory was that in the beginning God created man in the person of Adam with freedom of will, which, being exerted in opposition to that of God, resulted in Adam's fall and his doom, together with the human race as a whole, to Eternal punishment. Through the mediation of Christ, however, a chosen few known as the "elect" were to be saved; but nothing they did on earth could make the slightest difference as to what happened to them in the hereafter.

Said Jonathan Edwards in a public address in 1741:

"The God that holds you over the pit of hell, much in the same way as one holds a spider, or some loathsome insect, over the fire, abhors you and is dreadfully provoked; his wrath towards you burns like fire; he looks upon you as worthy of nothing else but to be cast into the fire; he is of purer eyes than to bear to have you in his sight; you are ten times more abominable in his eyes than the most hateful venomous serpent is in yours. You have offended him infinitely more than even a stubborn rebel did his prince; and yet, there is nothing but his hand that holds you from falling into the fire every moment . . . yea, no other reason can be given why you do not this very moment drop down into hell."

Even a radical like Dr. Colman, a very dangerous radical from the orthodox viewpoint of 1728, who was influential in swinging Boston to Unitarianism, began his funeral lecture upon Cotton Mather with an emphatic assertion of the doctrine of election. Likening Mather to Enoch, he preached from the text "And Enoch walked with God, and he was not, for God took him," explaining that Enoch's translation into Eternal Glory "must be resolved into the good pleasure of God, His wise and sovereign will; and to be sure it was not for any merit or desert in Enoch's body walking with God. Enoch deserved to have died for his sins as well as any before or after him. . . . Elias was a man of like passions with others. . . . It was not due to the righteousness of either that they were taken without seeing death. Before that God formed them in the belly he designed them their translation. . . .

"Whither are we going?" he asked. "What are we doing? How do we live and act; and what will become of us a few days hence? Will God take us; take us on the wings of angels and in their arms to His own presence and glory; or will death drag us out of the body and devils take us away to their abodes of darkness and of fire unquenchable?"

"Bye and large," as their descendants are wont to say, one wonders how far the bulk of the New England population literally accepted the terrifying doctrines enunciated by their ministers? Did the Puritan boys who listened to Dr. Colman worry themselves over the preacher's assertion that unless they were of the elect death would "drag us out of the body and devils take us away to their abodes of darkness and of fire unquenchable"? Did they actually believe the hypothesis of Infant Damnation and Original Sin? How can we tell? If some one will first define "belief" for us—so that it will not have a relative, but a static, meaning—we might attempt an answer. Is it not conceivable that to the followers of many highly intellectualized religions their "credo" is merely a working hypothesis?

However strong the belief of the original Puritans may have been, the fury of its fire rapidly dwindled among their descendants, in spite of the fact that they continued to indulge in the metaphysical subtleties of doctrinal argument, both in the pulpit and outside. Knowing the technical requirements for membership in some of our largest present-day churches, I suspect that the majority of the younger Puritans were not much more disturbed over mere dogma than the rank and file of modern congregations. At any rate, before another century and a half had gone by the ministers of those self-same denominational churches were preaching on "The Love of God which passeth understanding" with no mention of hell whatsoever. Hell, as a "working hypothesis," no longer worked!

The War of the Revolution had put Calvinism in dire jeopardy. The new government was thoroughly secular, required no religious qualifications for office and by the first constitutional amendment prohibited an established religion. "The eyes of New America were towards the future," says Gilbert Seldes in his "Stammering Century." "The great hope offered by Congregationalism was redemption from sin; America had definitely begun to be interested only in Progress. Wherever we turn, the irreligion of the early republic is evident. In the churches themselves, the movement away from Calvinism, theocracy and the trinity, towards religions of universal forgiveness, is marked!"

Francis Asbury, the Methodist, claimed 300,000 converts between the 1770's and the 1820's. There ceased to be an established church, and the "elect" were no longer accorded the advance distinction in this world which they had previously enjoyed by virtue of their divinely appointed position in the next. Heaven, "no more a free gift, had now to be earned." There was a marked split between the Unitarians and the so-called "orthodox" which disrupted social relations. Congregationalists and Unitarians, who had formerly been friends, did not dine together or go to each other's houses. "Orthodoxy" ceased to be fashionable, yet the Calvinist idea that wealth was a sign of grace remained imbedded in the Puritan mind, and in place of "the elect" the rich, irrespective of religious affiliation, came to be accepted as the "best people." The Puritan is to no slight degree responsible for the early importance attached to wealth in the United States. "The New World, which had been exploring the mysteries of Heaven, began to press across the frontiers of the West, to search out the mysteries of the Mississippi basin or of the Oregon. The American Republic had come into existence at the beginning of the scientific era which was to reach its climax with the trans-continental railway and the publication of the Origin of Species."

The American approached his job of conquering nature with enthusiasm and resolve; it was necessary to the national salvation. "His single means (of satisfaction) and his single thought" said the French engineer Chevalier, while conceding our intermediate objective of money making, "is the domination of the material world,—industry in its divers branches, business, speculation, action, work." The independence and individualism of the Puritan, fostered by the American system of government, were favorable to business enterprise. "Widely conceived" (I quote from Seldes' illuminating chapter "Times of Refreshing") "this was the great American preoccupation. It produced a manufacture suitable to a wide domain. It assumed transportation and the conquest of the wilderness. It involved big business by swift stages. In the half century before the Civil War, the United States was becoming pre-eminently a manufacturing country. By the time Lincoln took office the dominance of industry was obvious. For such a revolution to take place, the minds of the entire population had to be turned unwaveringly to a single object. Call it conquest of the frontier, or progress of mechanics, or desire for gain; when compared with the earlier absorption of the colonists in the affairs of the next world, it amounts to the same thing."

But before long a "vicious circle of work and profit" began to circumscribe the American mind and character. "We think of trusts and strikes, of Russian communism and radical labor, as phenomena of our own day and cannot imagine that they had their counterparts a century ago." But they did. There were reformers who said, "there is a greater freedom than man now possesses, there is a tyranny of money and materialism. The system which glorifies only money is not the only system." The demolition of Calvinistic dogma left a void for the spiritual yearnings of many people. The Rappites at Harmony, Indiana, and later at Economy, Pennsylvania, the Owenites at New Harmony and their offshoots at Macluria and Nashoba, the communist Oneida community, "Brook Farm," "Hopedale" and "Fruitlands," were early reactions against the worldliness of the age.

The followers of these cults were by no means all philosophers, the offspring of religious unrest, or reactionaries against materialism,—many of them were merely disgruntled radicals, or cranks. But all were opposed to the world as it was and to things as they were and sought by repudiating the common practices of humanity to achieve "salvation" on the one hand or "escape" upon the other. "The energetic wanted deliverance from difficulties; the feeble, deliverance from sin; the merely neurotic, deliver- ence from themselves." So they substituted the less pleasant for the agreeable, ate nuts and raw food, abstained from flesh, forbade carnal intercourse and the ownership of property other than communal, and eschewed all gaiety and pleasure. Thus they, in a measure, were able to rid themselves of the terror of sex, of the distaste for working for a living, from moral responsibility, from the fear of ill health and even of death. And, in the end, they perpetuated the perfectionism of the Calvinist and in a roundabout curious way returned to orthodoxy. The reformers of the nineteenth century sought to achieve their objects by preaching abstention, to-day they seek to do so by prohibition. The Puritan has outlived the philosopher.

# CHAPTER VII

## The Puritan Sabbath

I WAS brought up like the old setter: "Rover! Don't bark so loud. Don't you know it's Sunday?"

The influence of the Puritan Sabbath is felt throughout the United States and will continue to be for generations yet to come. It was the most salient feature of Puritan life. If I may venture a single generality—after my diatribe against generalities—the one commandment the Puritans kept was the Fourth and they kept it very well. They kept some of the others also, but not with the same enthusiasm. For our ancestors indeed the Sabbath may have been a sort of penance.

The Puritans used no such words as "Sunday" or "church," but always spoke of "The Lord's Day" and "the meeting-house," and to the Puritan, as well as to most of his descendants even down to the present, the meeting-house has been the centre of community life, secular as well as religious.

The custom of observing the Sabbath from sundown on Saturday grew out of the Puritan's logical interpretation of the words: "The evening and the morning were the first day," and still obtains in many hamlets and small towns in New England. The City of Hartford as late as 1855 required all stores to close on Saturday night. But what was sauce for the goose was sauce for the gander, and what was put on at one end came off the other, so that there was a concomitant shortening of the Sabbath itself after sunset, and "Sabbath evening dissipations and mirth making" sadly irked Jonathan Edwards. Even so it irked him not a tenth as much as it did the boys and girls who failed to find Saturday night very pleasant after having "tried all the week to be good."

Prior to 1595 it had not occurred to the people of England or elsewhere that Sunday was anything more than a "holy day" or "holiday" for rest and recreation. Calvin himself played bowls at Geneva on Sunday. But in that year a certain Dr. Bound advanced the theory, based on the Hebrew Scriptures, that although Sunday had not been divinely appointed as *the* Sabbath, the obligation to observe *a* Sabbath was ordained of God, and since the Christian world has seen fit to select Sunday as a holy day it must be observed like the Jewish Sabbath.

The Sabbatarian movement spread rapidly in England until it became a day of intense gloom. James I tried to cheer up his depressed subjects by issuing his famous "Book of Sports," which declared that dancing, archery, leaping, vaulting, May games and morris-dances were lawful, and honest mirth not to be prohibited after evening service; but it was wholly in vain, as was a similar effort on the part of Charles I in 1633. The English became stricter and stricter in Sunday observance and the Colonists followed suit. Finally in 1676 came the celebrated Lord's Day Act of 29 Carolus II, 7, forbidding all work and business on Sunday, "works of necessity and charity excepted," and this, the original "blue" law, became the basis of all later Sunday legislation in the United States.

It is still a crime to "play" on Sunday in New York, whatever that may mean, and all kinds of Sunday laws exist in every state which, besides occasionally irritating the inhabitants, create much legal confusion by permitting the setting up of the defense of contributory negligence in accident suits where the plaintiffs are technically in violation of Sunday statutes. The literal adoption of the Scriptural injunctions regarding Sabbath observance was in accord with the general Puritan tendency of the times.

The so-called "blue laws" were, in the first instance, merely the adoption, by the original settlers of the New

Haven and other colonies, of the Mosaic code as their principles of law and government. The Rev. Mr. Davenport, addressing those met to consider the nature of those institutions, said without dissent:

"The Scriptures do hold forth a perfect rule for the direction and government of all men and all duties which they are to perform to God and men, as well in the government of families and commonwealth as in the church."

Thus the Decalogue, with portions of Exodus, Leviticus and Deuteronomy, became the early colonial penal code. It has continued to be the basis of much of our legislation, even to the extent of a recent abortive effort on the part of a Western legislature to give it new vitality through a bill making it a crime to violate any one of the Ten Commandments, and beginning:

"Whoso shall have another God shall be fined one hundred dollars."

The famous Blue Laws of Hartford provided (according to the Rev. Samuel Peters, author of the "General History of Connecticut") that "no one shall travel, cook victuals, make beds, sweep house, cut hair, or shave, on the Sabbathday. No woman shall kiss her child on the Sabbath or Fasting day. No one shall read Common Prayer, keep Christmas or Saint days, make minced pies, dance, play cards, or play on any instrument of music, except the drum, trumpet, and jewsharp."

Whether or not these laws were his own invention as charged by the indignant Hartfordians, they were fully in the spirit of many which were actually enacted, and their influence is felt to-day in many parts of our country where no cooking is done on Sunday and all meals are "warmed over" from Saturday, where the barber shop is closed, and it is against the law, as in New York, to fish, shoot, "play," or "make a disturbing noise." These laws existed in all the New England states and there was not much difference between them.

Punishment varied from a fine to sentence to the whipping post or death, if done "proudly, and with a high hand against the authority of God,"—this last the literal wording of the New Haven law.

To amuse one's self on the Lord's Day was a "contumacious" act savoring of *lese majeste,* so to speak, and hence ratable with profane swearing and such other conduct as appeared to challenge the authority of the Almighty rather than mere weaknesses of the flesh, like rum drinking.

The barest glance at the examples collected by Mrs. Alice Morse Earle, in her interesting "Sabbath in Puritan New England" (to which I am indebted for the majority of the later citations in this chapter, particularly with regard to music), leaves no doubt as to the strictness of Sabbath enforcement. They also pull the gaunt mask from the jolly red face of many a "pious" New Englander who was fined because he tried to "show off" his new colt by "riding violently" to meeting. Persons were penalized for "unseemly walking," for "hankering about on men's gates on Sabbath evening to draw company out," while as late as 1831 in Lebanon, Connecticut, a woman was arrested on the way to and within sight of her own father's house for "unnecessary travling," although after lengthy litigation she succeeded in getting damages for false imprisonment.

Generally speaking, however, by the time of the Revolution it was found impracticable to punish Sabbath breakers by fine and imprisonment, and in 1776 the town of Belfast, Maine, adopted the modern and certainly more humanitarian method of social ostracism, voting "that if any person makes unnecessary Vizits on the Sabeth, They shall be look't on with Contempt."

The laws governing the keeping of the Sabbath were undoubtedly those which were given fullest effect and enjoyed the widest publicity. But even these, except in certain localities, unquestionably relaxed with the passing of the years, and in any event, those laws as they existed from two to three hundred years ago probably represented a creed rather than a code, as some of ours do to-day.

It is more than possible that the early colonists kissed their wives on Sunday and probably did even more reprehensible things without suffering for it. The fact that there are laws upon our statute books does not, as we all know, mean that they are obeyed. What sort of a picture of the United States will the historian of 2231 A. D., who forms his conclusions solely from the Constitution and the Volstead Act, conjure out of the past as to prohibition? I have little doubt that most people base whatever idea they have of the New England Sabbath on a few items that ceased to have any trace of validity—if they ever had any at all—more than a century ago.

There was doubtless as much difference in the keeping of Sunday in New England between 1731 and 1831, for instance, as between 1831 and to-day,—as much as there was at all times between the way it was kept in Boston and in Charleston. Individuals differed as much then as now. By the time my grandfather went to college in 1800 there had been a tremendous change in the general attitude from that which had existed before the Revolution. Religious people in those days claimed, just as they do now, that the war had demoralized everybody and particularly the young. The treaty of peace with England had hardly been signed and the British were still here, when the delegates to the General Court of Massachusetts declared that the Sabbath was too long and demanded that it be cut from thirty-six to eighteen hours. And it was!

Many were the jibes written and printed against this form of Sabbatarianism, and *The American Museum* for February, 1787, printed a poem entitled "The Connecticutt Sabbath," in which the author rebelled against having the Lord's Day stretched from one day to a day and a half.

> "And let it be enacted further still
>    That all our people strict observe our will;
>    Five days and a half shall men, and women, too,
>    Attend their bus'ness and their mirth pursue,

But after that no man without a fine
Shall walk the streets or at a tavern dine.
One day and half 't is requisite to rest
From toilsome labor and a tempting feast.
Henceforth let none on peril of their lives
Attempt a journey or embrace their wives;
No barber, foreign or domestic bred,
Shall e'er presume to dress a lady's head;
No shop shall spare (half the preceding day)
A yard of riband or an ounce of tea."

"The war changed everything," particularly in the towns, where the boys learned to swear and to gamble, the barber shops were kept open on Sunday, and theatres began to be popular. In the country people still kept the Sabbath strictly and had to go to church or suffer social ostracism, but the tythingman no longer went from door to door to summon them, there was wide disregard of the laws against travelling and a general loosening up.

After Sunday travel had been permitted in England for thirty years, Massachusetts and Connecticut still enforced the law against it; but travellers, inn-keepers, large numbers of citizens and even clergy connived at what might be called "vehicular bootlegging." Yet, to-day, there are localities where Sunday is observed with almost the same strictness as in Puritan times.

Every New England town had a tythingman, originally appointed not only to make sure that the Sunday laws were enforced but that people attended church and behaved themselves during divine service, where, armed with a long tapering rod with which to tap nodding and unruly heads, it was his business to "quiet the restlessness of youth and to disturb the slumbers of age." He had to see that the taverns were shut, that nobody did any work, that quiet was preserved in the streets and that there was no Sunday travel.

The Journal of Obadiah Turner contains an account of what once befel in Lynn, Massachusetts.

"June 3, 1646.—Allen Bridges hath bin chose to wake ye sleepers in meeting. And being much proude of his place, must needs have a fox taile fixed to ye ende of a long staff wherewith he may brush ye faces of them yt will have napps in time of discourse, likewise a sharpe thorne whereby he may pricke such as be most sound. On ye last Lord his day, as hee strutted about ye meeting-house, he did spy Mr. Tomlins sleeping with much comfort, hys head kept steadie by being in ye corner, and his hand grasping ye rail. And soe spying, Allen did quickly thrust his staff behind Dame Ballard and give him a grievous prick upon ye hand. Whereupon Mr. Tomlins did spring upp mch above ye floore, and with terrible force strike hys hand against ye wall; and also, to ye great wonder of all, prophanlie exclaim in a loud voice, curse ye woodchuck, he dreaming so it seemed yt a woodchuck had seized and bit his hand. But on coming to know where he was, and ye greate scandall he had committed, he seemed much abashed, but did not speak. And I think he will not soon again goe to sleepe in meeting."

Let us hope that it was the length of the sermons rather than their quality that induced so much Puritan drowsiness, but whatever the cause preachers were hard put to it to invent expedients to arouse the sleepers. One, a Mr. Moody of York, Maine, noticing that a large proportion of the males in the pews had dozed off, suddenly shouted "Fire! Fire!"

"Where?" excitedly demanded the instantly roused congregation.

"In hell,—for sleeping sinners!" retorted the ingenious pastor.

That the tythingman was no respecter of persons is shown by the following notice from *The Columbian Centinel* of December, 1789, when my grandfather was six years of age, entitled "The President and the Tythingman":—

"The President, (General George Washington), on his return to New York from his late tour through Connecticut, having missed his way on Saturday, was obliged to ride a few miles on Sunday morning in order to gain the town at which he had previously proposed to have attended divine service. Before he arrived however he was met by a Tything man, who commanding him to stop, demanded the occasion of his riding; and it was not until the President had informed him of every circumstance and promised to go no further than the town intended that the Tything man would permit him to proceed on his journey."

Even as late as the War of 1812 the tythingman was in many places a familiar figure, lying in wait at the cross-roads, toll gate or tavern, stopping and cross-examining all travellers as to their business. When the tythingman got lax or lazy a deacon or two used to be added to stiffen him up.

Josiah Quincy tells a story of how at Andover, about the time my grandfather left college, a gentleman in a buggy drove up one Sunday morning to the toll gate and complimented the deacon and tythingman on their strict and impartial enforcement of the law.

" 'But,' he added, 'the law, as you know, excepts those who travel on errands of mercy or necessity, and I regret to tell you that my mother lies dead in Boston.'

"On the strength of this assurance the Deacon let him go through, and that afternoon, when the gentleman came back on his return trip, gave him a friendly greeting. After the bar had been let down, and the buggy was safely by, the gentleman thanked the Deacon for his courtesy and then, as he whipped up his horse, touched his hat to him and said gravely:

" 'Goodbye, Deacon! Tell the busybodies of Andover that my mother is lying dead in Boston,—and you may add, if you like, that she has been lying dead there for the last twenty years.' "

Among the town records of Framingham appears:

"Duty of Tythingmen. The town voted, that if the tythingmen see any youths of said town disorderly in the public worship, and they will not forbear by being once stamped at by any of the tythingmen, in such case said tythingmen are desired to call them by name."

Habituated as I am to the traditional idea of Puritan decorum this particular resolution gives me both satisfaction and enlightenment.

It was as true of Framingham in those days as it is of all other localities even to recent date, that a man's "standing in the community" could be told by his "sitting" in the church, for in the town records may be read the following resolutions:

"That there should be a decent body of seats set up in the meeting-house, with a hanging table before the deacon's seat."

"That in dignity, the seats shall rank as follows: the table (Deacon's seat) and the fore seats are accounted the two highest; the front gallery equals in dignity the second and third seats in the body of the house; the side gallery equals in dignity the fourth and fifth seats in the body of the house."

There were separate galleries for unmarried men and women, and a "nigger heaven" high up in the rear with a grating, reached by a separate staircase. The deacons sat down in front directly under the tall pulpit with its funnel-shaped sounding-board.

Pew seats were usually—and until long into the nineteenth century—hung upon hinges to enable the worshipper to lean against the back of the pew for much-needed support during the praying or psalm-singing Marathons of that day. Boys especially took pleasure in slamming down these seats coincidently with the Amen, so that the noise could be heard for a great distance. In the Haverhill records appears the significant entry: "The people are to Let their Seats down without Such Nois" and "the boyes are not to wickedly noise down their pew-seats."

Once assigned a seat the owner was obliged to sit in it and nowhere else under penalty of a heavy fine. Small and "pestigeous" boys were usually herded by themselves, either on the stairs of the pulpit, those leading to the gallery, or in one of the high, shut-in pews, known for that reason as "the Devil's playhouses."

In Salem, in 1676, it was ordered that "all ye boyes of ye towne are and shall be appointed to sitt upon ye three pair of stairs in ye meeting-house on ye Lords Day, and Wm. Lord is appointed to look after ye boyes yt sitte upon ye pulpit stairs. Reuben Guppy is to look and order soe many of ye boyes as may be convenient, and if any are unruly, to present their names, as the law directs."

And speaking of boys—who clearly were then as now—Mr. Lawrence has unearthed a newspaper item of 1725, which inevitably recalls one of the incidents in Judge Henry A. Shute's "Real Diary of a Real Boy," to wit:

"Some evil-minded persons placed a Sturgeon of about eight feet in length on the Pulpit floor, where it lay undiscovered until the Lord's Day following; when it was so much Corrupted that it swarm'd with Vermine and caused such a Nausious and Infectious Stench that neither Minister nor People could by any Means assemble in the Meeting House, which occasion'd them to perform their Exercise in the Orchard."

Boys' pews lasted in the church at Windsor, Connecticut, near Hartford, until 1845. Sometimes there were even rough-and-tumble fights between the unruly and "pestigeous" and the tythingmen or deacons.

There was no heat in the meeting-houses in winter save for a few tin foot-stoves filled with charcoal for the more favored old ladies, and the congregation sat in coats and tippets, able to endure the cold only because they had hardly any more warmth in their own houses. Yet into these ice boxes new-born infants were brought to be baptized the first Sunday after birth, even were it within twelve hours of their advent into the world.

It was a long time before the descendants of the original Puritans were willing to allow the chill wind of their religion to be tempered by any sort of external warmth. Perhaps the idea of such comfort ran counter to their principles.

In 1783 a real stove was installed in the "Old South Church" in Boston, which was the occasion of the following verse in the *Evening Post* for January 25th of that year.

"Extinct the sacred fire of love,
Our zeal grown cold and dead,
In the house of God we fix a stove
To warm us in their stead."

The sermon over, the congregation retired to the "noon-house," usually a well-warmed building not unlike the modern "grange," where they spent the time discussing the sermon, eating lunch and perhaps indulging in a little gossip or even horse-trading. Out of the "noon-house," where in many places it was customary to read additional sermons between the services, developed the modern Sunday school, unknown until the first decade of the last century, the first, which was opened in Salem in 1808, being denounced by the Salem *Gazette* as a profanation of the Sabbath.

These noon-house gatherings afforded opportunity for social intercourse as well as spiritual uplift, and depending on circumstances, might savor of a political caucus, town or lodge meeting, sewing circle, *market overt,* or picnic where they swapped stories, cold doughnuts or pie of "pumpkin and Indian mixt." Also, no doubt, the women examined and criticized their friends' new clothes which up to that time had been obscured by the high backs of the pews, exchanged quilt-patterns and pieces, while the old crones smoked their pipes.

"Anne Bradford"—reads an old letter—"gave to me last Sabbath in the Noon House a peecing of the Blazing Star; tis much Finer than the Irish Chain or the Twin Sisters. I want yelloe peeces for the first joins, small peeces will do. I will send some of my lilac flowered print for some peeces of Cicelys yellow India bed vallants, new peeces not washed peeces."

This excerpt recalls another practice, which seems strangely out of character with most preconceived concepts of Puritan custom, but which obtained widely in the rural districts, of a newly wedded bride and groom getting up in the middle of the sermon and exhibiting their finery. The pair would stand up and turn slowly around this way and that to give everybody a good look, an interlude of entertainment no doubt much appreciated by the long-suffering congregation.

Even in old New England the evidence shows that a love of finery existed side by side with the belief in a brimstone lake, in which all those who yielded to frivolity in this world would receive a sulphur bath in the Hereafter, and proves that in this respect the Puritans, at least in the larger towns, were not so very different from other people.

The Abbé Robin wrote in 1783: "Piety, nevertheless, is not the only motive which brings American ladies in crowds to the temple. As they have no play to visit, and no public promenades, this is the only theatre where they can go to display their nascent elegance. Here they exhibit themselves dressed in stuffs of silk, and sometimes adorned with superb plumes. They wear their hair raised upon supports similar to those which were in fashion among French ladies a few years ago."

It would be a mistake to assume that because my grandfather was a clergyman and lived in a quiet country village his life was altogether peaceful. The very fact that the meeting-house was the community centre made it the focus of many a violent controversy between the partisans of old and new ideas both in the theory and practice of religion, and tradition says that my grandfather was not without his troubles in this respect. We who are used to trained choirs and expert organists can hardly imagine the discord existing a century ago among those who wished to praise God according to their own individual ideas.

The Rev. Thomas Walter wrote:

"The tunes are now miserably tortured and twisted and quavered, in some Churches, into a horrid Medly of confused and disorderly Voices. Our tunes are left to the Mercy of every unskilful Throat to chop and alter, to twist and change, according to their infinitely divers and no less Odd Humours and Fancies. I have myself paused twice in one note to take breath. No two Men in the Congregation quaver alike or together, it sounds in the Ears of a Good Judge like *five hundred* different Tunes roared out at the same Time, with perpetual Interferings with one another."

There was practically no way for the congregation to divide the lines without overlapping their neighbors until "singing by rule," that is to say by choir, gradually—very gradually—came in.

"Lining" or "deaconing," with its concomitant necessity of stopping for several seconds between each two lines for a reading and possible explanation of the next following, was a continual source of vexation. The practice had originated in the early dearth of psalm-books, but as the years went on it seemed foolish to continue a custom the only real purpose of which seemed to be to satisfy the vanity of the church elders. Presently the choir got to "singing down the deacon," that is, to start in and cut him off before he had finished the line. Of course the veterans put up a stiff fight, and one having been drowned out waited until the choir had concluded the psalm and then arose and said: "Now let the people of the Lord sing."

"Lining" often resulted in a hiatus fatal and contradictory to the original meaning. A curious effect must have been produced by the extraordinary assertion:

"The Lord will come and he will not,"

followed, after being sung, by the equally paradoxical

"Keep silence, but speak out."

One can condone my friend Loren Palmer's childish confusion when he heard his father's congregation singing about "the consecrated cross-eyed bear"—to him a mystical animal of most intriguing characteristics—which he later discovered to be "The Consecrated Cross I'd Bear."

"Lining" continued all through the nineteenth century in remote and poverty-stricken congregations, and perhaps still does to-day. There is authority for the rather surprising statement that in 1846 "the habit of lining prevailed" over three-fourths of the United States. Its "lineal" descendant is the frequent contemporary custom of the pastor's "giving out" (and reading) the hymn.

Many of the hymns of that era—as of later eras—were strange and terrible:

> "Far in the deep where darkness dwells,
>     The land of horror and despair,
> Justice hath built a dismal hell,
>     And laid her stores of vengeance there:
>
> "Eternal plagues and heavy chains,
>     Tormenting racks and fiery coals,
> And darts to inflict immortal pains,
>     Dyed in the blood of damned souls."

The practice of "fuguing," or part singing, which came in vogue at the end of the eighteenth century, gave great offense to many of the older members of the congregations, who regarded it as pure vanity on the part of the singers. One old preacher took his text from Amos "The songs of the temple shall be turned into howling," and on one of the pews in a Salem church was indignantly, if profanely, inscribed:

> "Could poor King David but for once
>     To Salem Church repair;
> And hear his Psalms thus warbled out,
>     Good Lord, how he would swear.
>
> "But could St. Paul but just pop in,
>     From higher scenes abstracted,
> And hear his Gospel now explained,
>     By Heavens, he'd run distracted."

Fuguing, which involved the repetition of a word or syllable, occasionally led to strange vocal results, such, for example, as that produced by the lines: "With reverence let the saints appear and bow before the Lord," which was sung "and bow-wow-wow, And bow-wow-wow, and bow before the Lord"—the bow-wowing continuing until all had had a chance at it for nearly half a minute.

The prejudice against instrumental music lingered long in New England. Cotton Mather declared it was entirely unauthorized by the New Testament, while a favorite text of his contemporaries was that from Amos, "I will not hear the melody of thy viols." When violin cellos or bass viols were at last allowed in the churches they were known as "Lord's fiddles." The opposition to the violin proper was based on its evil association with dance music. Frequently the interesting compromise was made that they could be used, *if the instrumentalists "would play the fiddle wrong end up."* Bass-viols began to be used in "advanced" churches about the time my grandfather graduated from college in 1805, and he must have commenced his ministry in the very thick of it. But the question of "bass-viol or no bass-viol" was still vexing New England churches as late as 1829, as we know from the records of the church in Wareham, Mass.

One who looks into the history of these old churches cannot fail to be astonished at the evidence that, however austere our forefathers may have been, they carried into their disputes a gusto and vehemence not usually associated with religion. We find deacons trying to howl down the choirs, blowing tin horns in meeting to drown out the viols, going out and "caterwauling" on the steps in imitation of the hymns within, and generally carrying on like disgruntled schoolboys.

Puritan churches were not all they are commonly supposed to have been. For one thing, dogs were always coming in and raising a rumpus, so that there were officially appointed "dog-whippers," toward whose salary dog owners were compelled to contribute. Naturally, expelling dogs from churches was not a peaceful business. The records are full of reports of complaints by tythingmen, together with admonitions directed to boys and girls who smiled, whispered, "snickered," laughed, whittled the pews, shoved each other over balcony rails and down-stairs, flicked kernels of Indian corn at one another, scuffled in the "Devil's play-houses," "damnified" the glass of the windows, "sported and played and by Indecent Gestures and Wry faces caused laughter and misbehavior in the beholders."

As I have already stated, my grandfather was distinctly progressive and early in favor of introducing instrumental music into his church, which he eventually succeeded in doing. The deacons usually opposed all musical innovations lest they should lose the chance to "line the hymn." It is said that one old deacon by the name of Haven—"Uncle Ben," he was called—proving particularly reactionary in this respect, the preacher, who was determined not to let the way of progress be blocked, drove the twenty miles into Boston one Saturday and procuring two musicians with a fiddle and a bass viol, smuggled them before service into the choir loft.

At that time the deacons, as a mark of their dignity, were allowed the privilege of placing their hats upon the "hanging table" or shelf before their seat. Among these prominently reposed "Uncle Ben's"—a big, white furry hat with a tall crown. Now the feeling between the instrumentalist faction, led by my grandfather, and the anti-instrumentalist faction, led by "Uncle Ben," had reached such a pitch that members of one party refused to speak to members of the other. On this historic morning "Uncle Ben" arrived early, clapped his hat down on the shelf, looked around, blew his nose like a foghorn and then, just to show how little he thought of the preacher, leaned back, and pretending to go to sleep, began to snore.

Suddenly without warning from the choir-loft came the sound of the sackbut and psaltery. For a moment the old man thought himself in a dream, but when the choir, accompanied by the fiddle and the viol, started in singing without giving him a chance to "line the psalm" he realized that he was awake and that some one had stolen a march upon him. With a snort he stood up, glared about, seized his hat and started to stalk out of the church. Half way down the aisle, in order to show his supreme contempt for those who had thus outwitted him, he attempted to put on his hat. He slammed it on his head, but—alas for his dignity!—it would not go on! In his anger he had snatched up by mistake a small boy's hat! Amid the snickers of the instrumentalists he stopped abruptly midway to the door. Could this be a sign from the Almighty? No doubt! Humbly "Uncle Ben" turned in his tracks, crept back to his seat, and sank down, never again to raise his voice against "the Lord's fiddle." In due course they even had an organ!

At the same time that he struggled with cantankerous and obstinate deacons over instrumental music, my grandfather fought the Demon Rum. Whether it was a natural revulsion due to his knowledge of how his great-great-great-grandfather John Train had got his living in 1635, I do not know, but he became a leader of the then comparatively new temperance movement in the early days of the last century. At that time everybody habitually drank hard liquor, the clergy along with the rest, and at noon most of the townsmen, including the minister, went to the tavern for a "toddy."

The drinking at baptisms, weddings and especially funerals was a public scandal; and "ordinations" were invariably very "wet," portable bars being sometimes established at the church-door, and strong liquor distributed free of charge to the entire assemblage. As late as 1825, at the installation of Dr. Leonard Bacon over the First Congregational Church in New Haven, free drinks were furnished at an adjacent bar to all who chose to order them, and were "settled for" by the church.

While we are on the subject I might add that flip, that "most insinuating drink," was made "of home-brewed beer, sugar, and a liberal dash of Jamaica rum, and was mixed with a 'logger-head'—a great iron 'stirring-stick' which was heated in the fire until red hot and then thrust into the liquid." Another favorite concoction was "Josselyn's New England Nectar," made of "cyder, Maligo raisins, spices, and sirup of clove-gilly flowers."

The bill from a tavern keeper for an ordination at Hartford in 1784, endorsed "This all Paid for exsept the Minister's Rum," reads:

|  | L. | S. | D. |
|---|---|---|---|
| "To keeping Ministers | 0 | 2 | 4 |
| 2 Mugs tody | 0 | 5 | 10 |
| 5 Segars | 0 | 3 | 0 |
| 1 Pint wine | 0 | 0 | 9 |
| 3 lodgings | 0 | 9 | 0 |
| 3 bitters | 0 | 0 | 9 |
| 15 boles Punch | 1 | 10 | 0 |
| 24 dinners | 1 | 16 | 0 |
| 11 bottles wine | 0 | 3 | 6 |
| 5 mugs flip | 0 | 5 | 10 |
| 3 boles punch | 0 | 6 | 0 |
| 3 boles tody | 0 | 3 | 6" |

The flowing of the bowl at these ordinations led to much gaiety among the clergy.

Ministers not only drank liquor; they distilled it. "Mr. Whiting had a score of appill trees from which he made delicious cyder. And it hath been said yt an Indian once coming to hys house and Mistress Whiting giving him a drink of ye cyder, he did sett down ye pot and smaking his lips say yt Adam and Eve were rightlie damned for eating ye appills in ye garden of Eden, they should have made them into cyder."

Many God-fearing and pious ministers owned and operated distilleries. The Rev. Nathan Strong, pastor of the First Church of Hartford, became a bankrupt owing to his failure as a distiller. He went into hiding and only showed himself on Sundays, when he was exempt from arrest. Nevertheless he does not seem to have lost caste, for ten years later Princeton gave him a degree as Doctor of Divinity. He used to say of himself and two cronies—also of the cloth, "Oh, we are all three in the same boat together,—Brother Prime raises the grain, I distill it, and Brother Flint drinks it."

One old pastor in Framingham by no means shared my grandfather's views on the subject of temperance, or rather perhaps he differed from him as to its nature. He was as reactionary as my grandfather was progressive. During one of the early "crusades" Dr. —— was visited by some of the young women of the neighborhood with a pledge. He read it over aloud:

" '—unless under the advice of my physician.' Yes, I will sign it," he agreed readily—"but I wish it clearly understood that I'm my own physician."

This worthy minister of the gospel visited the tavern regularly every morning for his toddy, which was served to him in an upper room. One very cold day he came in and said: "Landlord, we'll have our toddy extra hot and extra strong this morning." The landlord brought the toddy with two glasses, hung around a minute, and as no invitation to drink was extended to him, withdrew. Later in the forenoon the old gentleman was picked up from the roadside by a passing Samaritan and carried home. Next morning he called at the tavern as usual.

"Landlord!" he remarked. "What ailed yesterday's toddy? Something was the matter."

The landlord grinned a little.

"Well, Doctor, you said '*we'll* have *our* toddy extra hot and extra strong.' I thought '*we*' meant you and I, so I made double the usual quantity,—and you drank it all!"

"H'm! Yes!" ejaculated the Doctor. "In the future I shall be more careful in the use—h'm!—the use of the personal pronoun."

The most palpable evidence to-day of Puritan influence is the persistence throughout the country of baptismal or "font-names" dating from the English Reformation and particularly from the publications of the Genevan Bible in 1560, which was used as a well of nomenclature for seventy years by the English nation. C. W. Bardsley, Honorary Canon of Carlisle, in his amusing book "Puritan Nomenclature," says that "the Puritans objected to 'Peter,' 'Paul,' 'John,' and

other New Testament names because they were saints and in
the saints calendar: Hence 'the Hebrew Invasion', as it was
called, that filled England and America with Christian Joels,
Amoses, Pelatiahs, Obediahs, Abimelechs, Jonas, etc." and
which "was carried so far that a good Puritan would leave it
to a chance opening of the Holy Book to decide what appella-
tion his child should wear throughout life. This practice
often resulted in mistakes, words and phrases having a Biblical sound being assumed as a matter of course to have been
derived from the pages of Holy Writ.

"The incident is familiar of the Puritan who styled his
dog 'Moreover' after the dog in the Gospel; '*Moreover* the
dog came and licked his sores.' But the sterner Puritans were
not satisfied to have the Bible names which they would have
liked to monopolize shared by the population. They therefore took refuge in names indicative of their religious tenets,
the virtues they admired, the sins they eschewed. These
names were not fictitious but were actual baptismal names,
entered in the parish registers. Among them we find:

"Stedfast, Safe-on-Highe, Rejoice, Sin-denie, Fear-not,
Sorry-for-sin, No-merit, Accepted, Thankful, Joy-againe,
From-above, Dust, Faint-not, Reformation, Earth, Ashes,
Tribulation, The-Lord-is-Near, Free-gift, Hopeful, Purify.
The 'Grace names' Love, Mercy, Charity, Clemency, Tem-
perance, Truth, Constancy, Silence, Grace, Hope, Experi-
ence, Patience, Diligence, Obedience, Virtue, Confidence,
Comfort, Repentance, Humiliation, Humility, Abstinence,
Godly, Lively (referring to spiritual manifestations surely!),
Faithful.

"But they became tired of using mere names of the virtues, and after awhile turned to something more picturesque
and dramatic, affixing to their offspring ejaculations, exhor-
tations, or expressions of praise. Thus we have Fear-God
and Praise-God Barebone in 1596, and their two brothers
'Jesus-Christ-came-into-the-world-to-save Barebone,' and 'if
Christ-had-not-died-for-thee-thou-hadst-been-doomed Barebone,' commonly known as 'Damned Barebone,' for short.

"Thanksgiving for children is shown in Free-gift, From-above, More-fruit, Replenish, Increase and Increased, Deliverance, Much-mercy, Cherubin Diball, Seraphim Marketman (did they continually cry?), Thankful, Preserved (the name 'Preserved Fish' has only recently ceased to be found in the Brooklyn Directory), Beloved, Joy-in-sorrow, Lamentation, Safe-on-High Hopkinson, Help-on-High Foxe, Stand-fast-on-High Stringer, Aid-on-High, Restore, Have-mercy, Weakly Elkins, Helpless, Repent, Forsaken," and "Flie-fornication," a not particularly delicate reference to having been "born in sin."

There were also Wealthy, Pleasant, Handmaid, Miracle, Trinity, Unity, Providence, Inward, and Job-rakt-out-of-the-asshes.

In the Register of St. Helen, Bishopgate, may be read: "Sept. 1, 1611 Job-rakt-out-of-the-asshes, being borne the last of August in the lane going to Sir John Spence's backgate, and there laid in a heape of seacole asshes, was baptised the ffirst day of September following, and dyed the next day after."

While in the parish church of Old Swinford is found: "1676 Jan. 18 Baptized Daneell-Dallphebo-Mark-Antony-Dallery-Gallery-Cesar, son of Daneel-Dallphebo-Mark-Antony-Dallery-Gallery-Cesar Williams."

As Canon Bardsley says, "baptismal nomenclature today in the United States, especially in the older settlements, bears stronger impressions of the Puritan epoch than the English." Puritan names are perpetuated everywhere in this country.

As the Puritan threw off the shackles of religion in the old country so did he throw off those of convention in nomenclature and assert his freedom. "Oceanus" Hopkins was born on the *Mayflower*, "Peregrine" White was born as the vessel touched Cape Cod, and we have "Sea-born" Egginton, "Sea-mercy" Adams, "Sou'wester" and "Bonaventure." Once in America the Puritan occasionally relaxed his austerity in puns compounded of baptismal and surname. Thus

Robert New had his sons christened "Nothing" and "Something." Price became "Sterling" Price; Carrol, "Christmas" Carroll; Mixer, "Pepper" Mixer; Hopper, "Opportunity" Hopper; Ware, "China" Ware; Peel, "Lemon" Peel; Codd, "Salt" Codd; and Gentle, "Always" Gentle. But then in London they had Cannon Ball, Dunn Brown, Friend Bottle, River Jordan, and the two brothers Jolly Death and Sudden Death.

What were the Puritans really like? Do not for a moment imagine that I am attempting to answer the question even with respect to the generation represented by my grandfather. All that can safely be said is that they were probably, as a whole, not precisely as we usually suppose. There were Puritans and Puritans,—just as there are now. The fact that it is easy to dig up and assemble statutes and town orders, bawdy songs and profane ballads, curious excerpts from diaries, and scandalous matter derived from a period of nearly three hundred years, does not mean that the population of New England at any time during that era were generally profligate, riotous, or profane, any more than their "grim and sulphurous theology," their doleful hymns and their rigid observance of the Sabbath mean that, by and large, they got no fun out of life or never smiled.

# CHAPTER VIII

## When West Was East

IT was in the year 1900 that the Puritan, when moving from Boston to New York—as so many Puritans do,—discovered on the back shelf of a closet the little horse-hide box, about eighteen by twenty inches square studded with brass nails, containing the papers which his father had seen fit to cherish. These papers consisted of a diary, a few letters and documents relating to his professional career and to the Civil War, and covered, with many a long hiatus, a period from the time he went to college in 1833 to the Emancipation Proclamation of Abraham Lincoln in 1862. They shed an entirely new light on a father remembered dimly as a rather stern, whiskery and, as it seemed, very old man who always wore a low black sateen waistcoat draped with a heavy gold chain, a flashing diamond pin fastened in a white-pleated shirt, a black string tie, and high boots under steel-blue trousers which, when one sat on his lap, were always very tight about the abdomen.

The box and its contents seemed to offer a possibility of reconstructing him, as it were, *"ex pede Herculem."* But the letters and documents bore dates so far apart, that it was impossible to fill the gaps save by a process of deduction characterized by more ingenuity than logic, and to his surprise and chagrin the Puritan was forced to confess that he knew less than nothing of United States history during the period of his father's youth and early manhood, and, what was infinitely worse, that his knowledge of the march of events leading up to the great struggle over slavery was as vague as that of the present younger generation concerning those of the World War, and that most of the figures connected with it were but names to him. Ten minutes in the confessional of history exposed the shocking fact that he no longer recalled the nature of the Missouri Compromise; what Webster replied to Hayne or what the latter had said in the first place; while Henry Clay was but the name of a cigar once popular and remembered by virtue of the Pelmanistic couplet:

> "My name is mud and I live in the gutter,
> I'm cousin to Henry Clay."

The War with Mexico might have been between the Lydians and Phrygians for all he knew of it; and such things as "Fifty-four Forty or Fight!" and the "Wilmot Proviso" had no place in his "Ask-Me-Another"; so far as he was concerned Mr. Webster might never have made his "Seventh of March Speech"; the "Compromise of 1850," the Fugitive Slave Law, the Dred Scott case, "Bleeding Kansas"—just what were they all?—and—the Puritan hung his head—when *was* Abraham Lincoln elected President of the United States?

And yet it is quite possible that the Puritan was no more ignorant than most people about these and other important facts of our history. To the present day school boy Verdun has no more reality than Gettysburg,—perhaps less. He knows as little of the war in which his father was a "doughboy" as the Puritan did of that other in which his sire was one of the "boys in blue." It is literal fact that a Harvard freshman was recently unearthed who had never heard of the sinking of the *Lusitania.*

§

Although I am at the present writing fifty-four years of age, it so happens that I have met but two human beings who rejoiced in a parent of either sex born before my father. He first saw the light in the year 1817; that is to say, according to the customary historical reckoning by "battle, murder and sudden death," he came into this world but two years after the Battle of Waterloo and four years before Napoleon's apotheosis on St. Helena; George III was King of England, Louis XVIII was the ruler of France, and James Monroe

was the fifth president of the United States. Applying the
materialistic or "bathtub" measure of progress, there were
no telegraphs or railroads, no gas lights, coals had not reached
Framingham other than as interesting geologic specimens,
guns were discharged by means of flint locks, the pantaloon
was still regarded as something of an innovation, and at
about this time a celebrated headmaster dismissed the afternoon session of his school with the words: "There will now
be a prayer meeting; those who wish to lie down in everlasting burning may go; the rest will stay."

The War of 1812 bore somewhat the same relationship
to a small boy of my father's period as the World War does
to the children of to-day; and the burning of Washington by
the British was far more vivid to him than the sack of Lou-
vain can possibly be to them. England was the mother of
tyrants, Bunker Hill a great American victory; John Adams,
Thomas Jefferson and John Randolph of Roanoke were familiar figures; the treason of Aaron Burr, the former vice-
president of the United States, only less odious than that of
Benedict Arnold; and his killing of Alexander Hamilton in
a duel at the Elysian Fields still a fireside topic. "Men, who
were giving up wigs, still wore the enormous cravats which
had been introduced by George III to hide the swelling on
his neck. The long trouser was coming in, and with it the
shoestring." A popular jingle, widely current, throws light
both upon contemporary literary standards and sense of
humor:

> "O, Aaron Burr! What hast thou done?
> Thou has shooted dead the great Hamilton!
> Thou got behindst a bunch of thistles
> And shot him dead with a pair of hoss-pistols!"

This epic, popular in my father's boyhood, I learned from
him eighty years after the tragic event it so quaintly celebrated.

Yet during the thirty-five years that had gone by since
the birth of my grandfather in 1783, the United States had

experienced a development and a prosperity that staggered the imagination of the survivors of the Revolution. Since then the population had leaped from three and a half millions to six. Instead of thirteen states there now were twenty-four. Where there had been no city of 40,000, there were now four of that size, and two, New York and Philadelphia, of over 100,000. The hardships of the old semi-frontier life were disappearing. The War of 1812 had driven the coastwise traffic inland and developed an enormous carrying trade. Thirty thousand persons had emigrated from Europe in 1817. Everywhere there were canals, turnpikes, steamboats on lakes and rivers. On the Hudson alone there were 13 steamboats, burning 1,600 cords of wood a week, with a $1 fare from New York to Albany. Anthracite coal was just coming into use. Beyond the Alleghanies hamlets were turning into cities almost overnight, and owing to the ease of transportation the whole country was rapidly becoming a market for eastern manufacturers.

In 1816 Peal's Museum in Philadelphia installed a mysterious looking apparatus devised by a certain Dr. Kugler for the making of "carbonated nytrogen," advertising, as an added attraction to the "velocipede," two-headed calf and pickled mermaid, that on certain nights "the hall would be illuminated by gas-lights, which will burn without oil or wick." People paid, sniffed, marvelled and forgot. In 1820 the Masons built a hall and lit it with Dr. Kugler's newfangled gas, but the Lodge Works made such a stench that the public rebelled, candle makers and oil sellers organized a lobby, and the Masons' petition to be allowed to lay pipes and furnish gas to subscribers was rejected by the common council. So Philadelphia went gasless until 1837, although Boston adopted it for lighting in 1822, and New York the following year.

In 1817 the Conestoga wagon which covered the ninety miles between Philadelphia and New York City in three days was called "The Flying Machine."

In my father's boyhood a stage-coach trip to New York

from Boston was a real adventure. Josiah Quincy, who in the company of Judge Story made the journey in 1826, thought himself fortunate, travelling only in the "day time," to reach his destination on the fourth day, in time for a late dinner. Says he: "The stage left Boston at 3 A. M., and at 2 A. M. a man was sent around to the houses of those who booked for the passage. His instructions were to knock, pull the bell and shout, and disturb the neighborhood as much as possible in order that the person who was to take the coach might be up and dressed when it arrived at his door. When the coach arrived there was no light inside, and the passengers waited until daybreak before they could see who were their fellow-passengers."

Samuel Breck says that it sometimes took him nine days to go from New York to Boston. A person planning to take the trip would talk of it for weeks, or even months, in advance. On the fateful evening the old vehicle would come lumbering up to the door and his trunk would be strapped on the rack behind. All the baggage having been collected a return trip would be made to the stage office for the mail and the start would be actually made at about 10 P. M.

"After riding all night—and a bitter cold night it was and snowing fast—" says one traveller, "we arrived at the town of Sturby on the Worcester turnpike. Here we had breakfast and at this place we changed from wheels to runners. At noon we reached Hartford, Connecticut, and had a good hot dinner. From here the sleighing became poor. Many times during the evening the gentlemen had to get out and walk. Arrived at New Haven for supper—another wild night. We had our breakfast at a tavern on the old Boston Post Road. Every time the stage stopped for a change of horses or for meals, the gentlemen went for something in the shape of a hot toddy, the price of which was three cents.

"The price of meals was, breakfast and supper, 25c each—dinner 37½c. You could make the latter price by paying a quarter and ninepence, which was 12½c. Most of the taverns set a good table with plenty of food well cooked.

"On arriving in New York we drove through the Bowery, Chatham Street, Broadway, Cortland Street to the stage house, arriving at noon, having been 38 hours on our journey. The fare, including meals, was $17.50. Tired and lame we were too when the trip was ended."

In 1817, to paraphrase Prof. Edward Channing's comment on a still earlier period, the stage coach, the prairie wagon, the wind propelled sloop or schooner, or a steamboat that could make but four miles an hour were the only means of travel; a man was lucky if he could go by steamboat or stage coach 50 miles a day; thirty years later in 1850 a man was unlucky if he could not travel 50 miles in an hour behind a locomotive; to-day a racing motor can whirl him well over 200 miles in the same space of time, and he can climb in an airplane higher than the Himalayas. Had it not been for the application of steam to transportation it is more than likely that the loosely knit, sectionally minded and jealous states would have fallen apart into two or more main groups, or unscrambled themselves into their original component parts. The steam railroad disseminated news, conquered suspicion, made friends of strangers, and bound the country together with tracks of steel. With the railroad the states became really united, one and inseparable. But the railroad did more than that; it broke down all sorts of barriers, economic, spiritual and intellectual, and changed the whole trend of American civilization.

"In view of the divergent interests of the several parts of the country and of all the social and political prejudices that attended on these divergences, was it going to be possible," asks Prof. Channing, "to administer a constantly growing consolidated federal government for any length of time? Had not the steamboat, the railroad, and the telegraph come when they did would the Union have long continued?"

Yet in spite of the fact that there were steamboats the suggestion that steam might be utilized for land locomotion was to most people startling if not incredible. In 1815 the New

Jersey Legislature had granted to John Stevens the first railroad charter in America, but he was too far ahead of his time.
Nobody would put money into any crazy idea involving a
line of parallel rails laid horizontally on the ground over
which wheeled carriages were to be propelled by steam!
Stevens, although discouraged, kept at it. Few people could
comprehend what a railroad might be. In 1823 a correspondent of a newspaper wrote the editor asking "What is a railroad?" and the editor replied: "Perhaps some other correspondent can tell."

The possibility of train travel was first treated as fantastic. Edward Everett Hale, in his "A New England Boyhood," says: "When I was nine or ten years old, my father,
who was thought to be a fanatic as a railroad prophet, offered in Faneuil Hall the suggestion that if people could
come from Springfield to Boston in five hours, an average of
*nine* people would come every day. This prophecy was then
considered extravagant."

The editor of the Boston *Courier* wrote satirically in
1827: "Alcibiades, or some other great man of antiquity, it
is said, cut off his dog's tail, that *quid nuncs* (we suppose such
animals existed in ancient as well as in modern times) might
not become extinct for want of excitement. Some such motive, we doubt not, moved one or two of our *natural* and *ex-
perimental philosophers* to get up the project of a railroad
from Boston to Albany;—a project, which every one knows,
—who knows the simplest rules in arithmetic,—to be impracticable but at an expense little less than the market value
of the whole territory of Massachusetts; and which, if practicable, every person of common sense knows would be as
useless as a railroad from Boston to the Moon. Indeed, a
road of some kind from here to the heart of that beautiful
satellite of our dusky planet would be of some practical utility,—especially, if a few of our *notional*, public-spirited men,
our railway fanatics, could be persuaded to pay a visit to their
proper country."

The aid of verse was called in to satirize those who were

willing to hazard their lives by riding on the fire breathing and stench emitting monsters.

> "In my young days when I was leetle
> The only steam came from the kettle.
>
> .   .   .   .   .   .   .   .
>
> The Gals on good old dobbins rid then
> But folks don't do as they used to did then.
>
> .   .   .   .   .   .   .   .
>
> Higho, I grieve, I grieve
> For the good old days of Adam and Eve."

On April 5, 1834, the Boston *Patriot* announced the first successful run of a locomotive in New England.

"A Locomotive Engine was yesterday employed in hauling gravel on the Boston & Worcester Rail Road. The engine worked with ease, was perfectly manageable, and showed power enough to travel at any desirable speed. The distance traveled was about three miles, and the train usually traversed this distance, both with loaded and with empty cars, in about ten minutes, the engine blowing off waste steam a great part of the time, and evidently capable of carrying a much greater load, or moving with greater rapidity."

Regular passenger service having been established between Boston and Newton, the speed was regarded as too fast for safety and by vote of the directors was reduced to eighteen miles an hour. But even that part of the public which was not too timid to ride disliked "the familiarity" of train travel. Samuel Breck wrote in July, 1835:

"This morning at 9 o'clock I took passage in a railroad car from Boston for Providence. Five or six other cars were attached to the 'loco' and uglier boxes I do not wish to travel in. They were huge carriages, made to stow away some thirty human beings, who sat cheek by jowl as best they could. Two poor fellows who were not much in the habit of making their toilet, squeezed me into a corner, while the heat soon drew from their garments a villainous compound of smells made up of salt fish, tar and molasses.

"By and by just twelve—only twelve—bouncing factory girls were introduced, who were going on a party of pleasure to Newport.

" 'Make room for the ladies,' bawled out the superintendent. 'Come, gentlemen, jump up on the top; plenty of room there.'

" 'I am afraid of a bridge knocking my brains out,' said a passenger. Some made one excuse and some another. The whole twelve were, however, introduced, and soon made themselves at home sucking lemons and eating green apples . . .

"Talk of ladies on board a steamboat or a railroad car. There are none. I never feel like a gentleman there. To restore herself to her caste, let a lady move in select company, at five miles an hour, and take her meals in comfort at a good inn. The old-fashioned way with one's own horses and carriages, with liberty to dine decently in a decent inn and be master of one's own movements, with the delight of seeing the country and getting along rationally, *that* is the mode to which I cling."

Almost immediately there was objection to smoking.

"What! Puff the cigar in the cars," said the "Practical Christian," "those beautiful railroad cars! Smoke and chew, and chew and smoke, and spit this dirt all about? What avails laws, rules and regulations unless enforced? Can't help it, indeed! Ladies and gentlemen are annoyed, painfully annoyed! Even that tobacco smoke at the head of the cars passes directly through the whole train, diffusing a stench intolerable."

A cabal of stage coach proprietors and tavern keepers, who were the chief profiters of horse travel, vigorously opposed the introduction of the railroads, utilizing every means to influence the public against them. The idea that railroads would prove a general curse to the land was so skilfully encouraged that for a long time it was the custom to talk of the "calamity of the railways." The Boston *Traveller*, a "stage coach paper," issued on Tuesdays and Fridays for the express purpose of giving all the latest news about stage routes, led the campaign.

Almost everybody hated a railroad and the good people of Dorchester, outside Boston, hearing that one was in contemplation, "*Resolved,* That our representatives be instructed to use their utmost endeavors to prevent, if possible, so great a calamity to our town as must be the location of any railroad through it; and, if that cannot be prevented, to diminish this calamity as far as possible by confining the location to the route herein designated."

It was not until 1841, as Prof. George Lyman Kittridge points out in his invaluable "Old Farmer & his Almanac," that "the editor . . . first inserted railroads into his Map of New England, thus admitting them to a kind of parity with the stage routes which the map was meant to illustrate."

§

I know little of my father's boyhood, although I remember his telling me many stories, of the sort I assume that most boys are told by their fathers, concerning the rigors of his early upbringing. These included a chilly yarn about being obliged to get up on cold winter mornings to break the ice in order that the family might have water with which to wash and cook. Thinking it over at this later day I am confused as to just where this ice, which required breaking, was, although considering it was only a little over a decade since my grandfather had begun to preach in the old "Free Light" shanty, the household must have been fairly primitive.

That Framingham winters were cold I have no doubt or that my father and uncle shivered in their not altogether wind-proof attic. Indeed my father's description of the uses to which "Silas," a half-witted hired boy, known as "The Human Stove," was put on winter nights was too specific in its details to be otherwise than convincing. As seven o'clock approached Silas would be sent upstairs, where, after a sufficient lapse of time, he would be followed by my father, who would get undressed as quickly as he could and with a "Silas, turn over and give me your warm place!" leap into bed, and poor Silas' powers of radiation would be transferred to a spot further on from which he would in due course be ousted by my uncle Arthur.

Probably it was Silas, and not my father, who lit the fire in the morning with flint and steel, for friction matches did not come into use until between 1830 and 1840. Instead there were fancy tongs about six or eight inches long for men to lift coals from the fire to light their pipes with, or there would be a dish full of pine splinters beside the fireplace for the same purpose. John Quincy Adams used flint and steel with which to light his fires as late as 1848.

My grandfather's salary at this time was but $200 per annum and the family life must have been proportionately frugal, the menu consisting largely of "mush" made from Indian corn meal, the then staple of New England diet. To this I owe the misfortune of my father's failure to understand my repugnance for what had been his own diet as a child. I hated "mush," but he always insisted that it should be served and, when I would not eat, he would push my nose down into it and, with what was no doubt a purely factitious glare, roar: "Eat, Boy!"

In spite of mechanical progress the same marked difference between city and rural life still obtained as in the previous century and continued until the introduction of the railroads. From the point of view of to-day, however, Boston still resembled a large country town, as did also New York. As late as the year of my father's birth there were only nine "blocks" of houses in Boston, all the rest being separate, with light on four sides, and with ground or lanes about them. Stages clattered in from the country and there were taverns with big stables everywhere. Buggies were as yet unknown, and people rode in covered two-wheeled chaises hung on "C" springs. Brick for sidewalks was just coming into use and the streets were paved in the middle with round stones, called "cobble-stones," from the neighboring beaches. The social life was finished and formal. In the better houses the furniture was expensive and carpets of English make covered the entire floors; the less pretentious had rag carpets after about 1820 or, more often, sanded floors. All cooking was done at open fires. People dined at from two to three o'clock; ultra-fashionables at six. There were no policemen; only a handful of constables. Watchmen cried the hours of the night, as "Twelve o'clock, and a cloudy night. All's well!" They gave the alarm when necessary by sounding their rattles and shouting "Fire!"

In its general aspects country life had not changed during the period between the birth of my grandfather in 1783 and that of my father in 1817. The industrious farmer was independent of the outside world in almost everything. He worked with his men, who were his sons and the sons of other farmers, who lived at his house, ate at his table and were apt to marry his prettiest unmarried daughters. There were no servants except "indentured servants," bought on the dock as they landed from the old country. The girls often hired out as "help" on neighboring farms, but without loss of social equality. In fact they considered they were conferring a favor, as, economically at least, they were. There was no such thing as great wealth, the term "income" was unknown among the agricultural class, a small increase in stock at the end of the year meant that the farm was doing well, and if he owned property worth $10,000 the farmer was accounted a rich man. The "wood lot" provided fuel and building materials, the "wimmen folk" carded, spun and wove, made blankets, woollen stuffs, stockings, mittens and linen. In every house could be heard the clang of the loom and the buzz of the spinning wheel, while the odor of the dye pot was in every nose.

The men pitched horseshoes and tossed cents (heavier then than now) beside the tavern and the women had "spinning bees" and "quilting bees." Winter evenings they had spelling matches or singing schools under the direction of a singing leader or a singing master. But with the advent of the lecture course and the rise of the Lyceum, came the passing of the spelling bees and the huskings with their hard cider and kisses on the finding of red ears among the cobs. The first Lyceum in Massachusetts was established in Millbury in 1826, and within five years every village had its own.

The roads were terrible,—bog holes in spring, dust heaps in summer, so the farmer transported his produce in winter, loading his big double sleigh with frozen hogs, tallow, butter, cheese, dried apples, honey, home-made cloth and driving often a couple of hundred miles to Boston, selling and swapping his goods, and bringing back salt, sugar, tea, coffee, molasses, codfish, and good old Jamaica rum. He was a thrifty fellow, however, and spent little at taverns on the way, for he would carry his own supplies and feed, and pay only for his night's lodging and the stabling of his horses.

Life in Framingham continued, until the coming of the railroad, much the same as in post-revolutionary days. There were no longer, of course in that neighborhood, any slaves. Abolition was not an issue, although slavery was a problem. The situation of the free black at that time was intolerable. Nowhere did he have the rights and privileges of citizenship. Prejudice excluded him practically from all occupations. In the District of Columbia, as in most slave-holding states, any Negro who could not show manumission papers, or prove his freedom by documentary evidence, could be seized and sold. In the North anti-slavery feeling was general but, until 1830, usually took the form of proposals for deportation and colonization.

It was the "Era of Good Feeling," for Massachusetts had come into the fold. Her statesmen no longer ranted about the tyranny of central government or "southern domination"; she had become ardently nationalistic and given President Monroe (the last of the Virginia dynasts) a cordial and even enthusiastic welcome during his tour of New England. Monroe was followed by John Quincy Adams, the second Massachusetts man to be president, yet, after the two Adamses, more than a century elapsed before the Bay State furnished another.

Gradually the belief spread that the ownership of one man by another was a vicious, inhuman institution. From the indifference which had allowed slavery to lapse without a formal statute, Massachusetts gradually acquired an almost fanatical hatred of the South's "peculiar institution." John Quincy Adams, who was destined to lead the fight against slavery and the obnoxious "gag rule" in the national House of Representatives, recorded in his diary as early as 1820 that, if the slavery question should dissolve the Union, it would shortly be followed by universal emancipation. In 1831, William Lloyd Garrison established his paper, *The Liberator*, in Boston, which in strident terms announced, "—urge me not to use moderation in a cause like the present. I am in earnest—I will not equivocate—I will not excuse— I will not retreat a single inch—*and I will be heard.*"

Yet through the opening scenes of the great struggle between freedom and slavery all the wealthy, the "safe," the moderates and most of the holders of high office were against him. At the Harvard Centennial Celebration in 1836 the toast was drunk: "Massachusetts and South Carolina; they stood by one another nobly in the darkest days of peril and adversity; may long years of mutual prosperity find them undivided." This was the mutual prosperity of slave owners and slave traders and of the merchants and manufacturers in the North who profited by slavery. Daniel Webster referred to those who threatened this prosperity as "fanatical and factious abolitionists," and even James Russell Lowell, in his class poem in 1838, made fun of the abolitionists, although later he changed his attitude.

Garrison stands alone as the hero of abolition. Lincoln was not an abolitionist, and although he gladly used emancipation as a war measure he did so cautiously. Only two years before he had regarded other measures as adequate. The Great Proclamation in September, 1862, gave the Confederate States until January 1, 1863, to return to the union without their arms *but with their slaves*. It was, in fact, not respectable to be an abolitionist in Boston until the Civil

War was almost over. People were willing to turn out to prevent a fugitive slave from being returned, who would knock one down if one called them "abolitionists."

Yet by the end of 1835 there were already 300 anti-slavery societies in the United States, and in another twenty years the pulpit, the press and finally the mob had united in a fierce denunciation of slavery.

Puritanism as such exhibited no particular reaction to the slavery question. Carl Wittke in "Religious Influence in the 19th Century" says that the churches were luke warm when not altogether silent upon the subject, and points out that the Civil War caused a split in many of the denominations and that the northern and southern churches were loyal to their respective governments.

"In 1837 great difficulty was experienced in getting a church in Boston in which to conduct the meetings of the Massachusetts and New England Anti-Slavery Societies. The Presbyterian General Assembly put off acting on the slavery issue; a Methodist bishop of New Hampshire repudiated the Abolitionists; an Episcopal minister of Vermont pointed out that Abraham kept slaves at Ur of the Chaldees; the American Bible Society refused to accept money from the American Anti-Slavery Society for the distribution of Bibles among Southern slaves; and the Baptist Board of Foreign Missions held that slave-holding Baptists could nevertheless be sincere followers of Christ. The Abolitionists, in fact, were for years regarded as dangerous agitators who were bent only on disrupting the nation.

"Small wonder that Birney called the American church 'the bulwark of slavery,' and Wendell Phillips asserted that abolition would have come decades earlier had it not been for the churches."

As the child of a humane and progressive Baptist minister my father doubtless had been brought up to believe that slavery was wrong, but it is not probable that the menace of the coming struggle, in which he was later so actively to be plunged, had begun to loom large upon the horizon of the little country town where he learned to plait straw in the chimney corner, studied the catechism and Noah Webster's "Grammatical Institute of the English Language," and as a special treat for good behavior was allowed to enjoy a rollicking half hour with *The Latter-Day Luminary,* a Baptist quarterly of Philadelphia, or the bi-monthly *American Baptist Magazine and Missionary Intelligencer.*

My father very well remembered the visit of General Lafayette to the United States in 1825 and told me how my grandfather, who was a patriotic citizen, had driven him and his elder brother, Arthur, into Boston in the yellow hulled family chaise, a momentous journey of twenty-one miles requiring four hours. He was dressed for the occasion in a green bombazine frock and trousers, ruffled collar, bootees of leather tanned and manufactured in Framingham, and shining with "black-ball" well laid on for the journey. On his head he wore a hat of Dunstable braid, plaited by his mother, and made into a hat by a neighbor, but on arriving in the great city, he became self-conscious about his home-made hat and my grandfather good-naturedly bought him a cap in place of it.

"The next morning," he said, "we went out to Roxbury and near the old Punch-bowl Tavern we first saw Lafayette, my father holding me up in his arms so that I might see the procession over the heads of the crowd, my brother, who was five years older, being able to take care of himself. On my breast I wore a badge of white satin ribbon, on which was printed the likeness of the hero of the occasion and beneath it the motto 'Welcome Lafayette.' I was so thrilled at the mobs of people, the cheering and the general enthusiasm, that I was nearly beside myself with excitement and managed only with the greatest difficulty to stand on my father's shoulders by holding one of his hands in each of mine. It gave me, however, a perfect position—as good as a stage box,—for it put me at least three feet above anybody else, and when the procession hove into view I jumped up and down to the great discomfort of my father and screamed at the top of my lungs: 'Lafayette!—Lafayette!—Welcome Lafayette!' I had a magnificent view of him and, if I could paint, could draw a perfect likeness of him to-day as he rode by in his barouche. Afterwards we went over to Charlestown to the laying of the corner-stone of the Bunker Hill Monument, where I heard Mr. Webster deliver his oration and saw General Lafayette sitting among the veterans of the Revolution. The famous scene is indelibly burned into my memory."

A hundred years later I happened to be walking one afternoon on Riverside Drive, New York, where I accidentally met Miss Anna Hyatt, the sculptress. She had just come, she told me, from a great reception at the Hispanic Museum, given in honor of another famous general of France, and was wearing on her bosom a blue silken badge, exactly similar save in color to that which my father had worn on his memorable trip to Boston to see Lafayette, save that it bore the words, also stamped in gold: "Welcome Joffre!"

When in 1833 my father, at the age of sixteen, set out for Providence to begin his freshman year at Brown University, he also drove in my grandfather's "one-hoss" chaise. There were about 200 students, among them boys from as far afield as Chicago and Savannah. One even came from Wales. With the exception of algebra and geometry the first year was given over entirely to the classics. In the sophomore year he took up English grammar, surveying, navigation, nautical astronomy, trigonometry and its application to measuring heights and distances. In the Junior year he had mathematics, natural philosophy, chemistry and "vegetable physiology"; in the last year moral philosophy, astronomy, psychology, Greek, Butler's Analogy, geology, the "Evidences of Christianity," and the American Constitution. French, German and Hebrew were elective and charged for extra.

It was a required curriculum guaranteeing a mental discipline and a practical knowledge that makes me thoroughly ashamed of my own "elective" cultural browsings at Harvard sixty years later, where I spent such time as I devoted to my college course on fine arts, English literature, botany, geology, and other "snaps." So far as I am now able to determine my four college years resulted in nothing but a complete intellectual demoralization, and I left Cambridge with a less well-trained mind than when I entered it. It would have been far better for me in every way had I been obliged to buckle down and do some real work, as my father was. I should be glad to know some "nautical astronomy."

The winter term bill for his senior year is a commentary on the change that has taken place in economic conditions.

"Class Graduating September 1837

Rev. Charles Train to Brown University for College
Bill of Charles R. Train, Dr.

| | |
|---|---:|
| To Tuition | $12.00 |
| Room rent | 3.00 |
| University Library | 1.00 |
| Steward's Salary | 2.00 |
| Servants hire, printing, etc. | 2.00 |
| Repairs | .55 |
| Commons bill 8 weeks @ $1.62 per week | 12.96 |
| Public Fuel | .50 |
| Interest due to May 1st | .68 |
| Absent from prayers without excuses—once | |
| Absent from recitations without excuse— twice | .06 |
| | $34.78" |

In spite of absences from prayers and recitations without excuse he apparently graduated in good standing in 1837, secured his degree, attended the Harvard Law School for one year, and was admitted to the bar in 1841. It was during this latter period that he "fell." It was noised abroad that he had been guilty of the sin of dancing—not merely "hopping up and down." Among the letters, preserved in the little horse-hide trunk to which I have referred, is the following:

"Framingham, May 4, 1841.

Dear Brother in Christ:

At our last regular church meeting, the Church, not from any ill will or ill wish towards you, but from a sense of duty, and your spiritual good, authorized their clerk to write you, and state that common report says, when you were residing in Milford, Mass. you was the prime-mover of a resolution for a ball, attended the same and acted as a manager. This report comes well substantiated. We have reason to believe that your general character did not give much, if any, evidence of Piety. The Church wish you well and that you may be directed into the path of duty.

Yours,

F. Gay, Clerk.

They desire an answer immediately."

I have often wondered what that answer was. Three "short and ugly words," perhaps! The inappropriately named clerk was probably justified in the charge that the applicant "did not give much, if any, evidence of Piety." Clergymen's sons! I remember hearing my father tell in later years how, as a senior, he had angled from his window in "Hope College" on the Brown campus with a corn-baited line for President Wayland's geese, which were artlessly allowed to wander at large. He even boasted of having caught one, hauled it up squawking and fluttering through the air and into the window, wrung its neck, plucked and roasted it. Something of a feat if true,—particularly the end of the story!

But we know that he danced "in Milford, Mass."! What were the evidences of impiety in the hands of Mr. Gay, I wonder. And why did the Church desire an answer? Probably in order either to be assured as to his orthodoxy, or to secure oral admission from him as to his religious shortcomings, for while he was at the Harvard Law School he had many violent discussions with my grandfather upon doctrinal points, as a result of which the latter told him never to enter the church again so long as he was the pastor. In all likelihood Mr. Gay's letter was the first step preparatory to his being dropped from the rolls, custom requiring the delinquent to be given a hearing if he so desired. Pained and humiliated must my grandfather have been to have his son thus publicly expelled from his own church! What happened as a result of the invitation, I do not know. When I knew my father he was a devout Episcopalian and one of the wardens of St. Paul's Church in Boston.

The times, however, were changing fast. The first train had run through the village five years before, consisting of an engine, the "Yankee," weighing six tons, and dragging seven cars about the size of stage coaches with doors at the sides. It paused at South Framingham for a while, then loitered on to Farm Pond to take on water, which was passed up in buckets. The fare to Boston, seventy-five cents in summer, went up in winter to a dollar. But, at whatever price, the lurid delights of the gay city were at last easily accessible.

The young people discussed topics which shocked their elders and led them to believe not only that the new generation was going to the dogs, but that maidenly virtue would shortly no longer exist. Such complaints, however, were by no means new.

In 1815 a subscriber writing on "Modern Manners" in *The North American Review*, had inquired: "Allow me to ask if the violation of decorum, the want of etiquette, the rusticity of manners in this generation must not be a source of exquisite regret and mortification to those who have seen the last? What idea can the unfortunate young people of the present day have of ancient polish and refinement? So extensive is the deterioration of society, so deleterious the consequences of abandoning established systems that even the well-intentioned know not how to conduct themselves?"

People rode and drove on Sundays, although both were as much against the law as the sale of alcoholic spirits is today. The common man was beginning to think for himself. The "good and the great in their beautiful prime" may have still trod musingly the precincts of Harvard and other universities, but they no longer dominated the entire intellectual life of the community. The old austerity of life was being rapidly ameliorated. The theatre could not longer be evaded as a topic, for everybody knew that Mr. Edwin Forrest was playing in New York where Phineas Taylor Barnum had opened a museum, and "The Divine Fanny" Elssler had triumphed over the scruple against the exhibition of female nether limbs and, amid showers of roses and bouquets, had brought audience after audience of fashionables to their feet in frantic applause by her marvellous dancing of "Le Tarentule" and "La Cravovienne," departing from America with $84,000, of which $24,000 had been earned in fifteen performances. The railroad had dealt a body blow to practical Puritanism. Within the next quarter century the conflict over slavery was to damage it beyond recognition.

There was a multitude of general literary magazines, from *Godey's Lady's Book*, *The New England Magazine*, in which later Holmes began his "Autocrat of the Breakfast Table," *The Dial*, and the New York *Knickerbocker*, to those popular annuals, *The Token and Atlantic Souvenir*, *The Rose of Sharon*, *The Diadem*, *Friendship's Offering*, *The Remember Me*, and *The Christmas Blossoms and New Year's Wreath*.

It was an age of invention. The framers of the Constitution had by a single paragraph contributed towards the future development and scientific progress of the United States in a way no one of them could have envisioned, by providing, under Sec. 8 of Article 1, that Congress should have the power "to promote the progress of science and useful arts by securing for limited times to authors and inventors the exclusive rights to their respective writings and discoveries." This was a new idea, destined to immense results. By the creation of the Patent Office in 1791 American inventiveness was stimulated to a degree that made the new country soon outstrip all competitors in the old world.

Four years later, in 1795, Eli Whitney, sojourning in the

South soon after his graduation from Yale, perceiving the importance of having a machine by which the lint could be separated from the seeds of the cotton boll other than by hand, invented his famous "gin," thereby enabling the labor of a single man to produce fifty pounds of lint in one day as against a single pound per day theretofore. The economic and political results of this discovery cannot be overestimated. From that time on invention followed invention until there was no department of endeavor that had not profited by human ingenuity.

During the first decades of the nineteenth century the textile industry of New England was developed through many devices connected with weaving- and spinning-machinery, and New England farmers' daughters put away their spinning wheels and hand looms and went to work in the mills of Lowell, Waltham, and other cities. This marked the decline of the home industries and had an important bearing on women's changing status.

There were many inventions which astounded the world fully as much as the most spectacular of modern times. Philip Hone, commenting in 1839 upon the marvels of the daguerreotype, was moved to a rather curious flight of the imagination: "The manner of producing them (the daguerreotypes) constitutes one of the wonders of modern times; and like other miracles, one may almost be excused for disbelieving it without seeing the very process by which it is created. It appears to me a confusion of the very elements of nature. It is nothing less than the palpable effect of light occasioning a reproduction of sensible objects. . . . It appears to me not less wonderful that light should be made an active operating power in this manner, than that some such effect should be produced by sound; and who knows whether, in this age of invention and discoveries, we may not be called upon to marvel at the exhibition of a tree, a horse, or a ship produced by the human voice muttering over a metal plate, prepared in the same or some other manner, the words 'tree,' 'horse' and 'ship.' How greatly ashamed of their ignorance the bye-gone generations of mankind ought to be!"

The invention of the electric telegraph and its first public use in 1844 had led to the wide-spread publication of daily newspapers, yet as late as 1861 the physical "make-up" of the daily press was essentially the same as that in the eighteenth century. Page 1 was given over to advertisements and other business notices, and pages 2 and 3 contained mail correspondence from one day to one week old. The "Latest News by Telegraph" was carried on page 4, and consisted entirely of news dispatches from Washington. These dispatches were run, apparently, as they were received on the wire, without regard to so-called news value in the modern sense.

The period was marked also by a multitude of inventions of domestic conveniences. The Yankee had a passion for inventing numerous gadgets of all kinds and descriptions, and these became known to the trade as "Yankee notions." This is the origin of the "Notion Counters" found to-day in all department stores. Among the patents granted between 1790 and 1839 were six methods for destroying bedbugs, and one for preventing them from climbing up the bedposts; a bedstead with a "revolving rail," "secret" bedsteads, and "windlass bedsteads" (folding beds?); 234 washing-machines, including a number of combination washing-machines and churns, and one combination "washing-machine and corn-sheller"; portable waterclosets; self-igniting cigars; artificial teeth; anti-bilious cordials, "magic lotions," and nostrums for the cure of rheumatism, cancer, consumption and other ills; together with a "method of administering medicine by steam"!

There was brewing and distilling apparatus galore; the Seidlitz powder, the soda-fountain, the razor-strop, the fountain-pen, an adding machine (invented in 1834), the alarm clock, clocks that ran by "atmospheric air," artificial marble coffins, rat traps, a mode of catching ducks, a mode for improving the shape of horses, a mode of carrying fish in warm weather, and mills to be run by "dog power." Further, the records show that one John Grout, Jr., of Massachusetts, was granted a patent for a telegraph on October 24, 1800!

Among boots and shoes we find them "furred," "iron-bound," "mathematical," water-proof and "perpetual polished," and made from skins with the hair on.

There was a widespread horror of being buried alive, and an inventor obtained a patent for a wooden shaft, to be attached to the head of the coffin, having an intricate system of pulleys and ropes on the inside, with a huge bell on the outside. The corpse held a tassel in his right hand, and, should he awake, could pull the cord and jangle the bell, whereupon the grave diggers would come a-running and dig him out.

Another inventor sought to relieve wearers of tall hats in the summer time by placing a tiny electric fan in the crown. There are patents for many "anti-snoring" devices ranging from a cylindrical piece of wood with a slot in it and fastened between the teeth by means of strings around the ears, to small blocks of wood worn between the shoulder blades to prevent the sleeper from turning on his back.

One inventor sought to protect farmers against wild animals encountered in the fields by affixing a long bayonet to the whiffletree of the plow. There is a patent for a collapsible hoop skirt, which the inventor declared to be a device intended to prevent the indecent display of underclothing of a woman in a sitting posture (the noncollapsible skirts he regarded as immodest because the hoop was pushed forward and upward when a woman sat down and revealed her underwear), and there is record of a public patent having been granted for a hair restorer the chief ingredient of which is "the juice of baked pork and beans."

All this output of ingenuity had had its effect. The America into which my father had been born was experiencing the first tremors of the Industrial Revolution. Already we had lost our dependence upon European manufacturers. The first successful power loom for weaving in America had been con-

structed by Francis Lowell in 1814 and put into operation
at Waltham; the period from 1815 to 1842 witnessed the
gradual growth of American factories and the entry of these
interests into politics. The country began to throb with industrial activity, particularly in the neighborhood of Framingham and the towns north of Boston, but while with the
advent of the factory system its inherent evils appeared here
as elsewhere in the world, conditions were never as bad as
in English factory towns.

Americans generally were paid higher wages than Europeans. Farm hands received from seven to fifteen dollars a
month with board, according to the season and locality. Between 1830 and 1860 the men factory workers in Massachusetts, where wages were considered extremely generous, received five dollars a week, children between one and two
dollars, and women from one dollar and seventy-five cents
to two dollars a week, the latter figures including board. The
average working week was nearly eighty hours long. Wages
elsewhere were lower, yet the absence of conspicuous poverty
was frequently observed by European travellers, and Harriet Martineau so glowingly recorded her impressions of factory life in Waltham in 1835 that they seem like a dream
of the Elysian Fields or recollections of an officially conducted trip through modern Soviet Russia.

But in spite of the relatively superior conditions of American factory workers to those of Europe, the mills were usually unsanitary and unhealthy places in which to work; those
in New England generally had working days of thirteen
hours; in Connecticut they ran fourteen and fifteen hours;
while at Paterson, N. J., women and children were required
to be at work at four-thirty in the morning. In 1832, the
child workers in factories constituted two-fifths of the total
number of employees.

Craft and trade unions made an effort to correct these
evils and labor organizations pleaded for political and economic reforms, yet until 1834 every citizen in Massachusetts had to contribute to the support of some religious sect;

ministers with unsure livings were afraid to support unpopular causes; and about that time the Appellate Court decided that a free black woman was not entitled to the privilege of the ladies' cabin on a steamer.

There was little or no improvement in prison conditions. In Massachusetts, up to 1864, there were no separate gaols for women or juvenile delinquents. Under the common law any child over seven years old was deemed capable of committing a crime, consequently there were mere children in adult jails. Until 1829 prisoners re-committed to the state prison were tattooed on the arm with the words "Massachusetts State Prison." The lash was used for punishment in every state in the Union except Pennsylvania, and under the system of solitary confinement prisoners often went insane or committed suicide.

The treatment of the insane was, and had been from Colonial days, a disgrace. In 1837 a committee of the New Hampshire legislature stated that they had found inoffensive insane people wandering at large the butt of boys and drunkards, had found others in cages, in outbuildings of private houses, in county jails along with felons, in almshouse cellars "never warmed by fire or lighted by the ray of the sun," and in one Massachusetts prison a man was discovered "confined in a dark room in a cellar where he had lived for seventeen years; he had protected himself against cold by stuffing hay into the cracks of the door, his food being passed to him through a wicket."

Education for women was still scoffed at. In the early nineteenth century it was believed that the only reason for giving a woman an education was to fit her for marriage; and that to give a girl the same course of study as a boy was the height of absurdity, if not wicked. "In 1829, a scandal was caused in New York by the public examination of a girl on the subject of Geometry, the clergy, as usual, prophesying the dissolution of all family bonds." Female education was accused of an anti-domestic tendency "to which we may trace the restless craving for excitement and public pleasures, which so strikingly characterize the aggregate of female society at the present day."

The duties of a woman were to be obedient, to subject herself to her husband and to defer to him in all things; she was advised to cultivate the art of conversation, so as to be pleasing; she was told that "there is an inequality in the sexes, and that for the economy of the world the men, who were to be the guardians and lawgivers, had not only the greater share of bodily strength bestowed upon them, but also of reason and resolution," and that while unchastity was "superlatively criminal in a woman," in a man it must be viewed "in a far less disadvantageous light." Therefore, if a woman's husband was unfaithful, she was supposed to feign ignorance of his philandering, and by being pleasant and compliant, and by exerting herself more than usual to enhance her charms and make herself attractive to him, try to win him back to his lawful fireside. A woman was counselled to separate from her husband only as a last resort.

In many of the books written for women was printed or paraphrased Dean Swift's famous letter to a young woman on her marriage in which he informs her that the "great affair of your life will be to gain and preserve the friendship and esteem of your husband" and that love is "that ridiculous passion that has no being but in playbooks and romances." Further remarking, "So your sex employs more thought, memory and application to be fools than would serve to make them wise and useful. When I reflect on this I cannot conceive you to be human creatures, but a sort of species hardly a degree above the monkey; which has more diverting tricks than any of you; is an animal less mischievous and expensive; might in time be a tolerable critic in velvet and brocade, and for aught I know would equally become them."

Woman having as yet no rights received all the privileges. Her purity was a shield and buckler that enabled her to go anywhere in safety. The young of both sexes mingled with a freedom that made Europeans gasp.

American girls had always, even in Colonial times, enjoyed an amount of freedom scandalous to foreign visitors, one of whom wrote:

"The sweetheart comes to the house whenever he pleases, he takes his beloved out walking when he likes . . . young people sit spooning after their elders go to bed."

While another says:

"You will see a young girl drive off in a light carriage and injurious suspicion never interferes with the pure pleasures of this trip to the country."

The front parlor, with closed doors, was given over to courting. Matrimony, home life and a family was the ideal of both beau and belle, and literally the end also. The "young marrieds" disappeared from society to return only when it was time for their own "rosebuds" to "come out."

"Ladies" did not visit sculpture galleries except in pairs and fled at the approach of a man, all statues were draped, and the use of such words as "breast," "leg," "thigh," would have brought a deep blush to the cheeks of any true woman. Yet even within the last five years I have been personally reproved at the dinner-table by one of the leaders of intellectual society for speaking of a king's mistress as such, in the course of which my hostess cautiously referred to her as an "M."

Something of the amazing squeamishness that was rampant in the early nineteenth century may be realized from Mrs. Trollope's book "Domestic Manners of the Americans," where, among other things, she describes a visit to the Pennsylvania Academy of Fine Arts in 1831.

"One of the rooms of this academy has inscribed over its door,

ANTIQUE STATUE GALLERY

The door was open, but just within it was a screen which prevented any objects in the room from being seen from without. Upon my pausing to read this inscription, an old woman, who appeared to act as guardian of the gallery, bustled up and adressed me with an air of much mystery, said,

'Now, madam, now, this is just the time for you, nobody can see you—make haste!'

"I stared at her with unfeigned surprise, and disengaging my arm, which she had taken, apparently to hasten my movements, I very gravely asked her meaning.

" 'Only, madam, that the ladies like to go into that room by themselves, when there be no gentlemen watching them.'

"On entering the mysterious apartment, the first thing I remarked was a written paper deprecating the disgusting depravity which had led some of the visitors to mark and deface the casts in a most indecent and shameless manner. This abomination was unquestionably occasioned by the coarse-minded custom which sends alternate groups of males and females into the room. Were the antique gallery thrown open to mixed parties of ladies and gentlemen it would soon cease."

By 1839 a new and trifling type of woman was displacing the hard-working "helpmeet" of the more frugal early days, —the "fashionable females" with "nothing to do but harass servants and gouge money out of husband and father." "A double revolution in the status of women was taking place. The ideal good wife was changing on the one side into the idealized and silly lady and, at the same time, in other economic conditions, into a factory worker or a member of the learned professions."

The extent to which prudery was emphasized as a necessary virtue can now hardly be credited. It was *de rigueur* for a woman to faint at the sight of anything unseemly or the utterance of any "improper" word. They were actually taught how to do so at will with proper grace. The mother of one of my friends attended a "School for the Vapors" established in New York City for this sole purpose. What brought woman out of the category of the sensitive plant were the great "movements" of the nineteenth century, such as abolition, temperance and, curiously enough in so chaste a world, "free love."

I have no means of knowing whether my father in those

early years of his career strayed farther from Framingham than Lowell, Fitchburg, Worcester, or possibly Springfield. It is unlikely that he would have thrown away the money on an adventure to New York, although as an up-and-coming lawyer he could not have been oblivious to the fascinations of the rapidly growing city only 200 miles away at the mouth of the Hudson, which was already beginning to challenge Boston as the literary centre of the New World. Certainly he had no suspicion that the son of his old age would shake from off his feet, not only the dust of Framingham, but—O, sacrilege!—of even Boston itself for the garish glitter of Manhattan. But, then, he could not have hopped on an express and got there in five hours; neither could he have gone all the way by train; he would have had to go first to Boston, connect with a train for Providence and transfer to a steamboat (owned or controlled probably by "Uncle Daniel" Drew) which would land him at the Battery Pier some time next day, or by rail to Springfield, stage to Hartford, rail to New Haven, and boat to New York. But that would have cost money, although owing to the competition between "Corneel" Van Derbilt, Drew, "Liveoak George" Law and others, fares were ridiculously low. In 1840 one could go the 150 miles from New York to Albany in a luxurious steamer, occupy a "sumptuous" cabin and enjoy a hearty dinner and breakfast—all for the sum of $2. As Philip Hone notes in his invaluable diary, it was a wonder people did not live on board instead of staying at the Astor House.

The Age of Coal had arrived, at least on water. It was soon to come on land as well. From an entire output of 365 tons shipped from the Lehigh mines in 1820, and only 7,000 tons sent to New York for domestic use in 1830, by 1839, nine years later, Pennsylvania was mining 1,000,000 tons and shipping 122,000 tons to New York City, most of it to heat the boilers of steamboats. For coal-burning steamers had demonstrated their infinite superiority over wood burners and the old boats were being scrapped on every hand in favor of the new, which were so much cleaner, safer, and faster.

But while, save for the twice daily toot of the locomotive and the greater prevalence of the newspaper, existence retained its former tranquillity in the country towns of New England, enormous changes had taken place in the cities throughout the United States owing to the increase in wealth, the influence of European travellers and imports, and extended facilities in transportation. The installation of the fast packet lines—including the "Train Line" from Boston to Liverpool—had brought the old and the new worlds together and resulted in a stream of English and continental visitors such as Miss Martineau, Mrs. Trollop and Charles Dickens, curious like their successors to see what America was like and then go home and write it up. The exploitation of America by literary English did not begin with the advent in the early twentieth century of Major Pond's British cohorts, but nearly a century ago. Its nature has changed little. These visitors, depending on where they came from, where they went, whom they met, and what they were like themselves, gaped, admired, sneered, marvelled.

New York itself was like an overgrown country boy in patent-leather shoes lying on his back in a cabbage patch. No panic or fire could stop or even impede its expansion. With over 200,000 inhabitants it was a hodge-podge of wealth and poverty, of rusticity and elegance, with a melange of architecture in which one-story wooden cottages stood cheek by jowl with five-story residences of brick. People were just beginning to move uptown to Lafayette Place, Waverly Place, Washington Square and Lower Fifth Avenue, but the fashionable centre remained about Park Place, Chambers, Franklin and White Streets, while Bowling Green was still occupied by aristocratic mansions. Croton water, although discussed for years, was not introduced until the holocaust of 1835. Cholera in 1832 took toll of 3,000 lives in two summer months. Half of those who fell ill, died.

Broadway was the Rue de la Paix of America, thronged

with gaily dressed folk, swarming with brightly painted
omnibuses, horsemen, coaches and hand carts, but it was
wretchedly paved, inadequately lighted by gas and full of
mud holes. There were no day police, but each ward had
a couple of constables, while after sunset there was a night
watch who wore no uniform save a leather hat, carried a
pole and lantern, and cried the passing hours. The town
was alive with venders shouting their wares and soliciting
trade. While there were sixteen bonafide millionaires, the
scale of living among the well-to-do was, generally speaking,
only that of modest comfort. Puritan and Dutch influence
was still strong among those who regarded themselves—
and were regarded by others—as the socially elect,—both
influences making for thrift, sobriety, and lack of ostenta-
tion. Life among the old families was simple, prim, with a
considerable outward formality, and marked by an extraordinary delicacy. Those were the days when ringletted ladies
fainted at the sight of a mouse and possibly at that of a
tomato or "love-apple" as it was called, and social intercourse in mixed company was inevitably "elegant" and almost painfully "refined."

Yet occasionally, as recorded by that contemporary Pepys,
the Honorable Mr. Philip Hone, somebody threw a tremendous party, and a company of two or three hundred
heavily upholstered ladies and gentlemen crowded into an
elongated drawing room beneath crystal chandeliers whose
shimmering candles were reflected from the silver surfaces
of enormous mirrors hung in cornices of gilt, indulged in
heavy or facetious platitudes, and, after treading a few measures of a quadrille and partaking of oyster stew, cold chicken
and possibly of very sweet champagne, went home early in
order that papa might have his breakfast with the family at
seven o'clock as usual next morning. The satin-clad ladies
invariably carried several beautiful bouquets and the gentlemen all wore white gloves, sideburns, and monstrous lawn
ties that stood out like a cat's whiskers.

Although it was all, from the present-day point of view,
as simple and banal as a strawberry festival in an Ohio

church basement, an enthusiastic press was even then on hand in the person of one of Mr. James Gordon Bennett's young reporters, ready to distort its staid dullness into an orgy of Oriental grandeur, to catalogue the distinguished guests, extol the beauty and chastity of the maidens present and evaluate their fortunes.

The women, as Mr. Meade Minnigerode notes in his "Fabulous Forties," were all tall, graceful, beautiful, and "chastely correct," the enjoyment "rational," the "collations" "sumptuous," the society "select" and "highly respectable," the music "ravishing," and the concatenated bank accounts colossal. "Superb and select soirees" there were a-plenty, perhaps the most noteworthy being Mrs. Mott's fête in Honor of Ferdinand, Prince de Joinville, third son of Louis Philippe, for which "Dr. Mott's splendid mansion in Depeau Place . . . was fitted up in a style of princely magnificence, and completely crowded with an array of fashion and loveliness such as had seldom been seen assembled on any occasion," and where Mrs. Mott wore a marvellous "robe of Damascus manufacture, of ruby colored satin richly wrought in gold, a scarf of gold tissue from Constantinople about her classical shoulders, the corsage of her dress being ornamented with diamonds to match a magnificent train of pure brilliants," while her daughter was "the cynosure of all eyes, her lovely arms burdened with bouquets of the most beautiful japonicas and rare exotics presented by her numerous admirers, attired in a rose-colored crepe over the same colored satin trimmed with rouleaux of a similar material with a valant of the most costly Brussels lace, full half a yard in depth, tastefully looped up with bouquets of the most delicate of flowers," her marble brow encircled by a wreath of roses.

After a lapse of nearly a century hath it not a familiar sound?

Even to a gentleman of Mr. Hone's familiarity with the *vie mondaine* these parties seemed very grand and he almost rivals the reporter in his description of a "splendid and expensive entertainment where the sparkling of diamonds, the reflections of splendid mirrors, the lustre of silks and satins, and the rich gilding of tasteful furniture were flashed by the aid of innumerable lights upon the dazzled eyes of a thousand guests."

Watering-place life was popular at Newport and Saratoga, but in those days nobody thought of taking a regular "vacation," and the question of "where shall we go this summer?" did not come up early every spring as a matter of course in the ordinary family. Rich people from all parts of the country went for a week or two to some big hotel, largely for social or marital purposes. And they took an incredible amount of trouble to get there, driving long distances by stage-coach and, prior to the use of steamboats upon the Hudson, sailing by sloop from New York to Albany. The first inn had been built at Saratoga in 1791 by Gideon Putnam, upon the site of the present "Grand Union Hotel." Others were erected shortly thereafter, and between 1820 and 1830, at which time the resort had gained great favor, several huge wooden barnlike structures were built.

"The chief attraction of Saratoga," wrote a visiting Englishman, James Silk Buchanan, in 1841, "is the gay and ever-changing company that is found here from all parts of the Union, and especially of the opulent classes, into which it is the constant aim and desire of those who are not opulent to get admitted. Hundreds who, in their own towns, could not find admittance into the circles of fashionable society there —for the rich and leading families of America are quite as exclusive in their coteries as the aristocracy of England— come to Saratoga, where, at 'Congress Hall' or the 'United States,' by the moderate payment of two dollars a day, they may be seated at the same table, and often side by side, with the first families of the country; promenade in the same piazza, lounge on the sofas in the same drawing-room, and dance in the same quadrille with the most fashionable beaux and belles of the land; and thus, for the week or month they may stay at Saratoga, they enjoy all the advantages which their position would make inaccessible to them at home."

Mr. Hone greatly enjoyed Saratoga and its society, mentioning it for the first time in his diary on July 16, 1839.

"We are here located (as we Yankees have it) at the United States Hotel," he writes, "and no watering place in this or any other country can boast of a pleasanter establishment, or one better conducted." He was not sure whether he preferred the "balls" or the "hops." "The balls are understood to require more dressing, and a greater degree of etiquette prevails, so that the young ladies do not engage in them with so great avidity as in the hops; but, on the other hand, there are champagne and ice-cream, and blanc mange, whose agreeable presence is confined to the most dignified of these amusements."

Lest the reader should imagine such elegance to have been widely disseminated, I quote a paraphrase from "Middletown" to show how little change in the life of the ordinary frontier town had occurred between 1783 and 1845:

A local physician can still remember the pioneer culture out of which Middletown sprang. It is a useful date line. The log farmhouse of his father was ceiled inside without plaster, the walls bare save for the three pictures of Washington, Jackson and Clay. Meals were cooked before the great kitchen fireplace, and at night the room was lighted by the fire and tallow dips. Few owned watches and sun time was good enough to mark the day's work. When the family hearth went out, a boy ran to the neighbor's and fetched back fire between two boards. The homely wisdom of the period prescribed that children should be passed through the trunk of a hollow tree to cure "short growth"; hogs must be slaughtered at certain times of the moon or the bacon would shrink; babies must be weaned by the signs of the zodiac; a small bone from the heart of a deer—the "Madstone"—was good for hydrophobia and snake bite; erysipelas was cured by charms; there were those who could "blow the fire out of a burn"; a pan of water under the bed checked night sweats; bleeding was a sovereign remedy for fits and fevers; in the treatment of measles, a tea made of sheep's dung, popularly known as "nanny tea," was a favorite household remedy. Social callers were unknown but all day visits were made on horseback or in the springless farm wagon. There were no daily papers and most news traveled by word of mouth. Men would gather and talk for hours on the Providential portent of the great comet of 1843, or of the time ten years before when the "stars fell." People travelled many rough miles to hear champions argue disputed political or religious points. Hospitality was universal; whoever appeared was urged to take his place at the table. Nine-tenths or more of all that people consumed was produced in the immediate neighborhood.

Immediately following the entry in Mr. Hone's diary about the champagne and blanc mange is one of even greater interest:

"An extract from a St. Louis newspaper states that the hunters had come in with 24,000 buffalo-robes and a quantity of beaver, worth altogether $100,000. Twenty-four thousand buffaloes! What a sublime idea for any man who has never seen a buffalo or a drawing of one, or heard him described; only imagine a drove of 24,000 oxen—but the imagination cannot keep pace with the magnificent scale on which the works of nature are represented in the regions of the great West. I suppose this immense number of huge living animals would look on the prairies like a flock of sheep on Hemstead Plains."

It is hard to say whether Mr. Hone is referring to himself as having never seen a buffalo, or a drawing of one, nor heard one described. His comment somehow suggests that of Gelett Burgess, who never "saw a purple cow" and never "hoped to see one." After all, the second largest city in the state had been named by the Senecas after the animal which once frequented the near-by salt licks. Mr. Hone probably knew all about the buffalo, although at that time the world west of the Mississippi was as wild as the society of Saratoga was sophisticated, concerning which he notes next day that there are 2,000 visitors, comprising among others "many distinguished men (of whom we may feel sure that Mr. Hone rated himself as one) and fine women; antiquated belles of a by-gone generation, enjoying with gayety and cheerfulness the scenes of their former triumphs; fine married women and lovely girls, the ornaments of the present and the hopes of the future; and men uniting as in one brilliant focus the talent, intelligence, and civic virtues of the various parts of the country."

On August 12, after a visit of over three weeks, he makes his last Saratoga entry:

"This is the meridian of the Saratoga season. All the world is here: politicians and dandies; cabinet ministers and ministers of the gospel; office holders and office seekers; humbuggers and humbugged; fortune hunters and hunters of woodcock; anxious mothers and lovely daughters; the ruddy cheek mantling with saucy health, and the flickering lamp almost extinguished beneath the rude breath of dissipation. In a few days this brilliant company will be scattered over the face of the land, and who can tell for how many of them this will be the last season?"

It was all very different from what was going on in the little country town where my father, in spite of his excommunication from the Baptist Society, had continued to practice his profession. He had married, as was the custom of the time, as soon as he went to work; and, as was also the custom, had had five children in reasonably rapid succession. The early years of his young manhood must have been almost as arduous as those of his own father thirty-odd years before; but in spite of his lack of orthodoxy, or perhaps possibly because of it, he prospered and became popular among his fellow townsmen, so that they sent him as their representative to the General Court in 1847 and '48, when he became district attorney of what was known as "the Northern District" of Middlesex County for a three-year term.

That he had already attained distinction is shown by the fact that Lemuel Shaw, the famous Chief Justice of Massachusetts, rated him second only to the great Rufus Choate as a jury lawyer.

Then occurred something which must have set the little family aflutter and the town agog. The mail brought a letter from the Hon. Daniel Webster, then Secretary of State, announcing that, on August 2, 1852, President Fillmore had appointed him a "Justice of the Supreme Court of the United States for the territory of Oregon." Now, great as was the compliment, the office carried with it the obligation of residence on the part of the appointee, and the territory of Oregon was a wilderness of forest, desert and mountains, inhabited by few save desperadoes and hostile Indians.

Twenty years before, when its boundary was still under dispute with Great Britain, a bill had been introduced into Congress providing for the establishment of a territorial government, military occupation and the erection of a fort. It had been amended so as to give the President power only to send out an expedition to explore the country, to build forts and garrison them, and to extend the jurisdiction of the United States over Oregon as to citizens of the Union. But the bill was lost.

"When," declared a Mr. Mitchell, member from Tennessee, "we contemplate the vast extent of the fertile territory which spreads to the east and south of the Rocky Mountains, we may well be led to wonder what can lead any adventurer to seek the inhospitable regions of Oregon, unless, he wishes to be a savage.

"At what period do gentlemen suppose the population of this happy republic will have filled up the fair and fertile territory within our present limits? At what distant date will the pursuits of agriculture and the train of the mechanic arts have taken full possession of this immense region? That day is so distant that no gentleman of the most prolific mind can ever look forward to it! Not even within the reach of fancy itself can the advocates of this bill point out the time when Oregon Territory will have to be organized.

"But it is said that if we do not take possession, some other power will. Well, suppose they do; what will we lose? It is a territory we ought not to inhabit, and one I hope we never

shall inhabit. Why? Because it is situated at such an im-
measurable distance from the seat of Government that there
never will, there never can be, any intervening links to unite
it with the rest of the country. It is utterly impossible to
conceive, if we do plant a colony in Oregon, that it ever will
form part and parcel of our Government.

"It seems to me to be the decree of Nature herself that
the Rocky Mountains shall be the western boundary of this
Republic. She has interposed a country of four hundred miles
in extent, of the most barren, sterile character, a country
without timber and without water, a country wholly unfit for
the occupation of civilized man, while above and beyond it
the mountains rear their snowy and impassable tops, many
hundreds of feet higher than the summits of the Council
Bluffs. They stand like a Chinese wall, and must forever
and effectually guard us from all attacks from that quarter.
Should any foreign power ever be so senseless as to take
possession of Oregon, she can never injure the United States
on that side."

Even if it were possible, said he, to settle such a country
and eventually organize it into a state, it would in a few
years drop off from the Union, because there would be no
way to connect it with the rest of the Republic. It would take
any delegate or representative an entire year to go and return,—to be specific, averaging 25 miles a day, 368 days!
His mileage would cost $4,000!

"No, sir!" he concluded, "let those restless spirits who
cannot be content to cultivate their native soil, let such beings
go to Oregon, but let them go at their own risk."

These speeches were delivered in 1828, one hundred years
ago. They were sincere. When my father was offered his
Oregon judgeship in 1852 a quarter century had passed, and
a delegate from the Territory of Oregon sat in the House,
but it was still the era of the covered wagon.

There were no railroads across the Rockies. A traveller
wrote from Pittsburg in 1851: "I arrived here last night
after a very tedious and disagreeable journey from Phila-

delphia, by railway and canal, with little food and less sleep; two nights being spent in the rail-cars, and the third on the floor of a canal boat." In 1853 it took a resident of Bath, Maine, fourteen days and a half to make the trip to Peoria, Ill., and cost him and his wife $141.50, which he could now do in two days for $35. In 1846 J. Edgar Thompson, chief engineer of the Pennsylvania Railroad, met Canal Commissioner Burns in Hollidaysburg. "I asked him," said Burns, "how he expected to take cars over the mountains. 'By locomotives,' said he. Then I saw the man was a fool. I thought I would find out how big a fool he was, so I asked him how long he expected a train to be in running from Pittsburg to Philadelphia. 'Fifteen hours,' he said. Then I knew the man was a howling idiot."

The traveller from New York to Chicago in 1853 changed cars at Albany for Buffalo, changed at the Pennsylvania line for another gauge to Erie, where he changed again to the Ohio gauge for Cleveland. Here, if he were clever, he tried to beat his fellow passengers to the open scow sculled by a ferryman in order to catch the train for Toledo, where, in turn, unless he were within five minutes of his connection, he might be delayed as much as thirty-six hours.

The prospect of such a trip, even if only as far as Chicago, with a wife and five children might well have given any man pause, but when there was added to it the vision of a journey by wagon over 2,000 miles of wilderness, where he would have to spend the rest of his life among gamblers, cattle lifters and Indians, the game seemed hardly worth the candle.

This office, not so much of an honor as it might appear to be upon its face, he finally declined. My father's appointment is not without interest since, although confirmed by the Senate, it was clearly made without consultation with, or the approval of, the appointee, and moreover, although the commission duly signed by both Millard Fillmore and Daniel Webster hangs upon the wall of my library, *there was no such office*. The Territory of Oregon had been organized four years previous. Congress had provided for a Supreme Court in each territory, consisting of three judges appointed for a four-year term subject to confirmation by the Senate. These were not courts of the United States within the meaning of the Constitution, as Chief Justice Marshall had held as far back as 1824, but were simply judicial tribunals provided for by Congress under its Constitutional power to make rules and regulations for the government of territories of the United States. The title "Supreme Court of the United States for the Territory of Oregon," as recited in the commission sent my father, was entirely unwarranted (see Clinton v. Englebrecht, 13 Wallace 434), and should have read "a justice of the Supreme Court of the Territory of Oregon." Yet the commission is signed by one of the greatest lawyers in our history.

My father had acknowledged the receipt of the commission which accompanied Mr. Webster's letter of August 2, but, observing that it did not take effect until December 15, had written asking for time in which to make up his mind. Meanwhile Daniel Webster had died on October 24, 1852, and Edward Everett had succeeded him as Secretary of State. To him my father wrote on January 17, 1853, declining the appointment. He was, possibly, the only man ever designated by a President of the United States to a judgeship,—whose appointment was confirmed by the Senate,—without his knowledge and consent; certainly he was the only man ever elevated to "the Supreme Court of the United States"—even for a territory!—who held his commission nineteen weeks until it went into effect while he was trying to make up his mind, neglected to qualify or take oath, and resigned after thirty days!—He did not "wish to become a savage"!

# CHAPTER IX

# Pigs and Pantaloons

HAD my father accepted the appointment offered him by President Fillmore in 1852, as a judge of the Supreme Court of Oregon, he and his family would have made the greater part of the journey west of Chicago in a covered wagon. Incidentally, had he listened to the call of ambition rather than that of Puritan caution, he would probably have become King of the Great Northwest and I, as his heir apparent, might be now a multi-millionaire. He would, at first at any rate, have had to serve his own warrants, make his own arrests, enforce his own injunctions, and act as his own hangman until the honest folk outnumbered the desperadoes. And he would also have had to be a dead-shot and quick on the trigger. Anyhow, he didn't go.

The frontier was still a long way east of the Rocky Mountains and, in point of view of manners and customs, the country as a whole had a frontier flavor. Congress had not yet made an appropriation to determine the best route from the Mississippi to the Pacific. Mail was carried by six-mule coaches from Fort Independence, Missouri, to Santa Fé, each under guard of eight men armed with Colt's revolving rifles, long Colt revolvers, short Colt revolvers, and hunting-knives. The water-tight coaches carried eleven passengers, ran day and night, and made the trip of 850 miles in two weeks, floating across the rivers as boats. The "Pony Express" was not to be inaugurated for another decade.

Many people thought that the best way to overcome the difficulties of "The Great American Desert" and to compete with the agility of hostile Indians, in a region "no white man is supposed to have passed," was to make use of camels.

Experiments with a few imported into Texas seemed to support the idea and in 1855 Jefferson Davis, then Secretary of War, urged Congress to authorize the importation of a thousand of these semi-mythical animals. But, in spite of their theoretical superiority to mules, the camels faded out of the western picture.

California had been admitted as a state in October, 1850, and the "Great Caravan" had started on its perilous and heart-breaking trek for the golden Eldorado across the plains from St. Joseph, the Bluffs, Weston, Independence, Parkville and Kansas City. The St. Joseph *Gazette* estimated that not less than 75,000 persons would start, and the reports from Fort Laramie showed that, by July 8, 42,000 souls and 9,720 wagons had passed that way. Of these, according to the Philadelphia *Ledger* of June 21, 1850, 20,000 had set out from Iowa, and large numbers from Ohio, Indiana, Illinois, Michigan and Wisconsin. Most of these last were Puritans.

§

Puritans, to most of us, mean the early settlers of New England, their immediate descendants, or possibly a few later ones who are still living there. The words Puritan and Puritanism inevitably suggest a locality—New England. Few of us, unless we stop to think of it and perhaps even not then, realize how far the enormous and constant stream of emigration inland from the Northeastern coast, which began in Colonial times and continued for two hundred and fifty years throughout the last century, has disseminated Puritan blood and Puritan traditions. It has been estimated that 70 per cent of the inhabitants of the United States have a strain of Puritan inheritance.

We are also apt to overlook the fact that the Puritans did not confine their settlements to what is geographical New England, but at an early date overflowed from Massachusetts and Connecticut across to Long Island, until by 1660 there were eleven villages scattered throughout the Island, whence at least some of the inhabitants must have in due course worked their way south towards and to New York.

And, as the frontier was pushed back from the seaboard, the frontier Puritans—as differentiated from the coast Puritans, who had developed an aristocratic leisure class—went with it. These frontiersmen, trekkers on wheels and runners, sweeping across lake Champlain, over the Hudson to the Susquehanna, and up the Mohawk to Genesee and Buffalo, carried New England with them and planted it along Lake Erie, in the "Western Reserve," in Indiana and Illinois, so that to-day the middle-west is more like old New England than New England itself.

The occupation of Illinois and Indiana came next, then Michigan. In 1837 it seemed as if all New England were pouring into the state, for New England had "Michigania" on the brain.

"Come all ye Yankee farmers who wish to change your lot,
Who've spunk enough to travel beyond your native spot,
And leave behind the village where Pa and Ma do stay,
Come follow me, and settle in Michigania,—
Yea, yea, yea, in Michigania."

Finally the tide swept over Wisconsin, which from the very first until to-day has been dominated in its history and institutions by persons of Puritan descent.

So, as Lois Kimball Matthews has illuminatingly described in her admirable "Expansion of New England," the Puritans spread over New York, Pennsylvania, Ohio, Indiana, Illinois, Michigan, Wisconsin,—building towns, cities, states, and through their infiltration, as the frontier moved farther and farther west, affecting the character of the entire population,—their influence diluted in some localities, submerged in others, dominant in the main, persistent in all, but everywhere bringing with them their town meetings, their schools, their churches, their New England thrift, enterprise and prosperity.

New York City was surrounded by Puritan settlements—the New England towns on Long Island; Westchester and Bedford just over the Harlem River to the north; Rye and Greenwich on the Connecticut shore; and, across the Hudson, the solid Puritan escarpment of North Jersey. From these adjacent points there was a steady drift into the city, as well as a substantial immigration direct from New England itself. In addition there was a sort of backwash from the northern part of the state, while the Hudson afforded a capillary attraction towards the Metropolis. Hence you will find in every Hudson River town a substantial number of unmistakable Puritan names,—like Deliverance Appleby of Tarrytown.

In New York Puritan influence ran counter to that of the easy-going Dutch and the aristocratic Tory. Hence, while it left a pronounced mark upon the city and its inhabitants, it did not dominate it. There were sections of New York City—to say nothing of Brooklyn—that were more Puritan than Boston; and there are social groups there to-day who would feel more at home in the Framingham of 1840 than within sight of the present glitter of Broadway.

In 1850 Puritanism in New York found itself confronted by a vast and unruly horde of ignorant foreign immigrants, by a mushroom growth of holders of new fortunes made in crooked finance, western speculation, and the California gold rush, by the direct influence of English and continental life and view-point, the example of the aristocratic and ease-loving Southerners who came north to spend their summers, and by the loose ideals of a frontier now brought within an ease of contact hitherto undreamed of and to which the city played the part of saloon and bawdy house.

New York was still in 1850 a city of dramatic contrasts, of crudeness and luxury, where pigs rooted in the gutters and cattle were driven in huge droves through the streets, while gentlemen in claw-hammer coats, side whiskers and ruffled shirts sipped their Madeira around tables of polished mahogany and told the same rough stories that are told to-day, and ladies in tight bodices, jewelled toques, high-backed combs, and ringlets, crooked little fingers daintily as they gossiped while waiting for the men to come in.

Fifth Avenue was already becoming the synonym for Society in America. Every house had a front "parlor," gaudy and overpowering with velvet carpets, glass chandeliers, gilded mirrors, lambrequins, "hassocks," fringed sofas, and atrocities known as *"objets d'art,"* consisting of imitation majolica and *capo da monte*. The spittoon was everywhere in evidence, a conspicuous adornment of the most elegant of parlors; and while gentlemen were usually politely requested to "refrain from hawking and spitting" in public places, such as restaurants and churches, the practice was regarded with leniency and the appeal was honored in the breach rather than in the observance.

There were but ten theatres in the five largest cities in the country north of New Orleans, but only one enjoyed any real prosperity and that was in New York. The cheapest seats were in the "pit," as the orchestra stalls were then called, and the gallery gods sat in their shirt sleeves where now the agencies charge sometimes as high as $18 a seat and habitually as much as $8.80. Seats were evidently not reserved, for gentlemen are told to surrender them to ladies who come too late to secure them, and are warned in contemporary books on etiquette that *"A gentleman never sits with his hat on in the theatre*. Gentlemen do not generally sit even in an eating-room with their hats on, if there is any convenient place to put them." The "museum" (of stuffed birds, local relics, shells and curiosities), the "cyclorama," the waxwork, the "trained flea" and the "educated pig," the automaton chess-player, fireworks, and the biblical tableau with Adam and Eve heavily aproned in enormous fig leaves, were what "folded up the customers" in those days. But a "musee" with a stage annex was looked at askance as being but the camouflage of evil,—like the sandwich that went with the drink under the old Raines Law.

Opera had been introduced into the United States in 1825 at the Park Theatre in New York with Rossini's "Barber of Seville," but the word "opera" was at first considered too daring in Boston and the phrase "lectures on music with illustrations" was substituted. Opera, however, was too de luxe for the times and concerts were in better demand. Sentimental music—the more sentimental the better—was popular. There was music in the home and the sound of the sackbut, psaltery, lute and dulcimer was heard in the land in the shape of guitar, piano, flute and harpsichord. But as a whole we were too serious a people to be really merry or have much lightness in our humor.

It was a period of enormous commercial expansion and corresponding spread-eagleism. The burst of invention, which had begun with the development of steam locomotion on land and water, had steadily increased throughout the 40's and culminated for the time being in the 50's. In no preceding decade had there been any material progress comparable with that ending in 1850, which saw the invention of vulcanized rubber, the type-revolving press, the sewing-machine and the harvester, and was followed before the Civil War by the first successful fire engine, the fire-alarm telegraph, the breech-loading rifle, and the laying of what Queen Victoria called "The Electric Cable" under the Atlantic, although it presently proved a failure. Railroad mileage in the United States increased from 6,000 in 1850 to upwards of 30,000 by the end of 1860. Even so, railroads were generally regarded as a rather fancy, dangerous and expensive method of travel, and unlikely to supersede canal boats as freight carriers.

In 1851 Congress for the first time authorized postage stamps, fixed the prepaid postal rate at three cents for a distance not over 3,000 miles, and ordered the Mint to strike a three-cent coin for convenience in paying postage. This was the generally forgotten origin of the "Three-Cent Piece." A tremendous demand for stamps followed, and many people, being unfamiliar with their use, licked off the gum so that they would not stick. This caused much dissatisfaction and led to the custom of moistening the envelope instead of the stamp, a method the present followers of which generally assume to be "more hygienic."

Two years later Miss Leslie, a well-known writer, thought it worth while to call the attention of her readers to the possibly unappreciated conveniences afforded by the United States Post Office. "The practice of inclosing letters in envelopes is now universal; particularly as when the letter is single no additional postage is charged for the cover. The postage now is in almost every instance pre-paid, it being but three cents when paid by the writer, and five if left to the receiver. Therefore, none but very poor or very mean people send unpaid letters. Letter-stamps for the United States post should be kept in a little box on your writing-table. You can get them always by sending to the post-office —from a dollar's worth or more, down to fifty or twenty-five cents' worth, at a time. In a second box, keep stamps for the city or penny post, which transmits notes from one part of the town to another. And in a third, stamps to go on the covers of newspapers.

"Sealing with wax is found to be very insecure for letters that are carried by steamers into warm climates—the wax melting with the heat, and sticking the letters to each other, so that they cannot be separated without tearing. Wafers are better.

"It would be very convenient to use the post-office stamp as a seal, but the clerks in that establishment charge extra postage for the trouble of turning the letter to mark the stamp. This subjects the receiver to the payment of two additional cents.

"Be careful not to allow yourself to get entirely out of post-office stamps. Replenish your stock in time. If the gum on the back seems too weak, go over it afresh with that excellent cement, 'Perpetual Paste.' Embossed or bordered envelopes are not often used except in notes of ceremony—or when the acquaintance is slight. The same with ornamented note-paper. Intimate friends and relatives use paper that is handsome, but plain. Letters of business are generally enclosed in yellow or buff-coloured envelopes. Some of these yellow envelopes are large enough to contain a folio sheet when folded."

The American's tone was boastful, his oratory bombastic and highfalutin'. He was inquisitive, politically minded, argumentative, shrewd, always looking for a "bargain" or a "good chance," a hasty eater, a poor masticator, an incessant and unerring spitter. His purpose in life was to amass and accumulate. Almost the only way to achieve social distinction was by giving away money,—stingily saved or doubtfully acquired earlier in business life—and to acquire this (later to be distributed as a penance or to purchase social indulgences) the American delved until his dying breath. There were no clubs of the English sort. Men met at each other's houses. Teas took the place of the dinners of to-day —or of yesterday. Evening calls were the chief social diversion. There was an enormous desire for education, so that (coupled with the paucity of amusements) it led people to spend entire days in Barnum's looking at bottled mermaids and moth-eaten specimens of taxidermy. There was a positive mania for lectures and the lyceum became a national institution. Yet Henry Adams, writing fifty years later, declared that "in essentials like religion, ethics, philosophy; in history, literature, art; in the concepts of all science, except perhaps mathematics, the American boy of 1854 stood nearer the year 1 than to the year 1900."

"In the larger cities," says Seldes, "almost every report of social intercourse indicates a feebleness of imagination and a lack of grace. Except for dancing, upon which most of the churches frowned, almost all forms of entertainment were practised by one sex in complete isolation from the other. Dinner parties were rare, and at a small dinner, a family and friends, one ate or, if one talked at all, it was of business." Most amusements were frowned on by religion. Social pleasures were dreary, and life must have been insufferably dull to have led the American women to put up with the dullness and discomfort of the hotel life of the period. Women were habitually languid, if not ill. Pregnancy was treated as a disgrace. "Romantic love" was the subject of literary fiction. But the necessity of propagating children crushed the finer emotions of married life, made the American woman cold and artificial, and broke down her health. Eliza Southgate wrote to Moses Porter that not one woman in a hundred married for love, and contraceptives "intended for married ladies whose health forbids too rapid increase in family" were advertised with startling frankness.

The American ate heavily between two long stretches of work, and usually in silence so far as speech was concerned. Meat was served three times a day, and fruit was taken away from the table and munched while otherwise engaged. Beefsteak, fish and fowl appeared simultaneously at breakfast. Harriet Martineau, whose three-volume work on "Society in America" was published in 1839, describes an American breakfast as consisting of "a pie-dish full of buttered toast, hot biscuits and coffee, beefsteak, apple sauce, hot potatoes, cheese, butter, and two large dishes of eggs."

The New York business man breakfasted at seven and expected his wife and daughters to be on hand to fill his teacup and cut the bread. The main meal was usually at two or three, or on ceremonial occasions as late as four. There was a plethora of food. Even the great transcendentalist Emerson regularly ate pie for breakfast.

The hotels offered an impressive hospitality at from $2 to $3 per day, the Everett House in Union Square serving a dinner from two o'clock until half after five, and offering a choice of soup, fish, six boiled dishes, eight roasts, ten entrees, five cold dishes, thirteen vegetables, eight pastries and fourteen kinds of dessert. Champagne cost a dollar per bottle, claret fifty cents, Hock a dollar, Burgundy two-fifty per quart.

The following is an ordinary bill of fare at "The Revere House" in Boston at this period:

## REVERE HOUSE.

### BILL OF FARE.

Soup.
Chowder.

Fish.
Baked Cod Fish, Claret Sauce.

Boiled.

Leg of Mutton, Caper Sauce.          Corned Beef and Cabbage.
Turkey and Oysters.                  Ham.
Chickens and Pork.                   Tongue.

Cold Dishes.
Boiled Ham and Tongue, Pressed Corn Beef.
Boned Turkey.

Side Dishes.
Mutton Cutlets, Madeira Sauce.
Fillet of Beef, with Olives.
Blanquette of Veal.
Escaloped Oysters.
Macaroni, Baked.
Ducks, with Turnips.
Chickens, a la jardiniere.
Tripe, a la Maitre d'Hotel.
Calf's Liver, a l'Italienne.
Lobsters, Anchovy.
Currie of Chicken.
Pig's Feet, Piquante Sauce.
Rice Croquettes.
Hominy.

Roast.

Beef.                                Chickens.
Ham, Champagne Sauce.                Turkey.
Leg of Mutton.                       Geese.
Veal.                                Ducks.

Pudding and Pastry.
Cabinet Pudding.

| Apple Pies. | Squash Pies. | Quince Pies. |
|---|---|---|
| Damson Meringues. | Jelly Puffs. | Macaroons. |

Dessert.

Lemon Ice Cream.

| Apples. | Almonds. | Raisins. | English Walnuts. |
|---|---|---|---|

Breakfast, half-past Seven to Ten; Dinner, Ladies' Ordinary, half-past Two; Gentlemen's Ordinary, half-past Two; Tea, from Six to Nine; Supper, from Nine to Twelve.

SUNDAY—Breakfast at Eight; Dinner at half-past One; Tea at half-past Five; Supper, Nine to Ten.

On special or festive occasions the guests fared even better. Thus at "Taft's Hotel," at West Roxbury near Boston, twenty gentlemen sat down in January, 1853, to a meal of nineteen separate roasts of game.

## TAFT'S HOTEL, WEST ROXBURY.

### GAME SUPPER FOR TWENTY GENTLEMEN.

January 14, 1853.

### BILL OF FARE.

Roast.
1. Wild turkey, from Illinois.
2. Wild goose.
3. Canvas-back ducks.
4. Red-head ducks.
5. Black ducks.
6. Grey ducks.
7. Black-head ducks, from Virginia.
8. Brant, from Delaware.
9. Blue-bill widgeon.
10. Sprig-tail ducks, from Georgia.
11. Mallard ducks, from North Carolina.
12. Blue-wing teal.
13. Green-wing teal.

14. Widgeon teal.
15. Grouse, from Illinois.
16. Quails, larded.
17. Partridges, larded.
18. Spruce partridges, from Canada.
19. Venison with grape and currant jelly.

Puddings.
Custard.      Bread.

Pastry.

Meat pies.                    Squash pies.
Apple pies.                   Lemon pies.

Ice Creams.
Sherbet, Lemon, Vanilla.
Calf's-foot Jelly, Blanc Mange.

Dessert.
Grapes, Pears, Apples, Raisins, Dry Fruit.

Coffee.

In spite of the absence of any notation to that effect we may assume that wine was not wanting.

A dinner to a visiting Englishman is thus described:

"Dinner was served at four precisely. The table-service was of the plainest description, not a vestige of plate except the silver forks; and the viands of no very *recherche* kind— home raised chickens and a Virginia ham constituting the staple of the meal; but everything, from the okra soup to the orange fritters, was first-rate of its kind; the indispensable Manzanilla was supported by excellent champagne, decanted and iced to the freezing point (a test of good wine, for no inferior quality will bear it); and when, at last, Masters commended to his guest a prime bottle of Latour, and a swelling slender-necked decanter of the old Vanderlyn Madeira, Ashburner felt thoroughly comfortable and content, as a man should, who is drinking well after having dined well. He was a pretty fair hand at the bottle, as most Englishmen are; indeed, he crowded his host very hard, who was a fastidious, but not a profuse drinker, and liked to sip his Bordeaux leisurely. Before their united efforts the jug of claret and the decanter of Madeira speedily vanished; and then came some sublime coffee, during the discussion of which Masters extemporized a dissertation on the method of preparing that beverage, 'which it is singular your countrymen never understand how to make'; finally a *chasse* of white Curacoa assisted the guest to swallow his host's lecture."

At that time there was no such thing as athletics. People took little exercise and never walked if they could ride. The national health was poor; people discussed their dyspepsia instead of their operations.

"Sam Slick" took a fall out of the Yankee of the period. The dyspeptic Honorable Alden Gabble, an aspiring diplomat, went to Dr. Abernathy on account of discomfort after meals. "What's the matter with you?" said the doctor. "Why," says Alden, "I presume I have the dyspepsia." "Ah!" said he, "I see—a Yankee—swallowed more dollars and cents than he can digest . . . I'll be damned," said he, "if I ever saw a Yankee that don't bolt his food whole, like a boa-constrictor. How the devil can you expect to digest food that you neither take the trouble to dissect nor the time to masticate. It's no wonder you lose your teeth, for you never use them; nor your digestion, for you overload it; nor your saliva, for you expend it on the carpets instead of on your food. It's disgusting; it's beastly. You Yankees load your stomachs as a Devonshire man does his cart, as full as it can hold, and as fast as he can pitch it in with a dung-fork, and drive off; and then you complain that such a load of compost is too heavy for you. Dyspepsia, eh? Infernal guzzling, you mean. I'll tell you what, Mr. Secretary of Legation, take half the time to eat that you do to drawl out your words, chew your food half as much as you do your filthy tobacco, and you'll be well in a month."

Apart from the menace of the anti-slavery issue there was widespread social ferment in the 50's. The United States,

instead of the three and a half millions at the time of my
grandfather's birth, had now a population of over twenty-
three millions, of whom nineteen millions were whites, three
millions were slaves working upon 74,000 cotton, 16,000 tobacco, and 8,000 hemp plantations, and owned by 347,500
individual masters. There were nearly thirteen million people living on the Atlantic slope, eight and a half million in
the Mississippi Valley, and seventeen hundred thousand in
the Gulf states. There were two and a quarter millions of
foreign-born. There were a million Irish, half a million Germans, 250,000 English, 70,000 Scotch, 54,000 French, 30,-
000 Welsh, 10,000 Prussians. In Chicago there were 13,000
native Americans as against 15,000 foreigners, and in St.
Louis 36,000 natives to 38,000 outlanders.

New York contained over half a million souls of which
133,000 were foreign-born Irish, presenting terrific problems in municipal government. At that period there was practically no assimilation between the native and foreign-born
population, who stuck closely together according to nation-
ality and did not show themselves receptive to American
ideas and usages. Each nation had its own militia and newspapers. Of 6,000 militiamen 4,000 were organized in Irish,
German and French regiments having their own flags and
uniforms and speaking their native tongue. In addition to
race feeling, there was a tremendous amount of radicalism
and a violent anti-Catholic movement, frequently culminat-
ing in riots and more or less stimulated by the "Know Nothing Party," the "Wide Awakes," and others of a supposed
patriotic and nationalist order.

James Truslow Adams says that, from 1833 to 1853, law
and order were abandoned in a nationwide persecution of the
Irish and Catholics. "In 1834 the Ursuline Convent near
Boston was burned to the ground and sacked by anti-Catho-
lics. . . . Similar riots occurred within a few weeks at other
places, and in a few years the militia had to disperse a mob
of 2,000 marching on the house of the Papal Nuncio at Cincinnati. The Irish quarter in Chelsea, Mass., was attacked;

the chapel at Coburg was burned, that at Dorchester blown up, and that at Manchester, N. H., wrecked; at Ellsworth, Maine, the priest was tarred and feathered; the convent at Providence was attacked; and at St. Louis a riot resulted in ten deaths. But it is unnecessary to detail more, such incidents being all too common throughout the country."

In a subsequent chapter I comment upon the reflection of these outrages and the possible fear of retaliation in my mother's habitual warnings to me as a child never to speak of Roman Catholics or the Irish within their hearing. So far from the idea of religious liberty had the descendants of the Puritans strayed in but two hundred years! Yet the Irish furnished the labor for the railroad building which was now the chief enterprise of the country. Until 1851 the rate was from 75 cents to 87½ cents per sunrise-sunset day. Labor rightfully and vociferously demanded an improvement in conditions, wages, and the length of the working day. By violent means and sabotage the workers raised this to $1 per day in 1852, but a rise in prices had followed the influx of gold from California and this soon became inadequate.

Gangs of young ruffians held the cities in thrall. The fire-department houses were the headquarters of loafers and the centre of disorders of all sorts. There was a fight at almost every fire, and the fighting would continue long after the fire itself had been extinguished—sometimes for a couple of days. The New York police were compelled to wear uniforms for the first time in 1853; and submitted indignantly, declaring it an invasion of their rights as free men. Thieves, disguised in red shirts and fire hats, entered all burning buildings and looted them of their contents. There was no surface transportation other than by omnibuses, of which there were 650 owned by 27 companies, until 1851 when a horse-car line was opened from the City Hall as far as Twenty-third Street via Fourth Avenue. According to the New York *Tribune* of March 27, 1855, the Sixth Avenue Line had at that date only 50 cars, 300 horses and mules, and took in but $13,350 per annum. Competition for franchises was carried on by political rings through barefaced bribery and the corrupt control of the judiciary.

The whole city was thrown into excitement in 1853, first over Jake Sharp's grant from his pocket Common Council of the right to operate a horse railroad down Broadway, which fortunately was frustrated, and, later, over that given to the Manhattan Company which was only prevented from tearing up Broadway through threats of force from a citizenry aroused by placards reading: "Broadway in Ruins! Citizens to Your Posts! A Flagrant, Shameless Wrong to be Perpetrated!"

Among those punished for contempt of court in the Broadway franchise scandal was Alderman William M. ("What are you going to do about it?") Tweed. Yet these gangs of political highbinders were "pikers" compared with those of later date.

It is difficult to judge the general morality of an era, and this is particularly true of a country of the size and varying characteristics of the United States between 1850 and 1860. That the standards of pecuniary honesty were low seems to have been accepted by the abler students of economic conditions in America, such as de Tocqueville, and this view is shared by our own historian James Ford Rhodes. In view of the operations of the Tweed Ring in New York, the municipal corruption unmasked in the "muckraking" crusades in the first decade of this century, the revelations of the recent oil scandals, and the complacence of the public attitude towards the facts disclosed, it is clear that either what the foreigners thought about us was sound or that the mercury of our moral thermometer has sunk surprisingly fast in the last seventy years.

In the matter of sexual morality the situation is more complicated and the evidence more in conflict. As bearing on this subject Rhodes stresses what he calls the "Puritanism of 1850–60," but the "gospel of work," supposed by him to have so effectually distracted the male attention, may—

and probably was—counteracted by liquor and lack of exercise. At all events, in view of the acknowledged conditions in New York City, where prostitution was carried on wholesale with the most blatant effrontery, his conclusions are not much more convincing than Dr. Bow's *Review* of March, 1857, which said: "In eighty years the social system of the North has developed to a point in morals only reached by that of Rome in six centuries from the building of the city. . . . Already married women, moving in the fashionable circles of the North, forgo the duties of domestic life, bestow their minds upon dress and equipage, and refuse to no inconsiderable extent to undergo the pains of child bearing. . . . Already the priceless gem of chastity in women has been despoiled of its talismanic charm with men."

The maison de joie found in the decade before the war, just as it did after, an amazingly large clientele among the most select and supposedly respectable male members of New York society, and the Victorian attitude towards sex, and the hypocrisy regarding it, had astonishing, and sometimes unsuspected, results.

The extravagance of the 40's had been stimulated by the influx of gold from California, the tremendous boom in shipping and the mania for speculation of all kinds, particularly in banking and railroads,—an extravagance which the panic of '54 did not stem and which ended with the collapse of credit in that of '57. But, side by side with this financial exuberance and sensual indulgence, there was a growing interest in humanitarianism, temperance, woman's rights, spiritualism, "free love," and particularly in religion, which culminated in the "Great Awakening" of 1858, declared by the New York *Observer* to have been "the most extensive and thorough ever experienced in America" and during which, throughout the North, great throngs listened emotionally to discourses on "the doctrines of depravity, regeneration, atonement, election, the influences of the Holy Spirit, the judgment and future retributions." Everywhere were held "Monday meetings" for business men. Henry

Ward Beecher preached in Burton's Theatre to 3,000 en-
thusiasts, and the great revival led the playhouses to be
temporarily abandoned.

This epidemic of religious emotion is generally presumed
to have been an after effect of the terrible panic of 1857,
and took its name from a similar wave of religious hysteria
which swept the country in 1730–40, when George Whitefield, the English revivalist, stormed the country with Meth-
odism. It is noteworthy that Boston was slower than the rest
of the country to kindle to this display of religious fireworks.

"The expansion of feeling induced by such a religious
movement thus brings into notice the survival of other aspects of Puritanism as well as the continued use of the Puritan
phraseology," says Rhodes. "The influence of Puritanism in
New England, New York, Northern Ohio, and the Northwest
in the decade we are reviewing (1850–60) was great. Its inestimable value in politics and morals has not been too highly
rated. But this picture is not complete unless its unlovely side
be shown. The spirit of Puritanism has been hostile to art,
partly because art has ministered in religion to what is es-
teemed idolatry, and partly because it appeals to the sensuous
nature which according to the Puritan ideal should be re-
pressed. It may be questioned whether there is in the life of
any other people a period at once so rich in intellectual and
literary activity and so unproductive in other forms of art.
The Puritan frowned upon anything that was mere diversion,
and it was quite in keeping with his character that 'Paradise
Lost' should be preferred before 'Hamlet' and 'The Merchant of Venice.' The poet of the austere Commonwealth
spoke to people who had an aversion to the broadminded observing poet of the joyous Elizabeth age; they could not
forget that he was a writer and an actor of plays."

So the American Puritan read Shakespeare in an expurgated and denatured edition, and found in Gough, a temperance lecturer with a dramatic delivery, a substitute for the
theatre.

Chief in importance of the three great reform movements was "abolition," increasing so rapidly in numbers and influence as to distract public attention from that of "temperance," which otherwise might have succeeded in imposing prohibition upon the United States in 1855. The cause of temperance was at its apogee in that year, but the menace of the struggle over slavery soon out-shadowed it and prevented its successful culmination in national legislative enactment.

Had "prohibition" then become law it is possible that it would have become the fact also. At all events, interest in temperance as a spiritual and intellectual movement declined, and did not again reach anything like its pre-Civil War condition, until the practical capitalists of a mechanistic era, perceiving that efficiency and drink made a poor partnership, seized the opportunity afforded by another war to break it up. Nevertheless, in spite of a subsidence of interest in the temperance cause as a campaign, there was a gradual and widespread decline in drinking,—a paradox not unlike that presented to-day by the general growth of church membership in an age destitute of much curiosity about dogmatic religion.

"The hidden spring of Suffrage, as an actual political movement is, oddly enough, in Prohibition," says Seldes. "From 1800 to 1860, a very few women wanted to vote, but a much larger number wanted to vote against slavery. For half a century longer, although the desire for the ballot *per se* increased, the majority of women still wanted to vote only against the saloon."

The Woman's Rights Conventions held regularly after 1850 were largely augmented by abolitionists, temperance agitators and all classes of social reformers. A distinctive costume, consisting of gaiters, loose "Turkish" trousers, short skirt to the knees only, short jacket and straw gipsy hat, had been originated by Amelia Bloomer (whose name every woman wears), and a host of ladies from Lucy Stone, Susan B. Anthony and Elizabeth Stanton, down to others of ques-

tionable sincerity, put on the uniform of emancipation. But
the public hooted them, voicing its derision in a parody of
"Dickery, dickery dock, the mouse ran up the clock":

> "Gibbery, gibbery gab, the women had a confab
> And demanded the rights to wear the tights,
> Gibbery, gibbery gab."

The New York *Tribune* described Mrs. Amelia Bloomer
at one of her lectures as "attired in a dark brown changeable
tunic, a kilt descended just below the knees, the skirt of
which was trimmed with rows of black velvet. The pantaloons were of the same texture and trimmed in the same
style. She wore gaiters. Her headdress was cherry and black.
Her dress had a large open corsage, with bands of velvet
over the white chemisette in which was a diamond stud pin.
She wore flowing sleeves, tight undersleeves, and black lace
mitts. Her whole attire was rich and plain in appearance."

Dr. Mary Walker, however, whom I well remember, was
a fanatic who believed that if women wore trousers the
millennium would have arrived. She wore men's clothes, including white shirt and black tie, and appeared at the Court
of St. James's in "black silk trousers with velvet side-stripes
and a loose black silk coat with velvet bands on the pockets."
But her advocacy of "pants," which the women instinctively
feared would render them less attractive to the opposite sex,
led them to set the dogs on her. She made one contribution to
man's welfare which should not be overlooked—the inside
neckband to prevent the collar button from chafing the neck.

*Harper's New Monthly Magazine* said: "The most serious importance of this modern 'woman's rights' doctrine is
derived from its direct bearing upon the marriage institution.
The blindest must see that such a change as is proposed in the
relation and life of the sexes cannot leave either marriage or
the family in their present state. It must vitally, and in time
wholly sever that oneness which has ever been at the foundation of the marriage idea, from the primitive declaration of

Genesis to the latest decision of the common law. . . . That which makes no change in the personal relations, the personal rights, the personal duties, is not the holy marriage union, but the unholy alliance of concubinage."

There is no discernible connection linking the woman's rights movement with Puritanism, but early pioneering hardships made it necessary for the woman of the new country to assume more responsibilities in all departments of life than the woman of the old country and tended to remove many of her disabilities both legal and social. It was necessary for all to exert themselves to the utmost, intellectually as well as physically, women as well as men, in conquering the wilderness. This hitherto undreamed-of use of woman's faculties raised her status in her own eyes as well as in the eyes of the men, and made the woman's rights movement obvious and inevitable. This new activity of women gained such impetus before the wealthy class began to arise, that not even the creation of surplus wealth and leisure, which has in past histories been the chief cause of the female parasite and "nitwit," could put her back in her place as a "lady" and a sheltered doll. The real forces back of the woman's movement in America were physical rather than religious or moral.

America was flooded in the 50s with visitors from Great Britain and the Continent, few of whom individually returned home to give any adequate picture of the new country which had twisted the lion's tail so successfully. Taken collectively we may gain from them a pretty fair idea of certain parts of America and of certain strata, or if the word be an ungrateful one, of certain groups of society. Few of these travellers penetrated into the homes of the more well to do, the more cultured or the more aristocratic, any more than American travellers in England, France or Italy do to-day, if indeed they penetrate any homes at all. But what they did see helps us to know something of what America was like in the middle of the last century,—the city streets, the railroads, the hotels, the physical aspect of the country, and an occasional flash of native social manners and customs. What faults they found in us were, as Mr. Allan Nevins points out, precisely those noted by the travellers who had preceded them, "our unresting hurry; our tendency to live in hotels and boarding houses; our excessive sensitiveness to English censure; and the failure of nearly everyone (particularly the young women, who kept late hours, ate hasty meals of pastry cakes, and ice cream, studied too hard, and took insufficient exercise) to look after bodily health."

In a quaint and amorphous work entitled "The Upper Ten Thousand" by C. Astor Bristed (1852) one of the characters enlightens a "friend with a quantity of railroad statistics and gossip, such as, that the American trains averaged eighteen miles an hour, including stoppages,—about two miles short of the steam-boat average; that there were more than seven thousand miles of railroad in the country; that there was no division of first, second, and third class, but that some lines had ladies' cars—that is to say, cars for the gentlemen with ladies, and the ladies without gentlemen —and some had separate cars for the ladies and gentlemen of colour; that there had been some attempts to get up smoking-cars after the German fashion, but the public mind was not yet fully prepared for it."

"The most peculiar thing of all about these railways," writes Mr. William Chambers, who returned to Great Britain in 1853 to tell his countrymen about "Things as They Are in America," "is the passenger-carriage—always called a 'car' by the Americans. The object, which in exterior appearance most nearly resembles an American railway-car, is one of those houses on wheels which accompanies travelling shows and menageries; the only difference being that the car is double the length. The car is, in reality, nothing more than a long wooden box, painted yellow, with a roundish shaped roof; a door at each end; and a row of windows at each side.

"Cars differ somewhat in their interior organisation. Some have a small apartment at one end for ladies, or nurses with children. More commonly, they consist of a long unbroken sweep, with two rows of seats, and a pathway of eighteen inches between."

In view of the well-known fact that when Miss Fanny Elssler, the famous ballerina, visited New York in 1840 she brought her own table napkins with her lest in barbarous America she might have to lick her fingers after eating, it is not perhaps surprising that Mr. Chambers found so much to marvel at. He hastily corrects those who belittle the architectural grandeurs of the metropolis and waxes eloquent in his description of its magnificent hotels and stores, some of which rose to a height of five or six stories and were built "in an ornamental style of architecture more like the palaces of kings than places for the transaction of business." . . . Advancing northward from the commercial part of the town, he found himself in the quietude and splendor of a London Belgravia, where the edifices are "entirely of brown sandstone, and of a richly decorated style of street architecture; all the windows are of plate glass; and the door handles, plates and bell pulls silvered, so as to impart a chaste and light effect. The furnishings and interior ornaments of these dwellings particularly those in Fifth Avenue are of a superb kind; no expense being apparently spared as regards either comfort or elegance. In one mansion where I experienced the most kindly hospitality, the spacious entrance hall was laid with tasselated marble pavement; the stair and balustrades were of dark walnut-wood; one of the apartments was panelled in the old baronial fashion; and in a magnificent dining-room, the marble chimney piece, with exquisitely carved figures illustrative of Burns' Highland Mary, cost, I understand, as much as $1,500."

Mr. Chambers, it should be observed in passing, was a Scotchman. At the Astor House, where he noted with racial satisfaction that board cost but two dollars per day, he revelled "in a kind of elysium of princely drawing rooms and boudoirs, in which velvet, lace, satin, gilding, rich carpets and mirrors, contribute to form a scene of indescribable luxury. . . . Passing by you see highly-dressed ladies reposing on satin couches, or lolling in rocking chairs. One, who has just come in and still has on her bonnet and shawl is rattling over the keys of a piano. Another is reading a novel. Several are outside in the corridor seated on velvet covered ottomans, talking to each other or to the gentlemen belonging to their party. These corridors are every whit as elegantly furnished as the rooms, and are jocularly spoken of as 'the flirtation galleries.' "

"Peacock Alley"? But even the Waldorf-Astoria has been torn down!

"Let us just look around the lobby of the Astor, beginning with the left-hand side. There, at a wicket in the hall, like an open window, stands a man to take your hat and upper coat, and put them away in a bin till you want them. Adjoining in a niche in the lobby, is a man with brush in hand ready to clean and burnish your soiled boots. A little further on is a light closet, with basins of water and towels, to save you the trouble of mounting to your bedroom before going in to dinner. A few steps beyond, and passing the flight of steps which lead to the bar, we come upon an enclosure like a sentry-box, in which is seated a clerk with the machinery of an electric-telegraph; and on handing him a slip through his wicket, he will, for a trifling sum, despatch a message for you to almost any city throughout the United States.

"We now pass the waiter's form, and study the apparatus of the general book-keeper, which occupies the right side of the lobby. Behind the counter of this officer, we perceive a large case of pigeon-holes, with a number over each, and appropriated for receiving letters or cards left for the guests. Knowing your particular number, you have only to glance at the little depository under it, to know if anyone has been calling, or if any letters have arrived for you. At one end of the counter, there is a letter-box into which you drop all letters for post, which is another means of saving trouble. But the most curious thing of all, is the arrangement by which the official behind the counter knows who signals from his apartment. To have some hundreds of bells would produce inextricable confusion. All the wires in the house centre at one bell, placed in a case in the lobby, with the whole mechanism exposed on one side within a sheet of plate-glass. The other side of this case is covered all over with numbers in rows. Adjoining each number is a small crescent-shaped piece of brass, which drops from the horizontal, and hangs by one end, when the wire connected with it is pulled, the bell being by the same action sounded. The attention of the book-keeper being so attracted, he directs a waiter to proceed to the apartment indicated, and with his finger restoring the bit of brass to its former posture, it is ready for a fresh signal. A more neat and simple arrangement could not well be imagined. The fronts of these bell-cases are of white enamel, and being set in a gilt frame, have a pleasing ornamental effect."

And the luxury of the barber shops! "I never could understand why the not overindulgent Americans, lodging in the great hotels, or travelling by river steam-boats, require to be shaved by professional tonsors. At all events, there, in the barber's apartment, in every hotel, are seen seated a number of gentlemen—under the hands of coloured operators. And in what luxurious attitudes!—leaning back in a couch-like chair, and the feet exalted on a velvet-covered rest, we have a picture of ease and lassitude which I should fancy is only to be matched in the dressing-rooms of nobles and princes."

He is astounded at the marvels achieved in America by the telegraph system on some lines of which it is stated on good authority that "as many as 700 messages are sent in one day. So rapid is the transit, that the news brought to New York by a European steamer, at eight o'clock a. m., has been telegraphed, by way of Cincinnati, to New Orleans, and the effects there produced on the market returned to New York by eleven o'clock—being a circuit of nearly 4000 miles in three hours."

He is less pleased with the Broadway and Fifth Avenue stages, which many of us very well remember in the early years of the present century, and which apparently had neither changed nor altered in any respect between 1850 and 1900.

"I was amused with the manner in which the fare is taken in these vehicles. The passenger who wishes to be set down, hands his money through a hole in the roof to the driver, who forthwith relaxes the cord, and the door flies open. As there appeared to be no check on two or more departing when only one had paid, I suppose the practice of shirking fares is not very uncommon. I cannot say that the omnibus-system of New York is an improvement on our own. The drivers are still more unconscionable in their reception of extra passengers, particularly if the applicants be ladies. In such cases, the gentlemen either stand, or take the ladies on their knee."

Also he found the city excessively dirty. "The mire was ankle-deep in Broadway, and the more narrow business streets were barely passable. The thing was really droll. All along the foot-pavements there stood, night and day, as if fixtures, boxes, buckets, lidless flour-barrels, baskets, decayed tea-chests, rusty iron pans, and earthenware jars full of coal-ashes. There they rested, some close to the houses, some leaning over into the gutter, some on the door-steps, some knocked over and spilt, and to get forward you required to take constant care not to fall over them. Odd as this spectacle seemed on Saturday at noon, it was still more strange on Sunday, when bells were ringing, and people were streaming along to church. Passing up Broadway on this occasion, and looking into a side-street, the scene of confused debris was of a kind not to be easily forgotten—ashes, vegetable refuse, old hats without crowns, worn-out shoes, and other household wreck, lay scattered about as a field of agreeable inquiry for a number of long-legged and industrious pigs."

And now we come to what the student of comparative conditions must regard as highly significant. Mr. Chambers declares that in 1853 municipal corruption and inefficiency had put New York City at the mercy of footpads and plug uglies.

"You could not take up a newspaper without seeing accounts of unchecked disorders, or reading sarcasms on official delinquencies. In the New York *Herald* for November 28, 1853, the following passages occur in an article on Rowdies —a class of brawling reprobates who molest the public thoroughfares:—

" 'The insecurity of human life in New York has become proverbial; and it is a grave question with many, whether it is not practically as bad to live under the despotism of a felonious rabble as the tyranny of an aristocrat. Our police, with a few exceptions, are the worst in the world. It is a notorious fact that they are seldom in the way when crimes are committed, and when they see them by accident, they are very likely to skulk away and avoid all danger and difficulty. If a bank or some wealthy individual has lost a large sum of money, they will probably get hold of it, because they calculate upon a handsome reward. But when they know they cannot make anything extra—anything beyond their salary—there is not one in a hundred of them will give himself the least concern about the lives or limbs of the citizens who pay them for protection. We perceive that their pay has increased of late. We don't find that it has contributed very much to increase their vigilance. The whole evil lies in a nut-shell—it is the accursed system of politics that prevails at primary elections, and thence spreads its ramifications over the entire social fabric. Strike at the root, and the poison-tree will fall.' "

Save for the slight change in the vernacular, this item from *The Herald* of three-quarters of a century ago might have appeared in any New York or Chicago paper during the last five years. "The poison" tree has not yet fallen.

In the twenty years before the Civil War the cause of temperance had greatly advanced and, while there was much elegant drinking about the mahogany and even more inelegant guzzling in bar rooms, there was on the whole far less universal indulgence in strong drink than thirty or forty years before. Mr. Chambers, who doubtless was accustomed

daily to his "ain wee drap," states that the temperance of
those he saw at the hotel dining tables filled him "with no
little surprise."

One might suspect our guest of being merely polite were
it not for the corroboration of Mrs. Mary L. Duncan, who
wrote in 1852 of "America as I Found It," that she was
much impressed with the outward evidences of temperance
in America at least at the hotels. "The cool, calm, unloaded
atmosphere of the hotels is refreshing, and the table where
80 or 100 people dine, presents no liquid but cheering iced
water.

"I have happily nothing to do with travellers' hints about
brandy and water in the bar-room, out of sight, but am satisfied that those guzzling habits are now counted dishonoring
and injurious, which thirty years ago led people to drink a
little half a dozen times in the day. Now, no man puts the
bottle to his neighbor, and besets him with entreaties to
drink. No lady now, in making a round of calls, is in danger
of coming home half tipsy, by means of the cordial at one
house, the choice wine at another, and the Roman punch at
a third. If people will drink, they must do it secretly. They
must retreat to the bar-room, or inhale their sherry cobbler
behind the folding-door."

As contrasted with the rum-soaked condition of the country up to about 1825, the temperance movement had made
tremendous progress by the middle of the century and, as
has been heretofore noted, its effect was marked in the matter of drinking at the public tables of hotels and restaurants.
Yet plenty of it went on in private or in the barrooms, which
certain ladies frequented at summer resorts just as they go
into the gambling houses at Palm Beach to-day, and it was
customary and even *de rigueur* to get tight on certain occasions to the very end of the century (as to a more limited
extent it is even now), while to be able to carry one's liquor
was the attribute of a gentleman at all times. A single quotation from Martine's conservative "Handbook of Etiquette"
(1853) shows us the general attitude at the only period

before 1918 when prohibition nearly became the law of the land.

"At dinner-parties which are given to gentlemen, for the purpose of conviviality, one may indulge in as much wine as he pleases, provided he does not get *drunk*, and make a nuisance of himself. Where drinking, and toasting, and bumpers, are the order of the feast, as at a public dinner, given in honor of a distinguished man, or at the inauguration of some public enterprise, far greater latitude is allowed, in all things, than on more private and select occasions."

These were, and continued to be for another half century, the days when people "took wine" with one another. The etiquette of this familiar ceremony was clearly laid down in all the books.

"It is considered well bred to take the same wine as that selected by the person with whom you drink. When, however, the wine chosen by him is unpalatable to you, it is allowable to take that which you prefer, at the same time apologizingly saying: 'Will you permit me to drink *claret?*' or whatever wine you have selected.

"In inviting a lady to take wine with you at table, you should politely say, 'Shall I have the pleasure of a glass of wine with you?' You will then either hand her the bottle you have selected, or send it by the waiter, and afterwards fill your own glass, when you will politely and silently bow to each other, as you raise the wine to your lips. The same ceremony is to be observed when inviting a gentleman."

It was not considered an offense if a lady "politely" refused an invitation to take wine with one of the opposite sex. Miss Leslie gives the following advice in her "Behavior Book" (1853):

"If you have no conscientious scruples, and if you are acquainted with the gentleman, or have been introduced to him (not else), you may comply with his civility, and when both glasses are filled, look at him, bow your head, and taste the wine. If you are placed between a lady and gentleman who are taking wine together, lean back a little that they may see each other's faces. It is not customary, in America, for a lady to empty her glass,—or indeed, at a hotel, or boarding-house, to take wine with the same gentleman after the first day. . . . On no consideration let any lady be persuaded to take *two* glasses of champagne. It is more than the head of an *American* female can bear. And she may rest assured that (though unconscious of it herself) all present will find her cheeks flushing, her eyes twinkling, her tongue unusually voluble, her talk loud and silly, and her laugh incessant. Champagne is very insidious; and two glasses may throw her into this pitiable condition.

"If a stranger whom you do not know, and to whom you have had no introduction, takes the liberty of asking you to drink wine with him, refuse at once, positively and coldly, to prove that you consider it an unwarrantable freedom. And so it is."

In order that her reader may know how to be perfectly lady-like Miss Leslie also adds:

"While at table, all allusions to dyspepsia, indigestion, or any other disorders of the stomach, are vulgar and disgusting. The word 'stomach' should never be uttered at any table, or indeed anywhere else, except to your physician, or in a private conversation with a female friend interested in your health. It is a disagreeable word (and so are all its associations), and should never be mentioned in public to 'ears polite.' "

It is quite probable that the amount of drinking that went on in both England and America in the eighteenth century was the original reason for the strictness of the Victorian etiquette regarding women. Respectable women had to be protected from insult on the part of indiscriminating or intoxicated males. Miss Leslie gives careful instructions to be followed by ladies travelling alone.

"On arriving at a hotel, ask immediately to see the proprietor; give him your name and address, tell how long you propose staying, and request him to see that you are provided with a good room. Request him also to conduct you to the dining-room at dinner-time, and allot you a seat near his own. For this purpose, he will wait for you near the door, (do not *keep him waiting*), or meet you in the ladies' drawing-room. While at table, if the proprietor or any other gentleman asks you to take wine with him, politely refuse.

"If you are to pursue your journey early in the morning, desire, over-night, the waiter who attends your room, to knock hard at your door an hour before the time of starting. Before you go down-stairs, ask for the chambermaid who has attended you, and give her a fee (not less than a quarter-dollar), putting it into her own hand yourself, and not commissioning another to convey it to her. Do not omit giving a quarter-dollar at least, to the waiter who attended your room, and one also to him who has served you at table.

"Refrain from making acquaintance with any strangers, unless you are certain of their respectability. If a gentleman of whom you know nothing, endeavors to get into conversation with you, turn away, and make no reply. Avoid saying anything to women in showy attire, with painted faces, and white kid gloves. Such persons have frequently the assurance to try to be very sociable with respectable ladies who are travelling alone. Keep aloof from them always.

"If you have breakfasted early, it will be well to put some gingerbread-nuts or biscuits into your satchel, as you may become very hungry before dinner."

Miss Leslie warns against having anything to do with a woman with a "profusion of long curls about her neck, who has a meretricious expression of eye, and who is overdressed. It is safest to avoid her. Also, you will derive no pleasure or advantage from making acquaintance with females who are evidently coarse and vulgar, even if you know that they are rich, live in a large house, and are of respectable character. Young girls who are loud, noisy, bold, and forward (however fashionable they may be), it is best also to avoid."

Unfortunately with the decline in drunkenness there had been a corresponding increase in the use of masticatory tobacco. Gentlemen were not allowed to smoke indoors, so they chewed instead, and spat freely into the receptacles provided about the rooms. America from having been awash with rum was flooded with tobacco juice.

"Spitting," says one author, "is a filthy habit, and annoys one in almost every quarter, in-doors and out. Since vulgarity has had its way so extensively amongst us, every youth begins to smoke and spit before he has well cut his teeth. Smoking is unquestionably so great a pleasure to those accustomed to it, that it must not be condemned, yet the spitting associated with it detracts very much from the enjoyment. No refined person will spit where ladies are present, or in any public promenade; the habit is disgusting in the extreme, and one would almost wish that it could be checked in public by means of law." That it has been, in fact, may perhaps be taken as a mark of progress.

Should the reader be inclined to accuse the writer of hyperbole in his statement that "every youth begins to smoke and spit before he has well cut his teeth," let me but refer him to what Mr. Charles William Jonson, who wrote "The Stranger in America," observed in 1807, which may be the origin of Mr. Martine's remark.

"Often have I, with horror, seen boys, whose dress indicated wealthy parents, intoxicated, shouting and swearing in the public streets. In the use of that stupefying weed, tobacco, apeing their fathers, they smoke segars to so immoderate a degree, that sickness, and even death, has been the consequence. This is fully elucidated by the following paragraph, copied from a late newspaper, printed at Salem, in Massachusetts.

" 'Died in Salem, Master James Verry, aged twelve, a promising youth, whose early death is supposed to have been brought on by *excessive smoking of segars!!!*'

"That this pernicious custom was habitual in an infant, not four years of age, I was myself a witness. This little boy is the son of Thomas Taylor, a segar-maker, in Alexandria, near Washington. While conversing with the father, I observed the son smoking a large segar, made of the strongest tobacco. I expressed my astonishment; on which the infatuated parent, with an exulting smile, replied, that the child had contracted the habit above a year ago, and that he smoked three, four, or more, daily, which he was regularly supplied with, 'or he would cry for them.' In addition, he would steal them when opportunity offered, and, in fact, he was seldom without a lighted segar in his mouth. What was most surprising, the child was fat and healthy; thus for a time, and at this early age, proving that 'habit is second nature.' "

But it should not be assumed that the nineteenth century had a monopoly in infant precocity. Even as I write in 1930 there has been going on in the daily press a sort of contest between parents who boast of the ability of their three, four and five year old offspring to smoke an equivalent number of cigars daily, with statements as to their favorite brands, and I note that in Memphis, Tenn., Kenneth Azdel, aged six, has just been taken to a hospital by his parents to be cured of the cigarette habit. *Time* for May 26, 1930, has the following: "At Houston, Texas, W. H. Strebeck, barber, vaunts: 'I'll match my kid against any other youngster his age for intelligence.' His 'kid' Edwin, 2 years, 7 months, has been smoking three big cigars a day since he was one."

Spitting must have been almost as offensive as described by English travellers since it is so unanimously and vividly condemned. One illustration from Miss Leslie will more than suffice:

"English travellers are justly severe on the tobacco-chewing and spitting, that though exploded in the best society, is still too prevalent among the million. All American ladies can speak feelingly on this subject, for they suffer from it in various ways. First, the sickening disgust without which they cannot witness the act of expectoration performed before their faces. Next, the danger of tobacco-saliva falling on their dresses in the street, or while travelling in steamers and rail-cars. Then the necessity of walking through the abomination when leaving those conveyances; treading in it with their shoes; and wiping it up with the hems of their gowns. We know an instance of the crown of a lady's white-silk bonnet being bespattered with tobacco-juice, by a man spitting out of a window in one of the New York hotels. A lady on the second seat of a box at the Chestnut-street thea-tre, found, when she went home, the back of her pelisse entirely spoilt, by some man behind not having succeeded in trying to spit past her—or perhaps he did not try. Why should ladies endure all this, that men may indulge in a vulgar and deleterious practice, pernicious to their own health, and which they cannot acquire without going through a seasoning of disgust and nausea?"

Lest the modern reader, who is accustomed only to chew-ers of gum, should imagine that the habit was limited to the lower orders, was local in character or confined to the ex-treme South or West, let me quote the Hon. Thomas C. Grattan, Her Britannic Majesty's consul at that centre of cultivation and refinement, the city of Boston, to the effect that in 1859 at the best houses there the men guests at eve-ning dinners spat freely upon the floor. "The heavy meal at nine o'clock, the quantity of Madeira, the nuisance of the tobacco smoke, and the accompaniment of spitting on mats laid down for the occasion, were too much for me."

G. W. Stevens, an English visitor during the presidential campaign of 1896, in a sketch of Mr. McKinley says:

"I rang and walked in; Mr. McKinley was sitting in a rocking chair in a little office not ten feet from the door. . . . Clear eyes, wide nose, full lips—all his features sug-gest dominant will and energy rather than subtlety of mind or emotion. He had on the frock coat in which he was pres-ently to address deputations, and loosely tied brown slippers in which he was not. He also was not unmindful of the spit-toon."

While we are on the general topic of tobacco, why not dispose of the subject by an authoritative statement from "The Gentleman's Book of Etiquette" published by Mr.

Cecil B. Hartley in 1860 and widely quoted as an authority:

"One must never smoke a pipe in the streets; one must never smoke at all in the coffee-room of a hotel. One must never smoke, without consent, in the presence of a clergyman, and one must never offer a cigar to any ecclesiastic.

"But if you smoke, or if you are in the company of smokers, and are to wear your clothes in the presence of ladies afterwards, you must change them to smoke in. A host who asks you to smoke, will generally offer you an old coat for the purpose. You must also, after smoking, rinse the mouth well out, and, if possible, brush the teeth. You should never smoke in another person's house without leave, and you should not ask leave to do so if there are ladies in the house. When you are going to smoke a cigar you should offer one at the same time to anybody present, if not a clergyman or a very old man. You should always smoke a cigar given to you, whether good or bad, and never make any remarks on its quality."

It should be remembered that this was in 1860, when, the reader will naturally observe, it was far less bother for a gentleman to pull out his plug and bite off a satisfactory chunk than to be obliged to remember and comply with all the above technicalities. And perhaps clergymen might chew?

But why, with all this universal spitting and drinking, was the comparatively mild and innocuous habit of smoking held in such abhorrence?

My own theory, for what it may be worth, is that the use of smoking tobacco, being an innovation introduced into England about the time of the Reformation and hence frowned upon as an unclean habit fit only for such lewd fellows of the baser sort as frequented pot-houses, never fully recovered from the odium thus cast upon it until recently. Smoking never has had the same prestige as drinking; indeed it does not offer the same opportunities for distinction. An aristocratic Englishman's life in the eighteenth and nineteenth centuries centred largely about the punch bowl. Few sportsmen went to bed sober and beginning with their claret at

dinner they only waited until the departure of the ladies to
fuddle themselves in earnest. They remained behind to
drink; we stay to smoke, as does the Briton of to-day. Smoking, indeed, at the time of the colonization of America, was
a crime punishable with fine and imprisonment if committed
within five miles of a habitation.

On the other hand everybody drank, including the clergy.
Smoking, however, except in private, remained under the
ban of strict etiquette until the end of the nineteenth century. As drink went out, men sought a substitute and, since
they could not smoke, they chewed. This continued until the
horrors of expectoration had made the United States such
an object of ridicule and disgust that the very women for
whose sake the anti-smoking rule had been invoked, in des-
peration made it clear that they preferred the lesser of the
two evils.—That is my theory, but in all honesty I must
confess that pipe smoking was not unknown among women
in the middle of the last century and that there were several
instances of women who smoked cigars and pipes among
distinguished female members of New York society as late
as 1875.

By 1850 the Puritan attitude towards diversion was rapidly losing ground. The rest of America did not share the
gravity of Boston. The Yankee country man with his shrewd
and satirical comments on political affairs had already appeared in print. Will Rogers' literary grandfather "Major
Jack Downing" (Seba Smith) had produced his famous
"Select Letters." Artemas Ward and Petroleum Vesuvius
Naseby had begun to convulse the commoner sort including
a lank youth named Abraham Lincoln, and Mrs. Partington
was making the highbrows chuckle with such excruciatingly
comic stuff as:

"I am not so young as I was once, and I don't believe I
ever shall be, if I live to the age of Sampson, which, heaven
knows as well as I do, I don't want to, for I wouldn't be a
centurian or an octogon and survive my factories and become
idomatic by any means. But then there is no knowing how

a thing will turn out until it takes place, and we shall all come to an end some day, though we may never live to see it."

Humorous books were widely read and quoted,—the "Widow Bedott Papers," the "Sparrowgrass Papers," "The Travels, Voyages and Adventures of Gilbert Go-Ahead," the "Squibob Papers" and "Josh Billings' Farmer's All-minax."

Jenny Lind, the Swedish nightingale, had torn the hearts from the breasts and lifted the souls of a crowd so vast that Castle Garden overflowed upon the Harbor and many of the would-be audience took to boats. The Academy of Music had opened in New York, and Boston and Philadelphia had a regular season of Italian opera. Such actors as Edwin Booth and Edwin Forrest had enthralled thousands, but—so long as a majority of church-goers regarded the theatre as "an un-mitigated evil,"—concerts, minstrel shows, lectures and still more lectures, supplied the place of the drama in most places, the lyceum offering almost as many "stars" as the stage in the persons of Henry Ward Beecher, Wendell Phillips, Ralph Waldo Emerson and nearly two hundred other minor luminaries.

The old-fashioned garden of American letters was now in full bloom. During the preceding ten years Emerson had written his first volume of poems and essays; Poe, the "Black Cat," "The Gold Bug," "Marie Roget," "Annabel Lee," "The Raven," and "The Bells"; Hawthorne, "Grandfather's Chair," "Mosses from an Old Manse," and the "Scarlet Letter"; Lowell, his "Fable for Critics" and the "Bigelow Papers"; Cooper was publishing the best American novels yet written, Longfellow was doing the work which endeared him to the public, and Prescott had established himself as the greatest of the historians of the period if not of our entire history. *Putnam's Magazine,* setting a high standard of re-finement and good taste, was specializing in native writers. Emerson, Lowell, Longfellow and Holmes were launching *The Atlantic Monthly. Harper's,* a magazine that then paid nothing to the English author, but gaily pirated his work since there was no copyright, had given America "Bleak House" and "The Newcomes," besides the "Easy Chair." Of large circulation there were also *The Saturday Evening Post, Godey's Lady's Book, Graham's Lady's and Gentleman's Magazine,* Peterson's *Lady's National,* while there were many others such as the *Dollar Magazine, Miss Leslie's Magazine, Metcalf's Magazine,* and the *Nineteenth Century.*

Nothing was printed which, to quote a no less eminent authority than Mr. James Ford Rhodes, "a young girl might not read." Had he been accursed with a greater sense of levity than is seemly in historians, he perhaps might have added with equal truth that probably nothing was printed which any young girl *would* read to-day. Certainly the matter contained between the covers of those early magazines bore little relation to actual human life. It was graceful, informative of matters usually inutile, frequently superficial and banal. But they were popular, and *Harper's* is said to have had a million readers and very likely did.

Yet in spite of the fact that the rigidity of Puritanism was yielding to the influence of Europe and of economic change, nearly half the population of the country remained of Puritan descent, while New England under the outward restraint of the Puritan tradition kept on the even tenor of its way. The country as a whole was markedly religious and the clergy were treated as direct representatives of the Almighty.

Even in New York, then as now supposedly the Babylon of America, too much theatre-going could not be safely indulged in by serious people without being reflected in their standing. The Sabbath still began in effect on Saturday night, while in certain sections of the city chains across the street prevented the peace of the day from being disturbed. Sunday train travel was frowned upon, the Brooklyn *Independent* opposing the running of horse-cars on Sunday on the ground that it would demoralize the town and encourage the "pursuit of secular business and pleasure on the Lord's Day."

"In the novel 'Home,'" says Seldes, "a family was described as spending Sunday morning in Church and the afternoon in religious conversation on a sailboat. So much offense was taken at this frivolity that the edition was withdrawn and the sailboat deleted."

A letter to the *Independent*, October 2, 1851, said in part: "I am sorry to find that the stockholders of the Saratoga railroad still run their cars upon the Sabbath. It is an odious and monstrous violation, not only of the laws of God, but of all the decencies of Christian society. And yet I have noticed ladies traveling in them, thundering into Saratoga on the Lord's Day! Women traveling in public conveyances on the Sabbath! There is something in this peculiarly degrading and shameful. It ought to be only the lowest of the sex that will stoop to such debasement."

According to a computation by Professor Channing, by 1850, 40 railroads, controlling about 4,000 miles of track, had stopped running cars on Sunday. Pittsburgh, a Presbyterian stronghold, for years tolerated no Sunday excursions. Even to-day the traveller who happens to be indulging in a harmless game of solitaire must put away his cards while the train is crossing the State of Connecticut.

The expurgated edition of Shakespeare's works by Thomas Bowdler was still in common use, in which "nothing is added to the original text; but those words and expressions are omitted which cannot with propriety be read aloud in a family."

New fortunes, however, were accumulating with a resultant desire on the part of their possessors to get something for their money. Said the New York *Tribune* in 1854: "With the princely fortunes accumulating on the one hand, and the stream of black poverty pouring in upon the other, contrasts of condition are springing up as hideous as those of the Old World."

One of these contrasts was the building of the *North Star* by Commodore Vanderbilt, and his famous trip around the world in 1853 taking his wife and his sons and his sons' wives with him, but leaving a bevy of grandchildren, among whom were several future financiers and leaders of society, at the old home on Staten Island without any means of communication with their parents during his absence. The voyage of the *North Star* was an odyssey of luxury and grandeur. A side-wheeler of 2,500 tons, she was the largest yacht as yet built and the first of any size to be propelled by steam.

Like Noah the modern Crœsus took along one of each of his descendants after his or her kind with its mate in this ark, which, although not pitched within and without with pitch, possessed a gorgeous saloon with hanging kerosene lamps and a central sofa upholstered with a beautiful new material just then coming into fashion and known as "plush."

But out on the Western plains Sioux, Apaches and Pawnees crept up to the campfires of pioneers and split their skulls as they slept, while back in Framingham, Mass., the town closed up tight at six o'clock Saturday night, and the family having partaken of soda biscuits, corn-meal mush and apple sauce, read aloud the catalogue of the progeny of Amos or Bildad, crept upstairs, blew out their candles and pulled the quilt over their heads in preparation for the Holy Day to come.

# CHAPTER X

## Pantalettes to Pajamas

WITH all their bombast and swagger the mid-Nineteenth Century Americans exhibited the same sensitiveness to British social opinion as did their descendants. To this mother complex may in part be attributed the extraordinary influence of Queen Victoria upon the social life of the United States for over fifty years. She had married her cousin Albert of Saxe-Coburg in 1840 and from that moment had exalted domesticity into a religion. The life at Buckingham Palace resembled a highly ceremonial prayer meeting.

"It was," says Strachy, "indeed a model Court. Not only were its central personages the patterns of propriety, but no breath of scandal, no shadow of indecorum, might approach its utmost boundaries. For Victoria, with all the zeal of a convert, upheld now the standard of moral purity with an inflexibility surpassing, if that were possible, Albert's own. She blushed to think how she had once believed—how she had once actually told *him*—that one might be too strict and particular in such matters, and that one ought to be indulgent towards other people's dreadful sins. But she was no longer Lord M's pupil: she was Albert's wife. She was more—the embodiment, the living apex, of a new era in the generations of mankind. The last vestige of the eighteenth century had disappeared; cynicism and subtlety were shrivelled into powder; and duty, industry, morality, and domesticity triumphed over them. Even the very chairs and tables had assumed, with a singular responsiveness, the forms of prim solidity. The Victorian Age was in full swing."

During that age brown, yellow and black women, as well as white,—Asian, African and American—venerated the plump little queen at Windsor as the personification of all the virtues their sex could possibly be heir to. Victoria's invisible empire extended far beyond 54′ 40″, the confines of the Sudan, or the Khyber Pass. We Yankees could declare ourselves independent of British royalty till we burst, boast that we'd got the ships, we'd got the men and got the money too, with which to wipe Windsor Castle off the map, but for all that we were even more dominated in our social relationships by England from 1850 to 1900 than from 1725 to 1775.

The very intensity of the Queen's prejudices gave them sanction. She knew no half way measures, no compromises. She was an army with banners so far as decorum was concerned. The irreverent might have called her stubborn. So long as she lived Victoria would not permit smoking under the royal roof, and Ambassadors, invited to Windsor, were said to have been reduced, in the privacy of their bed rooms, to lying full length upon the floor and smoking up the chimneys. She carried her enthusiasm for wifely fidelity so far that, in addition to allowing no divorced lady to approach the court, she "frowned severely upon any widow who married again."

As for Women's Suffrage, the mere suggestion of it sent the blood rushing to her head. The hereditary Puritanism of America was highly sympathetic to the prudery of the British Court. It is hard to realize now the extremes to which "niceness" was carried in those days; and even greater than the actual niceness itself was the terror of not being thought nice. To "avoid the appearance of evil" became the great social commandment. People even tried "to cheat themselves in their own diaries." This became the basis of what is commonly called "Victorian hypocrisy."

To deny that such a thing existed is as absurd as to insist that there has been no evolution in manners and customs in the last eighty or ninety years. The really interesting question is how far these have been merely surface changes rather than indicative of a fundamental difference in attitude. In other words were the Victorians, in spite of the fact that they wore white gloves to dinner while we do not, essentially different from ourselves?

Fundamentally are we not the same whether we handle things with gloves or without? Is there, so to speak, any difference between a "limb" and a leg, a "male cow" and a bull, an "interesting condition" and pregnancy, "a statutory offense" and adultery, "unmentionables" and drawers, the pelvic or abdominal arch and the tummy, or any of the other euphemisms of the Greatest Euphemistic Era of all History? I trow not. The only difference that I can observe between what wise men and women thought, and reasonably human men and women did, in 1850 and to-day is that there was a universal conspiracy of silence regarding what is known as sex. This was because sex, in the opinion of Queen Victoria, was the serpent which could, and, if it got anything like half a chance, would destroy The Home. I say "the only difference"; I take that back. There is another difference and that is that men of presumably decent bringing up were about three times as tough as they are now.

Queen Victoria's solicitude concerning the protection of female virtue bore its finest flower in 1863 when in Lady Gough's book of "Etiquette" it was laid down that:

"The perfect hostess will see to it that the works of male and female authors be properly separated on her bookshelves. Their proximity unless they happen to be married should not be tolerated."

Although American prudery did not reach the point of discriminating as to the sex of books, the influence of Queen Victoria was an undoubted factor in the tremendous increase of chaperonage from 1860 to 1890. Her squeamishness in regard to the proprieties may seem less mawkish if we realize that she grew up in an epoch when drinking was still carried on to such an extent that footmen were kept on duty in many of the great houses—such, for example, as that of Coke of Norfolk—to assist intoxicated guests to their feet after morning prayers.

Of the various ways of attempting to get an accurate picture of the social manners and customs of a given period, a resort to books on contemporary etiquette is perhaps the least satisfactory. It is in effect somewhat as if, in order to determine how the Children of Israel behaved during their forty years' hike through the wilderness, we were content merely to consult the Ten Commandments.

A cursory examination of some 150 books on etiquette has left me profoundly skeptical as to their accuracy or the personal knowledge of the authors of the subjects which they discuss. In fact I emerged from a fortnight's perusal of detailed instructions as to the use of fish-forks, the manner of conducting a lady out to dinner or into a rowboat, the proprieties of calling, the home distillation of pomatum, and how to eat an orange, with the distinct conviction that almost without exception such books are, and always have been, catchpenny contrivances written by hack writers in dusty libraries and compiled from all preceding lore of the same sort since the days of Ptolemy Philadelphus.

I allege this the more joyfully for having been able to trace not only, mind you, the same injunctions, but the identical paragraphs, word for word, lifted in successive decades by assiduous authors on etiquette from their equally unscrupulous predecessors,—those of the 90's filching them from those of the 80's and 70's, and these in turn having incorporated them bodily from those of the 50's and 40's. A reading of these extraordinary treatises results in the inevitable conclusion that either manners had hardly changed at all, or that their writers were hopelessly ignorant people and incorrigible thieves. The latter statement is true at any rate, for having read all about what a young lady should wear when going boating (a dashing, dangerous sport regarded with considerable suspicion in 1837), I picked up the identical paragraph in 1868, and happened upon the same old friend bobbing up in a most unexpected manner in a later treatise by a lady of impeccable social position.

Usually the larceny is disguised by some alteration in the phraseology, but the source is easy to discover, although the original owner of the material be lost in the obscurity of the dim past. Thus we may learn from "How to Behave, a pocket manual of Republican Etiquette and guide to correct personal habits," published in 1850, that "if a lady chooses to seat herself upon the ground, you are not at liberty to follow her example unless she invites you to be seated. She must not have occasion to think of the possibility of any impropriety on your part. You are her servant, protector, and guard of honor. You will of course give her your hand to assist her in rising."

One might perhaps suppose that in the next twenty years, especially after the general loosening up following the Civil War, this excessive sensibility to the possible dangers of recumbency might have become somewhat mitigated. But no! In "The Bazar Book of Decorum, a Treatise on Etiquette," published by Harpers in 1870, we are emphatically instructed by the author, Robert Tomes, M.D., "if you are walking with a woman in the country,—ascending a mountain or strolling by the bank of a river,—and your companion being fatigued, should choose to sit upon the ground, on no account allow yourself to do the same, but remain rigorously standing. To do otherwise would be flagrantly indecorous and she would probably resent it as the greatest insult."

Now I have no desire or inclination to quarrel with the learned medico upon the niceties of deportment of sixty years ago, but I find it hard to believe that any young lady would have resented it as an insult, if, having decided to sit down, her escort should have done the same, although I well remember when it was not considered good form for a gentleman caller to seat himself uninvited upon the sofa beside his hostess.

I feel the more strongly about the matter by reason of Dr. Tomes' excessive accuracy in other respects, notably the arc which should be described by a gentleman's hat in salutation: "When you salute a lady or a gentleman to whom you wish to show particular respect, in the street, you should take your hat entirely off and cause it to describe a circle of at least ninety degrees from its original resting place."

These humorless books on etiquette besides rehearsing the same stale anecdotes, the same stilted quotations from Lord Chesterfield's letters, and the same sententious adaptations of the antique philosophy of Polonius, are not only repetitive, redundant and plagiaristic, but seek to pad out their shopworn aphorisms with banal disquisitions on female virtue, male chivalry, temperance, the iniquity of Woman's Rights, personal cleanliness, cosmetics and the care of the skin. Their counsels run the gamut from variations on the Sermon on the Mount to eulogia upon the Saturday-night bath. They give complete instructions as to the proper course to pursue from somewhat before the cradle to well after the grave. The previously mentioned pocket "Manual of Republican Etiquette" (I hasten to explain that it contains no reflections upon the manners and customs of the Democratic Party) modestly proclaims itself "an exposition of the principles of good manners; useful hints on the care of the person, eating, drinking, exercise, habits, dress, self-culture, and behavior at home; the etiquette of salutations, introductions, receptions, visits, dinners, evening parties, conversation, letters, presents, weddings, funerals, the street, the church, places of amusement, traveling, etc., with illustrative anecdotes, a chapter on love and courtship, and rules of order for debating societies." And all for the small sum of fifty cents.

In spite of the fact that these books on etiquette are insufferably stupid, an occasional jewel is found in the toad's head of their banality. Sometimes indeed it is possible to reconstruct a whole social era out of a tiny tidbit. Thus we are solemnly informed by Miss Leslie that "the fashion of wearing black silk mittens at breakfast is now (1853) obsolete. It was always inconvenient, and neither useful nor ornamental."

That manners in the United States were pretty static in the last century, seems to be shown by the fact that there are but two differences of opinion recorded in the entire library of 150 works so far examined, and that these differences were speedily dissolved in a general genteel harmony. In "Sensible Etiquette of the Best Society" by Mrs. H. O. Ward, published in Philadelphia as late as 1878, we find that it was still a matter of dispute as to whether a gentleman should give his right or left arm to a lady. The lady authoress raises the question and later cites herself as an authority, first quoting:

"A gentleman offers his *left* arm to the lady whom he is to lead into dinner.—'Social Etiquette in New York,' *Home Journal,* and

"Dinner announced, the host offers his *left* arm to the lady.—Mrs. Dahlgren's 'Etiquette of Social Life in Washington,' immediately following these citations with

"A gentleman offers his *right* arm in conducting ladies, whether on the street or in the house. By so doing, the right hand of the lady is left free to hold her parasol, or, if in the house, to use her fan, attached to her chatelaine, and to guard her train from being stepped upon. Some writers decree that the right arm is to be offered on one occasion, and the left arm on others. This is absurd, as no man could remember the distinctions with our mode of life. Both common sense and gallantry assign the lady's place where it is for her greatest convenience, on his right. In America a gentleman should, as a rule, keep on the left of a lady, in order to guard her from the jostling of passers-by. It is for the protection of ladies in this way that the rule is so universally followed of giving the right arm.—Mrs. H. O. Ward."

We of the later generation know that Mrs. Ward won.

The other mooted question was how to eat asparagus. Martine's "Handbook of Etiquette" settles it.

"An epicure," he says, "will eat even macaroni with his fingers; and as sucking asparagus is more pleasant than chewing it, you may, as an epicure, take it up *au naturel*. But both these things are generally eaten with a fork."

There was also, as pointed out in 1856 in "How to Behave," a little confusion as to what should be done with the old knife and fork anyway, since "to hold them in your hand would be awkward, and to lay them on the table-cloth might soil it; but the author of the 'American Gentleman's Guide,' whose acquaintance with the best usage is not to be questioned, says that they should be retained, and either kept together in the hand or rested upon your bread, to avoid soiling the cloth."

I should here record, for the peace of mind of posterity, that the books of etiquette written at the time when elevators were first used in America show that the same discussion, as to whether gentlemen ought to keep their hats on in the presence of lady passengers, went on then as now. And also, then as now, it was about an even break, which is the reason the same question is still being argued.

After all, etiquette is in most cases but the shield of cowards, and when few are any longer to the manner born, it matters little that we may be thought to belong to the hoi polloi. So we all naturally drift towards the easier, more comfortable and expeditious ways. The technique of etiquette changes little, and then, usually, owing to some physical or mechanical reason, such as the introduction of lawn tennis, the bicycle, or the automobile;—in a word such changes come of necessity and not by reason of any alteration in the general point of view, which instead presently adapts itself to the new conditions and perhaps starts thereafter on a frolic of its own.

Moreover, such changes as do come, come quickly. One day the women are wearing their hair long and the next day short. The changes usually occur because an influential minority decides for one reason or another that that is the way things should, or shall, be done. It is all a matter of how much sway over the public mind and imagination these leaders,—whether they are dressmakers, social eccentrics, fashionable fools, or movie stars,—exercise. The movies will undoubtedly have a tremendous effect upon

American manners and customs for a long time to come. Everybody knows how to kiss these days under Greta Garbo's and Clara Bow's expert tutelage. And what the public learns from the screen about contemporary manners will, on the whole, be a good deal more accurate than "Manners that Win" or "How to Behave" or any other works which needs must be ultra-conservative in order to show clearly the gentility of the writers and which, as well, are generally five or ten years out of date when they venture beyond mere commonplaces about the correct way to eat soup.

How manners may perhaps be made is illustrated by the experience of a scion of an impeccable Gotham family who took a "research" job as social arbiter for one of the best-known companies in Hollywood. The picture had been written for, and around, the star who was on the screen at least four-fifths of the time, always of course in a different dress. One scene showed her as hostess at a dinner party. The company were assembled, the dining-room doors thrown open, the butler appeared, bowed and announced that dinner was served, whereupon the star, who occupied a throne in the centre of the screen, arose, took the arm of one of the guests, and started to lead the procession into the festal hall.

When the New Yorker, in performance of the duty for which he was being paid, explained, as tactfully as he could, that it wasn't done that way in the best families at least where *he* came from, and that the hostess went in not first but last, the lady withered him with a "Me—*last!* How could the star go in after everybody else? Of course I go in first! I don't believe you know a damn thing about it." Or rather this is a refined, euphemistic and emasculated version of the way she put it.

The heroic youth insisted that he was, in spite of logic and obvious desirability, nevertheless right, whereupon the lady disdainfully ignored him, called her own butler to the telephone in San Francisco, and being promptly assured of her infallibility, proceeded to enact the scene in her own way. That scene will be watched in breathless admiration by 40,-

000,000 people and hereafter, in spite of my friend Mrs.
Post and all other final authorities, the American hostess will
be going in to dinner ahead of her husband on the theory
that if you see it on the screen it's so, and that gents should
follow ladies. Incidentally the social arbiter was fired then
and there,—as he deserved to be—for questioning the right
to priority of a Queen.

When William Randolph Hearst recently sent a moving-
picture company to shoot a film of native life at Tahiti, the
director found to his annoyance that the dusky belles had all
abandoned their picturesque costumes in favor of such as
they had seen worn upon the silver screen by Pola Negri
and Gloria Swanson, whose coiffure they had likewise copied, so that it required a substantial financial bonus to induce
them to discard their new finery for their former innocent
habiliments.

Books on etiquette do not reflect actual conditions, since
they assume to tell only what *should be* done and not what
*is*. Their function is to lead erring sinners against politeness,
if not to repentance, at least into the right way of eating,
drinking, and paying calls; it is not their business to tell us
what the sinners have been up to. Therefore it is useless to
expect to find in any such book the slightest suggestion of
the existence of any widespread contemporary habits or customs that were, or are, contrary to law or ethics. Yet etiquette has nothing whatever to do with morality. There is as
much etiquette in the doing of that which is naughty as that
which is accepted as proper, in fact usually more so. But the
authors of books on etiquette quite naturally do not wish to
array themselves against the forces of law, order, purity or
religion, or to alienate their readers through allowing them
to suppose that they are in sympathy with the sons of evil
or the daughters of joy by explaining how the naughty things
are done.

Thus all we can expect to find in a book on etiquette is a
statement of how perfect examples of sober, law-abiding
and godly people do, or at least should, conduct themselves,

—although it by no means follows that the majority of those of the widest social experience are any of these. For example, it would be quite hopeless to turn to any book on etiquette published since 1918 in order to find out what was the etiquette about serving wine. We know perfectly well that at the present writing (1930) for every host in what is known as "smart society" in New York City who does not serve cocktails and whiskey, and frequently sherry, champagne, and liqueurs at his table, there are at least ninety-nine that do. If one wishes to know whether it is customary to pass cocktails before lunch you will not find out by reading Mrs. Emily Post's "Etiquette," and no doubt that is as it should be; the danger lies in the possibility of the future historian or student of manners concluding that in this thirteenth year of the Eighteenth Amendment the people of the United States drank no liquor.

In "a house which has the remains of a cellar," Mrs. Post admits that the miraculous pitcher still flows. But how about the cellar which has no such liquid surplus?

"A water glass standing alone at each place makes," says she, "such a meagre and untrimmed looking table that most people put on at least two wine glasses, sherry and champagne, or claret and sherry, and pour something pinkish or yellowish into them."

Mrs. Post is either disingenuous about what she allows her readers to infer most people do, or she jolly well knows what that pinkish or yellowish "something" is. This is written not for the purpose of criticizing an excellent book of its kind, but to show that the kind affords very little information as to the habits, or even the customs, of the people it purports to describe.

Picturesque as they often are, most of these books about behavior give us little light on the state of social intercourse at the time they were written, for they are generally compiled for those who do not know how to conduct themselves, by persons almost equally ignorant, are hopelessly out of date and even more hopelessly misleading by reason of their entreaties not to do things which no reasonable human being who ever went into any sort of decent society would think of doing anyway. I will guarantee that a shrewd selection of excerpts from any book of etiquette published prior to 1900 would lead to a fair inference that the members of most social circles in the United States habitually conducted themselves like chimpanzees. Even Emily Post gives us a hideous moment with her "If food is too hot, quickly take a swallow of water. *On no account spit it out!*" "Ah, ha!" some historian of A. D. 2000 will exclaim, if the print is still legible, "those same spitters we read about in 1853 were at it in 1925!"

Lastly no deductions can be made from the prohibitions contained in such books, for the prohibitions are directed towards the most ignorant of the author's clientele and the books themselves are written for people who do not know how to behave,—not for those who do. The oft-repeated admonition never to "eat peas with a knife" does not indicate that most people offended in that respect at the time the opus was published, any more than Mrs. Post's various protests against "spitting out" things which one has accidentally taken into one's mouth and does not wish to retain there proves that most people get rid of the objectionable substances in that way.

I stress the characteristic of books on etiquette which obliges the author to outgild the lily of conventionality wherever morals are involved. As he is laying down the law he must prove his authority as a law-giver. He can afford to take no chances. He will always be found in the rear guard and not the vanguard. This has always been true of such books. Up to a certain point they tell the truth about current habits and customs; but beyond that point, since they must be moral to be authoritative, they begin to preach, asserting in defiance of the blatantly obvious that "no true lady" or "true gentleman" will do thus or so. Smug propriety is their stock in trade. Lectures on the glory of womanhood crowd recipes for "escallopped oysters," youth restoratives, and how to receive a proposal of marriage. No books on etiquette prior to 1900 ever advocated the slightest independence on the part of women. The instant the author leaves the domain of fact and enters that of ethics, naturally he is no longer an observer and recorder but an advocate. We are not interested in whether gentlemen or ladies ought, or ought not, to carry flasks or drink cocktails at tea time, but in whether or not *they do*. Young people will not seek information about these things on the shelves of libraries, but among their contemporaries and associates. "Sure they do! Don't I see them?" has far more sanction than a pedantic paragraph in a "Book of Behavior" no matter how luxuriously bound.

But while we shall not find out from any book of etiquette published in 1855 how people actually behaved at that time, such books are of inestimable value as giving us a glimpse of contemporary opinion, even if ultra conservative with regard to the rights of women, the reading of novels, the amount of liberty to be allowed the young, etc.

Thus we find that women aged almost as quickly in 1860 as in revolutionary times. A young girl had to get married within two or three years after her *début*, and if not, back she went on the shelf. Says Mr. Martine succinctly: "Young ladies do not receive calls from gentlemen unless they are very intimate with them, or have passed the rubicon of thirty summers."

It was the accepted doctrine that a girl became an old maid at twenty-five, was withered and ready for a retreat or nunnery at thirty, and fit only for "the boneyard" at thirty-five, at which age she was supposed to wear a cap. Once married she vanished into the purdah of American uxoriousness, carrying upon her head the symbol of servitude, however unbecoming, her wildest public debauch a reckless afternoon "tatting" in a rocker. Women's place—socially at least—was on the piazza. If you are inclined to doubt this, read Miss Leslie in "The Behavior Book."

"Most American ladies beyond the age of thirty-five look

better in caps than without them, even if their hair shows no signs of middle age. Before that time, the females of our country begin to fade, evincing one effect of torrid summers and frozen winters. A tasteful and simply elegant cap (not one that is elaborate in its design, and loaded with ornament) imparts a grace and softness to a faded face, and renders less conspicuous the inroads of time."

Did women fade sooner in 1853 than they do now? And if so, why? Was it because they took so little exercise, or paid less attention to their diet or corsetted themselves so tightly, or being told that they were old, conducted themselves accordingly and hence actually became so? Or was it only an apparent maturity, induced by the use of caps and encouraged by jealous husbands or mothers anxious to marry off their younger sisters? No doubt all these played their part.

Augustus K. Gardner, M.D., in an article on the "Physical Decline of American Women" in *The Knickerbocker* of January, 1860, wrote, "we shall attempt to tell why woman is a haggard creature, dull-eyed and sallow, pinched in form, an unfit mother, not a help-meet, but a drag on the energy and spirits and resolution of her partner in life. Look at the dress of women. Were man to so direct the fashion of women's dress, in order to enable him by physical force to overcome her and tyrannize over her, he could not more completely fetter her than she shackles herself. Her sleeves are placed so low down upon the waist that she is unable to raise her hands to the top of her head or use them freely in any direction; her limbs are restrained in their motions by a profusion of flowing skirts, and her breathing interrupted by lacings or corsets, which displace the organs and slowly destroy life. It is in vain, however, to hope for any relief from the tyranny of fashion. Were these injuries caused by any edict of church or state, long ere this they would have been abrogated. Against the decrees of fashion there is no appeal."

The tradition of the fragility of woman, the idea that she was a sensitive plant which instinctively shrank from any contact with the coarse facts of life, and was physically unadapted by nature to violent exercise persisted until the end of the century. The author of "Social Customs" says as late as 1887:

"Tennis and other athletic exercises, now so much in favor with young girls, no doubt assist greatly in producing a good muscular development, although tennis is such violent exercise that one cannot recommend women to make use of it, except with a good deal of caution."

Mrs. Hale of Boston, who described the "Manners of Happy Homes and Good Society All the Year Round," evidently thought things were in a pretty bad way in 1868 and that the young folks were going to the dogs. The girls deceived their parents, and while not exactly lambs in wolves' clothing perhaps, were certainly wise little serpents in the plumage of doves. What was more, she knew the exact reason for it—novel reading. Too many trashy books.

"There are evils under the sun that Solomon never dreamed of," she asserts. "In our land, one of these evils is a deluge of books. Works of fiction, perhaps from being 'light reading,' are floating on the top waves, filling our homes with an everflowing stream of 'the last new novels,' and threatening to wash away from the minds of the young all love for works of truth and soberness. I am not intending to discuss the evils of this mania for fiction. That there are injurious effects from this habit of indiscriminate novel-devouring, everybody will allow. How to prevent it, is the question. This involves the whole system of home life."

How to prevent it! Yes, Mrs. Hale, that is still the question, but not only in regard to novels. Her anecdote about a certain Mr. Tuttle,—it is a short story in fact rather than an anecdote,—introduced to demonstrate the poisonous effects of this sort of literature, is singularly unconvincing.

I shall condense Mr. Tuttle to as few lines as possible in order to make Mrs. Hale's point—whatever it is.

Mr. Tuttle was a rich man, "on change," with a wife and two lovely daughters, but he was entirely devoted to business and rather neglected his home although, as Mrs. Hale points out, he was really a good fellow, and basically sound in his ideas in that he heartily disapproved of novels for young girls. True to his principles he absolutely forbade his daughters to read the insidious and pernicious things. But temptation was too strong for them. They were unable to resist, and hence entered upon a subtle course of deception which utterly ruined their characters. One day there was an awful scene in which they were unexpectedly exposed to their father. Thereafter, obviously at any rate in Mrs. Hale's opinion, they were ruined, that is, as we have said, their characters were, and—Mr. Tuttle shortly *failed in business*.

I either do not fully understand this story or there is something wrong with it. Mrs. Hale, in her eagerness to demonstrate the dangers of novel reading, leaves it to be inferred that the loss of the Tuttle girls' virtue was due to the naughty books, whereas it was clear that the real cause of their downfall was that they disregarded the Fifth Commandment and became little sneaks. It is here that the confusion creeps in. The Misses Tuttle's sin of disobedience and deception *preceded* the novel reading and was not *post hoc propter hoc*. Yet Adam did not fall until he and Eve had nibbled at the apple. So why blame the apple? It was the weakness of poor human nature. Suppose Mr. Tuttle had forbidden them to go out rowing and they had disobeyed him? Would that demonstrate the iniquity of aquatic sport?

Mrs. Hale was probably forced to abandon logic and resort to deliberate obscuration in order to conceal the real truth, which was that the Misses Tuttle, even before their father's prohibition, had tasted of the forbidden fruit and found it too delicious to be resisted. They had, in a word, already been ruined by the insidious books before having been forbidden to read them. But that might have made the novels appear far too alluring! Even the apple needed the aid of the serpent, and there was no serpent at the Tuttles'. So Mrs. Hale leaves us a little worried over whether the Misses Tuttle were all that they should have been in the first place. And why did Mr. Tuttle fail in business? Is not that what might be called "a cruel and unusual punishment" to be visited upon a well-meaning man who merely found being "on change" more amusing than sitting at home with Mrs. Tuttle, and who certainly tried to do the right thing as to novels? Besides, Mrs. Hale does not tell us anything about Mrs. Tuttle.

Omitting any further discussion of the morals of the Tuttle girls, it may be worth while to inquire just what these deleterious novels to which their father made objection probably were. Well, in the same year that Mrs. Hale described those "happy homes all the year round," Dickens, Thackeray, George Eliot and George Meredith, Trollope, Charles Read, Wilkie Collins, and Marryatt were being widely read; the Rev. E. P. Roe was producing "Barriers Burned Away" and "The Opening of a Chestnut Burr"; Bret Hart had written the "Luck of Roaring Camp," was under salary to *The Atlantic,* and was about to bring out his first collection of short stories; William Dean Howells was writing "Their Wedding Journey," Henry James his earlier short stuff, John Esten Cooke's "Hilt to Hilt" and "Mohun" were still popular, and Edward Everett Hale's "Man Without a Country" published in 1863 was already a classic; Edward Eggleston was just about to bring out "The Hoosier Schoolmaster," and the type of novel most generally in demand were Charlotte and Emily Brontë's "Jane Eyre" and "Wuthering Heights," William Harrison Ainsworth's "Windsor Castle," G. P. R. James' "Richelieu," Disraeli's "Vivian Gray" and "Coningsby," Bulwer Lytton's "Last Days of Pompeii," Charles Lever's "Charles O'Malley," Blackmoor's "Lorna Doone," Dinah Craik's "John Halifax, Gentleman," and Kingsley's "Hypatia" and "Westward Ho." Rough stuff! as the modern girl might say! However, the Misses Tuttle might possibly have gotten hold of something warmer for all we know. At any rate their tragical history shows the care with which parents sought to keep unsullied the fair white texture of their daughters' minds.

But it is against those immodest and unwomanly women

who sought to demoralize society by insisting that they had such things as "rights" that the authors of the books on etiquette pour out the full vials of their scorn.

"Would the true wife desire to supersede her husband?" asks Mrs. Hale. "Would the good, intelligent mother, who has trained her son to the glorious ambition of serving his country, and gaining a noble fame,—would she, were it in her power, pluck the laurel from his brow, and place it on her own? Would she be willing that any woman should enter the lists against her son? If not, is it right for this mother to encourage the competition of her own sex against the sons of other mothers?"

"No! A thousand times no!" we hear the readers shouting. Mrs. Hale knows her audience and confidently continues:

"Greatness is most perfect when it acts with the least reference to *self;* power is most efficient when moving the will through the heart. Let us American ladies cultivate the virtues, the knowledge, the accomplishments, which will influence, imbue, and aid men to do the work of the world to the glory of God; then the women will truly shine forth as 'the glory of the man.' "

But while Mrs. Hale, a married lady, makes woman's abstinence from fame and glory seem a real self-sacrifice, her spinster confrère, Miss Leslie, lets the yellow cat out of her bag by admitting that woman would have no chance anyhow. She was no Lucy Stoner! No bloomers for her!

"Men make fortunes, women make livings. And none make poorer livings than those who waste their time, and bore their friends, by writing and lecturing upon the equality of the sexes, and what they call 'Women's Rights.' How is it that most of these ladies live separately from their husbands; either despising them, or being despised by them?

"Truth is, the female sex is really as inferior to the male in vigour of mind as in strength of body; and all arguments to the contrary are founded on a few anomalies, or based on theories that can never be reduced to practice. Because there was a Joan of Arc, and an Augustina of Saragossa, should females expose themselves to all the dangers and terrors of 'the battle-field's dreadful array'? The women of the American Revolution effected much good to their country's cause, without encroaching upon the province of its brave defenders. They were faithful and patriotic; but they left the conduct of that tremendous struggle to abler heads, stronger arms, and sterner hearts."

After all, she consoles herself, there is such a thing as being womanly. "We envy not the female who can look unmoved upon physical horrors—even the sickening horrors of the dissecting-room."

In spite of this jealous guarding of the young from contamination and the great concern over the preservation of female virtue on the part of "womanly women," it is interesting to note that all this solicitude does not seem to have had great effect.

The young had things pretty much their own way. They herded together, ignored their parents, ran the parties to suit themselves, raced up and down the hotel corridors, flirted, and even hung about the barrooms of Saratoga in a way that would not be countenanced to-day. Mr. Buchanan, that conservative and observant Englishman already quoted, wrote in 1857:

"The young, indeed, of both sexes carry on matters just as they please, so that the old seem either to be left on the shelf altogether, or only brought upon the stage to look on, bestow their approbation, and pay the expense. Here at Saratoga, in all the parties we visited, whether balls, concerts, or promenades, the married ladies were seemingly only valued as persons necessary to give countenance to the assembling of the young; while these usurped all authority and influence, and monopolized the exclusive attention of the men."

"Our very girls are brusque and blunt with selfish egotism," said *The Galaxy* in an editorial on "Manners of the Day" in 1868. "This anyone must see who observes their intercourse with their own sex. Ask any woman of thirty-five who was brought up among cultivated people, if she did not receive more consideration, more deference, even as a girl, from women of her mother's age than she now receives as a woman from young girls, unless she is a great dispenser of society favors, that is unless they have something to gain by deference and it will pay to be polite?"

The English girl of the period, *The Saturday Review* said, "is a creature who dyes, paints, and enamels,—studies the arts of vice, that she may render herself attractive to those accustomed to its pleasures,—is immodest in dress, behavior, and conversation—and whose whole object in life is to marry the man who, of all she knows, has the largest fortunes and the least brains." . . .

"This of course touches England primarily, but it concerns us also," commented *The North American Review*. "The same complaints are made here,—less in degree, but in kind the same; since the days of the 'Potiphar Papers' every Saratoga and Newport season has brought to light an increasing love of luxury, fastness and display. Will the Saratoga woman of ten years hence be such a woman as *The Saturday Review* describes in these terms: 'Belladonna flashes from her eyes, kohl and antimony deepen the blackness of her eyebrows, 'bloom of roses' blushes from her lips'? Is she of this sort now?"

The sympathies of a newspaper correspondent at Saratoga were deeply aroused in 1865 by the "sickly languid appearance of a young lady who had a seat directly opposite me every day at the dinner table; her form was emaciated, her skin perfectly transparent, and a death-like hue seemed to pervade the whole atmosphere about her; the eyes shone with unnatural brilliancy and under them was perceptible the inevitable blue-black coloring,—the tell-tales of a debauchee."

He wanted to meet and, no doubt, to do something for her, until to his horror he learned that "she for whom my whole soul has yearned in sympathy for a week was daubed all over with paint, and most shockingly disfigured herself to gratify a prurient taste to be in the extreme of fashion.

Looking around me at the dinner table today I saw no less than six ladies disfigured by a daub of blue-black paint on the lower eyelids. The next fashion possibly may require ladies to wear rings in their noses. It is bad enough to wear paste diamonds and pinchbeck jewelry; but when earth's angels begin to paint about the eyes, wear false busts, and false hair in a bag behind their heads, to what extremes may we not expect the dear creatures to go!"

"We have heard the same report from Newport," comments the editor of *Godey's Lady's Book*. "The ladies paint under their eyelids to give a more brilliant effect to the eye. What is Republican America coming to? These places—Saratoga and Newport—are the Sodom and Gomorrah of our Union."

Those who are appalled at current stories about flask-toting collegians and intoxicated flappers should turn back to *The Round Table* of 1866 and read the article about "Drunkenness among Women," which created an enormous sensation not only all over America but in Europe.

The writer stated that while, fortunately, the hard-drinking times had passed away, and the recent temperance movement had banished liquor from many sideboards, the drink habit was spreading among women. "It is not alone at the watering places that the ladies thus indulge. At their own homes, at the stores, and at those public nuisances called ladies' restaurants they are accustomed to drink liquors. The sight of a tipsy or intoxicated woman is not uncommon at the seaside and it is by no means extraordinary upon Broadway. We have the best authority for stating that . . . the vice of fashionable drinking is now more prevalent among the ladies than among the gentlemen of this country. . . . Certain dress-makers make it a point to furnish their customers with drink, and some of the most fashionable *maisons des modes* are, in fact, fashionable drinking houses. . . . Whiskey and brandy are the favorite drinks with these ladies. It may be true that a woman is very far gone upon the downward road when she can order and drink such stimulants in a public saloon; but still hundreds of women in our best society do this every day. In dress-makers' bills the significant item 'small trimmings' often covers up the expense of liquors which the lady has ordered through the modist who panders to her vitiated taste. At the watering-places a bribe to the waiter procures a secret supply of liquor, which, by the connivance of the landlord, is charged as 'extra luncheons.' . . . Mothers of families are breaking the hearts of their husbands and daughters by this vice. Girls of eighteen, the daughters of our most respectable merchants, have been seen grossly intoxicated in Broadway stages and upon the public streets. . . . The artificial life of most American women and the exhaustion that follows their reckless disregard of the rules of health create the necessity for stimulants, and when the habit of indulgence is once formed the inebriate asylum seems to be the only permanent remedy."

The editors of *The Round Table* replied to the widespread criticism evoked by this article by reasserting its truth. "By careful inquiry and investigation we are now satisfied that it would be possible to print the names of a greater number of respectable females—women, that is, of respectable families—than would fill the space occupied by this article (three columns), who within the last five years, in the city of New York, have fallen victims to drink. . . .

The whole of society was deteriorating according to *The Galaxy:* "In the course of the last twenty-five years, the period during which our wealth has notably increased, there has been a great and widespread deterioration in our manners and in the tone of our society. . . ."

As for the theatre! They had the same uproar on Broadway over the equivalent of sex plays in 1868 as they did sixty years later in 1928. It had reached a low ebb indeed, not so much on account of the nudity—after all the critics were strong men!—but just general lack of taste! The stage was becoming thoroughly commercialized, decent people wouldn't go any more, it would be ruined.

To the same general effect is the lamentation of J. S.

Redfield in *The North American Review* for October, 1868, entitled "Modern Women and What Is Said of Them": "If our politicians are every year becoming more and more corrupt, our theatres every year more and more indecent, and our society more and more abandoned in its luxury and frivolity, we shall very soon reach a point at which there will be little sacred for life and property,—if that in some quarters of the country has not been reached already. The soberest of American cities has had its winter's excitement furnished by the Cancan, the officers of the law in New York act or remain inactive according to the relative length of the plaintiffs' and defendants' purses, while the high whirl of Newport and Saratoga serves as a ready Lethe for all moral obligations. A rather disheartening picture might be drawn in this way of our probable future; and yet we cannot believe in its truth.

"The purpose of what we have written is to correct for our readers the false notion widely entertained, and as we have seen, in highly intelligent quarters, that an advancement in intellectual culture and material well being—that is, in civilization—is necessarily or even probably accompanied by an improvement in manners. As to complaints of deterioration," the writer not unwisely adds, "they are as old as the world. Who can doubt that Shem, Ham and Japhet mourned over the low tone of morals and manners after the great rain, and wondered if they should ever see a real old Antediluvian gentleman again?"

# CHAPTER XI

## Puritans and Popinjays

NEW YORK before the Civil War was in every way, from a present day viewpoint, a provincial city. Even the best houses had no central heating, the rooms being warmed by "Franklin" stoves, or "base-burners" bearing fancy names, the streets were dirty, poorly paved and dimly illuminated, rooms were lighted with lamps and candles, there was no plumbing save in the houses of the rich, and what are euphemistically known as "modern conveniences" were located in every back yard and were neither modern nor convenient, particularly as the cesspool was usually buried within a few feet of the pump from which the family water supply was drawn. The danger of contamination to the well was such that most families sent their servants to fetch water from some spot less likely of pollution, usually a street pump often at a considerable distance, such as the famous "Tea water" in Pearl Street. For those who lived on lower Fifth Avenue there was a pump at the corner of Tenth Street and University Place and another near where Jefferson Market now stands. Whether water-carrying came within the scope of a domestic's duty was apt to be a serious bone of contention between master and man.

One of my acquaintances recalls the issue being raised by an Irish coachman who, asked to bring a pitcher of water from the pump distant about 200 yards, strenuously objected to playing the part of Gunga Din, sending word that he had been hired to take care of the horses and not as a water carrier.

"Very well," remarked his employer, "tell James to harness up and bring around the carriage."

When the equipage arrived in front of the door the master emerged from the house carrying the pitcher, and ordered the coachman to drive to the pump, where he filled it himself and then drove back to the house.

"Now, James," he said, "you can take your choice. You can walk to the pump yourself and fetch home the water or when we need it you can harness up and drive me there." James wisely elected the easier alternative.

Few carriages were privately owned in the decade before the war, and the acquaintance to whom I refer tells me that he not only knew each one by sight and to whom it belonged, but the first name of every coachman. None of the latter wore livery, the first to be seen in New York being introduced in 1866 by Pierre Lorillard, Sr. Even had anyone desired to make a display it would have availed him naught since all his associates knew exactly what he was "worth."

The servants for the most part were negroes or untrained Irish immigrants who, including cooks, received from $1.50 to $3 per week. "Fire towers" throughout the city enabled watchmen to detect incipient conflagrations and ring the bell for the volunteer fire companies, much as fire wardens to-day keep vigil on the forest hilltops. Owing to the use of candles ladies' headdresses sometimes caught fire at evening receptions. Originally napkins were not changed in restaurants but were used by successive guests; Delmonico won high commendation by his innovation of supplying a fresh napkin for each customer. In 1850 a violent scandal was caused at the Second Assembly Ball by the dancing of the german in place of the quadrille by four ladies, of impeccable social position, wearing enormous hoop skirts.

There were few accretions to this society save from within. It grew from generation to generation, but only by natural multiplication. Outsiders rarely married into it or broke through the Chinese Wall of Knickerbocker exclusiveness. Proud of its lineage it was "indifferent alike to outside approval or condemnation, shunning publicity, disapproving the spectacular and sensational," and once a girl married she could never escape, for divorce was not recognized.

Family life was simple in the extreme. Ladies did their

own marketing, bargaining shrewdly. Everybody was respectable. Everybody belonged to some church and attended divine service.

But this "Age of Innocence" was not destined to last. During the decade between 1850 and 1860 the prosperous, the adventurous, the socially ambitious poured into New York from all parts of the country just as they do now. It became the shoddy Paris of a vast untamed continent. They came to seek their fortunes, to buy clothes, to attend the opera, to marry off their daughters, to take the packets to Europe. Society began to expand, while remaining excessively provincial, and the exclusive old families withdrew more and more into themselves. They retained social control when they saw fit to exercise it, but there was considerable polite grumbling about its autocratic attitude being out of place in a democracy. Only the grumbling was very polite.

That the New York society of this era was provincial rather than cosmopolitan is indicated by the serious suggestion of Mr. Nathaniel Parker Willis, a social and literary chit-chatter of much contemporary fame, that its members should call upon such presentable strangers as strayed within the city gates.

There ought to be, he opined, an early autumnal social season for the benefit of the southerners who visited the city at that time. He had noticed at a special performance of the opera that "few of our own fashionables were present, and yet a more thoroughly fashionable audience was never assembled in that house. There were Virginians, Louisianians, Carolinians, Kentuckians and Washingtonians,—the picked society of these Southern and Western latitudes.

"As our country's great centre of transit, we should think the society of New York might accommodate itself to the October presence of Southerners, with advantage. A brief gay season of early parties, on the off nights of the Opera, might take place in this month. What the French call *l'ete de St. Martin*, and we 'the Indian Summer,' might be, socially, the most delightful month in the year. It would be the etiquette, as it used to be in Boston about the time of Harvard Commencement, to call upon all presentable strangers; and this custom would promote an intimacy and good feeling between Northern and Southern society, which would be no trifling link in binding the country together."

Moved by the innocent beauty of Signorina Tuffi, this social pioneer made so bold as even to advocate the reception of professional opera singers—of guaranteed virtue—into the houses of the elect.

"Why," he asked, "would not any society be improved, by taking up, as persons to cherish and make much of, the gifted and accomplished creatures whose natural superiority marks them out for this profession? They are not all of good character, it is said—but, because all painters are not of good character, are painters, therefore, as a class, excluded from society? To invite an Opera-singer to a party in New York, except as a person hired to perform for the amusement of those present, would be considered by most people as rather a venturesome risking of the censure of 'mixed company.' "

But lest we lack an *argumentum ad hominem* to demonstrate the social naïveté of that time there rises to our assistance the stately figure of Isaac Brown, sexton of Grace Church, and a sort of cro-magnon precursor of no less a figure than that of Mr. Ward McAllister.

"This out-door Manager of the Stylish Balls of our great city is a fine-looking and portly person, who, in a certain sense, is Usher also to the most select portal of 'another and better world,' being the Sexton of Grace Church, the most fashionable and exclusive of our metropolitan 'Courts of Heaven.' Mr. Brown, we should add, is a person of strong good sense, natural air of command, and as capable of giving advice, upon the details of a party, as was ever the famous 'Beau Nash,' of Bath, to whose peculiar functions Mr. Brown's are the nearest modern approximation.

"Mr. Brown comes, at the summons, and takes a look at the premises. He is then consulted as to the guests. His knowledge of who is well or ill, who is in mourning for a death or a failure, who has friends staying with them, and what new belle has come out with such beauty or fortune as makes it worth while to send her family a card, is wonderfully exact; and, of course, he can look over the list of the invited and foretell the probable refusals and acceptances, and suggest the possible and advisable enlargements of acquaintances. But this is not all, and we have mentioned thus much, only to explain the combining circumstances that give Mr. Brown his weight of authority. Besides all this, he makes a business of keeping himself 'well booked up,' as to the strangers in town. How he does it we have no idea; but, upon the quality, manners, place of belonging, means, encumbrances, and objects of travel, of all the marked guests at the principal Hotels, he can give you list and programme, with a degree of prompt correctness that is as surprising as it is useful. Of course it is the list from which invitations are made, and (as no man who can afford to give a Ball can afford also to make morning calls) Mr. Brown takes the cards of the father of the family and leaves them 'in person' on the distinguished strangers. A man of more utility, or in the distribution of more influence, than our friend Mr. Brown, could hardly be picked from the New York Directory."

This influx of strangers, to which reference has been made, originated in the popularity of the famous watering places of Newport and Saratoga to which every family of social pretensions or marital aspirations then made an annual hegira. Not infrequently wealthy planters drove in their own coaches from their homes in the South, paying visits by the way like the continental grandees of old.

At these resorts every social class was represented, every type that has since been caricatured in every decade from the impudent, flirtatious "flapper" to the bar-room wit and "wise cracker" or the wealthy sportsman, who drove trotters instead of playing polo as to-day. Fashionable life consisted of "a profuse American breakfast, a promenade on the wide porticos, cigars and ten pins, the bar-room and billiards, lounging and gossip, a bad dinner at two or three, which the ladies dressed for, a drive after dinner, dancing until two in the morning for men and women, and gambling the rest of the night for men."

America as a whole was fiercely democratic and entrance into society at a fashionable watering place presented little difficulty if the applicant was reasonably presentable and had money. The avowed purpose of going to Saratoga and Newport was to make new acquaintances. The result was a stampede of vulgar and showy undesirables, some of whom fell by the wayside but many of whom, nevertheless, managed to make the grade. Exclusiveness was frowned upon as un-American, and to quiet people, who were dissatisfied with the friends they already had and who did not care to make new ones on crowded piazzas and in packed drawing rooms, it was politely indicated that they had better stay away. Many went to Europe every summer, just as they do now, but everybody else sought the hotels, for in that era cottage life in the summer was practically unknown. Money was an open sesame.

Here mingled the entire "would-be," and much of the genuine, aristocracy of America: planters of the old school from Georgia and the Carolinas, in Panamas and grass-cloth suits, swapped stories on the piazzas and spat harmoniously over the railing into the street; coldly disdainful matrons from Boston and Philadelphia swished by in hoops and feathers, followed coyly by their emotionally agitated virgin offspring; speculators from New York, gamblers from Kentucky, rice merchants from Charleston and New Orleans with their families, and hundreds of immature fops and dandies promenaded through the halls, listened to the band, and waited for the dining-room doors to be thrown open.

There seem to have been few, if any, young men of the athletic type of the present day. Most of them were coxcombs, aping the style and manners of "young men about town, chiefly remarkable for foppery of dress, and the assumption of beards, mustaches, and other exotic fashions, as if they were either foreigners themselves, or had travelled so long on the Continent of Europe as to bear about them the marks of their sojourn at Rome, Naples, and Paris."

That foppery was characteristic of American men who went into society seems definitely established. In *The Southern Literary Messenger* of May, 1849, under the title "Advice to Young Ladies," we find: "The belle of the day is invariably surrounded by a crowd of fops and flatterers, whose only chance of attracting notice is to flourish in the sphere which her presence illumines. The rules of social intercourse oblige her to receive them civilly: while policy and convenience prompt her to encourage them by particular marks of favor and condescension. They are useful—these exquisites—in their way. They can handle a fan, or a bouquet—they can register engagements for the quadrille—select a box at the opera—have a pretty taste in jewelry and costly books—and sometimes sport fine horses in a new-fangled and dashing equipage. Some can trill opera airs melodiously from beneath a well-dyed moustache; and many more are skilful in the foreign dances; which display to such advantage the voluptuous elegance of form."

Multi-hued raiment for men was not confined to the United States, however. When Lord Palmerston arrived at Osborne after the death of the Prince Consort in 1861, it was with whiskers perfectly dyed "and dressed in a brown overcoat, light gray trousers, green gloves, and blue studs."

Contemporary colored plates in Thackeray's "Pendennis" show young bloods in black frock coats with white cuffs folded back, double-breasted waistcoats of red brocade, green stocks with large pins, green-checked trousers, strapped down to shoes with suede uppers and patent-leather tips.

Bristed in "The Upper Ten Thousand" satirizes these sad young popinjays, but even discounting his exaggerations by fifty per cent, it is hard for us to picture one of them as he must actually have appeared in all his glory. Take for instance "Mr. Edwards, a little man, about five feet and half high. If he could have stood on his bushy black beard it

would have lifted him full three inches higher. Besides this
beard he cherished a small moustache, very elaborately
curling-tonged at the ends into the shape of half a lyre. To
look at his figure you would take him for a boy of nineteen;
to look at his face, for a man of thirty: He was probably,
about half-way between the two ages. Everything about him
was wonderfully neat: a white coat and hat, cream-coloured
waistcoat, and pearl-coloured trousers; miraculously small
feet in resplendent boots, looking more like a doll's extremi-
ties than a man's; a French kid glove on one of his little
hands and on the other a sapphire ring. Then he had a watch-
chain of great balls of blue enamel, with about two pounds
of chatelaine charms dependent therefrom; and delicate little enamelled studs, with sleeve-buttons to match."

When Mr. Edwards went a-riding, "he wore white cord
trousers, a buff waistcoat, and a very natty white hair-cloth
cap. His coat was something between a summer sack and a
cutaway,—the colour, a rich green of some peculiar and indescribable shade. His spurs were very small, but highly polished; and, instead of a whip, he carried a little red cane
with a carved ivory head. In his marvellously-fitting white
buckskin glove he managed a rein of some mysterious substance that looked like a compound of indian-rubber and
sea-weed."

Another of Mr. Bristed's characters appears for breakfast "very flashily got up in a blue cutaway with gilt buttons,
wide blue stripes down the sides of his white trousers, a check
shirt of enormous crimson pattern, and a red and white cra-
vat; no waistcoat, and wide embroidered braces, the work of
some lady friend."

One of the beaux of Saratoga—a professed cosmopolite,
Hunter by name—"carefully eschewed the indigenous habits of dress; and while all the other men appeared at the
balls in dress coats, and black or white cravats, he usually dis-
played a flaming scarlet or blue tie, a short front coat, and
yellow or brown trousers."

Making every allowance for Mr. Bristed's Dickensonian

style these abortive young dandies must have been very wonderful as well as terrible, and the ease with which a sweet young girl could collect about her a coterie of previously unknown young men filled the ever socially alert Mr. N. P. Willis with alarm,—in spite of the fact that the girls and their mammas had come to Saratoga for that very purpose. "The chances are, that not one of them was presented by her father or mother, or by any elderly friend of her family. A game at billiards or a chance fraternization over juleps in the bar-room is, in fact, the easiest and most frequent threshold of introduction to ladies at a watering-place."

Mr. Willis becomes indignant over the miserable plight of "a youth who has habits of self-culture of his own—who neither drinks at the bar, nor lounges in the billiard-room, and is both unwilling to owe the acquaintance of a lady to such a medium, or too proud to seek it and run the risk of a supercilious refusal—and how is this kind of stranger, who is perhaps the most truly valuable acquaintance a young lady could possibly make, to procure a presentation?

"We go back to a principle," he affirms, "that does not apply to society at a watering-place alone, when we say that a young lady should receive no new acquaintance, except through her parents, or through some one properly exercising parental responsibility. It is the fault, in the manners of our country, which, *more than any other, needs correction,* that an acquaintance with a young lady may be begun, and pursued, with little or no inquiry or care as to the wishes of a mother, no cultivation of the mother's friendship, and no attentions to her, whatever, when met, with or without her daughter, in society."

The brilliant author immediately offers the corrective,— a committee on introductions appointed by the manager of the hotel, consisting of six of the "most respectable visitors, to preside generally over the gayeties and social arrangements of the house. It would be convenient if they would allow themselves to be designated by a ribbon in the buttonhole, but, at any rate, their names should be written up in the office of the hotel, and it *should be etiquette for any gentleman or lady to speak to them without an introduction.* Every new comer, in that case, would start, at once, with six accessible acquaintances, or persons inclined to be courteous, with which provision any stranger who had tolerable tact and good manners would find no difficulty in getting on."

Yet *per contra*, Mr. Willis was as against exclusiveness as he was averse to indiscriminate acquaintanceships. He had no use for snobs and thought that hotel life should be just one big happy family; energetically, if somewhat inconsistently, decrying *"the fashionable exclusiveness, exercised so insultingly and tyrannically at American watering-places.* Thousands of most respectable persons avoid Newport and Saratoga, from disgust at the assumption of a few ruling fashionables, their monopoly of everything in the way of privilege, and their systematized plan of creating an exclusive circle."

Perhaps the issue had better be left to the reader after he has been introduced (properly) by Mr. Bristed to the Robinson family of New York, who were among the "upper ten thousand" fashionables at Saratoga in 1850.

"These Robinsons were evidently the leaders in every movement of the fashionables, but why they were so was not so clear. There was a father in some kind of business, who occupied the usual position of New-York fathers; that is to say, he made the money for the rest of the family to spend, and showed himself once a fortnight or so—possibly to pay the bills. There was a mother, stout and good-humoured, rather vulgar, very fussy, and no end of a talker. There were three or four young men, sons and cousins, with the usual amount of white tie and the ordinary dexterity in the polka; and two daughters, both well out of their teens. The knowing ones said that one of these young ladies was to have six thousand a-year by her grandfather's will, and the other little or nothing; but it was not generally understood which was the heiress, and the old lady manœuvred with them as if *both* were. This fact, however, was not suffi-

cient to account for their rank as *belles,* since there were
several other girls in their circle quite as well, or better off.
Nor had their wit or talent any share in giving them their
position; on the contrary, people used to laugh at the *betises*
of the Robinsons, and make them the butt of real or imaginary good stories.

" 'And yet,' said the Englishman, 'these people are your
leaders of fashion. You can't do anything without them.'

" 'As to that,' replied Sedley, 'fashionable society is a
vast absurdity anywhere, and it is only natural that absurd
people should be at the head of it. The Robinsons want to
be fashionable—it is their only ambition—they try hard
for it; and it is generally the case that those who devote
themselves to any pursuit have some success in it, and only
right that it should be so.' "

Which, we may perhaps be permitted to add, is as true
in 1930 as it was in 1850.

Of course it was all of the supremest unimportance. History was not being made at Newport or Saratoga but
along the Mississippi, the Great Lakes and the Ozarks. Columbia's teeming womb was stirring and in the travail of the
Civil War was about to give birth to a great nation. These
superficial aspects of American life of the eastern seaboard
taken by themselves could hardly rate as an indication of
the degree of civilization that America had reached. Yet to
the student of manners they are pregnant with the germs
of characteristics which later influenced the whole trend of
American life. In Mr. Bennett's odious young reporter is
perhaps personified the regard for riches that made Thomas
W. Lawson's "Frenzied Finance" ultimately upset the financial apple cart and caused the voice of Theodore Roosevelt
to echo down the corridors of political history as the big-
game hunter of malefactors of great wealth. We see here
nearly a hundred years ago the same characters, the same
motives, the same self-advertisement and ballyhoo, the same
methods, the same theatrical properties as we do now—save
that the mirrors and spittoons have disappeared and we drink
gin and whiskey in place of claret and Madeira. There is lit-

tle difference in the character of the personnel of what used to be known as "flash" society in the 50's and to-day; not an iota between the drug-store sheik who blows smoke in the face of his girl companions and the vulgar fop of the last century who could gracefully ring a cuspidor ten feet distant through his teeth.

Meantime the plain people in other parts of the country lived their frugal laborious lives and brought up their large families, oblivious to the fact that the great American social "band-wagon" had started. They had other and more vital things to think of. The menace of slavery was dimming the sunlight like the corona of a coming eclipse. With the increase of sectional excitement after 1850 the Southern gentleman bowed rather more stiffly to the New York dandies on the piazzas of Saratoga. The coaches of the rich Georgia planters, when they drove to Newport, carried no more black body servants, for the repeal of the "slave sojournment" laws of Pennsylvania and New York, the Fugitive Slave Act and the passage of the Personal Liberty Laws made it dangerous to bring negroes to the north. And when the new Republican Party came into being in 1856 and declared that slavery was a relic of barbarism the more hotheaded of the Southerners gave up their vacationing altogether. But the fast, flash, cheap life continued at full fling.

"About a million and a half of dollars," said Harper's *Easy Chair* in October, 1857, "are left at Saratoga alone every season for the privilege of doing penance in the cells of its mammoth hotels during the hot weather and grumbling about it during cold weather." A year later: "Saratoga! A caravanserai crowded with rich people, and drinkers and dancers; belles bowling in muslin and flirting in a public parlor; very young men gambling and getting drunk, and sick with tobacco; an army of black waiters manœuvring in the dining hall; people polking themselves into perspirations; a scraggy green square patch with starved Germans tooting on wind instruments after dinner; and people full of ditto languidly toddling around."

But all was not lowbrow or vulgar at Saratoga in the last

mid-century. Far from it! That is, if you were an intellectual, as George William Curtis tells us in "Lotus Eating" (1852). After breakfast, "if you choose, you may sit apart and converse, instead of bowling, upon metaphysics and morals. After dinner the band plays upon the lawn, and we all promenade upon the piazza, or in the walks of the court, or sit at the parlor windows. We discuss the new arrivals. We criticise dresses, and styles, and manners. We discriminate the arctic and antarctic Bostonians, fair, still, and stately, with a vein of scorn in their Saratoga enjoyment, and the languid, cordial, and careless Southerners, far from precise in dress or style, but balmy in manner as a bland southern morning. We mark the crisp courtesy of the New Yorker, elegant in dress, exclusive in association, a pallid ghost of Paris—without its easy elegance, its *bonhommie*, its gracious *savoir faire*, without the *spirituel* sparkle of its conversation, and its natural and elastic grace of style. We find that a Parisian toilette is not France, nor grace, nor fascination. We discover that exclusiveness is not elegance."

In spite of all this elegance and gracious *savoir faire*, everybody in those days got up between six and seven o'clock and by half past seven the drawing rooms were already filled with two or three hundred guests waiting for the dining-room doors to open. Breakfast was hearty and, according to Mr. Buchanan, was practically swallowed whole by the ravenous guests, "the longest time taken by the slowest being never more than 15 minutes, some of the quickest getting through the meal in 5 minutes, and the average number occupying about 10.

"Elegance of manners," he sadly reflects, "in such a scene as this is quite out of the question. People eat as if they were afraid that their plates were about to be snatched from them before they had done; mastication may be said to be almost entirely omitted; and in nine cases out of ten, persons do not remain in their chairs to finish the meal, short as it is, but rise with the last mouthful still unswallowed, and dispose of it gradually as they walk along."

Then came a promenade to the springs, polka in the drawing rooms, bowling, with frequent visits to the bar-room on the part of the gentlemen, billiards and gossip until it was time to dress for two o'clock dinner, when "the hurry and bustle of the breakfast scene are again repeated, with little of table enjoyment to reconcile the parties to the heat and noise of the room. The fare is coarse and bad, the dishes few in number, and wretchedly cooked, besides being all lukewarm; and the miserable sprinkling of bad vegetables being almost as cold as if they had been dressed on the preceding day; no covers for the dishes or warm plates for the guests; no appointed carvers; an insufficiency of attendants; and, altogether, an ill-managed and an ill-enjoyed dinner." Moreover, "the bedrooms were generally exceedingly small, scantily provided, and altogether inferior to what the scale and style of the house, in other respects, would warrant the visitor to expect."

In short the board was not worth the $2 per day that the swells paid for it. But nobody cared, for the band played and the belles and dandies skipped about the drawing rooms "polking," and everybody dressed up at least thrice every day and promenaded past the spitting Southern colonels, and chatted and gossipped and flirted and danced until two o'clock in the morning, and got "engaged" and—

Then one April morning in 1861 the boom of the guns from Fort Sumter and Fort Moultrie told the young bloods of Charleston that there would be no social season at Saratoga that summer.

# CHAPTER XII

## Puritans and Cavaliers

IT was into a brash, bombastic, Yankee world of chandeliers and mirrors, spittoons and white gloves, of "side whiskers and sentimentality," that my Puritan father, now a prominent country lawyer and politician of forty-two years, was projected from the quiet village of Framingham by his election as a Republican representative to the Thirty-sixth and Thirty-seventh Congresses, which sat from March 4, 1859, to March 3, 1863. He had already been a delegate, along with other Puritans and near-Puritans, to the first National Convention of the Republican Party, held in Philadelphia in 1856, which nominated John C. Frémont, "The Pathfinder," for President, and where Abraham Lincoln of Illinois, who had assisted in launching the new party at the preceding Bloomington Convention, had received 110 votes for the vice-presidential nomination.

Fate could not have selected a more tempestuous moment for my father's political début. Slavery was already the paramount issue, inextricably entwined with all other issues however irrelevant in appearance. During the preceding ten years its shadow had grown black and menacing as a thundercloud; already the lightning had begun to play and distant mutterings were to be plainly heard.

John Brown had been executed on December 2, while the newly elected representatives were assembling, and the first Congress to organize in the recently completed marble wings of the Capitol convened two days later while his body was being lowered into its grave. From the start it was a turbulent session, given over to abusive oratory, threats of violence, recriminations, challenges upon points of honor, the lie both circumstantial and direct. The Southern members charged the Republicans with responsibility for John Brown's raid, and were not unjustified by appearances. Indeed, it was generally believed in the South that Seward had been directly implicated in it. Ex-President John Tyler writing to his son on December 6 said: "Virginia is arming to the teeth. . . . But one sentiment pervades the country: security *in the Union,* or separation. I fear the debates in Congress, and, above all, the speaker's election. If excitement prevails in Congress it will add fuel to the flame which already burns so terrifically."

The physical arrangement of the new hall contributed to the tension, for the desks and chairs had been moved out and benches substituted, so disposed about the speaker's rostrum as to occupy the smallest possible space consistent with comfort. This close physical juxtaposition undoubtedly added to the heat of the debates, and the proceedings were continually interrupted by brawls, hisses and shouts of "treason," "liar," "perjurer" and challenges to fight, which the challenged either refused or check-mated by selecting weapons unsatisfactory to the challenger, such as bowie knives, or rifles loaded with buck-shot.

The sentiment in the North was strongly against duelling, and while the Northern men very generally carried arms, they knew that they would have small chance against experts skilled in the code of honor and with the use of the long, silver-mounted, hair-triggered weapons that reposed in their rosewood boxes on most Southern mantelpieces.

Not only were the members of both sides supposed to be "heeled," but it was commonly reported that they also had friends similarly armed in the galleries. Senator Hammond wrote: "I believe every man in both houses is armed with a revolver—some with two—and a bowie-knife."

I take it that Senator Hammond must have been something of an alarmist. I do not believe my father carried a gun or any knife larger than the jack-knife he used for cutting the plug tobacco which he, in common with the Southern members, habitually chewed. But I have no doubt that he was badly scared. His letters indicate that at this time he would not have been loath to surrender any dreams of political distinction which he might have had before coming to Washington.

He wrote to his friend James W. Clark (December 15, 1859):

"I don't like Washington; it is a mere caravansary without character, or permanency, as it seems to me, and my opinion of those whom the world calls great, has gone through as many mutations as your own. There are here some men of ability and fine attainments, but they are exceedingly rare. The House of Representatives is a mere unorganized mob, and the discussions which have all been on the Democratic side, do not come up to Massachusetts stump speeches. Some of the members are drunk and some not, but all imagine that they must indulge in the same blatant nonsense in denunciation of Republicans and abolitionists, and laudation of niggers and southern interests.

"We sit from four to six hours and it is tiresome work. The proceedings were enlivened last week with the scrimmage of Crawford of Georgia and Kellogg and Logan of Illinois which created a temporary excitement and ill feeling. This has all died away and we go on without any fuss. While you would imagine from the papers that we are all ready to cut each others throats, we are making each others acquaintance and waiting for the good time coming. I think it cannot be denied, however, that a single imprudent act on the part of the Republicans would precipitate a fight on the floor, which would at once envelope us in a civil war, which would end in the extinction of slavery and probably of the south. This is the reason we have refused to participate in any debate until after the organization. The clerk has no power except that of putting questions to the house. We have no Sergeant at Arms, and everything depends upon the comity of members. We shall by and by elect Sherman and go on with the business. In case of a fight, I shall be found after it is over among the slain, for my seat is in the arena near the speaker's desk and I cannot get away if I would, but I anticipate none.

"I am afraid now that we shall not organize so that I can be at home at Christmas, which I should regard as a calamity. How I wish to see my wife and babies I can't tell. There is more comfort at home in five minutes, than here in a session."

Although the Republicans had a plurality they lacked a majority and could not organize and elect a speaker without support, and the House, as my father had feared, did remain in session between Christmas and New Year's, and not until January 30, 1860, was a speaker elected on the forty-fourth ballot.

Four weeks later Abraham Lincoln, the possibility of whose nomination for president had theretofore been treated as a joke, delivered at Cooper Union in New York the speech that introduced him to the country at large as a commanding figure, and on May 18 the Republican National Convention chose him over Seward. Threats of disunion were rife. Repeatedly upon the floor of the House Southern members declared: "We will never submit to the inauguration of a Black Republican president!"

Yet such threats were not new either. Twenty years before, Philip Hone had noted:

"Another sign has been exhibited in the House of Representatives; another movement toward the accomplishment of my recent melancholy prediction. That indomitable, pugnacious, wonderful man of knowledge, without tact, John Quincy Adams, has presented a petition from some people in Haverhill, Mass., praying for a separation of the Union, as the only means of obtaining the right of petition, the maintenance of which they consider of more importance than the union of the States. A monstrous doctrine, the very whispering of which has a sound as of thunder, more awful than that of foreign war! But, after all, it is precisely the same threat, founded on better ground, as that made by the Southern anti-tariff nullifiers; but now that the brat is born of

Northern parents, these patriotic hotspurs are horrified beyond all example; their indignation knows no bounds. 'Treason!' "

The Massachusetts delegation to the House of Representatives numbered among its members Charles Francis Adams, Henry L. Dawes, and Alexander H. Rice, afterwards Governor of Massachusetts. The senators were Charles Sumner and Henry Wilson. My father served upon the so-called Covode Committee, appointed in March, 1860, to investigate the abuses alleged against the President and his immediate circle, which after three months of secret hearings amassed evidence of a shocking amount of corruption, now only of interest as disclosing methods of repaying contributions to campaign deficits similar to those used later during the Harding administration. The report, submitted by him, did not, however, formally propose the impeachment or censure of anyone and to-day the Covode Committee is not only generally forgotten but its name is not even mentioned in the leading histories of the time. In view of the grossness of the scandals unearthed, which included the compulsory assessment of officeholders, the bartering of contracts and blatant jobbery of every kind, the fact that no action was taken is significant, indicating an unwillingness to raise an issue which might precipitate a conflict resulting in the disruption of the Union.

What part, if any, my father took in the campaign resulting in Lincoln's election I do not know. I have no record of his activities between the adjournment of the first session of the Thirty-sixth Congress, on June 25, 1860, until it reconvened for its second session on December 3. Lincoln's election had occurred on November 6, 1860, but already, for over a month, the movement towards secession backed by armed resistance had assumed a definite and organized form with the active support of the governors and officials of the Southern states, many United States Senators, Representatives in Congress, and three members of President Buchanan's cabinet.

The possibility of saving the Union from disruption was the sole topic debated. The flames of sectionalism had heated the boiler of the war engine until it was ready to burst at any moment.

Meantime the commissioners from South Carolina had arrived in Washington and sought audience with President Buchanan. The poor old man was at his wits' end what to do. In his message of December 4 to the re-assembled Congress he had said: "The question fairly stated is: 'Has the Constitution delegated to Congress the power to coerce a State into submission which is attempting to withdraw, or has actually withdrawn, from the Confederacy?' "

As to which Mr. Seward remarked: "I think the President has proved two things: That no State has the right to secede unless it wishes to; and that it is the President's duty to enforce the laws unless somebody opposes him."

Buchanan was in fact a broken-down old gentleman whom many persons considered senile, although this last was far from being the case. General Benjamin F. Butler urgently advised the President to have the commissioners hanged, "but [to quote Butler in "Butler's Book"] to say that he was astounded at the boldness of the proposition would be but a feeble description of his condition of mind and body."

Butler was well known as a Democrat and had many friends in Washington. One night after dinner, one of these took him for a walk and showed him a long, low, dimly lighted building near the present British Legation.

"He took me," says Butler, "to the further end of one of them and there, looking through a small aperture which I reached by standing upon a keg, I saw from seventy-five to one hundred men drilling with arms.

"I stepped down and said: 'Well, what is all this about?'

" 'We are getting ready for the fourth of March,' said he.

" 'Drilling a company of the district militia to escort Lincoln?'

" 'Yes,' said he with a laugh. 'They may escort Lincoln, but I guess not in the direction of the White House.'

"I looked at him and said: 'You are not in earnest.'

" 'Never more in earnest in my life. We don't intend to have the black Republican —— inaugurated to rule over us here in Washington.' "

The electoral votes were counted on February 13, 1861, and Lincoln was declared elected. Seward wrote: "Treason is all around and among us, and plots to seize the Capitol and usurp the Government." He was told "that there are two thousand armed conspirators in the city, and the mayor is secretly with them." The Richmond *Enquirer* on December 25 had demanded: "Can there not be found men bold and brave enough in Maryland to unite with Virginians in seizing the Capitol at Washington?"

Nathan Crosby, a prominent citizen of Lowell, Mass., had written my father on January 29, 1861:

"It seems to me a dream and I am writing in a dream. What is now to be done? I am only stating my leading thoughts and points of anxiety. It is that Washington be kept from revolt, or capture at all hazards and costs. Our northern passenger steamers should be brought into the Potomac filled with our soldiers, who are impatient to go with ammunition and rations to lay quietly there until the danger be past and Lincoln's administration started.

"I am afraid of your Mayor's arrangements and his men, and so I should be of any soldiers in Maryland. Flood the River and the region with loyal men from the west and north with provisions and boats so that a quick locomotion could be given to them.

"The border states will not join in the crusade and their only hope will be in possessing the city with its officers, capital, archives. This will give them the government in view of the nations, and without them I think we are lost. We should lose our prestige of government, our navy and army would follow. We should have no rolls of officers or men to try no one for treason; no records, no power, nothing! They would establish a provincial government. . . .

"Everything depends on keeping the city.

"Now, if Buchanan will not and Scott will not or cannot hold it, the Republicans at Washington should form a committee of safety; * * * if the compromise is not satisfactory to the south, my fear is that a row will follow, which will end in the abdication of Buchanan and a provincial government established, or thousands of men in arms will run in, seize the city, and martial law be proclaimed until national government is established.

"My dear sir, I have written in the greatest haste in the midst of a long civil trial so as not to miss another day's mail.

"Ponder and answer as you may find occasion.

Yours truly,<br>N. Crosby."

Lincoln started on February 15 for Washington by a circuitous route two days after the official declaration of his election, making many speeches which "had better not have been delivered. The journey," Rhodes declares, "can only be looked upon as a sad failure." The general opinion was that this man, who was faced with a task greater, as he himself said, than that which rested upon Washington, was a "Simple Susan." Yet he was greeted everywhere with enthusiasm.

A friend of my father's, Mr. Robert B. Caverly, wrote to him on February 18, as follows:

"Albany,
　Feb. 18, 1861.
"Dear Train:
"Having a moment's leisure at this locality I write to you. Old Abe has just now been received here. His journey to the Capital is to be a success. The people are rising in mass, —the further he goes the greater will be the numbers. At this place there were at least 15,000 in the crowd. The Park at the Capital here was every inch of it packed and all the trees were filled with living beings. If you have not seen Lincoln you will be disappointed at seeing him; with his

present heavy beard he is really a noble looking man. His likenesses are decidedly a mistake. In every state through which I have passed I have not failed to hear men say they did not vote for Lincoln, but that they intended to support him, that they think he will be an honest President, etc. They go in for 'defending the Constitution as it is, and enforcing the laws as they are.' I suppose Congress will make all possible speed in providing for an increase in the army, etc. and in doing all other necessary things to evince to the world that this is a government not always to be sneered at and trifled with. Some of our Republicans begin to distrust Seward, but for myself, I have no doubt but that in all his votes, etc., he will be entirely right 'on the goose.' From what I saw and heard on my journey, I am led to believe that the border states could not be hired to go out of the Union. Why then, should we pay them anything in the way of 'compromise' to keep them in? We owe them nothing and the people in all the rural districts in this latitude may be set down as unanimous against any compromise and in favor of a rigid and decisive enforcement of the laws.

"Hoping that you will be instrumental in doing much good to the nation at this eventful crisis; as the people out west say to 'Old Abe' 'You shall have our prayers.'

In haste,<br>
Truly your friend,<br>
Robert B. Caverly."

This letter is interesting not only for its picturesqueness but for the curious and now obsolete use of the word "disappointed" and the phrase regarding Seward's being "entirely right 'on the goose,' " a jocular reference possibly to the ritual of some semi-secret political organization like the "Know Nothings," such as "riding the goat," or to some situation in the "Royal Game of the Goose" utilized for the teaching of arithmetic in my father's childhood. It is interesting to note Mr. Caverly's awe at 15,000 people being massed in the park of the Albany Capitol, in view of the 142,000 estimated to have listened to "Al" Smith's speech of acceptance there in 1928.

Lincoln was duly inaugurated on March 4. Fort Sumter surrendered on April 14. From that date, until the arrival of the Eighth Massachusetts and the Seventh New York regiments on April 27, the President greatly feared the capture of the city. Why it was not taken between April 12 and April 25 is still a subject of military debate, for Jefferson Davis had, under General Beauregard near Charleston, four or five thousand well-drilled troops which was a greater force than could have been assembled anywhere else in the United States within ten days. He could have cut the wires to Washington and rushed 4,000 men by rail across North Carolina, through Virginia and over Long Bridge in thirty-six hours, with practically no opposition. "The prize to be won," as Butler says, "was gloriously magnificent. The capitol of the nation, with its archives, its records and its treasures, and all of its executive organization was there." He might even have captured Lincoln and his secretaries, for their only hope would have been in a flight by sea to Philadelphia, and there was no vessel to utilize for their escape.

Lincoln had issued his proclamation asking for 75,000 volunteers for three months on April 15. "The North had sprung to arms but there were no arms." An incredible state of unpreparedness existed everywhere, in south as well as north. The North had no rifles; the South no powder. Even on July 1 the total strength of the Union Army was 186,000 of which but 30,000, in wretched condition, were available for the defense of Washington. Yet already, to quote John Ford Rhodes, the cry of "On to Richmond" was heard everywhere and Lincoln, yielding at last to popular clamor, consented to allow the forcing of a battle.

On Sunday, July 21, 1861, McDowell's "Grand Army" of 30,000 was routed by Beauregard and Johnston at Bull Run. Lincoln received a dispatch reading: "General McDowell's army in full retreat towards Centreville. The day

is lost. Save Washington and the remnants of the army.
. . . The routed troops will not reform." Hope of taking
Richmond, says the historian, gave place to fears of losing
Washington. It was widely believed and emphatically as-
serted by many in the North that the defeat of the army
was due to the fact that the attack *had been made on Sunday*.
Puritanism still operated through a literal interpretation of
the Jewish Scriptures in 1861!

And then the North and the South girded their loins for
what was clearly to be a lengthy struggle. The irrepressible
conflict had come.

There is nothing in the little leather box containing my
father's literary remains relating to the progress of the War
until the summer of 1862. During the intervening period
McClellan had for four months dallied and hesitated, failing to take advantage of Grant's brilliant victory at Fort
Donelson in February by marching on Richmond; in March
the *Merrimac* had thrown consternation into the Union
Fleet, and Secretary Stanton had had a bad quarter of an
hour during which he feared lest the "horrible marine Chi-
mera" might take Fort Monroe and bombard Washington;
Lincoln had given an unparalleled exhibition of patience
waiting for McClellan to do something, only to see him
driven back from within sight of the spires of the Confederate capitol, the Peninsula Campaign a failure.

July and August, 1862, to continue to paraphrase Rhodes,
were months of depression. Had it not been for Lincoln the
North might have abandoned the contest. But the President
had no thought of allowing those already dead to have died
in vain. His July 1 call for 300,000 three-year men was received with enthusiasm and the singing of "We are coming,
Father Abraham, three hundred thousand more." Too many
military cooks were spoiling the campaign of the Army of
the Potomac. Halleck, Pope, Lincoln, Stanton, Chase and
McClellan—all had fingers in it. Then Jackson slipped behind Pope, severed all his communications with Washington,
and smashed him at the Second Battle of Bull Run. Halleck
ordered Pope's demoralized army back to the trenches about

the city and because of the "great danger to Washington" called for troops and gunboats to reenforce the Capital. All clerks and employees in the civil departments and in the public buildings were put under arms. Lincoln, greatly distressed, offered to resign his office, but, against strong opposition in his cabinet, relieved Pope and reinstated McClellan. At that moment came the news that Lee was leading his army across the Potomac into Maryland. The fate of Washington wavered in the balance.

Congress had adjourned on July 17, 1862, after having sat continuously from December 2, 1861, for two hundred and twenty-eight days, and my father had returned home to Framingham. But the national crisis did not permit of his remaining there. An able-bodied man of forty-five, he could not, even if charged with heavy public responsibilities that would soon recall him from the field, refrain from throwing himself into the struggle. So he bade his wife and five children good-bye and started back to Washington, arriving there on September 2 at one of the darkest moments of the war.

His diary from September 2, 1862, to November 10, 1862, jotted down in pencil on horseback, train and at the camp fire, lies before me now. It is hardly decipherable, but such parts of it as are legible furnish a vivid, if fragmentary, picture. His friend Brig.-Gen. George A. Gordon had been commanding a division under Pope in the Army of the Potomac, and was among those who reached the city on September 2 after the Second Battle of Bull Run. The first entry in the diary reads:

"Sept. 2. Met Gordon just in from the Pope Campaign on the Rappahanock, and volunteered on his staff. Saw Secretary of War about a Commission."

He wrote to his wife in Framingham:

"Washington
September 3, 1862.

"Dear Wife:
We did not arrive until nine o'clock last evening being detained on the road by multitudinous trains packed with

troops and freight. We got nothing but cold vittals to eat, and Rice and I slept together at the house on the street where Mr. Seward lives for want of a room at the hotel. Today I have been looking after the wounded and sick and helped Mr. Abbott in returning the body of Fletcher Webster to Boston. He was found on the field after the battle stripped of all his clothes. . . . General Gordon I saw for a few moments. He has not been undressed for fifteen days. Banks is sick, but not seriously. Pope's campaign has been a failure, and we are today worse off than we were at the commencement of the rebellion. Our army is now safe in the intrenchment front of the city, and the next you will hear of Stonewall Jackson will be across the Potomac. *But!* we will whip them yet. My valise has not yet come and I am wearing a borrowed shirt. Expect me home when you see me.

"Much love to all,      Yours in haste,      Charles."

On September 4, after having conferred with both the President and the Secretary of War, he received his commission and made his preparations to leave for the battle front.

"Willards Hotel,
     September 4, 1864.
My dear Wife:
"I wrote you a hurried letter yesterday. Today has changed all my plans. Gordon came in all worn out, and without a staff officer left. Of course, I at once volunteered to go on his staff and give him all the aid in my power. I did not wish to join him except in a military capacity, because if I should happen to be captured I could not be exchanged as a civilian. I at once went to the President and he gave me a commission as Captain and assigned me to Gordon's brigade. I have bought me a Buffalo robe, woolen drawers, four flannel shirts, one half dozen woolen socks, pair of blankets, and leave for the field tomorrow morning.

I shall be detained until Gordon's staff are able to rejoin him, perhaps a month. I am at liberty to leave at any time, as I volunteered, work without pay, and bear my own expenses. Banks is here sick, but hopes to go on tomorrow. If he does I shall go with him; if not, I shall go alone.

"My dear Martha, we are in an awful condition the only comfort I have is that there can be nothing worse. Pope is an imbicile—But we shall come out right yet. Don't tell our friends what I say. Lincoln is a fool, Stanton an ass, ——— a corrupt scoundrel, and Smith and Blair haven't brains enough to drive an omnibus. Bates isn't fit for a nurse.

"Kiss the children. May the Lord have you in his holy keeping is the prayer of your devoted husband,

Charles R. Train."

Lee had marched into Maryland, since, as he could not invest the fortifications about Washington, he must either fall back to a better base or cross the Potomac and "give the people of Maryland a chance of liberating themselves."

Singing "Maryland, My Maryland" the Army of Northern Virginia, led by Stonewall Jackson, had reached Frederick City on September 6. In the North all was consternation. Washington, Baltimore, Harrisburg and Philadelphia were panic-stricken. Leaving Frederick City where he had found but a cold reception Lee divided his army and sent Jackson back to capture Harpers Ferry, while he himself continued towards Hagerstown. Unfortunately for the South a written order disclosing the division of his forces was found and placed in the hands of McClellan, who at once threw his army forward. Lee, apprehensive of McClellan's rapid advance, turned aside from Hagerstown and after vainly attempting to hold the passes of South Mountain took up his position behind Antietam Creek. My father had joined Gordon, whose brigade had expected to remain over Sunday at Frederick, but in consequence of McClellan's decision to take advantage of the division of Lee's army it was ordered forward to near Middletown. Here the men could watch

the progress of the battle of South Mountain. It was my father's first experience of actual warfare and its effect is reflected in his diary. He had been violently ill almost as soon
as he had reached the front, from an intestinal attack, but
had recovered by September 13. The diary reads:

"September 13th—
Marched on Frederick. Camped at twelve o'clock and
rode into the town with Gordon. This is a very old town,
oaks, great wealth and comfort. Made several calls with
Gordon. The people are very glad to see us; like Gordon,
and are very hospitable. Saw Mrs. McPherson and daughter, a very interesting girl. Arranged to go to Church.

"September 14th—
Instead of going to Church as we had arranged ordered
to march. We had a magnificent reception as we came
through Frederick. The houses decorated with flags; ladies
waving their handkerchiefs, throwing their arms around Mc-
Clellan; kissing McClellan; gave us water to drink, and one
lady gave Gordon a bouquet of flowers. Maryland is un-
mistakably loyal. All day on the route. In sight of battle of
South Mountain. Saw cannonading on the ridge. R——
killed,—a clear suicide, ought not to have rushed to the
front and exposed himself. This is the first of a series of
victories. Slept on the ground and dreamed of gifts from
home; thread, needles, etc. I wish I could see the dear ones
at home and hug them all.

"September 15th—
Went to battlefield in the morning with Gordon. The
dead lying in heaps. It is dreadful. Saw a man on the fence,
another on his knees. The men fall in their tracks and don't
change a muscle."
He returned that day with General Gordon to Washington, where he notes that he "left two shirts, one woolen
shirt, three collars, one pair of socks to be washed." Evi-

dently the business which took them there was quickly disposed of for he is back at the front again next morning.

Lee's advance into Maryland had been checked. McClellan was in control of South Mountain and it seems to be the consensus of military opinion that he should have fallen upon his weaker adversary at once, on the 15th, and crushed him before Jackson could come up. But he characteristically allowed his passion for absolute preparation nearly to deprive him of his advantage.

McClellan began in the afternoon by sending Hooker across the creek, where a preliminary skirmish lasting until dark showed Lee where the main advance would occur next day. "The bloodiest single day of fighting in the war," as Longstreet called it, followed. "Never," says Rhodes, "was the horror of a civil war given more ghastly demonstration than on this border battlefield, where members of the same families and life-long friends were arrayed against one another." The carnage was fearful, although it was, according to General Francis A. Walker, "a day of isolated attacks and wasted efforts."

By some curious chance General Gordon's draft report of the battle to General A. S. Williams is among my father's papers. He describes it as a "bloody and obstinate" contest. "From sunrise to sunset the waves of battle ebbed and flowed. Men wrestled with each other in lines of Regiments, Brigades and Divisions, while regiment, brigade and division faded away under a terrible fire leaving long lines of dead to mark where stood the living.—We slept," he writes, "upon the bloody field of our victory."

My father fought throughout the day, carrying dispatches under fire. "I owe especial thanks," reports General Gordon, "to the Hon. Charles R. Train, who volunteered his services on my staff at a time when a fatiguing labor and a most arduous service had deprived me of all aids save one officer. This gentleman also, has shown his willingness to lay down his life in his country's cause. The invasion of the loyal North called him from his congressional duties and his home at a moment's notice. No fatigue though excessive, no danger though most perilous deterred him from moving forward whenever he could render assistance in beating back the invading foe."

The diary reads:

"September 16th—
Marched on the enemy. Halted until dark, then to the front and slept on our arrival at three a. m.

"September 17th—
Heavy cannonading at daybreak all along the line extending some nine miles. We went on to the fight as soon as we could eat,—Second Mass., 3rd Wisconsin, 27th Indiana, 13th New York, 107th New York. Oh God! Oh God! What sights and sounds. I went in rear of the left wing, Gordon making a most rash but magnificent charge. Wasn't killed, thank God! We were separated in the confusion and did not find ourselves for three hours. We cried when we met. At dark we had driven the enemy back the whole line and lay behind our battery.

"September 18th—
Buried our dead.

"September 19th—
The enemy have left during the night. Rode over into their lines. The stink is awful. I vomited an hour. They have not buried their dead. I vomited an hour and thought I should die. Went to all the hospitals and to B—— to take care of Dwight. Arrived in time to see him die. A good and brave man. Gordon sends me to Frederick to telegraph. Will leave to go to Washington—if I can get there. Met Dennis W. T. He turned back with me, and Childs took my horse, and I rode on the carriage. Major Jones gave us a chair in his car and I reached Washington at ten a. m."

Lee had retreated across the Potomac into Virginia, his army a "horde of disordered fugitives." The North once more breathed freely. The victory of Antietam, if it had really been a victory, inspired the Union leaders with renewed hope. Lee was not invincible, after all. Maryland's loyalty had been demonstrated, and no longer apprehensive that his act would be construed as a last card played in despair, Lincoln on September 23, 1862, issued his Emancipation Proclamation.

§

While the descendants of the Puritans and Cavaliers were dying to save or to break the Union of the States, were starving in prison camps or suffering in hospitals that lacked even the roughest comforts for the wounded, there were countless others to whom the war meant nothing more than mere excitement, an excuse for laxity in conduct and the chance to make more money.

The temptation to draw parallels is well nigh irresistible. We, who have for ten years watched the results upon America of the World War, may perhaps be viewed leniently if we tend to find that consequences not dissimilar followed other conflicts in prior eras. The United States has been through three great wars, all of which profoundly affected its economic and social life. The Revolution had resulted in a notable and widespread impatience, particularly in the larger towns of New England, with the stricter expressions of Puritanism, but the economic effect of the war with England upon the people was quite different from that of either the War of the Rebellion or the World War. It left the country impoverished; while the two latter did not. On the contrary they enriched large numbers of people in all classes from bounty-jumpers to middlemen and manufacturers.

The Civil War, even while it was in progress, resulted in a wave of material prosperity, particularly in New York City. As Boston during the Revolution had its Tories; so New York during the Rebellion had its thousands of "Copper Heads," as Southern sympathizers were called. The city was "rank secessionist," semi-officially antipathetic to the Union cause, the State remaining 18,000 men shy on its quota to the end of the war. Early in 1861 Mayor Fernando Wood had proposed a resolution in the Common Council that New York should secede from the Union and become a free and independent city under the name of "Tri-Insular,"—from the fact that it occupied parts of the three islands of Long, Staten and Manhattan; and Governor Seward's disinclination and delay in asking for troops to put down the draft riots, which could have otherwise been ended in twenty-four hours, had resulted in the loss of over a thousand lives. Had it not been for the bravery of Col. O'Brien, who was murdered and mutilated after Indian fashion by the mob, and his Eleventh New York Volunteers the 5,000 rioters might have burned the city. This was in 1863, when after a year or two of abstinence from balls, theatres, card parties, the war had become a bore and the inhabitants, many of whom had grown wealthy in the meanwhile, had returned with zest to their social entertainments.

The New York *Herald* of February 1, 1863, asserted: "War and high prices could not terrify the Gothamites, as long as life remained in them they would keep up their reputation for jollity and good fellowship." Among these jolly Gothamites was one Mr. Ward McAllister concerning whom something will be said later. The same thing was equally true of Washington after the first two years of suspense were over. F. W. Seward, who was Assistant Secretary of State, wrote to a friend towards the end of 1863:

"Gayety has become as epidemic in Washington this winter as gloom was last winter. There is a lull in political discussion; and people are inclined to eat, drink, and be merry. The newspapers can furnish nothing more interesting to their readers than accounts of parties, balls, and theaters, like so many court journals. Questions of etiquette are debated with gravity. People talk of 'society' who never before knew or cared about it. A year ago the secretary of state was 'heartless' or 'unpatriotic' because he gave dinners; now the only complaint of him is that he don't have dancing. It is a sign of a changed state of feeling everywhere, that all the Northern cities have given up mourning and grumbling and are devoting themselves to festivities and fairs."

A correspondent of the Springfield *Republican* on February 20, 1864, declared that "a soldier in the Army of the Potomac does not endure a severer strain on his constitution than a woman in 'society' in Washington. I don't believe that he is as utterly worn out at the end of a march as she at the close of a week of the 'season.' Think of it, shopping, dressing, calling, all day; parties, dancing, late suppers, late sleep, repeated week after week. At present Washington is mad with gayety, reeling in the whirl of dissipation, before it sits down to repent in the ashes of Lent. There are three or four grand parties a night; theaters, operas, fairs, everything to make its denizens forget that war and sorrow are in the land."

Incidentally this state of affairs was not confined to the North. Extravagance, gaiety, and vice were rife in Richmond in 1863 and 1864. The Richmond *Dispatch* of April 13, 1863, said: "The greed of gain now so prevalent in the Southern Confederacy is more wicked and infamous than the same vile passion in Yankee hearts," and an officer wrote six months later, "the demon of gain and the love of filthy lucre has seized the hearts and souls of our people." Balls and "hops," public and private, were frequent and one editor, who called attention to the fact that five dances were being given when flour was $125 a barrel, ended his diatribe against the prevailing prodigality with "On with the dance! Who prates of famine and want?" Diamonds, silks, laces, gloves and ribbons were in great demand. The city was "wide open," and swarmed with gamblers, prostitutes, thieves, while noon-day murders and hold-ups, in addition to drunken brawls, occurred in the open streets, and forty gambling halls absorbed not private fortunes but public funds.

In New York, according to David Emerson Fite to whom I am indebted for the foregoing citations, the opera and thea-

tres played to packed audiences, while there were no less than
three houses in the city devoted to "black-face" comedians;
there was a pronounced revival in the interest in horse racing,
enormous purses were offered, and huge amounts of money
changed hands on the results; there was an unprecedented
demand for pearls, diamonds, camel's hair shawls, Brussels
and velvet carpets, and imported dresses; billiard matches
were played for $1,000 per side; while prize fighting became
almost a national sport in spite of the fact that the combatants
usually hailed from Ireland.

The summer resorts were as crowded as if there were
no war in progress. Compare the following description of
Saratoga in the Boston *Journal* of 1864 with what went on
in Palm Beach during the World War:

"Of fashions here there is no end. Indeed it makes one's
heart sick to see the folly which reigns triumphant. Dancing,
dressing, and flirtation are the chief diets of men, women,
and children (if there be such creatures as the latter nowa-
days). One would hardly think after gazing on a $4000
dress 'just from Europe' on a woman professing to be a patriotic American, that the Sanitary Commission was in need
of stores and that the country's heart was being torn asun-
der. Girls, none too young to be in the nursery, make their
three or four toilettes a day, having hats and gloves for each
dress, and assume affectations that would disgrace an actress
at the Bowery. In flirtation the married women are decidedly the most *au fait;* in fact, from the manner of a certain
set of New York fashionables, one would suppose that he
had dropped into one of the Spas of Europe. Shoddy seems
to be preeminent, and there are government officials here
who are doing their best to aggravate the evil that is now
cursing the land. Honest men may make money out of the
government, but no man who has any respect for himself or
regard for his country will revel at Saratoga when the times
demand sobriety and economy. What the women spend in
dress, the men spend in 'liquoring up,' until they can't stand,
in horses and in gambling. The 'Hell' here is very elegantly

kept up and patronized by gentlemen. We heard of several young men in society who 'fought the tiger' so persistently as to be (using the elegant vernacular of the place) entirely 'cleaned out,' and obliged to borrow of the bank to get home. One gentleman lost $1000 in one evening with the greatest nonchalance. Surely we are improving on the morals of our Puritan fathers. The races attracted nearly all the sporting community of the country."

Everybody had money, and all were in a hurry to spend it,—"Easy come, easy go!" The newly rich wanted to get their money's worth. They sought it on the social band wagon, which prior to the war had been more or less retarded by Puritan and Dutch conservatism but which now, with the profiteers harnessed in the traces and satisfied that money could get them anywhere, started merrily on its way.

The end of the Rebellion marked the end of an era. The struggle henceforth was not between Puritan and Cavalier, but between Puritanism and Mammon.

## CHAPTER XIII

# The "Dreadful Decade"

## 1865–1875

FOR nearly a decade Mammon had the upper hand.
The great convulsion of the Civil War deflated the
enthusiasm of the reformers and marked the end of
the self-denying and renunciatory period of upward striving;
and, like all wars, the Civil War was followed by a wave of
hysteria in which ideals and pruderies were alike forgotten,
and vulgarity and carnality, political bribery and corporate
crime held sway. Speculation, aided by the inflation of the
currency, was rampant in real estate, railroads and industry.
Wall Street was filled with giant gamblers, and the money
made there was lavishly and often corruptly spent.

"As the nation turned aside from whatever idealism there
had been in the war," says James Truslow Adams in his brilliant study of "The Adams Family," "it was to throw itself
into an insane rush for power—money, land, mines, politics,
railroads, any form of control that would lead to power for
the individual. No one appeared to have any idea what he
was going to do with wealth and power when he got it. There
was merely a mad urge to get it. There was no time to think,
or someone would get it first. The opportunities were stupendous and life was short."

It was the era of piratical railroading, of "Jubilee Jim"
Fisk, "Uncle" Daniel Drew, Jay Gould, the Grant and Ward
failure, the Beecher-Tilton trial, and a bitter radicalism intensified by the horror of city slums like "The Five Points."
The North was still suffering from war shock, the South was
prostrate in the throes of Reconstruction, in Washington the
President was under impeachment, in New York Boss Tweed
was looting the city treasury protected by his pocket judges,

while the "Black Horse Cavalry" rode roughshod over the legislature at Albany. Society, under its veneer of cant, hypocritically turned its eyes away from the gaudy gambling houses and brothels of East Fourteenth Street where its sons and husbands spent their evenings.

The prostitutes who had followed the army swarmed throughout the town, although it is hardly credible, as openly stated by Bishop Stimson at Cooper Institute in 1866, that they equalled the total local membership of the Methodist Church in number. This extraordinary announcement drew from Superintendent Kennedy of the Metropolitan Police the indignant reply in writing, that he had not made any census of persons of that character since January 24, 1864, when there were only 599 houses of prostitution, 2,123 public prostitutes, and 72 concert saloons of ill repute. "The number of waiting girls was not then taken."

Whatever the police census may have shown as to prostitution I am informed by certain persons who had the best possible opportunities for observation that the morals of "high" society itself, among both men and women, were looser during the decade after the Civil War than they have been at any time since. One has only to glance at the daily newspapers of the time for a general confirmation. Abortionists advertised themselves openly in the press, the New York *Herald* being conspicuous in this respect.

Considering the low state of public and private morals, the corruption of federal and municipal government, and the purely materialistic ambitions of the leaders in the financial and business world, the period well deserves the epithet, coined by Don Seitz, of "The Dreadful Decade." One reason for its dreadfulness was the fact that the influence of woman had not as yet made itself fully felt. It was unfortunate that some of the leading exponents of "women's rights" were also the violent advocates of extreme individualism and "free love." Sensitive women, however ambitious for their sex, were loath to associate themselves with persons whose private lives were at least open to suspicion. Yet at that, the "siren sisters" Virginia Woodhull and "Tennessee" Claflin were hardly more notorious than several well known women recently received in New York society.

But while the war had intensified all the most obvious and picturesque attributes of the great cuspidorial epoch, and New York City, so far as morals were concerned, probably deserved the epithet so often accorded it of being a "whited sepulchre," those in the upper reaches of high society still recall fondly the Halcyon days from 1865 to the panic of 1873 when there were no restrictions upon sport, and few upon personal liberty, when horse racing was in its glory, the Four-in-Hand Club the fashionable resort, the Knickerbocker Circle small and select, when "claret would age and grow mellow . . . and the private cellars were full of old Madeiras," and the charge of the "400" as yet unheard of.

"If I as a sportsman," says Mr. Frank Gray Griswold, "should be asked what were the best years during my lifetime in and about New York for a man of my tastes and inclinations, I should say the first few years that followed the Civil War—from 1865 to the panic of 1873. . . . The most popular sport at that time was yachting. The yachtsmen of the day owned large sea-going schooners and raced them in the open sea. The luxury loving yachtsman did not appear in force until 1881. Yachting revived quickly after the Civil War and the seasons of 1865 and 1866 were full of interest.

"At the Union Club in October, 1866, George A. and Frank Osgood bet Pierre Lorillard, Jr. and others $30,000 a side that the '*Fleet Wing*' could beat the '*Vesta*' to 'The Needles' on the coast of England. James Gordon Bennett heard of the match and asked to be allowed to enter the '*Henrietta.*' A three-cornered race for $90,000 was the result. On Christmas Day under every stitch of canvas '*Henrietta*' with her colors floating in the breeze flashed by the Needles at 3.45 p.m., 13 days, 22 hours, 46 minutes from Sandy Hook and won. This was the first ocean yacht race."

Outwardly also, as well as inwardly, New York had its dreadful aspects. The river of wealth, which had begun to roll into the City shortly after the discovery of gold in California, was swollen after 1865 by that of the war millionaires, who now joined with their precursors in what "society" referred to as "The Gold Rush." These newly rich told their architects that they might go "the limit,"—and they did. Rococo palaces of gray stone, some of them later taken over and used for clubs, rose on the corners of Fifth Avenue, until the crash of Black Friday standardized good taste in the more modest and conservative brownstone.

It was at this time that the fret saw began to do its fiendish work along the eves and balustrades of houses in the upper reaches of the city and on the Hudson. This was followed by the cupola, universally pronounced "coopilow." Dwellings sporting these excrescences were generally known as "Italian villas," although the newly invented horror bore no resemblance to anything Italian, but, "in no other style of building could a dollar be made to make more show than in the cupola house of our reign of terror."

Future paleontologists will identify the age by the remains of the cast iron dog and stag on the front lawn, the horse block and "summer house," and the cigar store Indian, then in healthy middle age and not tottering to senility as I knew him. Women, according to Valentine's Manual, wore camels-hair shawls, hoop skirts, "scalloped boots," "bosom pads" of horse hair or rubber, wire bustles and dinky little hats, while the men outshone them in velvet coats, "spring-bottom" skin-tight pants, "reefer" coats, kid gloves of varied hues and pancake derby hats. To pin the label more exactly it was the heyday of the cameo, the "what not," the worsted motto, the painted fire board, and the tall vase filled with pussy willows or cat-tails tied with yellow ribbon, which decorated everything from the coal scuttle to the whisk broom. Offenbach was the Gershwin of the opera, Detaille, Rosa Bonheur and Bouguereau, the accepted exponents of pictorial art, and every parlor had its "cosy corner," its curio cabinet and bamboo or scrollwork easel holding crayon portraits of heavily whiskered males and dour ladies of aggressive rectitude.

It was a world without subways or elevateds, elevators, telephones, typewriters or electric lights. The horse cars had "hill horses" (a third horse to help on the grades) and "drawing room" cars costing an extra dime. The gas lamps so dimly illuminated the streets that armed gangs could board the cars, slug the conductors, and rob the passengers without being seen.

In those days Corporal Thompson's Madison Cottage— "At the Sign of the Buckhorn"—adjacent to Madison "Park," was the rendezvous for the trotting men. On the southwest corner of the square, where the Fifth Avenue Building now stands, was Franconi's canvas hippodrome, while diagonally opposite, on the northeast corner, was the low shed of the Harlem Railroad. Here cars for Boston started from one side, and for Albany from the other, being dragged by horses to 32nd Street, where engines were attached in the open street.

Already, according to *The Galaxy* in 1867, ten men owned one-tenth of all the taxable property in New York City.

| | |
|---|---:|
| Wm. B. Astor | $16,114,000 |
| Wm. C. Rhinelander | 7,745,000 |
| A. T. Stewart | 6,091,500 |
| Peter and Robert Goelet | 4,417,000 |
| James Lenox | 4,260,000 |
| Peter Lorillard | 4,245,000 |
| John David Wolfe | 3,997,000 |
| M. M. Hendricks | 1,690,000 |
| Rufus L. Lord | 1,500,000 |
| C. V. S. Roosevelt | 1,346,000 |
| Total | $51,405,500 |

The Stock Exchange stood on William Street between Beaver and Exchange Place, and speculators frequently offered $100 per week for the privilege of listening at the keyhole during the calls. The late Henry Clews recorded that he bought his seat on the Exchange in 1857, all expenses included, for $500, and contrasted that price with the $35,000 which it was worth thirty years later in 1887. Had he been a clairvoyant or lived longer he might have noted the $625,000 brought by a seat in 1929.

"Commodore" Vanderbilt was the big figure in finance.

"I can't afford it!" he once protested, when asked by a friend for a contribution towards some supposedly worthy object.

"But your son William has made us a handsome gift!" expostulated the visitor.

"That's all right!" remarked the Commodore, "he's got a rich father!"

In 1863 he cornered Harlem and drove it from 30 to 179, at which price he made five or six millions. The following year he drove it from 75 to 150, and then to 285, allowing the speculative members of the New York Legislature to settle with him at that figure to the tune of 15,000 shares.

We were still a frontier country in manners and morals, and man swaggered supreme in the East as well as in the West. Although the Union Pacific was completed in 1868, the Northwest was still a wilderness, and a herd of cattle could be driven a thousand miles in a straight line without meeting an obstacle in the shape of a fence. There were only a few places between the Blue Mountains of Oregon and the North Platte in Wyoming where the barest necessities of life could be purchased, and one might travel for weeks without meeting another human being.

This was the jurisdiction which Millard Fillmore had offered to my father in 1852 and where, in consequence, I might have passed my childhood. In view of the network of rails that now gridirons the Northwest it may interest some readers to learn that as late as 1878 there were only thirty miles of railroad—from Wallula to Walla—in that part of the country. Millions of buffaloes roamed the plains unaware of the impending slaughter that was practically to extermi-

nate them within a few short years. In 1872 they were so thick
in the Arkansas Valley that the soldiers at Fort Dodge found
them a nuisance in the pursuit of other game animals; a year
later there was not one left. In 1872–3 the Santa Fe, Kansas
Pacific and Union Pacific carried East 1,250,000 buffalo
robes. Buffalo steak sold for from one to two cents a pound.
There was only an insignificant herd left in 1900, but happily, owing to the efforts of the government, there are now
nearly 5,000 of the animals in the United States.

The influence of Puritanism, as Mr. H. L. Mencken points
out in his admirable essay "Puritanism as a Literary Force,"
has passed through various metamorphoses in the United
States, and with its consciousness of sin, its hatred of the
flesh, its obsession with salvation, and its distrust of joy and
beauty as traps of sin and lures of corruption, continues in
spite of the decline of Calvinistic belief to be a potent influence among us. It is by no means local and "In the South
today," said John Fiske in 1900, "there is more Puritanism
surviving than in New England." Its religious manifestations are particularly obvious in the South and Southwest.
There are almost as many primitive Puritans in the United
States in proportion to the total population in 1931 as there
were in 1731. This "simon-puritanism" of the fundamen-
talist with its demonological doctrines of a jealous, merciless,
and vengeful deity, its obsession over morality, particularly
in sexual affairs, and the need of enforcing its own views by
fierce and inquisitorial laws is actively with us yet, and finds
its immediate expression in organized movements, under
highly salaried professional executives, to make any form of
personal immorality a crime punishable by fine and imprisonment, and "to erect the individual's offense against himself
into an offense against society." These reform movements
are now largely financial and carried on by high pressure
salesmanship and Wall Street methods, so that their evan-
gelical atmosphere is sometimes lost in that of big business.

When, as has already been noted, Unitarianism under-
mined and finally destroyed Calvinism, and the imaginative

genius of the Americans was diverted from religion into business, manufacture and the development of natural resources,—the character of the Puritan and his descendants did not necessarily change although he might become a Baptist, a Methodist, a Unitarian, or an atheist. He still distrusted whatever made for happiness unless disguised as improving. Hence arose the "lyceum," the "lecture illustrated by music" which concealed the opera, and the "museum," in reality a theatre with a side show of curiosities, like the "Boston Museum" of my childhood which, as in the case of the Raines Law Hotel sandwich, later legalized the joy-giving drink that went with it.

The neo-Puritan was as preoccupied with an hereafter as his predecessor before the Revolution, only it was now an earthly instead of a heavenly paradise towards which his eyes were directed. Whatever he may have "believed" regarding immortality and the saints, the reward he was surest of, the one that he sought first, was the same plenteousness in goods, crops and cattle, the same bursting barn and fecund flock, which to his fathers had been the signs of God's grace. In other words the Puritan, says Mr. Mencken, had become a Philistine,—an idolater worshipping the symbol, rather than what aforetime it had stood for, and as Philistine he exhibited (and still more or less exhibits) the same intensity of purpose, the same sense of obligation to spend his time profitably—to waste none of it, since "time was money,"— the same distrust of the amenities of life, the same feeling that what makes for pleasure must be evil and that conversely what is distasteful must be good, as his grandfather did. In a phrase a Philistine is nothing but a Puritan minus his Calvinism. The chief difference is that to-day his idea of salvation—instead of, as in 1783, being wafted to Heaven on the wings of angels—is a translation to Paris or Antibes in a Rolls Royce as his chariot of fire.

Of course they were not all like that, and the Puritans did not all turn into Philistines, however you may define one; but, generally speaking, the post-Revolutionary American in his intense absorption in the pursuit of money, and the improvement of his material condition, could neatly wear the cap of the Philistine, defined by Webster as "a person lacking liberal culture and refinement; commonplace; prosaic."

Mr. Mencken, developing this idea, claims that "as Puritanism, in the strict sense, declined in virulence and took deceptive new forms, there was a compensating growth of its brother, Philistinism, and by the first quarter of the Nineteenth Century, the distrust of beauty and of the joy that is its object, was as firmly established throughout the land as it ever had been in New England. . . ." Thus the repressive influence of Puritanism upon artistic expression nearly strangled American taste and, under the guise of "decorative art," gave us in due course the dado, the tasselled cushion, the wax flower, the gilded bamboo chair, the lithograph and the framed banality of the "motto."

On the spiritual side, however, the relief from dogma, the new doctrines of laissez faire, and the revolt from the materialism dominant during the earlier decades of the Republic had showed itself, as has been said, in all sorts of "isms" and communal experiments, from the vague yearnings of Emerson for contact with the infinite, to "movements" against slavery, intemperance, and the personal domination of property and of sex, although in contrast to the militant aggressiveness of the primitive Puritan the reformer of the first half of the nineteenth century usually tried to achieve his ideals by inhibition rather than by prohibition. In connection with these major movements, and stimulated by the new doctrines of liberty and democracy, there grew up others which were purely in the nature of revolt, of which that for woman's rights is the best example.

§

The general unrest and demoralization that followed the Civil War was favorable to the spread of the feminist movement. Slavery was no longer an issue and woman's entire energy could now be directed towards her own liberation. The blatant masculine profligacy of the later 60's provoked an indignant reaction. The female worm—taught to suffer meekly the lapses of her husband and keep the home fires burning for him—turned, let the fire go out and aired her wrongs upon the public platform amid the cheers of her oppressed sisters. Of course the close relationship between drink and what was commonly known as "vice" was obvious, so the temperance and woman's rights movements ran in the same leash. So, rather startlingly, did another—that for "free love." The reform movements of the 30's and 40's had brought together many strange bedfellows, but none so astonishing as the political partnership of prudery and license exhibited in the recrudescence of the feminist movement of the late 60's, which by preaching the equality of sex and the inequity of the double standard of sexual morality tended to condone "free love."

It was a picturesque paradox that involved Susan B. Anthony and Elizabeth Cady Stanton with Victoria C. Woodhull and her sister Tennie C. Claflin,—a curious "bundling party," at the conclusion of which primitive Puritanism in the person of Anthony Comstock crept from under the bed, called for the police, and set the stage for a revival of religious militancy which to-day has flowered into the wholesale activities of the Anti-Saloon League, the Lord's Day Alliance, the Society for the Suppression of Vice, Billy Sunday, and all his sisters and his cousins and his aunts. Less spectacular than the "Revival of 1858" which followed the panic of 1857, that which followed the panic of 1873 was far more lasting. Is there a connection between a lean purse and a love of God? Between fear and worship?

Two antithetical figures emerged from the excesses and extravagances of the "flash age," both crusaders, both fanatical, both absurd,—the protagonists of Puritanism upon the one hand and of revolt upon the other,—Anthony Comstock and George Francis Train.

Comstock first came prominently before the public eye in

the early 70's when he undertook to suppress *Woodhull and Claflin's Weekly*,—a so-called "radical reformatory paper" established by two amazing sisters, the one beautiful, the other fascinating, who, after an adolescence flavored with spiritism, free love, and quackery, had established themselves in New York and were carrying on a picturesque career of blackmail and brokerage under the ægis of Commodore Vanderbilt and behind the skirts of reform. "That they were women made their behavior a matter for scandal in a period which, for all its lawlessness and vulgarity, still kept sacred the shrine of woman's purity and her consequent subservience to a binding decorum." Attacking the "double standard" in sex, they "ventilated scandal" and tarnished the reputation of Henry Ward Beecher. Whoso would know more in detail of such matters should read "Anthony Comstock—Rounds-man of the Lord" by Heywood Broun and Margaret Leech.

The *Weekly* was ostensibly a vehicle for disseminating the gospel of the equality of the sexes, of which the two charmers made themselves the exponents and by which, in one way—and perhaps another—they earned their living; and, although Victoria at a national convention of miscella-neous reformers was put in nomination by the "Equal Rights Party" for President of the United States and presented the views of the Women's Rights Association to the Judiciary Committee in Washington, early in '72, scandal was so busy with their names that by the autumn they found themselves deserted by their more conventional associates.

Victoria had been intimate with Theodore Tilton, a bril-liant young writer, friend of Henry Ward Beecher and a member of "Plymouth Church," and from him she learned of the probable infidelity of the latter with Mrs. Tilton. Claiming that her views had made her a scapegoat for just such hypocrites as she alleged Mr. Beecher to be, and that it was her duty to expose iniquity in high places, especially behind the altar, she boldly published the story of the preach-er's passion for another man's neglected wife in eleven and a half columns of fine print. Although Mr. Beecher was of sufficient prestige to ignore the charges for awhile, the exposure rent Puritan society and ended in Tilton's bringing a suit for $100,000 damages against the preacher for alienating the affections of his wife. It was the sensation of the decade, rivalling, if not surpassing, the prosecution of Tweed. The jury split; Beecher, in spite of the persuasive evidence against him, weathered the storm; Tilton died; and both the sirens turned pious and made brilliant marriages in England.

The story, while gaudy and typical of the "flash age," is itself only relevant to our purposes as an introduction to that personification of primitive Puritanism—Anthony Comstock, whom I knew for many years while I was acting as assistant district attorney of New York County. Comstock was a crusading fanatic against pornography, who, although a nuisance, was entirely sincere. The consciousness of the power behind him gave him the confidence, if not the courage, to brave humiliation and insult, and I am told by one of our judges that he has seen him practically kicked down the stairs of the Criminal Courts Building by men who had, *au fond,* considerable respect for him. He was an enthusiastic smut sleuth with a hound's nose for obscenity in either art or letters. I suspect that he enjoyed his calling, for he used gloatingly to exhibit with both pride and gusto to myself and other assistants of the district attorney peculiarly atrocious trophies of his various raids in the form of nasty photographs and obscene articles. Quantitatively his career was a huge success, for he caused to be destroyed nearly 15,000 pounds of stereotyped plates, over 60,000 articles of rubber, 5,500 indecent playing cards, 3,000 boxes of pills and powders, 194,000 obscene pictures, 134,000 pounds of improper books, and jailed enough sinners to have filled a train of sixty-one coaches, allowing sixty to each coach. I quote Miss Leech in order to dissent most emphatically from one of her conclusions about him.

"Anthony Comstock was adapted to the folkways of his time and place. Often in the fight against obscenity he stood

alone. Always he was in the van. But somewhere behind him
an army of Puritans was solidly massed. For this reason he
was feared and hated—because he was so strong. Had his
crusades run counter to the *mores* of his people, he would
have been a pitiful figure, a martyr to his lonely ideal. But
in him the people cursed the spirit of enforced righteousness
made palpable—fleshly and menacing, with ginger-colored
whiskers and a warrant and a Post Office badge. He was the
apotheosis, the fine flower of Puritanism."

With apologies to a lovely lady, Anthony Comstock was
nothing of the kind. On the contrary he was a reincarnation
of the antique witch finder with the burning fanaticism of a
St. Paul and the relentlessness of a Torquemada. He was not
a "fine flower" so much as a thistle. He was the protagonist
of the militant prohibitory Puritan as contrasted with the in-
hibited ascetic,—a sturdy fighter of the Devil both in others
and within his own conscience, but like his prototypes of "the
stern and rock bound coast of New England not satisfied
until he knocked the Devil down and put him in the stocks."
He was the type of Puritan referred to by Harvey O'Higgins
and E. H. Reede in "The American Mind in Action" when
they say: "The Puritan hated the Flesh in himself and he
hated even more fiercely the Flesh appearing in the vices of
others. . . . His hate, reservoired within him, gets its drain-
age in raids on vice, in the persecutions and suppressions carried on by anti-vice societies and in campaigns of reform that
call for the punishment of evil doers." The will to make
others good, so evident in American life, is part of the individualism in the Puritan's religion. "If I, rather than the
Holy Church," says Henry Seidel Canby, "am responsible
for morality, then I must see to it that my brother behaves
himself."

*Woodhull and Claflin's Weekly* was no less anathema to
Comstock than its provocative editors, and he promptly seized
the opportunity afforded by its attack on Mr. Beecher to have
them thrown into Ludlow Street jail for sending an obscene
publication through the mails. That, as J. P. Morgan used to

say, was his "good reason"; his "real reason" was the attack on Henry Ward Beecher. From the first it was opera bouffe. The sisters engaged old "Bill" Howe, of the celebrated criminal law firm of Howe & Hummel, and the courtroom was turned into a bear garden. The charge was tenuous in the extreme, the police had overstepped the bounds of law and decency in rifling the sirens' trunks of private letters, there were preposterous delays, and the whole affair savored of persecution. For weeks the New York press revelled in what *The Herald* called a "sensational comedy of free love" and a good time was had by all, including, one may suspect, even the two wild women themselves.

Besides its bearing on the recrudescence of Puritanism in the last quarter of the century I am interested in the Comstock-Woodhull-Claflin affair as responsible for the last vivid appearance before the public eye of my far distant kinsman George Francis Train. George Francis—like myself—was a descendant of that first John Train who came to America in 1635, established himself at Waltham, built his mill and sold rum to the Indians. His father, Oliver Train, of Waltham, was a cousin of Enoch Train, the founder of the famous "Train Line" of packets established between Boston and Liverpool in 1843, and the "discoverer" of Donald McKay, who built *The Lightning, The Monarch of the Seas* and other celebrated clippers in the early part of the nineteenth century. George Francis entered the shipping business at the age of sixteen as an employee of the Train line. He seems to have risen quickly to a position of great importance and to have been instrumental in extending its business to California. According to Miss Leech, whom, with her generous permission, I again quote to avoid the imputation of family egotism—"he was a man of great ability. At the age of twenty, he had attained a notable position in the shipping business at a salary of $10,000 a year, a considerable figure in 1849. He created a fleet of forty sailing ships. He acquired 5,000 lots in Omaha, said to have been worth $30,000,000. He introduced street railways into Europe.

He projected the Union Pacific Railway, and organized the Crédit Mobilier to finance it, though he was not implicated in the scandals with which that gigantic venture was tainted.

"In 1872, he was a man of forty-three, possessed of considerable wealth, with a famous show place in Newport. Handsome, with a magnetic personality, he might have carried everything before him. Having paid a visit to France during the Second Empire, he had been on cordial terms with Louis Napoleon and the Empress Eugénie; and the Queen of Spain was also among his friends. But his communistic views and eccentric habits of thought and behavior were constantly leading him into strange adventures. In earlier years, while taking a trip around the world, he had been offered the presidency of Australia by the discontented miners of that colony, who had projected a revolution. In 1870, anticipating —and by his own claim, inspiring—Jules Verne, he had gone around the world in eighty days. While in France after this trip he had organized the Marseille Commune, known as the 'Ligue du Midi.' Returning to the United States he announced himself as an independent candidate for the presidency in the campaign of 1872, in which Grant and Greeley were the main contestants. He, later, however, concluded that the post of 'dictator' was more desirable."

Train was making a speech from the steps of a Wall Street bank when he heard of Comstock's arrest of the Claflin sisters. Instantly his chivalric soul was fired, and leaping to their support he offered to go their bail, declaring "I am satisfied the cowardly Christian community will destroy you, if possible, to cover up the rotten state of society." "He became a frequent visitor at Ludlow Street, scrawling on the wall of the sisters' cell one of his characteristic couplets, which denounced the baseness of the attack on their reputations.

"Unable to get a public hall in which to proclaim his sympathy for the lady brokers, Train proceeded to publish an issue of a newspaper, which he called '*The Train Ligue.*' In this he repeated certain of the statements included in the proscribed number of the *Weekly*,—purposely exaggerating them, in an effort to get himself arrested as a test case. He also vociferously demanded the prosecution of the Bible Publishing Company for printing 'disgusting slanders on Lot, Abraham, Solomon and David.' But Comstock did not rise to the bait. Train was forced to further efforts. He issued another number of '*The Train Ligue*,' containing certain outspoken sections of the Old Testament, printed under sensational headlines. Our crusader, returning from a Western trip, was aroused to action by this new and blasphemous offense. The Federal authorities refused to proceed in the case; but from the State courts, so delinquent with regard to the *Weekly*, Comstock was this time able to obtain an indictment, and the knight errant was thrown into the Tombs.

"New inspiration was afforded to the representatives of the press; and accounts of Train's prison fare, his epigrams, his long sealskin overcoat, and the flower in his buttonhole ranked high in the news of the day. This was surely a willing victim,—he refused to give bail, declaring that he was entirely guilty, that the liberty of the press was at stake, that two thousand newspapers would fall with his, and that the mob of the Commune would tear down the Tombs within thirty days. Incarceration was, moreover, no novelty to this quixotic soul, who was in late years fond of saying that he had been fifteen times in jail without a crime. But the '*Daily Witness*,' ever faithful to Comstock, fondly commented on his cleverness in effecting the capture.

"Train wished to plead guilty to the charge of obscenity —adding to his plea the words, 'based on extracts from the Bible.' But the court refused to permit a conditional plea, and directed 'Not Guilty' to be entered. Of this occasion, the *Sun* for December 23, 1872, reported: 'Mr. Train did not walk in with moody air and cautious tread, like an ordinary prisoner. He rushed in like a modern Achilles, his face lit up, his eyes bright and resolute, and his whole bearing indicative of soul-set determination.' He was attended by a woman in a long dress, with 'manly hat and hair,' who waved a silken banner which she called the rainbow flag of the new government, of which Train was to be dictator.

"In his cell in the Tombs, the prospective dictator cordially received the representatives of the *Sun,* and gave him an outline of his plans. With the establishment of the Commune, he would hang, first, the murderers; second, the thieves; third, the leading politicians; fourth, an editor or two; and fifth, Congress. He gave out a copy of some verses, signed 'Champion of the People.' That night he dined on prison stew and pronounced it excellent. His cell was on 'Murderers' Row,' and twenty-two of the 'murderers' formed a club and elected Train president.

"On the basis that he was mentally unbalanced, two doctors were appointed to examine him. Their report declared that he was 'of unsound mind, though harmless'; and this description he adopted as an appendage to his signature in issuing his frequent bulletins, which were subsequently printed in *Woodhull and Claflin's Weekly,* under the head, 'Hark! From the Tombs.' Continuing in his refusal to give bail, he stayed in the Tombs for fourteen weeks, suffering from the bad air and general insalubrity of that institution, and at every opportunity loudly voicing his disgust at such conditions. He earnestly wanted to be tried on the charge of obscenity. The authorities, however, were reluctant to make an issue of his case. They were clearly anxious to be rid of 'this dreadful person,' as the *Times* editorially termed him, adding that for months he 'obstructed business, distracted judges, and made a travesty of justice, uttering his vaporings and trumpetings.' Frequently he was left alone in the courthouse and in prison corridors. But George Francis Train had resolved to be a prisoner, and a prisoner he remained.

"At length, in the spring of 1873, his endurance was rewarded. He was brought to trial, and there began those hearings styled by the appreciative press 'the Train matinees.' In these performances, our drygoods salesman (Comstock) had a role to play; and even his attire, his black necktie and the black studs in his shirt bosom were faithfully reported in the newspapers. On April 15, he recorded in his diary his impression of the crowd in the courtroom. 'There was present the most disgusting set of Free-lovers. The women-part, thin-faced, cross, sour-looking, each wearing a look of "Well, I am boss" and "Oh, for a man." The men, unworthy of the name of men, licentious looking, sneakish, mean, contemptible, making a true man blush to be seen near them. This is Free Love.'

"Comstock's experience on the witness stand was not altogether pleasant. 'The Counsel for defense,' he wrote, on May 19, 'seemed very bitter against me, and was determined to disparage me before the Jury.' In this case, the defense made much of the fact that one-half of the fine was then allowed by New York law to the informer. But such sums Anthony had always wisely refused to accept, turning them over to charities. He must have had his moment of triumph, when he was able to make this point; and never, we may assume, did he tamely submit to the sneers of the inquisitor. 'He has a ministerial bearing,' notes the *Sun* of May 20, 1873, 'speaks deliberately and gesticulates freely. On this cross-examination, he frequently bit his lip and cast a withering glance at Mr. Bell (counsel for Train).'

"In his defense, Train's counsel had thought it wise to adduce medical opinion that he was insane. This admission, as it developed, facilitated a summary disposal of the case. Having instructed the jury to acquit on the ground of insanity, Judge Noah Davis—before whom in the fall of that same year "Boss" Tweed was to be tried—ended by remarking that he would send Train to the insane asylum at Utica. This entirely unexpected turn caused intense excitement in court; and presently the dictator rose to move the impeachment of the judge in the name of the people.

" 'Such a scene as for a moment ensued beggars description,' reports Anthony's diary for May 20. The *Telegram* for the same date has an account, probably apocryphal, of the crusader's subsequent conduct.

" 'Mr. Comstock, informer-general to the Young Men's Christian Association (runs this story), looked quite tri-

umphant at first, but was evidently unable to bear the
sight of his victim being carried off to a dungeon in a
lunatic asylum. He put his cambric to his eyes to keep
back the tears which had come unbidden, and was taken
out in weeps, leaning on the arm of his bosom friend of
some weeks, Mr. Luther C. Challis. As he left the room,
the coming dictator followed him with mournful eyes
and a pitying smile. All wrath had left the man's soul.'

"For his arbitrary action in this case, Judge Davis was
liberally criticized. It was said that the legal profession in
general believed that the charge of obscenity against Train
could not have been sustained. Some sympathy for the dictator, who had vainly suffered nearly five months of imprisonment, was expressed in the newspapers.

"By the time the Woodhull and Claflin case was ended,
Comstock was deep in other affairs. The drama of the
*Weekly* was played out, and the sisters and their champion,
George Francis Train, had crossed the vice-hunter's path to
pursue their separate ways. Eventually, the sisters went to
England, where both made brilliant marriages. Tennessee,
whose death occurred in 1923, became the wife of Sir Francis
Cook, who made a fortune importing India shawls (enjoying
the title of 'Marchioness of Montserrat'). Victoria married
John Biddulph Martin, a wealthy London banker. For years
she published a magazine, the *Humanitarian*. In 1893, a
middle-aged figure, she delivered a lecture at Carnegie Hall,
New York. She established herself successfully in England,
and is said to have forced the British Museum to take from
its shelves certain books which contained reflections on her
character.

"George Francis Train was marked for a less happy destiny, though even in ill-fortune the eccentric philosopher
seemed to find many compensations. Through the action of
the court in declaring him insane, he suffered severe property
losses; from wealth he was reduced to a meager competency.
He passed the last years of his life in the Mills Hotel in

Bleecker Street, New York, where he subsisted on three dollars a week, finding nutriment chiefly in peanuts. Until his death in 1904, he was a familiar figure in Madison Square, where he spent much of his time on a park bench, making friends with the children, and sharing his diet of peanuts with the squirrels."

§

During this prolonged pugilistic encounter between Comstock and the Devil, the buccaneers of Wall Street had been playing ducks and drakes with prosperity. Twenty-five thousand miles of railroads had been built between 1869 and 1873, nearly two hundred and thirty millions in securities were in default, and the speculative boom had collapsed, followed by panic and depression. The country came to its senses. A tremendous reaction set in. There was a renaissance of Puritanism—not the milder forms of religious enthusiasm of the second quarter of the century—but of the battling order,—an "army with banners,"—chief of them the Y. M. C. A. The movement extended from an attack on vice to one upon "Boss" Tweed himself under whose protection it flourished.

The "Chapter of Erie," the attempted "Gold Corner," the Crédit Mobilier scandal, the wholesale bribery of legislatures and common councilmen (Jay Gould in 1868, according to the testimony of Tweed, had carried to Albany in a satchel $500,000 to be distributed to thirty members of the "Black Horse Cavalry"), the Maritime Bank failure and the exposure of Ferdinand Ward had sickened all self-respecting people. There was a recrudescence of decency in business, as well as in morals. "Boss" Tweed himself was sent to the penitentiary.

A notable feature of this third "Great Awakening" in American history was the series of revivals conducted by Dwight L. Moody and Ira D. Sankey, the first an eloquent exhorter, the second a tenor singer "with a genius for the

direction of massed choirs." Many families named their
coach horses "Moody and Sankey."

The gold panic of '73 marked the beginning of a change in
the public attitude in regard to wealth, showing itself first in a
gradually growing hostility towards millionaires and merg-
ing by degrees into an animosity against mere wealth itself,
until the World War destroyed all social and economic con-
tinuity. During the period, when the American eagle was
screaming loudest, from the coming of the railroads to the
Civil War, we had hailed the new millionaires as proof positive of the success of our institutions, reflecting the old Puritan idea that material prosperity indicated the presence in the
near family neighborhood, if not of Providence Himself, at
least of one or more of the more rugged virtues. After the
panic and the exposures of stock market rigging no such fanciful idea any longer obtained, and it was perceived that a man
might accumulate ten or even twenty millions of dollars and
be nothing but a common crook after all.

I have quoted James Truslow Adams to the effect that
during the mad rush for money in "the flash time" after the
Civil War "no one appeared to have any idea what he was
going to do with wealth and power when he got it," but by
the end of the 70's most of those who had "got theirs" had a
very clear idea of what they wanted—at least their wives and
daughters had—namely, social position. The generation of
"getters" was followed by a generation of "spenders," and
nowhere has the influence of these two groups had a wider
influence upon the ideals of the population as a whole than in
the United States. For this reason alone is what we call "society" worth passing notice.

The Rev. Mr. White, a bucolic pastor from the upper part
of the state, hearing in 1868 of the vice, crime and general
deviltry that went on in the metropolis, felt himself called
upon to visit the city to see for himself if such things could
be. He returned home, not only to verify the worst reports
in all particulars, but to write a book which he called "Sunshine and Shadow in New York." It is rather hard to find the

sunshine owing to the superabundance of shadow, but it gives one a glimpse of what some people, perhaps erroneously, thought of certain aspects of New York society.

"With the elite of New York, so called, money is the principal thing. The best society of New York is not to be found among the elite. If you wish parties, soirees, balls, that are elegant, attractive, and genteel, you will not find them among the snobbish clique, who, with nothing but money, attempt to rule New York. Talent, taste, and refinement do not dwell with these. But high life has no passport except money. If a man has this, though destitute of character and brains, he is made welcome. One may come from Botany Bay or St. James; with a ticket of leave from a penal colony or St. Cloud; if he has diamond rings and a coach, all places will be opened to him. The leaders of upper New York were, a few years ago, porters, stable-boys, coal-heavers, pickers of rags, scrubbers of floors, and laundry women. Coarse, rude, ignorant, uncivil, and immoral many of them are still. Lovers of pleasure and men of fashion bow and cringe to such, and approach hat in hand. One of our new-fledged millionaires gave a ball in his stable. The invited came with tokens of delight. The host, a few years ago, was a ticket-taker at one of our ferries, and would have thankfully blacked the boots or done any menial service for the people who clamor for the honor of his hand. At the gate of Central Park, every day, splendid coaches may be seen, in which sit large, fat, coarse women, who carry with them the marks of the wash-tub. These people have money. They spend it in untold sums for balls, parties, and soirees, and in drawing upper New York into their gaudy mansions.

"Much of the society of New York is very select, intellectual and genteel. But the moneyed aristocracy, those who crowd gilded saloons and make up the parties of the *ton,* who are invited to soirees, fancy balls, and late suppers, are among the coarsest, most vulgar and illiterate of our people. Money is made easily by many in New York; fortunes are acquired in a day; families go from a shanty on a back street to a brownstone front in upper New York, but they carry with them their vulgar habits, and disgust those who from social position are compelled to invite them to their houses. At a fashionable party, persons are invited according to their bank account, and to their standing on 'change. A fashionable party is made up of representatives of all nations and all religions—men and women who can speak the English language and those who cannot, Jews and Gentiles, Irish and Germans, red-faced and heavy-bearded men, coarse-featured, red-faced, uncultivated women, who are loaded down with jewelry and covered with satins, who can eat as much as a soldier in the trenches. If they give a party, they give it to those who ridicule their position and manners. If they go to a party, they laugh in their turn."

It was at about this time that one enterprising—and possibly notoriety-seeking—lady, appeared at her own ball in a tiara of diamonds lit with gas jets, fed from a tank in her bustle by means of an elastic pipe skilfully concealed in the shower of "Niagara," or "cataract," curls worn on the back of her head.

# CHAPTER XIV

## The "Brownstone Era"

### 1873–1893

THE "Brownstone Era" spanned roughly the twenty years between the panic of 1873 and that of 1893, and included Grant's second term, those of Hayes, Garfield and Arthur, Cleveland's first term and that of Harrison. During this period, once the worst after-effects of the war were over, the United States began to find itself. In general the country was prosperous, comfortable and restored to commercial sanity; railroad jobbery had been curbed; the frontier pushed to the Pacific; there was a huge expansion in industry; a tremendous development in rural communication through electric railroads, telephones and the free delivery of mail; a gradual betterment in the economic conditions of the negro coincident with his "constitutional" disfranchisement; a tendency towards amalgamations of capital, forming virtual monopolies and "trusts," together with a growing distrust of corporate wealth, which took effect in the Interstate Commerce Act of 1887; while the power of labor made itself felt in strikes and riots. America was taking its place as a world power; New York City had regained its self-respect, for Tweed was in jail; a witty and charming group of poets and writers centred about the Gilders; *The Century Magazine* was at its zenith; Theodore Roosevelt was taking his first lessons in municipal politics.

In the 70's and early 80's only the principal streets of New York were cleaned, and the lineal descendants of the pigs observed by Charles Dickens still rooted in East Side gutters. The city was "half mining camp, half Mayfair," exhibiting many of the "frontier characteristics peculiar to the country

as a whole at that era," says James Collins Brown, to whom
the world is indebted for that invaluable hodge-podge of information relating to the Metropolis, assembled by him in
"Valentine's Manual." Above 59th Street the Ninth Avenue
"El" ran through an uninhabited, but fertile, region covered
with truck farms. Goats roamed the hinterlands of upper
Fifth Avenue and Central Park, on either side of which
stood hundreds of wooden shanties erected by squatters,
many of them at altitudes attainable only by ladders.

There was no Brooklyn Bridge and all access to Long
Island was the same as in the time of the British occupation.
Wagon traffic congested the streets, and the best way to get
from upper to lower Manhattan was by the Harlem boats, a
means of transportation to which, if present conditions do not
improve, the inhabitants may be glad to return. The din of
traffic was overwhelming, for the roadways were badly paved
and all wheels shod with iron. Street pumps were still in general use, and the main thoroughfares were lined with telegraph poles until the regime of Mayor Grant,—I still paraphrase freely from Mr. Brown—while swarms of sparrows
dropped caterpillars, grubs and other forms of manna upon
the pedestrians below.

The majority of buildings were from two to three stories
in height. "Central heating" was practically unknown and
most people kept the windows of their sleeping rooms tight
closed in order to prevent "the pneumonia" in winter and
"the malaria" in summer. Red flannel underwear, "chest
protectors," fur caps, "ear tabs," wristlets and "liver pads"
were in general use; week-day bathing was regarded as effete.

The chief social festival was New Year's Day, upon which
everybody called on everybody else and, after a glass or two
of rum punch, departed for the next visit leaving behind him
an elaborately decorated greeting card fringed with colored
silk. By the end of the day locomotion inevitably became so
difficult that gentlemen intending to dine out usually donned
their evening clothes in the forenoon before starting on their
round of calls. A hundred calls—with a like number of

drinks—was by no means unusual. This good old Spanish (or Puritan) custom finally necessitated a basket tied to the front door-knob in substitution for the inside refreshment formerly offered.

Horse trotting was the popular sport. William H. Vanderbilt with "Aldine" and "Early Rose" in a top road wagon had made a mile in 2.16½. When Frank Work beat it, Vanderbilt bought "Maud S." for $21,000 and, mating her with "Aldine," lowered the time in 1883 to 2.15½ and later to 2.08¾.

It was at this time—about half a century ago—that a so-called "blue-glass" craze came in, and "sun parlors" or "solaria," the top and sides of which were made entirely of blue glass, were generally recommended for the same purposes as the Vita glass and violet ray are to-day and apparently effected the same cures, thus once again showing that there is nothing new—under the sun.

The Metropolitan Opera House, although built by the richest people in society in 1883, was used at first for balls, flower shows, wrestling and boxing matches, which last sometimes resulted in riots. The word "vaudeville" was unknown. The leading playhouse was Daly's Theatre, where John Drew worked his way to fame at $30 per week, along with Ada Rehan who topped him at $35.

Almost every town in the country with more than a thousand inhabitants had at least one roller-skating rink where the people diverted themselves by rolling round and round, endlessly, on a smooth floor. It is estimated that at one time there was over $12,000,000 invested throughout the country in roller-skating rinks.

In the 1870's labor was poorly organized. Intelligent workmen in the large cities were glad of the chance to work ten hours a day for two dollars. Stage and horse-car drivers in New York worked from twelve to sixteen hours for the same amount; livery and hotel drivers for from ten to twelve dollars per week. A national organization with a pretentious programme, under the no less pretentious name of the

"Knights of Labor," sought to bring all of the working class together in one great movement, but the leaders could not sufficiently arouse the interest of prosperous trades in the less fortunate ones, and, its effort to stir up class consciousness having failed, they fell back "upon the trade or group consciousness of identical interest," organized trade unions federated on a national scale, and ultimately reorganized as the "American Federation of Labor."

Puritan influence made itself felt in a rigid Sabbatarianism which closed the town tight on Sundays, and allowed only drug stores and restaurants to remain open, while various fanatics still endeavored to stop the running of trains and street cars also. When the "Gotham Club," composed of young men who worked for a living and studied art in their leisure moments, tried to engage quarters in the "Y. M. C. A." building in order to have a Sunday class in water color painting—which must be done in daylight—it was turned down, and club members severely lectured on their evil ways by the "Y" secretary.

Women's colleges had just become firmly established. The daily life of the early college girl was very simple and decorous. A "waterproof" and a copy of Milton's "Paradise Lost" were among the required equipment of each Vassar student. Short sleeves and low necks were taboo, and the graduation dress of each girl was carefully examined to make sure that it did not show too much of her feet and ankles when she stood upon the platform. She was required to be in bed every night at ten o'clock, and among the early rules was one requiring her to take two tub baths a week. Furthermore, every Monday evening she was required to report whether she had taken them, as well as to give a verbal outline of the Sunday sermon.

Outdoor sports for women were practically unknown, except for horseback riding, croquet, and the like. Calisthenics or simple gymnastics were considered sufficient. One writer reports that the early students were greatly annoyed by letters from strange men, who had gotten their names from the college catalogue, and sought opportunities to make their acquaintance.

The most significant feature of the Brownstone Era, if not of the century, so far as social-economics is concerned, was the development of the woman's rights movement. Women came—or rather burst—into their own in spite of the ironic jeers of men. This triumphant consummation of a movement severely frowned on by the Great Dictator of Feminine Propriety was brought about, curiously enough, through two purely mechanical contrivances.

In 1870 Victoria wrote to a Mr. Martin:

"The Queen is most anxious to enlist everyone who can speak or write to join in checking this mad, wicked folly of 'Woman's Rights,' with all its attendant horrors, on which her poor feeble sex is bent, forgetting every sense of womanly feeling and propriety. Lady —— ought to get a *good whipping*. It is a subject which makes the Queen so furious that she cannot contain herself. God created men and women different—let them remain each in their own position. Tennyson has some beautiful lines on the difference of men and women in 'The Princess.' Woman would become the most hateful, heartless and disgusting of human beings were she allowed to unsex herself; and where would be the protection which man was intended to give the weaker sex? The Queen is sure that Mr. Martin agrees with her."

Almost needless to say, he did, and so did many millions of women on this side of the Atlantic who obediently reflected her attitude.

At the conclusion of the Civil War woman's place was still the home and she remained there except when invited out by man. The only occupations available to women of gentle breeding were those of school teaching and nursing. The others received barely enough to keep body and soul together. When peace came, says Allan Nevins in his "Emergence of Modern America," "New York had not less than fifteen thousand working women whose weekly pittance did not rise above three dollars and fifty cents or four dollars.

They were employed in shops, factories and large stores and they had reason to count themselves happier than the thousands of wretched women, sisters to Tom Hood's slaving seamstress, who carried materials home and made shirts and overalls for seventy-five cents a dozen. Girls in the dry-goods stores of the great Eastern cities, where civilization was proudest of its achievements, toiled from seven thirty in the morning till the closing hour of nine or ten, without seats, without rest rooms or facilities for a quiet lunch, without more consideration than dumb animals received; and for this health-ruining drudgery many were paid five dollars a week."

In 1865 no women were employed in the financial district of New York, and it is stated on good authority that in 1868 there were only five females in the city who made their living by writing shorthand. The invention which opened the door to the employment of women outside the salesroom, the factory and domestic service—was the typewriter. This, together with the introduction of the telephone and the bicycle, marked a new era in American life. There had been typewriters of sorts ever since 1829, but they were too slow and too clumsy to be serviceable. The first practical machine was invented by Christopher Latham Sholes in 1867, but it bore little resemblance to the modern instrument, being more like a home-made toy piano. The Remington Company, then engaged in the manufacture of firearms and sewing machines, undertook to make typewriters for the market and, since the job was taken over by its sewing machine department, the Remington Typewriter No. 1 was an amazing simulacrum of its regular output. Mark Twain was one of the first to adopt it and in 1875 wrote a characteristic testimonial:

"Gentlemen:

Please do not use my name in any way. Please do not divulge the fact that I own a machine. I have entirely stopped using the typewriter for the reason that I could never write a letter with it to anybody without receiving a request by return mail that I would not only describe the machine but state what progress I had made in the use of it, etc. etc. I don't like to write letters and so I don't want people to know that I own this curiosity breeding joker.

Yours truly,<br>Samuel L. Clemens."

Public opinion, which had theretofore opposed the employment of women in business, began to veer after the activity of the office had been so increased by the introduction of the typewriter that there were no longer enough men to perform the clerical work. Thus the typewriter blazed the way to woman's economic and social freedom.

At first good looks were a handicap, for the wives at home looked askance at the proximity of female beauty to their downtown husbands, so the girls are said to have adopted mannish clothes and to have made use of various expedients to make themselves look "old and unattractive" until firmly entrenched in the office. Most of them in fact were much older than the "stenogs" of to-day. To them, irrespective of age and appearance, is due the immense advance in the sanitary conditions of business offices throughout the country.

A second epoch-marking discovery was that of the telephone—with the aid of a dead man's ear—by Alexander Graham Bell, a teacher of deaf mutes in Boston. From teaching mutes to talk Bell turned to teaching an iron disk to talk, for the construction of the human ear pointed the way to the mechanism of the telephone receiver. The invention was greeted with jeers. Originally it had only a single wire, connected at either end with a sort of can, which served both to receive and to transmit. There was no means of signalling except to tap on the diaphragm. One tapped, listened for the "all ready!" shifted the can to the mouth, and spoke. This single crude mechanism for receiving and transmitting did service until 1879. Signs warned the user not to "talk with your ear and listen with your mouth." Persons of wealth indulged extravagantly in two instruments, using both simultaneously, one with which to speak and one with which to listen, dual functions later combined in the present "English" receiver.

"Poor Bell," says Herbert N. Casson in his "History of the Telephone," "instead of being applauded, was pelted with a hailstorm of ridicule. He was an 'imposter,' a 'ventriloquist.' The London *Times* alluded pompously to the telephone as 'the latest American humbug,' and gave many profound reasons why speech could not be sent over a wire, because of the intermittent nature of the electric current. Almost all electricians—the men who were supposed to know —pronounced the telephone an impossible thing; and those who did not openly declare it to be a hoax, believed that Bell had stumbled upon some freakish use of electricity, which could never be of any practical value.

"Even though he came late in the succession of inventors, Bell had to run the gauntlet of scoffing and adversity. By the reception that the public gave his telephone, he learned to sympathize with Howe, whose first sewing machine was smashed by a Boston mob; with McCormick, whose first reaper was called 'a cross between an Astley chariot, a wheelbarrow, and a flying machine'; with Morse, whom ten Congresses regarded as a nuisance; with Cyrus Field, whose Atlantic cable was denounced as a 'mad freak of stubborn ignorance'; and with Westinghouse, who was called a fool for proposing 'to stop a train with wind.' "

The telephone, with all other recent inventions, was exhibited at the Centennial Exhibition at Philadelphia in 1876. The exhibition covered an area of 236 acres, ran six months, and was visited by 10,000,000 people. Although Appleton's "Annual Cyclopædia" for that year gives a detailed description of its features, it is noteworthy that in the entire account no mention is made of the telephone, or of Bell, its inventor.

Although the telephone was in actual use in New York City by 1877, the telephone directory consisted of but a single sheet and was limited to business use, while in 1878 there were only fifteen residence telephones. The first pay-station booth was opened in 1885.

A report on the conditions in an exchange in 1879 gives an idea of the primitive method employed at that date:

"When a call comes in it is promptly answered by the man at the switch, who calls out the names of the parties to the clerk. The clerk writes the names on a slip of paper and hands it to the boy who makes the connections on the switch, and then passes the slip to the operator on the table. The operation, though a good check both on the operator and the public, strikes me as rather cumbrous and intricate. . . . I also notice that the switch boys frequently make mistakes in connections, and I am informed by the switchman that sometimes seven minutes elapse before the parties get to conversing with each other, and that sometimes a man had to wait so long that he had forgotten his call."

Says Mr. Casson: "To describe one of those early telephone exchanges in the silence of the printed page is a wholly impossible thing. Nothing but a language of noise could convey the proper impression. An editor who visited the Chicago Exchange in 1879 said of it: 'The racket is almost deafening. Boys are rushing madly hither and thither, while others are putting in or taking out pegs from a central framework as if they were lunatics engaged in a game of fox and geese.' In the same year E. J. Hall wrote from Buffalo that his exchange with twelve boys had become a perfect bedlam. By the clumsy methods of those days, from two to six boys were needed to handle each call. And as there was usually more or less of a cat-and-dog squabble between the boys and the public, with everyone yelling at the top of his voice, it may be imagined that a telephone exchange was a loud and frantic place.

"Boys as operators proved to be most complete and consistent failures. Their sins of omission and commission would fill a book. What with whittling the switchboards, swearing at subscribers, playing tricks with the wires, and roaring on all occasions like young bulls of Bashan, the boys in the first exchanges did their full share in adding to the troubles of the business." Thus the girls got their chance.

By 1884 the movement for women's rights had become remarkably vigorous in both the political and economic sphere. "The most detailed and sympathetic treatment of the woman's movement," says Nevins, "was that by the well-known English social worker and suffragist, Emily Faithfull in 'Three Visits to America' (1882)—When Miss Martineau visited America in the thirties she discovered only five occupations open to women, but now Miss Faithfull found more than 400 in Massachusetts alone. In fact merely between her first visit in 1872 and her second in 1882, the introduction of the typewriter and telephone threw open wide new fields of employment for women."

The 80's saw the installation of the first elevator, or "perpendicular stairway" as it was called, in the Fifth Avenue Hotel, and the same decade established the popularity of the bicycle, an invention which had a more far-reaching effect on American social life than any others save that of the telephone and automobile.

The bicycle of the 80's had a front wheel with a diameter about three times the size of the rear one, the tires being strips of solid rubber which were constantly coming off and having to be cemented or tied on again with string or wire. There were several types, among them three known as the "Kangaroo," the " 'Xtraordinary," and the "Bone-Shaker." The original model had been imported into this country in 1876; in 1878 the first American company for its manufacture was organized; and by 1884 there were about 30,000 bicycles in use.

The nation-wide craze for the "bike," which filled the streets with processions of riders, aroused the vociferous ire of tradesmen who believed that the newfangled machines would spell their ruin. "The loudest outcry," wrote Joseph B. Bishop in *The Forum* for August, 1896, "comes from the makers of watches and jewelry. Many of them have abandoned the business entirely and substituted for it bicycle making. They say that formerly when a son came of age, or Christmas Day came around, the favorite family present was a watch; now it is a bicycle. The girls used to save their pin money with which to buy earrings, or a breast pin, or a locket; now they hoard it for a bicycle. The piano trade for the current year is said to have fallen off fifty per cent. Furniture dealers cite cases in which they have heard mothers say to their daughters that they could have their choice between new suites of parlor furniture and bicycles, and the choice has invariably been bicycles.

"Possibly the worse sufferers of all are the horse and carriage trades, and the businesses connected with them. The practice of horseback riding is nearly extinct and saddle horses are a drug on the market. The livery stable business has been cut down from a half to two-thirds, and carriages are in such poor demand that several leading firms have gone to the wall. Riding academies have been turned into bicycle schools, and riding masters have been forced to begin life over again in other occupations. It is stated by the journals of the tobacco trade that the consumption of cigars had fallen off during the present year at the rate of a million a day, and that the grand total of the decrease since the 'crase' really got under way is no less than 700,000,000. There is no doubt that riding does interfere with the smoking habit. The tailors say their business has been damaged at least 25 per cent, because their customers do not wear out clothes so rapidly as formerly, spending much of their time in cheap bicycle suits which they buy ready made. Shoemakers say they suffer severely because nobody walks much any longer, since persons who formerly got their exercise in that way have taken to the wheel, upon which they ride in low priced shoes which are subject to very little wear. The hatters say they are injured because bicyclists wear cheap caps. One irate member of the trade proposes that Congress be asked to pass a law compelling each bicycle rider to purchase at least two felt hats a year. Railway and steamboat men say their excursion business has been diminished perceptibly by the tendency to go into the country and to the seashore on the bicycle rather than by rail or water. Trolley and other street car lines from cities to their suburbs say their receipts have been cut down so heavily as to amount in some instances to the destruction of all profit.

"Dry goods dealers complained of reduced sale of dress goods and expensive costumes; book sellers said riding prevented much reading; one news agency in New York said it lost in trade a million dollars in decreased sales; saloon keepers complained because riders were drinking only beer and "soft drinks"; barbers said that the men used to get shaved regularly on Saturday afternoons, haircut and shampoo, to take their girls to the theatre, but now "they go off on a bicycle and do not care whether they are shaved or not. You see where it hurts our business is that when a man skips a shave to-day, we cannot sell him a shave to-morrow; *that shave is gone forever.*"

A plumbers' union in Indianapolis adopted a resolution condemning the use of bicycles by plumbers, on the ground that by so doing they were able to get through their jobs more quickly.

In many cities, including Fifth Avenue, New York, as late as during the first decade of the present century, three-foot strips of asphalt were still laid next the curb for the use of wheelmen.

The art of "salesmanship" was but poorly understood. There was no such thing as "the advertising business," and the advertisements themselves were crude, illustrated by simple and uninteresting cuts, with no attention to typography and layout, or to clever copy. John Rogers was advertising his famous "Groups," and several other statuary companies, weak imitators of Rogers, were likewise advertising plaster figures with which to ornament the parlor. Much of the space was taken up by advertisements of plants, seeds and farm supplies, showing that the country was far less urban-minded than now. Cuts of bicycles portrayed whiskered riders on high front wheels blowing upon small trumpets to warn pedestrians out of the way. Scroll-saws and patterns invited the perpetration of fret-work crimes. Patent medicines, supported as always by the ever-present "testimonial," heralded their "all-sovereign" curative powers. Heavyweight flannel underwear extended North, South, East and West to the uttermost reaches of the human frame. Pianos were square, with heavy, carved legs. Parlor organs exceeded the pianos in advertising space. Another musical instrument was the organette, or the organita, which, though it descended from the organ, was an ancestor of the "player piano." It had reeds like an organ, and a turning crank worked the bellows and unwound the perforated paper roll that caused the contraption to play tunes.

Among the advertisements in *The Century Magazine* was one for "Carpenter's Library Organ," an unbelievable piece of furniture which combined an organ with bookshelves, mantel, huge clock and cupboards. It would have taken an enormous room to contain it, and how it could have been manœuvred into a house without removing at least one sidewall is a mystery.

Advertising copy was dull and crude in the extreme, and when the effort was indulged in to make it otherwise the results were often startling. From *The Century* for January, 1883, I cull this flower of native poetry in praise of a patent nostrum:

"Ferric Odyline

"Mysterious law our world controls,
To man unknown, by all unseen,
But science circumscribed the poles
And gave us Ferric Odyline.

The deadly drugs of other days
Prescribed by honest men have been,
But now the folly of their ways
They see in Ferric Odyline.

When Paralytics prostrate lay
    Or ambling Gout on crutch is seen,
Go tell them it will well repay
    The price of Ferric Odyline.

Rheumatic Pains endured for years,
    And Chronic Cough or Hardened Spleen
And Asthma, too, will disappear
    By using Ferric Odyline.

From youth's first dawn to hoary age
    The fruitful fields of life we glean,
And on the world's historic page
    All fix the Ferric Odyline."

Where are the drugs of yesteryear?

It was a complaisant period. The descendants of the Puritans might well have been satisfied with the evidences of God's favor which had been vouchsafed to them in their storehouses and in all unto which they had set their hands. He had made the Americans plenteous in goods, in the fruit of their bodies, in the fruit of their cattle and in the fruit of their ground. Under the firmly planted feet of Queen Victoria the world was solid and established. There was nothing much to worry about.

One could buy sugar for four cents a pound, eggs for a cent apiece, wheat for seventy cents a bushel, and get a full meal—"turkey dinner"—for a quarter. Whiskey was $2 per gallon and pure California wine seventy cents per gallon. Chewing gum had come into vogue among the adolescent; and ice cream soda had been invented, shortly to replace ice water as the national beverage. Collecting "cigaret pictures" had become a juvenile fad almost as popular as collecting stamps. New York was "wide open" and one could "play the wheel" without interruption from the police at half a dozen places in fashionable residential districts and enjoy a sumptuous supper at midnight, including wine, free of charge. Many people still considered it immodest for a woman to have a male physician attend her during childbirth. Midwives attended more than 60 per cent of accouchements. The medical profession itself apparently neglected this important field, and the early "baby doctors" came in for considerable derision on the part of their colleagues. Marion Harland is said to be the first one who brought the subject of pregnancy and its proper care into open discussion, in her magazine *Babyhood*. This started a movement for the reduction of childbed deaths and infant mortality.

It was an era of social metamorphosis when girls were just beginning to abandon the rocking chair on the hotel piazza for the tennis court. People hummed airs from "Pinafore" and "The Mikado," the safety bicycle was a novelty, John L. Sullivan and Chauncey M. Depew were accepted institutions, the new Scotch game of golf was regarded as ridiculous, Mrs. William Astor was the *dea ex machina* of a society whose temple was 840 Fifth Avenue, men still attended divine service, cocktails in private houses were unknown.

With the development of electric lighting, the use of the typewriter and the telephone, there had come a general feeling that the end of scientific ingenuity had been attained. The self-laudatory recapitulations of our achievements seemed to indicate that things were so good we had better leave well enough alone, that not much in fact was left to be done. The railroad, the telegraph and cable were believed to be the ultimate modes of communication. The most eminent scientists (including Simon Newcomb, the astronomer) declared that aerial flight was a problem beyond man's capacity to solve. The most imaginative balked at the possibility of the submarine. Even Edward Bellamy, whose immensely popular "Looking Backward," published in 1887, sought to picture the America of A. D. 2000, did not venture to hint at the possibilities of the radio, although his description of the development of the telephone is an almost uncanny suggestion of it.

In Chapter XI, page 111, is to be found the following:

" 'Come, then, into the music room,' she said, and I followed her into an apartment finished, without hangings, in wood, with a floor of polished wood. I was prepared for new devices in musical instruments, but I saw nothing in the room which by any stretch of imagination could be conceived as such. It was evident that my puzzled appearance was affording intense amusement to Edith.

" 'Please look at today's music,' she said, handing me a card, 'and tell me what you would prefer. It is now five o'clock, you will remember.'

"The card bore the date 'September 12, 2000.' and contained the longest programme of music I had ever seen. It was as various as it was long, including a most extraordinary range of vocal and instrumental solos, duets, quartettes, and various orchestral combinations. I remained bewildered by the prodigious list until Edith's pink finger-tip indicated a particular section of it, where several selections were bracketed, with the words '5 P.M.' against them; then I observed that this prodigious programme was an all-day one, divided into twenty-four sections answering to the hours. There were but a few pieces of music in the '5 P.M.' section, and I indicated an organ piece as my preference.

" 'I am so glad you like the organ,' she said. 'I think there is scarcely any music that suits my mood oftener.'

"She made me sit down comfortably, and, crossing the room, so far as I could see, merely touched one or two screws, and at once the room was filled with the music of a grand organ anthem; filled, not flooded, for, by some means, the volume of melody has been perfectly graduated to the size of the apartment. I listened, scarcely breathing, to the close. Such music, so perfectly rendered, I had never expected to hear.

" 'Grand!' I cried, as the last great wave of sound broke and ebbed away into silence. 'Bach must be at the keys of that organ; but where is the organ?'

" 'Wait a moment, please,' said Edith: 'I want to have

you listen to this waltz before you ask any question. I think it is perfectly charming'; and as she spoke the sound of violins filled the room with the witchery of a summer night. When this had also ceased, she said: 'There is nothing in the least mysterious about the music, as you seem to imagine. It is not made by fairies or genii, but by good, honest, and exceedingly clever human hands. We have simply carried the idea of labor saving by cooperation into our musical service as into everything else. There are a number of music rooms in the city, perfectly adapted acoustically to the different sorts of music. These halls are connected by telephone with all the houses of the city whose people care to pay the small fee, and there are none, you may be sure, who do not. The corps of musicians attached to each hall is so large that, although no individual performer, or group of performers, has more than a brief part, each day's programme lasts through the twenty-four hours. There are on that card for today, as you will see if you observe closely, distinct programmes of four of these concerts, each of a different order of music from the others, being now simultaneously performed, and any one of the four pieces now going on that you prefer, you can hear by merely pressing the button which will connect your house-wire with the hall where it is being rendered. The programmes are so coordinated that the pieces at any one time simultaneously proceeding in the different halls usually offer a choice, not only between instrumental and vocal, and between different sorts of instruments; but also between different motives from grave to gay, so that all tastes and moods can be suited."

Later on in the same book at page 273 we find:

" 'Now, as to hearing a sermon today, If you wish to do so, you can either go to church to hear it or stay at home.'

" 'How am I to hear it if I stay at home?'

" 'Simply by accompanying us to the music room at the proper hour and selecting an easy chair. There are some who still prefer to hear sermons in church, but most of our preaching, like our musical performances, is not in public, but delivered in acoustically prepared chambers, connected by wire with subscribers' houses. If you prefer to go to a church I shall be glad to accompany you, but I really don't believe you are likely to hear anywhere a better discourse than you will at home. I see by the paper that Mr. Barton is to preach this morning, and he preaches only by telephone, and to audiences often reaching 150,000.' "

Had Bellamy lived but a few more years he would have seen, or rather heard, the realization of what he prophesied in 1887, yet at the time even so simple an extension of the powers of the telephone as he foretold was regarded as fanciful.

The simple Knickerbocker society, which had ruled New York up to the Civil War, had been as unable to withstand the onslaught of the "Gold rush" which followed it as the modern suburb is to-day to "turn down" the slightly offensive millionaire who presents it with a golf course and invites its boys and girls on yachting parties. The more conservative had at first assumed what would now be termed a "high hat" or "snooty" attitude towards those whom they called "bouncers" and "silver gilts"; the newcomers, however, had not only persistence but more money than had ever been seen in the world before.

The intense outward propriety of what is commonly called the "Brownstone Era" was due not only to the influence of Queen Victoria, and to a revulsion among the better class against the crassness of the "Dreadful Decade," but to the striving on the part of its protagonists to achieve social respectability and recognition. For a while it was more Victorian than Victoria herself. It is interesting to speculate as to what would have been the outcome had the movie, the radio and the automobile been then invented,—but as yet not even the bicycle had come into popular use. There were no objective interferences with a return to Puritanism, no legitimate excuse for not attending church on Sundays, so for a decade—at least upon the surface—Puritanism came back and Wealth humbled itself, walked cautiously and passed the plate on Sundays, until in the twentieth century the sons and daughters of Mammon, perceiving that their money had bought them their much-coveted place in society, began to find convention irksome and started in to get their quid pro quo.

There had been no recognizable aristocracy subsequent to the Revolution in America, yet the Americans remained English-minded long after they had declared all men to have been created equal, and, the nearest thing to a lord being the owner of landed estates or their local equivalent, wealth in due course and quite naturally took the place of family. Sensitiveness to English opinion and regard for the English aristocracy has always been one of the most marked characteristics of American fashionable life. The visit of the Prince of Wales as Baron Renfrew, in 1861, paralleled in snobbery that of his grandson in 1926, and during the great ball given in his honor at the Academy of Music ten minute bulletins were published by *The Herald,* such as "10.10 the Prince is Approaching,"—"10.20 He arrives,"—"10.30 He is now dancing."

Since we have never had a College of Heraldry and hence no definite test as to who is and who is not entitled to "a place in society," it has been left to the claimants to assert their rights by whatever means seems to them most effective, and inasmuch as serious-minded people have little time or inclination to bother with the pretentious, their assiduity has usually achieved success. Yet nothing is more fickle than fortune in this regard, and while some have not the slightest difficulty in climbing to the top of the social heap, others, no less wealthy or desirable, never succeed—for no tangible reason—in getting off the ground.

The Puritan-Philistines, in most instances, succeeded in forcing their way in. No less an authority than Mr. Poultney Bigelow in his "Seventy Summers," four of which (from 1879–1884) he spent in New York City, has left us an account of how it was accomplished and the impression made upon his simple adolescent mind by ostentatious wealth. "At that time," says he, "there were a few millionaires, and they were tolerated, provided they were otherwise a social asset."

Happily Mr. Bigelow himself assisted in tolerating these millionaires by attending a ball given by one of them, where "the Cotillon favours were jewels from the great house of Tiffany, and these were passed about by flunkeys as though they had been bon-bons or glasses of lemonade.

"My education had not prepared me for such display. I had not then read Petronius or dreamed that the land of Washington could produce a Trimalchio, but I felt uncomfortable in offering costly jewels to a debutante of whom I asked nothing more than a turn in the dance. Next day the newspapers had fulsome details of this dance. The flowers that concealed the banisters were alone estimated at $10,000; the golden plates were estimated in cash, and the golden crests as well. Verily decadent Rome could not have done much more in the way of waste. Yet it was well that I saw it, or I could not have believed such things possible within a century of our being a British colony."

He also (young men will go everywhere, as one knows!) attended what he refers to as the "social eruption" of another family of which he "learned by picking up from the top of my father's wastepaper basket a beautifully engraved invitation to a reception at their palace just completed. I said nothing, but went from curiosity, nor was I disappointed. Everybody there seemed surprised at seeing everybody else there, and the usual greeting was: 'Hello, what brings you here?' It was a man-only reception, and the invitations had been broadcast amongst those that might have been selected in connection with a monster charity or patriotic demonstration. It was a quasi *ballon d'essai*. The guests went as to an auction, and indeed, we acted as though at one; for the public prints had from time to time published paragraphs regarding marvels of luxury. Even the bathroom was referred to as having the walls daringly decorated: nude nymphs, after the engaging manner of Boucher or Fragonard. I did not see these, for the bathroom was always packed; and if there was one part of the palace even more dense it was near the tables, where champagne flowed freely. The crowd was immense, a crowd whose component parts were social strangers one to the other, though many of them were familiar public figures at the Bar, in politics or on the race-track. There was a host— so I learned afterwards—but I did not see him at any time. No one there appeared to feel under any obligation save to come and see, and then go forth and advertise the wonders they had seen."

When people like Ward McAllister and Poultney Bigelow were willing to try anything once in the shape of a new millionaire's party, they could hardly expect to have him rejected by society. Yet all through the 80's, however civilized the newly rich had become, there was still a noticeable distinction between the Men of Money and the Old New Yorkers. Nevertheless, the "silver gilts" easily crashed the gates, ignored such of the older Knickerbocker families as at first disdained them, and established dynasties of their own. Today, when most people speak of the "old New York families" they usually have these in mind. Before me is a newspaper advertisement featuring the endorsement of something or other by a celebrated youth, who is described therein as a "scion of one of the oldest and most socially prominent families in America." I happen to know that at a dinner party less than fifty years ago, the young man's great-grandfather spat on a gold plate which he then wiped with his elbow.

These nouveaux riches, or Philistines, were essentially simple people, but their self-consciousness about their own lack of culture and the newness of their riches turned them for the time being into snobs. They were too close to their own past to recognize even their own true value. In America they were afraid of being inconveniently recognized by old friends, or by new friends that might not be of the right sort, but ten days on an ocean liner would take them to England where one American, if not as good, nevertheless looked just like another, and where, if one insisted on meeting only titled people, one could make no social mistakes.

The conquest of London proved as easy—easier even— than the conquest of New York. They returned home the intimates of royalties and bringing the English fashions with them. The "dude"—aping the cockney drawl, the monocle, the "Piccadilly swing" or the "Pall Mall glide" of the London "masher"—was a familiar figure on Fifth Avenue. The plebeian who had acquired wealth often aspired to patrician distinctions, and Tiffany was said to have a pattern book of crests from which the embryonic nobleman could choose his scutcheon. Naturally this excited the irony of the public and the expression "Quite English, you know!" was on everybody's lips. Comic songs ridiculing the phobia were popular, one especially, with the refrain:

> "O, the things that we say and the queer things we do
> Are 'English, you know!' 'Quite English, you know!'"

It was partly for this reason, no doubt, that the Victorian influence was so potent in the eighties and early nineties. Primarily, however, it was because the new leaders of society wanted to show that they were the right kind of people. Hence social conventionality reached its flood at this time, and there was an elaboration in the lives of the rich attained neither before nor since. The houses of commonplace and rather ignorant business men swarmed with menials in colored livery, chosen for their height and the shapeliness of their calves. Flunkies occasionally even wore powdered wigs. "Favors" of a most expensive sort were distributed to both male and female guests at dinner parties.

Social usage was modelled in every respect upon that of the "Mother Country." Nobody whose hands were sullied by "trade" (save in a few notably exceptional cases) was received. Respectability and propriety were the twin watchwords of society. Great country houses modelled on the "stately homes of England" advertised the wealth and "position" of their owners, European travel became common and a yearly trip to Paris to buy clothes a domestic necessity. Up to the 80's most city dwellers had not felt obliged to leave town for a vacation, which, when taken, rarely exceeded a month and was passed, as a matter of economy, convenience and greater sociability, in some huge caravansary at Newport, Saratoga or Bar Harbor, since, travelling being still a genuine undertaking and there being no such thing as "commuting," those who took the trouble to go away wanted to go far enough to make it worth while. Gradually the new millionaires began to feel that hotel life lacked proper distinction, and palatial summer "cottages" of brick and stone, in addition to their country houses nearer the city, were erected at these resorts where the formality of city life was continued, without any of its present mitigations in the way of exercise.

The effort to spend the wealth accumulated in and since the days of the 'Forty-niners, in gold, silver and copper, in hardware, cotton, pork, and dry goods, in steamships, railroads, and stockjobbery was at its height. The owners did not quite know how to do it satisfactorily, but they did the best that they could and had already organized themselves into an aristocracy of wealth consisting of less than 500 individuals—400 to be exact—with an acknowledged empress and a grand vizier (later exchanged for a court jester) who granted patents of social nobility and dictated the mode of fashionable life. The entry to this charmed circle was beyond the dreams of most aspirants, but they could at least gape in wondering admiration, keep informed of its goings on and perhaps, if fortunate, meet an acquaintance or distant relative of one of its members. "Swell" life attained a degree of notoriety and exercised a domination over the minds and souls of the vast unrecognized such as can be realized now with difficulty.

Yet even this "Era of Extravagance"—outside the mere lavishness of its expenditure—was strongly tinged with Puritanism. It was an age of conventionality, euphemism and prudery, of church going, Sabbatarianism and uplift, of

"Moody and Sankey," of Christian Endeavor and Comstockery, of national self-satisfaction—in short the "Brownstone Era,"—the era in which I first saw the light and passed my adolescence.

# CHAPTER XV

# The Puritan Shadow

I WAS born in the city of Boston in 1875, ninety-two years after the birth of my grandfather in 1783, and fifty-eight years after that of my father in 1817. It was an era of gas, sulphur matches, fixed wooden bathtubs lined with tin, nightgowns, chewing-tobacco, and the Republican party, when it was still regarded as elegant to produce from one's waistcoat pocket a small gold toothpick concealed in a gold case, and use it daintily after eating, when the spittoon was an omnipresent necessity, when ladies wore crinolines and bustles, when the waltz was regraded as something of an innovation, when one was not expected to smoke in the house, but to retire to the kitchen or woodshed, when clergymen did not smoke at all, and many married ladies over thirty-five wore caps with ribbons, and when it was *comme il faut* to carry one's hat into the parlor and keep on one's gloves when calling. Does the reader have polite doubts? Let him turn to that invaluable handbook for the socially aspiring, entitled "Manners that Win," published in 1880, where he may read:

"When calling, a gentleman leaves his overshoes, overcoat, and umbrella in the hall, but retains his hat. The lady rises to salute and receive him, unless for some reason, age or illness, she cannot, when she retains her seat and excuses herself from rising. If she offers her hand, he takes it respectfully but does not remove his glove."

The Civil War had apparently been fought only the day before yesterday. One had friends who had lost uncles and brothers at Shiloh and Gettysburg—saw, met, and sat on the knees of war governors and generals at the Union Club on Park Street.

There were, of course, no telephones, no electric lights, no safety-matches, no motors, no golf or country clubs.

We had bananas, but no grapefruit. Divorce was a social disgrace, irrespective of the guilt of either party, and usually led to social ostracism. Ready-made shoes of good quality could be bought for from $2 up, and ready-made "Plymouth Rock" pants for $3. They were advertised thus:

"When the pant hunter pantless is panting for pants,
And pants for the best pants the pant market grants,
He panteth unpanted until he implants
Himself in a pair of our 'Plymouth Rock' pants."

Statesmen, generals, and ministers of the Gospel publicly indorsed patent medicines. "Rogers' Groups" were to be found in every "parlor." The bustle was omnipresent. Women wore their hair in "water waves," "bangs," and ringlets; men used bear's grease. "Votes for women" and "women's rights" in general were jokes, and the ladies who aped men's clothing were treated not only as freaks but as of doubtful virtue. It was still eminently respectable to be a Sunday-school superintendent or United States senator, and clergymen were universally objects of admiration to the ladies.

No profanity was permitted upon the stage, and it was nearly twenty years later before the first outspoken "damn" sent a shiver down the backs of the startled audience, although presently, once the "customers" had become properly acclimated to such daring expletives, they inevitably and for many years received them with "sure-fire" applause and laughter. Not until 1900 did the first "God damn" appear under the imprint of a respectable publisher:—not until nearly quarter of a century thereafter was it heard across the footlights. The stage—except for the classics and old English comedies—was still looked upon askance; most actors and actresses were classed with harlots, saloon-keepers, and gamblers. Novels were decried as frivolous and often harmful. "Comic operas," even if advertised as "phantasmas," were not attended by the best people. The mother-in-law joke was still regarded as funny, and black-face minstrels played to packed houses everywhere.

On trans-Atlantic steamers sidewheels had only recently given place to propellers. In 1854 the clipper *Lightning*, built by Donald McKay for James Baines & Co., had, on her maiden voyage from Boston to Liverpool, to quote Samuel Eliot Morrison, "made the greatest day's run ever performed by a sailing vessel; a day's run that no steamship at that day could equal by a hundred miles, that no steamship equalled for a generation, and that barely fifty ocean steamers today could surpass," *i. e.*, 436 miles. This is an average rate of eighteen miles. No steamer on the ocean in 1875 could equal this, in spite of the fact that many, if not most, used sail as auxiliary to steam.

There were hitching-posts and horse-blocks on the residential streets of New York, Philadelphia, and Boston, and a common sight on Beacon Street in the latter city was a herd of several hundred cattle mooing, bellowing, and shoving each other across the sidewalks and even up the steps of the houses, while nurse-maids and pedestrians sought refuge in the vestibules. The Union Pacific Railroad had been completed only a short time, every farmer had his buffalo-robe, and Custer had just made his "last stand." Indians—real, live, dangerous ones in war-paint and feathers—still swarmed the Western plains and were the most popular subject of juvenile literature. That a woman should smoke or ride astride was almost as unthinkable as that she should appear in the streets totally nude, and would have excited as much of a riot. Cigarettes were not widely used and were viewed as decadent, "nasty," and in some occult way as suggestive of obscenity. This last was perhaps due to the lure of giving away with each box a photograph of some Amazonian stage favorite with the exuberant pulchritude so much admired by lewd fellows of the baser sort at that period. The annual circus parade was in effect a local holiday even in cities as large as Boston.

It was about this time that the word "chestnut" was first applied to any anecdote or story too familiar to be longer enjoyable to the hearer. For some unknown reason the term caught the popular fancy, swept the country and became embedded in the American language. Presently what were known as "Chestnut Bells" made their appearance. These were small, circular gongs, about an inch and a half in diameter, which could be attached by a pin to the facing of one's jacket. When anybody "got off an old one," the bell owner pulled a concealed chain and rang the gong twice—in imitation of the driver's bell on a horse car. Every one I happened to know possessed a "Chestnut Bell," just as later he had "Pigs in Clover," and it is a constant surprise to me that so few of the people of my own age I now meet have any recollection of them. Riding a bicycle was very recherché—although not the social equivalent of polo playing to-day. But it was considered dangerous and dashing and involved wearing a blue suit consisting of a bob-tailed jacket, short knickers, and dinky little cap. I can perfectly remember the awe inspired by my Latin teacher thus attired when perched upon his nickel-plated high wheel.

Everybody wore gloves to everything. At dinner-parties, and this was still true down into the twentieth century, men wore white gloves when shaking hands with their host and hostess and peeled them off before going to the table. It may have been that the hands got harder use then than now and gloves helped to conceal reddened joints and broken, blackened nails.

In those days there was nothing invidious in the terms "upper and lower classes," and they were used without embarrassment or apprehension that the speaker might be regarded as either snobbish or unchristian. It was not considered undemocratic to recognize the fact that God had been pleased to call people to different "estates of life" where they should order themselves humbly and reverently to "their betters." At least the betters had no doubt about it. There was enormous respect for anything "established." There was no "muck-raking," the cities were as yet unashamed, no historic character had been debunked. That George Washington could not tell a lie and did it "with his little hatchet" was as certain as that God made cherry-trees. Nobody questioned the literal interpretation of the Scriptures or the divine origin of capitalism. To advocate membership in a trade-union was to read oneself out of respectable society. Everybody went to church or, if not, concealed himself in the rear of the house, and, except just before and after morning service, the streets on Sundays were practically deserted.

Bishop William Lawrence in "Fifty Years" writing of 1870 says: "Through boyhood and to some degree in college I had accepted the Christian Faith as it had been taught me. While the Jesus of the Gospels was a vivid story, the chief emphasis was upon the Old Testament, and of course both Old and New Testaments, being inspired, were true to the word and letter. The world was created in six days in the year 4004 B. C., for Genesis and the date on the margin of the family Bible said so. Adam and Eve, the serpent, Noah and the flood destroying everybody and everything on the earth but the family and the animals entering the Ark two by two, Jonah and the whale, Joshua and the sun, Daniel and the lion's den, the three young men in the fiery furnace, were facts as real as anything that happened yesterday. A heaven of bliss and a hell of eternal fire were as vivid as the blue, serene sky over my head or a big bonfire by night."

Darwin's theory of the survival of the fittest was considered a huge, if impious, joke, which Gladstone had supposedly annihilated in his "Impregnable Rock of Holy Scripture" by proving to the satisfaction of almost everybody that the word "day" used in Genesis in the account of God's making of the world, if properly translated, meant really "period of time." Just how he disposed of Methuselah's nine hundred odd years, I forget. Any deviation from es-

tablished conventions was an indication of either insanity or
sin. New England still adhered frigidly to the belief that
whatever made for joy or gaiety must be in essence evil.

Life was still lived with Puritan frugality. Even among
the well-to-do there were practically no male house domestics. Few people kept more than two servants, who were
inevitably female Irish immigrants recently landed. We paid
Bridget, our cook, $4 and the "second girl" (there was no
first girl) $2.50 per week. The second girl swept off the
steps in the morning, washed out the vestibule, waited on
table, answered the bell, and helped with the family wash.
In winter any peripatetic choreman, who happened by, shovelled the snow off the sidewalk for twenty-five cents. My
father and the cook together managed the furnace, and my
mother did much of the dusting. We had roast beef once a
week and little meat the rest of the time. There was no "dinner" except on Sundays, its place being taken at night by a
nondescript meal of minced fish or fowl, hot breads, pies,
cookies, apple sauce and corn-meal (or "Indian") "mush."
Luncheon was negligible.

Every household in Boston in those days had a "Bridget,"
and in our immediate connection there were no less than four,
known respectively as "Big Bridget," "Little Bridget," "Old
Bridget" and "Young Bridget." These, being more or less
permanent, ranked much higher in family esteem than the
constantly changing girls above stairs. My mother, a sweet
little woman, about twenty years younger than my father,
while not intellectually gifted, had the charity and self-ef-
facement of a saint. Constitutionally timid she adjured me
never to use the words "Irish" or "Roman Catholic" in front
of any of the servants, although for my part I could not understand her reticence, since I felt that if I were Irish and
Roman Catholic I should not be ashamed of the fact. She
was convinced that the Romanists in America and the Russians in Russia were engaged in a colossal and far-reaching
conspiracy to overthrow the Government of the United States
and make America subservient to the Pope of Rome. How

the Russians got into it I never understood, but according to her they were hiding everywhere,—in the chimneys, walls, and between the floors, listening to everything that was said and preparing for a general massacre like that of St. Bartholomew. Indeed, reference to St. Bartholomew and the identifying white handkerchief were often on her lips.

My father, who was by now one of the prominent figures of Massachusetts both in politics and at the bar, had moved at the conclusion of his service in the army to Boston, where after the death of his first wife, Martha A. Jackson of Attleboro in 1867, he met and married my mother, Sarah Maria Cheney of South Boston, in 1869. He held many important public offices, and in 1872 was elected Attorney-General of the Commonwealth, a position which he held by annual election for seven consecutive years. In this last capacity he prosecuted many famous cases, including that of Jesse Pomeroy, and attained a high reputation for his knowledge of the law and as an advocate.

He was a man of quick intelligence, humor, self-possession, and fertile in resource. A schoolmate described him as "a genial, large-hearted, impulsive boy; sarcastic, transparent; never attempting to conceal his faults; nourishing no ill will; seeking no revenges; always ready to meet all consequences; just the boy—as in after years he was just the man—one would most like to have for a friend, or an enemy."

As he was popular with both men and women, and a great story teller, I think that what I then took for "gruffness" may have been largely put on for my benefit. At the Bi-Centennial Anniversary of Framingham in 1900 the orator of the day said that "if he had been willing to be untrue to his political principles and friends about forty-five years ago, and have made even a bow of allegiance to a then powerful political organization, he could have been Governor of the State."

I am glad that my father preserved his political integrity even at the cost of so high an honor.

In winter the streets were filled with "slush"—crushed

ice and snow, ground to the consistency of corn meal and of much the same color,—and for the comfort of the passengers the wooden floors of the horse cars were covered with straw into which one could thrust one's feet for warmth or which, if preferred, one could fashion into long stalks to tickle the ears and necks of other travellers. Over the windows inside were colored advertisements heralding the virtues and delights of "Ball's Corsets," "Pope's Bicycles," "Carter's Little Liver Pills" and "St. Jacob's Oil."

The great event of the day was the appearance at dusk of the lamp-lighter with his magic wand. There was an eerie quality about this stealthily hurrying figure different from that surrounding even a fireman, a policeman, or the red-cheeked drivers who drove their "pungs" down the back alleys and allowed small Puritans to ride on the runners or cling to the cleats along the sides. The back yards were the enchanted forests of those early years, and all my romances were tainted with a slight aroma of first-class swill.

Boston society in the 70's was the same sort of family affair as exists to-day in those comfortable mid-western towns originally founded by New Englanders who trekked there in covered wagons during the early years of the nineteenth century. When people returned home in the late afternoon they stayed there, and, apart from an occasional political banquet, my father never dined out. In fact I do not think that he possessed such a thing as a dress suit although he owned a blue "claw-hammer" with tails and brass buttons.

Existence was simple and methodical. Every morning at precisely half past eight o'clock each front door opened and the owner of the house, wearing a tan-colored "reefer," as the short box-coat of those days was locally called, and carrying a green baize bag supposedly holding papers, descended to the sidewalk and started to walk "down-town." At six, or six-thirty, in the evening he reappeared and, ascending the steps once more, disappeared for another ten hours. The ladies "went down-town" about ten o'clock, after having helped one of the "Bridgets" with the lighter house-keeping. On rainy days they took the horse-cars, whose warning tinkle could be heard for several blocks. Indeed, one could "watch out for the horse-car" from the bay window and still have plenty of time to cross the street and signal for it to stop. The drivers and conductors were family friends, often taking part in the conversations between passengers.

One was aroused each morning by the seven-o'clock car —"Jingle-clup-jingle-ingle-ingle-clup-clup. Whoa!—Clatter!—Giddap!—Clupitty!—Jingle-jingle-clup-clup—jingle-jingle-ingle-clupitty-jingle——"

How deep the snow was in those days! How huge the mounds piled along the curbs; higher even than one's head! And what a thud *The Transcript* made when the paper-carrier hurled it into the front vestibule against the door! There is no such snow, no such strong man now! I used to find all kinds of strange loot in that dusty vestibule which had accumulated in my absence—sample packages of starch and oatmeal, tiny bottles containing salving ointments and health-giving pills, and wonderful colored advertisements of all kinds, some containing the most side-splitting jokes, which were immediately taken away from me by my watchful mama.

One variety in especial I recall which at first gave me infinite delight,—a pseudo-magazine, in reality a circular, always bearing some such fancy name as *The Four Leaf Clover* or *The Pansy Blossom*, printed on cheap blue or pink paper, its front and next succeeding pages given over to poems, news items and a story. This last was always a thrilling narrative of love and adventure which, after working the reader up to a high tension, would end abruptly with the laconic statement "And then they took St. Jacob's Oil," or "Pitcher's Castoria," or "Carter's Little Liver Pills," and lived happily ever after, but leaving the problem otherwise unsolved. After a while I gave up reading them in view of the inevitable disappointment attending the denouement. But

I resisted only with difficulty and sometimes, when I succumbed, would invent a more literary ending for myself.

Looking back over the development of the modern magazine, the enormous success of which is due to advertising, I am satisfied that the man who invented these patent-medicine trick-stories is the father of all of them. For it was he, beyond peradventure, who discovered the possibility of attracting the attention of a possible buyer through the medium of fiction and, having thus "barked" him in, of selling him something. The next improvement—a great step in advance—was that of finishing the story in proper style, and printing the advertisement immediately following. Thus Tom and Agnes no longer remained indefinitely suspended over Niagara Falls taking "St. Jacob's Oil," which, however efficacious, every boy knew could not possibly save them, but instead were duly rescued, resuscitated and properly married, while the reader, without suffering from a sense of chagrin and disappointment upon being advised to take that sovereign elixir, was much more likely to listen favorably to the juxtaposed admonition to buy a bottle. And so again is honesty found to be the best policy. The most hardboiled magazine reader of to-day, unless indeed he reads the advertisements first, hardly is aware of the process by which he is lured into expending his substance on safety razors, union suits, shot guns, waterproof paints, and motors. It all started back in our vestibule on Marlborough Street in Boston with *The Four Leaf Clover*.

While perhaps no conclusion should be drawn from the effect of the Puritan tradition upon one Puritan boy brought up in a Puritan city fifty years ago, it is suggestive of the persistence and strength of an influence which most of us assume to have vanished long before that time. In all essentials and in most outward manifestations the New England of 1875 was practically as Puritan as it had been a century before. There was the same insistence upon Sabbath observance as when the "tythingman" went his rounds to see that everybody went to church, the same attitude of suspicion towards anything that made for mere gaiety or pleasure such as light fiction and the stage in contradistinction to what was supposedly educational and "improving," the same antagonism to the Roman Church, to divorce, to women's rights, to the frank pursuit of happiness. Queen Victoria contributed her share to the continuance of the Puritan shadow by making the last half of the eighteenth century as conventional as the Pilgrim fathers had made it dour. New Englanders found it hard to throw off the conviction of sin. Even their taste for rum was in the Puritan tradition.

Although my father was an Episcopalian—a sect to which still adhered a faint flavor of Popery in its inordinate celebrations of Christmas and Easter—and my mother a Unitarian—or in other words hardly a Christian at all—I was not permitted to indulge in any form of amusement upon the Lord's day, when even a walk must be a mild promenade with no unseemly outcries or cavortings. I was allowed on the Sabbath to read only the Bible and certain selected Sunday-school books bound in red and blue and tooled in gold; to talk only about spiritual or supposedly spiritual things.

At church I was cooped up in a long high-backed pew during long, dreary hours, without occupation except to draw surreptitious pictures of the minister in the back of my prayer-book. Sometimes I smuggled toy animals into church, but these my father always managed to take away, save on one occasion when I stuck a little feathered rooster upon the lady's hat in front of us, unbeknownst to my parents. Still it was fun to peek over the back of the pew, which I could just do by standing on tiptoe on the seat, and make faces at the people behind.

It was on Sunday in especial that I suffered from the consciousness of having been born in sin, the conviction that misbehavior on the part of little boys occasioned acute cardiac pain in the Almighty, and that His burning eye followed me into the most secret places, including the bathroom. Sunday was a miserable affair always, for it was the one day in the week when a hearty dinner of roast beef made me fret to get out into the open air and "work it off." Many an hour did I sit book in hand gnashing my teeth in a half-darkened room, vainly trying to interest myself in "Paul and Virginia" or "The Dove in the Eagle's Nest," while I yearned to be running across the fields or to be lying under the sky upon the beach. But no! God's eye was upon me! So I made the best of it, feeling that there must be something wrong about the whole business, exactly what I most annoyingly could not find out, since any attempt at discussion between me and my parents upon the subject of religious dogma was sternly rebuked. "Little boys mustn't try to understand such things." Later on the conviction stole upon me that my mother, at least, might be afraid to discuss "such things" because they were beyond the comprehension of even herself. As for the other six days in the week certain concessions were made toward liberalism by allowing attendance at Papanti's dancing school on Saturday mornings and, once or twice a winter, at some "operetta" given at the old Boston Museum, where I was hurried past the pickled mermaids and fœtuses by my anxious guardian, and where in later years I revelled in old English comedy given by a stock company composed, among others, of Junius Brutus Booth, Jr., Edgar Fawcett, George Wilson, Mrs. Vincent, Annie Clark, Edgar Davenport, John Mason, and, for a time, Richard Mansfield.

It was through such cracks in the wall that I first gained the knowledge that there were other worlds possessed of other standards where, by some curious paradox, people were not damned for doing the very same things that would have damned them in Boston and which, strangely enough, Bostonians were willing to pay to see portrayed upon the stage. From these plays I gathered that there was a thing called "love," not mentioned at home. That this had anything to do with sex was unsuspected and no doubt would have been stoutly denied by those in authority. But that obvious naughtiness might be rather charming, and that parents could even go so far as to laugh at it, aroused the first suspicions in my mind that the line between right and wrong might not be so clearly defined as I had been led to believe. Secretly I pondered and, pondering upon the nature of God, became at nine, as I believed, an atheist. Once upon the skids, my whole intellectual cosmos toppled with a crash.

The "Back Bay," where we lived, consisted of "made land" reclaimed from the tidal overflow of the Charles River, and in my boyhood was only partially built up. Vacant lots abounded in which to play "robbers and police," fight one another with burdocks, and build campfires in which we roasted potatoes. We fished for eels and catfish in Muddy River and Stony Brook, floated about on rafts, ran "tiddle-dies" in winter, and fought the gangs of "muckers" who periodically descended upon the fair plains of Common-wealth Avenue from the East and West Ends like the rav-aging Huns of Attila. We had our battles of Chalons too, for, if we were seen to be getting the worst of it, the cops or "Peelers," as they were called, usually came to our assistance and drove off the barbaric hordes.

I had no allowance, the dollar I received at Christmas being held sufficient for sumptuary expenditures, but I dug dandelions for five cents a quart and was paid for such kindling wood as I scavenged from houses in process of con-struction. I also was given the proceeds of the family rag bag and did a negligible trade in old iron and bottles. In order to eke out my otherwise insufficient amount of spend-ing money I stole animal crackers out of the biscuit tin and disposed of them for a penny a handful, and sold "soda" from my mother's bromo-seltzer bottle for two cents a glass.

Our Marlborough Street house was the Mecca of country relatives of my mother's, and also of my father's first wife, and my childish memories swarm with the ghosts of angular red-nosed maiden great-aunts and distant "cousins" of all sorts who showed an intense curiosity to see me in my bath. Some came for lengthy visits, even "for the winter." There were Aunt Susans, Aunts and Cousins Elizas, and Hetties, and Abbies. I disliked them all intensely for they treated my dear mother, as it seemed to me, with a certain condescension. Nevertheless she was kindness itself to all of them, although at least half had only the smallest of vicarious claims upon her, and in spite of the fact that they arrived at the most inconvenient hours, ate prodigiously, and sniffed.

The presence of this rather down at the skirts crew added to the sense of social inferiority which I directly inherited from my mother. This was increased by the intense economy practiced in our household where to save matches we always used "spills" from six to ten inches long made by rolling up the margins of old newspapers. In order to light the gas one thrust a spill or lighter into the fire and thus transferred the flame to the gas jet. As I write it occurs to me that, what I have always heretofore taken to have been an economy, may have been in fact done for convenience, it being much easier to reach the gas jet with a spill than with a match, which had the added inconvenience of being too close for comfort to the flame. But apart from the use of "spills" thrift was not only encouraged but enforced by the most rigid discipline, thus engendering a parsimony akin to avarice, and enhancing the conviction that my family came from a lower economic stratum than most of my fellows.

The part played by these two influences in my later psychology is interesting at least to myself. To arouse social self-consciousness in a child by depriving him of pocket money, or teaching him stringent economy, at a time when he should be unconscious of social or economic inequalities between himself and his companions, is an undesirable and dangerous proceeding. He should, on the contrary, be taught from the first the uselessness of money unless spent for good purposes. The idea that worldly prosperity in the shape of a large bank account is an evidence of God's regard for the possessor, is a tenet of Puritanism that has brought no credit or real benefit to the thin-lipped race who follow it.

I fancy that the narrowness of my own upbringing was due as much to parsimony as to religion. If my parents looked askance at the theatre, there was also the obvious fact that it cost money to go there; and if candy was a luxury, so by the same token was whiskey or tobacco. As I look back upon a childhood in which I experienced no spontaneous demonstrations of affection, where the good-night kiss was a peck rather than a caress, and in which praise was rarely accorded to any task, however well done, on the ground that its performance was but a duty, I thank God that with the advancing years the shadow of the Puritan falls more lightly as his figure grows more meagre. I believe that one of the worst injunctions to a child is to "take care of the pennies and let the pounds take care of themselves." On the contrary, he should be taught the value of the pounds and to let the pennies look out for themselves. I do not think that wholesale charity excuses retail penuriousness; and I firmly believe that more harm is done by stifling impulsive generosity than by bestowing alms unwisely.

I do not intend to convey the impression that there was no broader social horizon in the Boston of those days, but merely that my own—which was bounded by the car-tracks of Marlborough Street—was like that. Persons who lived on Commonwealth Avenue and Beacon Street may have been less provincial. Certainly I shared my little mother's almost painful awe of them, which soon bred in me an antagonism toward what were known as "carriage-people."

Until I was well along in my college course I lived in the ever-present expectation of social slights, carrying upon my shoulder a chip the size of a chopping block. Looking back upon it I am convinced that all this was utterly without basis and grew entirely out of my mother's intense self-consciousness and her lack of social experience.

All youth is naturally rebellious and cuts the teeth of revolt upon whatever social restraint is handiest. Under different circumstances I might have publicly burned the Bible or the Constitution of the United States, or at least have run away with a gypsy girl. As it was I smouldered at what I regarded as the "proud man's wrong, the oppressor's con-

tumely" of my mother and myself. I was quick to resent
fancied slights on her behalf, and although *au fond* I was
almost as shy and sensitive as she was, by a perfectly natural
process my outward manner became and, perhaps has continued to be, the precise antithesis of my inner self.

As I look back on my Puritan childhood I can see that its
chief results were (1) an overvaluation of money and "social position"; (2) a dislike, based on envy, of those who
had them; (3) an intense and abortive religious scepticism;
and (4) a yearning for whatever makes human life gracious, tender, carefree, and colorful. Save for my love of
the amenities, I was essentially Bolshevik—had such a term
then existed. To-day when the fumes of hell have lost their
sulphur, when gentleness has replaced severity in the treatment of children, youth is far more happy than fifty years
ago.

To be fair about it, I should say that it may well be that
I was treated far more tenderly than is my recollection. But
I do not think so. My father was a stern man of the ante-
bellum school, an adherent of the "spare-the-rod-and-spoil-
the-child" doctrine which he had strictly followed with regard to his offspring by his first wife. He had mellowed by
the time he had begotten me, the child of his old age, but
although his austerity was tempered by kindliness, his manner was brusque and I stood in awe of him—an awe shared,
I believe, to a great extent by my mother. That he was the
Attorney-General of the State, and one of the leading lawyers of Massachusetts meant nothing to me.

The influences affecting childhood are subtle, far-reaching, and often devastating. I have no hesitation in saying
that this early sense of social inferiority acquired from my
mother has dominated my life and that to it either directly
or indirectly all my subsequent development can be traced.
For it bred in me a recalcitrant individualism, that led me
to question and challenge everything that was conventional
and authoritative, and a fierce determination to demonstrate
that I was as good as anybody, if not better, which showed

itself in a pert cockiness and self-assertion that must have been far from attractive.

It was a bookish period and, outside the family connection, the people my father knew were of the literary tradition. Indeed, although I have never cared for the Boston accent, I am grateful for the accurate English I heard as a child. I suppose to-day we would have passed as a distinctly "highbrow" bunch. Even the tradespeople, I feel sure, would seem "literary" to me now, if I should meet them again.

My first lesson in the meticulous use of words occurred in connection with a series of burglaries in the neighborhood. Just behind us on Exeter Street lived a well-known Boston spinster, Miss Ella Day by name. One moonlight night, when I was about ten years old, I was aroused by the noise of a watchman's rattle and hurried to the window hoping to catch sight of the burglar leaping over the back-yard fences. Although I could see no burglar, I did see Miss Day's attenuated right arm projecting from her window with the rattle, which she was vigorously whirling, at the end of it. Thoroughly thrilled, I shouted across to her:

"Miss Day! Miss Day! What is it—robbers?"

Even now I can hear her thin, shaking voice with its slightly condescending acerbity:

"No—*burglars!*"

In those days Boston was Boston.

I pause for an instant to wonder a little whether that example of purism was not worth more to me than all the English courses I later slouched through at Harvard. No doubt, Miss Day would have refused to call a burglar a robber even at a pistol's point. Women have died for less! Yet my mother always said "You was," and my uncle habitually used "shew" for "showed"—which may demonstrate either our illiteracy or our antiquity.

It is just as difficult to predicate what is going to affect a man's mind as what will affect his life. There is an equal

amount of chance in both. A paragraph in a newspaper or an
article in a magazine may alter the whole intellectual existence of any one of us. So may a smash on the nose. As for
our lives—! No one can tell when a red-hot rivet may drop
on his head after a twenty-story fall or the girl he is going
to marry may appear around the corner. Whether mathematics, Latin or economics is going to help educate a man,
nobody knows or can know. The most learned are often the
least educated, and the most educated the least wise. And
how are you going to give a man wisdom except by giving
him experience? In the old days if a boy refused to learn his
parts of speech and insisted on dreaming under a haycock his
master used to beat him. To-day he hesitates to do so for fear
he may kill a poet. But of course, on the other hand, some
people believe that all poets and lawyers ought to be killed.

What dogma, emotion, experience or physical fact has had
the most far-reaching effect upon your life? Do not jump to
a conclusion too quickly! For myself I answer unhesitatingly
—a clam shell. There can be no question about it. A clam
shell has made my destiny. In the parlor of our little house
on Marlborough Street in Boston in addition to the cuspidor
by the fireplace there stood upon the centre table for the convenience of smokers a large clam shell used as an ash receiver. The inside of the shell was painted white and against
it were silhouetted in black the figures of two men—a tall
thin man and a short fat man. Both had on frock coats and
tall hats, and the tall thin man was bending over and giving
a light to the small fat man from the end of his cigar. That
clam shell excited a strange fascination for me, one reason
being that I thought the thin man looked like Mr. Edward
A. Kelley, a friend of my father's. For nearly fifty years that
clam shell with its little black figures must have lain dormant
in my mind even as once it must have lain dormant in the
mud. Certainly I never consciously thought of it during that
period. Then one evening I saw "Potash and Perlmutter"
and it occurred to me that an amusing dialogue or story of
a similar character might be written about two lawyers. As

I sat smoking in my library there came floating up out of the
depths of my subconsciousness the memory of that clam shell
—with a thin man in a tall hat and a short fat man getting a
light—"Tutt" and "Mr. Tutt." I had no plan, no plot; but
I jotted down on a neighboring pad an imaginary conversation between the two figures on the clam shell:

"Tutt," said Mr. Tutt.

Certainly it wasn't much,—neither very funny nor witty,
but the more I thought of the old clam shell the more vivid
the two characters became, until presently they were living,
breathing human beings who have since then had countless
legal adventures together, which have occupied a large proportion of my time for many years. To-day nobody remembers what cases I prosecuted as an assistant district attorney,
and comparatively few recall the names of the novels I have
written, but a great many people know "the Tutt family"
and, if I am remembered at all after I am dead, it will be
as "the fellow who used to write those Tutt stories in *The
Saturday Evening Post.*" If it had not been for Ephraim
Tutt I should not have given up the law for letters. I might
even—God save the mark!—have become a judge. To that
clam shell I owe the fact that I live in the city only four
months in the year instead of eleven, that for my living I
occupy myself with my own thoughts and those of other
light-minded men, instead of quarrelling over other people's
business and domestic affairs, that I have never run for public office, and that when I want to go to Asia or Africa I
shove a pad and pencil in my pocket and jump on the next
steamer. In fact I owe it more than I can ever repay. But,
then! Who knows but that the lime of that shell may contain
the residue of the bones of some of my ancestors and that
they are thus paying their debt to posterity? "Imperial Cæsar,
dead and turned to clay—!"

Upon the death of my father, when I was nine years old,
I was sent to the Boston public schools until I was twelve
and then to St. Paul's at Concord, N. H., of which Doctor
Henry A. Coit was head master, where I remained four

years. These were the happiest days of my youth. I loved
the country and the freedom from parental restraint and,
although the discipline was strict and there was a great deal
of compulsory chapel-going, the presence of boys of my
own age from all parts of the country opened up vistas into
a new and exciting world. Although I was still shy, small
for my age, and not popular, I nevertheless lost for the time
being my sense of social inferiority, which later, however,
returned at Harvard. But I had carried with me the dogged
resolution of unsurrender I had acquired at home, and
quickly found myself at loggerheads with the Rector on the
question of religion.

Mr. Owen Wister's study of Doctor Coit in a recent number of *The Atlantic Monthly* is a penetrating and brilliant
analysis of a truly noble, but essentially mediæval, character.
Yet, possibly because it is the mature appraisal of a discriminating mind, it in some respects fails to convey the
utter awe which Doctor Coit inspired among us younger
boys. His quickly shifting glance, the austerity of his sallow
countenance, the tap-tap of his cane as he unexpectedly made
a swift appearance around the corner of the "Big Study,"
the uncanny perspicacity which guided him correctly at least
four times out of five, his classic phraseology which frequently obscured a literary sarcasm, and the aroma of holi-
ness inevitably surrounding him struck terror to the heart
of the small boy.

Surely this was no mere saint, but God Himself! with his
eye in every place beholding the evil, if not the good. Yet
the tap of that ebony cane carried with it something of the
same menace as the tap of the stick of the blind pirate in
"Treasure Island."

Doctor Coit, although possessed of a sense of humor,
rarely betrayed it, always catching himself in time. He
walked aloof, speaking with the tongue of angels and not
of men. His twelfth-century attitude toward the dogma of
religion was singularly unenlightening to a youth of the
twentieth.

"That is a mystery, my child," he once said to me of the doctrine of the Trinity, "too holy to be discussed."

A cousin of mine had married a young Presbyterian clergyman in Concord, and I had received from the Rector a blanket permission to lunch with her on Saturdays, of which I frequently availed myself. One Friday he sent for me to come to his study.

"Clifford," he said kindly but sternly (he always called me Clifford after my half-brother who had died while at school in the 60's), "I understand that this cousin whom you visit in Concord is married to some one who calls himself a Presbyterian?"

"Yes, Doctor Coit," I answered. "He is the pastor of the First Presbyterian Church of Concord."

The Rector twiddled his long delicate fingers with that characteristic and unforgetable sweep of the thumb.

"Well, my dear!" he said, "no doubt he is a very esteemable person—but I would not go there too frequently."

Seeing my look of disappointment, he went on:

"There are many very worthy persons among the Presbyterians. Very likely the young man whom your cousin has married is one of them. But"—he looked at me sharply, and I can hear his voice as plainly as if he were sitting beside me now—"do not forget, my child, that in the life to come the Presbyterians will not be upon the same plane as the Episcopalians."

No doubt Doctor Coit had some doctrinal basis for his statement, rendering it less startling to students of theology than it seemed to a small boy.

Only recently I repeated this anecdote to an ecclesiastic of high authority in Doctor Coit's church. He smiled, then nodded, and said thoughtfully: "But I think I understand what he had in mind."

I did not relinquish my cousin, and the incident did not encourage my laggard interest in becoming confirmed, which the Rector anxiously desired and which I as obstinately postponed. Doctor Coit by his manner evidenced his displeasure at my recalcitrancy. Most of the other boys in my form had already been confirmed, and my refusal made me conspicuous as a back-slider. At length, Doctor Coit having appealed to my mother, I yielded, and in due course sullenly knelt at the chapel rail to receive the apostolic laying on of hands.

"I don't believe it! I don't believe it!" I kept repeating, and when Bishop Niles laid his hands upon my head I deliberately blasphemed. I looked for the veil of the temple to be rent in pieces, but God is merciful and nothing happened—that is, nothing visible to the eye of man.

The most terrible ordeal of the entire year was when the Bishop came to examine us in "sacred studies." This ceremony took place in the chapel, modelled upon that at Eton, which has a long narrow nave, where the boys sit in tiers upon either side. The questions and answers, prepared by Doctor Coit himself, were printed in pamphlet form, and had to be learned by rote. Each boy in turn arose and, standing alone with 400 pairs of eyes fixed upon him, answered a single question. Some fainted at the ordeal. There was none so callous that he could face it with anything but horror. Few failed, for the answers were simple; but, if a lapse of memory did occur, the victim never forgot the tone of shocked disgust with which the Rector would turn from him and utter the word: "Next!"

The questions and answers covered the chief incidents in the life of the Savior from Bethlehem to Gethsemane, and a nervous boy could easily become confused. There was no respite or *locus penetentiæ* for any such however. With the Bishop looking on from the choir the batting average had to be 100 per cent or nothing. My classmate Hamilton Fish, who later was the first Rough Rider killed in the Spanish War while charging up San Juan Hill, was not a favorite with the Rector and he had rather looked forward to reestablishing himself in Doctor Coit's good opinion by an assiduous study of the pea-green covered pamphlet for several days before the Bishop's visit. On the fatal morning he found himself quaking in his seat directly under the nose of the Bishop, separated from the Rector by the entire length of the chapel. As the question came nearer and nearer "Ham" became more and more nervous, until when it came his turn to arise he could hardly stand. The Rector recognized him, eyed him reprovingly for a moment, and in a somewhat forbidding tone inquired:

"Who was the father of Our Lord?"

With the blood that rushed to "Ham's" head his confusion became twice confounded. Desperately he snatched at the first straw of memory that floated across his befuddled brain—for the Rector would not wait.

"*Joseph of Arimathea!*" he gasped.

Never have I seen such an annihilating look as that with which the Rector turned from the unfortunate "Ham" to the boy upon his right.

"Next!" he thundered.

Compulsory religion had its compensations in various time-killing devices, rendered possible only by the long white sleeves of the choir cotta, in which one could conceal almost anything up to the size of a small elephant. One boy made a practice of cutting the columns of *The Scientific American* into strips, pasting them together, and rolling them into a long scroll which could be gradually unwound and read without detection during the sermon. Another always brought to chapel a complete aviary, composed of small imitation birds made of real feathers, which he would make hop and dance around on the shelf provided for our prayer-books and hymnals. You cannot send small boys to chapel three times a day and expect them to hold their attention exclusively to spiritual things.

As time went on my terror of Doctor Coit subsided and was replaced by a timorous affection. He was a great school-master, and doubtless a great saint, but I do not feel that from the point of view of character development his influence was any more beneficial to me than the Puritan environment in which I was brought up. In spite of having been confirmed, I was no more of a believer than when I had gone to St. Paul's, and my subsequent career at Harvard was not such as to increase my religious faith.

That Puritanism encouraged and accentuated a consciousness of sin in the young is one of the worst indictments against it. As Professor Julian Huxley has so well said: "Once it is recognized that the sense of sin is often, and especially in adolescence, a mental disease, something to be avoided if possible and got over (like the measles) with the utmost celerity, instead of being paraded as admirable, the great step will have been taken. It is nothing to be ashamed of, any more than measles; but, also like measles, it is nothing to be proud of. I believe that the religion of the future will have as one of its great aims the saving of man from an exaggerated sense of sin by prevention of childish conflicts."

"Action and reaction are equal and opposite." A story is told of a Harvard freshman who consulted Phillips Brooks, then "College Preacher" and as such accessible as a spiritual adviser to the undergraduates. The boy introduced himself with the statement:

"Doctor Brooks,—I am an atheist."

"I am sorry to hear that," said the preacher. "Won't you sit down and tell me about it?"

After about an hour the freshman arose and held out his hand. The great Christian did the same.

"Doctor Brooks," said the youth, "I have listened to everything you have had to say and I am still an atheist. But," he added graciously, "I should be sorry to feel that I had said anything that had disturbed your own beautiful faith!"

I cannot vouch for this anecdote, and I hasten to add that the freshman in question was not myself, but I reached Harvard in a state of unregeneracy, owing, I think, to the prejudice against religion engendered by the dreary Sunday afternoons of my childhood and the overdose of chapel-going I had suffered at boarding-school. The effect of the revulsion against ecclesiastical dogma, caused by my being dragooned as a boy of thirteen into confirmation on the theory that once driven into the fold I would probably stay there and that, while herded with the sheep, I would no longer dare to bleat like the goat I in fact was, has never left me.

In spite of the intellectual misery it occasioned me, however, I was still prepared to give religion a chance, and at my mother's request even went so far along the road to actual conversion as to become an usher at St. Paul's Church in Boston, where I had originally been baptized and which she still attended. Here every Sunday, arrayed in my first cutaway coat, I steered a fragmentary public into the seats and temporarily achieved a sense of personal importance by looking inquiringly at the pew-owners, who would obligingly hold up one or more fingers to indicate the number of vacant places to be filled. This sense of importance was rudely shattered on the Easter Sunday of my freshman year by one Mr. Robert Burgess, the Senior Warden, who with a few other dignitaries exercised the privilege of entering the church by a rear door, thus gaining his seat without the necessity of struggling with the common crowd.

Mr. Burgess was as distinguished in appearance as he was religious by nature, which last trait led him, according to common report, to use in place of ordinary visiting-cards others bearing Bible texts appropriate to the various seasons of the Christian year. It is said that on one occasion he caused to be sent up to a lady upon whom he was calling a card bearing the printed admonition "Prepare to meet thy God!" but that, as she afterward admitted, on coming downstairs she "found it was only Robert Burgess." He was a man of approximately seventy years with luxuriant white whiskers, the ends of which trailed impressively over either shoulder of his frock coat in a manner enhancing his general dignity. On this particular Easter Sunday the great man, entering as usual from the vestry, started toward his seat down the main aisle, at the head of which I was stationed. As he passed he bent his head and mumbled in my ear something I did not understand. Fearful lest I should incur his displeasure by failing to carry out some request, I followed him a few steps.

"I beg pardon, Mr. Burgess," I explained, "but I didn't catch what you said."

"Um-um-um!" he repeated over his shoulder, continuing his majestic progress down the aisle.

Much worried, and no wiser than before, I hurried after and overtook him as he was entering his pew.

"I'm awfully sorry, Mr. Burgess," I panted, "but I didn't hear what you were saying!"

Mr. Burgess stopped short, turned, glared at me, and in a voice which I felt must rock the church bawled:

"The Lord is risen!—*Can you hear that?*"

My humiliation was such that I shortly thereafter gave up being an usher and terminated all my ecclesiastical relationships.

In spite of the fact that I valiantly assured myself that I did not believe in a God, or look forward to either the bliss of heaven or the pangs of hell, the second-hand Puritan theology of my mother (which in spite of her being married to an Episcopalian held her completely in thrall) had become so embedded in my subconsciousness—as it doubtless still is to-day!—that although my language was Rabelaisian, my conduct was like that of Cotton Mather. No matter what I reasoned myself into or how I talked, I acted like a Methodist deacon. While I loudly asserted my disbelief in any judgment-day, and had successfully challenged the Almighty to do His worst, I could not escape either the conviction of sin or that of His all-seeing eyes being ever disapprovingly upon me. I longed to tread gay measures over the primrose path of dalliance, yet my feet led me along the straight and narrow way of virtue. I could not escape an underlying consciousness of wrong-doing in pleasures which my mind told me were entirely innocent. And I still have it! Although now my slight feeling of guilt is tempered by a subtle and delicious sensation of freedom. I may not have cast off the old Adam, but I am at least temporarily rid of him.

It was quite otherwise at that time, for now, added to my original sense of sin, was a new shame in a suddenly awakened consciousness of sex that filled a large part of my thoughts for the next four years.

I remember my friend Dr. Alexis Carrel telling me that during the World War he once unexpectedly met, in a shattered village near the front, a grizzled brigadier-general with whom he had gone to school as a boy and whom he had not seen since. With the guns booming only a mile or so away, the two sat down over a bottle of wine amid the ruins to compare notes on their respective careers.

"When we last knew each other in Lyons," remarked the bearded general, "I was but ten years old. I am now forty-one. Of those intervening thirty years I spent twelve in thinking of but one thing. My mind never left that subject from the time I was eleven until I was twenty-two. Those twelve years might just as well have been left out. I studied, I worked, I led a regular life, but I was so obsessed with the subject of sex that nothing I did was of any value and I accomplished absolutely nothing. It was only after I married that I was able to find myself and make any progress."

In a lesser degree this was true of my own life at Harvard. I continued to lead the existence of an anchorite, but my brain was continually filled with the visions of a Mahomet's paradise. I do not want to be unfair to my friends or to myself, and I certainly do not wish to have it supposed that what was true of us was true of the rest of my class or of the university as a whole; but the fact is that, as I look back on my four years at Harvard, it seems as if I spent most of my spare time in swapping dirty jokes and smutty stories. Among a certain group of my companions hardly a word was uttered that did not carry with it some obscene implication. There may be little value in such a confession as illustrating the effects of Puritan repression. Perhaps that is the normal way for boys to be, irrespective of their up-bringing and early environment. But I doubt if it is to such an extent. If at some period between the ages of eight and eleven I had been given a thorough psychologic purge, a sort of moral "spring cleaning" along with my regulation dose of sulphur and molasses, as a result of which I could have said, "So that is all there is to it!" I would not have spent so much time either in what Heywood Broun calls "vague speculations concerning the exciting horrors of the unknown" or in being ashamed at indulging in them.

I got little out of my college life, perhaps in part because I put little into it, but chiefly because I was the victim of a vivid sense of social inferiority which was intensified by the fact that I made no societies and was too proud and sensitive to seek my companions among those who did. Night after night I sat alone waiting in my room on the bare chance that the chanting company in the yard outside might pause before my door and "take me out." I have described that tense, half-fearful waiting, followed by bitter disappointment, when the crowd passed by, in the story of an imaginary Thomas Kelly, but his feelings were my own as well as those of hundreds of other boys both then and now. If they had stopped and I had heard that knock upon my door, my whole life might have been different, and—who knows?—perhaps not so good!

"Tra-lala-la-lala-lala-lala——"

If I heard the echo of that song to-day, no matter how faintly, it would send icy shivers down my back.

The majority of the fellows I knew were physically chaste, but more or less dirty-minded. Like most of their elders the boys who indulged themselves talked least about it. One of my close friends, however, who had been brought up as an aristocrat in a small town, was constantly boasting of his adventures; and the roommate of another actually maintained a mistress in a modest flat in the West End of Boston. Yet these were marked exceptions, and I am convinced both that the percentage of chastity throughout the body of the university was extraordinarily high and also that the great majority of the collegians of that day did not add to their knowledge of sex during their four years at Harvard by any actual experience. Of course this would have been true at that time neither of the smart, drinking crowd of *jeunesse dorée* nor of the riff-raff and cheap sports coming from the factory towns and tougher Boston suburbs, any more than it is to-day, but it is as true as that the average American husband of 1930 is faithful to his wife, which thesis I am prepared to defend with my dying breath. Taken by and large, those of my classmates who had had the advantage of a normal bringing up were undoubtedly a simple, clean-minded, democratic lot of boys whose attention was concentrated chiefly on athletics, and whose natural respect for women and distaste for coarseness led them to shun the not very alluring invitations to lechery offered by the shabby side streets behind Beacon Hill.

It was different as to drink. While a man could not go with women without losing caste, it was rather chic to get drunk, or at least "lit," once in so often. To be called "the funniest drunk Harvard ever had" was a title of some consideration and was regarded even by the "grinds" (the word "highbrow" had not yet come into use) with complacence. All elections, even to literary organizations, were apt to turn into mild orgies, and I vividly recall taking refuge under a desk on the occasion of my election as an associate editor of a college paper while a playwright, now distinguished on at least two continents, emptied the contents of a punch bowl above my head. No one in my time could have honestly repeated the entry, heretofore referred to in Professor Pierce's notebook of 1832, that he saw no one drunk on Commencement. There were usually a few drunks to be seen on that day, both indoors and out, in the decade from 1890 to 1900, although they were gentlemanly drunks, filled with loyal sentiment for dear old Harvard and maudlin affection for classmates whom in their earlier years they perhaps would have not condescended to recognize. More generally, then as now, they were in a mere state of spiritual exaltation.

Taken all in all, I had a wretched and wholly unprofitable time of it, and did not even attain the satisfaction of any scholarship, for, although I secured a "magna cum laude" and was a Commencement speaker, I did so by a skilful bunching of "snap" courses and sporadic cramming for examinations. All the elective system did for me was to enable me to loaf through my four years, sitting on the steps of my dormitory, smoking innumerable stogies which I ordered in boxes of 1,000 from Wheeling, W. Va., at $8 or $9 the box. I spent practically nothing on amusements and lived on an incredibly small amount of money for one who was not in need of charity,—$500 to $600 per year, if I remember correctly. Instead of buying tickets for the theatre the boys who sat at the same table with me in Memorial Hall commons (where we boarded for $3.90 per week) used to make a practice of going on as "supers," sometimes for nothing or, less frequently, receiving twenty-five or fifty cents a night. In this way I supported Irving, Terry, Duse, Sothern, Jefferson, Ada Rehan, Beerbohm Tree, Mojeska, Sara Bernhardt and in fact most of the dramatic stars of the end of the last century. I have been an archer, waiter, gaoler, tramp, page, scribe, man-at-arms, village bum, inn-keeper, and once—in "Izeyl"—the leading female citizen of a Hindu village.

On this occasion I confess that we did the Divine Sara dirt. She had taken the Tremont Theatre and advertised for "supers" who could speak French, on the strength of which we attended at the stage door early in the morning on the first Monday of her engagement and, by letting the best French scholar among us do all the talking, induced her director to sign us up in a body under the impression that we were emigrées. The first play of her repertoire was to be 'Izeyl" and, since I was young, small, and pink, the stage manager thought it good economy to make use of me as a girl, and I was accordingly made up for the part in a black wig, brown tights, and with a bunch of bushes tied about my waist. The wig and bushes were right enough, but unfortunately the tights had belonged to a much larger "woman" than myself and my feet reached only to the ankles. There were no others available and nobody regarded the matter as of the slightest importance anyway since I had only one thing to do,—namely, on receiving the cue *"Le roi!"* to rush out before the lights at the head of my group of maidens from Harvard and make obeisance before the palanquin in which Madam Bernhardt was being borne.

Standing in the wings, we heard the thunders of applause out front as Sara made her appearance; heard our cue; and burst upon the stage crying shrilly *"Le roi! Le roi!"* I was naturally in the lead and going strong. So were all the other "girls," and we would undoubtedly have made a big hit, had not my feet caught in the flapping ends of my brown tights, precipitating me headlong in the middle of the spotlight before the palanquin, where I lay helpless unable to get up. It was then that the great actress showed her genius. Descending from her seat in the palanquin she gently assisted me to rise, as if I had voluntarily thrown myself at her feet instead of having flopped there, and no one in the audience, I am sure, noticed the contretemps.

Thirty-six years afterwards, when Madam Bernhardt was making her last tour in the United States and when, owing to illness, she was obliged to make use of a wheeled chair, I met her at the house of a friend and told her of the incident.

"Yes, Madam," I assured her. "It is absolutely true that you raised me,—a fallen woman!—to my feet!"

Looking sadly at the wheels of the chair she said:

"Alas, M'sieur! I could not do it now!"

Later on, when Sir Henry Irving and Ellen Terry were playing in "Henry VIII," the same crowd of irresponsibles signed up for a week as halberdiers, priests, monks, gentlemen-in-waiting, falconers, etc. I, being the smallest, became temporarily a clerk or scribe with an inkhorn dangling from my belt. As such I hovered about the ante-chamber of the king's apartments, mingling on terms of equality with the Dukes of Norfolk and of Suffolk, the Earl of Surrey, the Lord Chamberlain, Woolsey, Cromwell and even with Henry himself. Thrilled at my own importance, I pretended to whisper and smile knowingly at the noble lords, enjoying myself to such an extent that at the "exeunt all save Woolsey" I lingered on, occupying myself with some "business" invented for the occasion, until the advent of Cromwell, whom Woolsey at once began to address in his famous speech:

> "What! amaz'd
> At my misfortunes? Can thy spirit wonder
> A great man should decline? Nay, as you weep,
> I am fall'n indeed."

So enthralled was I by the great scene that I moved nearer and nearer, until quite inadvertently I intervened between the Cardinal and a portion of the audience, so that the last portion of his speech was rendered somewhat as follows:

Woolsey: "O, Cromwell, Cromwell! Had I but served my God (sotto voce) *get that fellow off the stage d'y'hear?* —with half the zeal I served my King—(sotto voce) *get him off, I say!*—he would not in mine age have left me naked to mine enemies—(sotto voce) *off you fool!*"

Cromwell: "Good sir, have patience!"

Woolsey: (looking at me meaningly and hissing the words) "*God!*—So I have! Farewell the hopes of Court: My hopes in Heaven do dwell."

But my hopes dwelt only in escape, and by the time Sir Henry had made his exit (R) I had dashed off stage (L) and was in the supers' dressing room changing my scribe's costume for that of a Harvard freshman.

While I had been having my adventure, my classmate Herbert Ross had likewise been having his. Anxious as to what would happen to me if I remained on stage with Cromwell and Woolsey, he hung about in the wings until he found a place on the backdrop behind the Cardinal where, owing to friction, the paint had been worn so thin that it was possible to look through and see what was going on before the footlights. To this spot then he affixed his eye, and here Queen

Katherine, in the person of the beautiful Ellen Terry, found him,—a stalwart youthful halberdier apparently engrossed in the consummate acting of the great Irving. So delighted was she at his oblivion that she stepped up behind him, examined him with interest and finally inquired whether he had a knife.

You may be sure that he did have a knife, and, blushing at such attention from the most famous English actress, quickly opened the blade and tendered it to her, whereupon Miss Terry casually slit a large triangular piece in the backdrop.

"Now you can see!" she remarked with a smile.

Queen Katherine's maid who had observed the incident was much shocked at her mistress's recklessness.

"O Miss Terry! she protested. "Why did you make such a big hole!"

"But he had a big eye!" retorted Miss Terry with an arch glance at the collegian.

All in all we picked up a considerable knowledge of both the theatre and opera at an enormous amount of personal inconvenience which was amply repaid when, after doing our bit, we were passed into the house and allowed to take places among the standees. It is something to have lain at the feet of Julia Marlowe in Sherwood Forest, or that of Arden, clad in a suit of Lincoln green tights with a buckskin jerkin, caressing a lancewood bow with one hand while drinking a flagon full of air with the other. I know of nothing quite to equal the experience, except being blown through the floor by an exploding barrel of beer as I seem to remember having happened to me in Hoyt's "Temperance Town." More vividly I recall, however, the enormous eyes of the very beautiful girl I had to escort in one scene of that play to church, or prayer meeting, and the gobs of lampblack that made her lashes resemble the five points of two stars of liquid gray.

After the play we would go to the "Bell in Hand," an ancient low-ceiled and dirty bar, with sawdust covered floors, on "Pie Alley," a narrow passage leading off Court Street and much frequented by drivers and cabmen, where we drank beer and ale, witnessed an occasional fight, and heard a great deal of profanity. There was another favorite resort for cabdrivers on Tremont Street at which one could literally get a drink "for a song." At one end of the room was a platform with a rickety upright piano. Here any artist lacking the price of a glass of beer could entertain the company and, if not too raucous, could earn all he wanted to slack his thirst. I sang at this place many times—in quartette, duet and solo—usually songs appropriate to the occasion and company, such as "Brown October Ale," "Here's a Health to King Charles," "When Johnny Comes· Marching Home," "Come Landlord, Fill the Flowing Bowl," "Down Among the Dead Men," etc., etc., apparently to the entire satisfaction of the audience who at this particular place were always politely attentive.

I never saw any of my more fashionable classmates there and I do not fully understand why I should have exhibited myself under these conditions, for I always had the price of a glass of beer upon my person. I suppose I felt that I was seeing life and that singing for the edification of cabdrivers was a rather dashing performance, demonstrating that I was a Bohemian and not a Puritan! Back of it all was a spirit of bravado leading me to entertain the secret wish that somebody from my own class of society would find me there and realize that I did not give a damn if all the world knew what I was up to. In fact there was a period when, largely under the influence of Robert Louis Stevenson, I studiously neglected my already abandoned personal appearance, smoked corncob or long China pipes, drank peculiar concoctions of beer, ale and ginger pop out of a pewter tankard, and studied by the flickering light of tallow candles stuck into empty bottles.

My generally defiant attitude, expressive of my supreme indifference to the social neglect of my classmates, my grotesque attempts at a Bohemian existence, my beer and my "stogies," did not result in anything more devilish than a coated tongue and bad taste in my mouth the morning after an outré excursion to some newly discovered saloon or rathskeller. I was and still am—no credit to myself!—strictly temperate by virtue of necessity, due to the fact that, though my spirit might have been willing, my stomach was weak and any admixture of drinks would quickly turn it.

It was not until my senior year that I so far escaped from my Puritan inhibitions as to conclude that, simply as a matter of human experience, I ought to get thoroughly "soused" at least once before leaving college. I had won second money in the Boylston Prize-Speaking Contest and, being in funds, took advantage of my opportunity by going into Boston alone and purchasing a box at an opera given by the Castle Square Opera Company. Sitting by myself in state while the curtain was up, for the occasion was too serious for company, I descended between the acts to the bar, where I proceeded to work my way through "The Barkeeper's Handbook"—beginning with A, for ale, B, for burgundy, C, for champagne, etc.—until by the end of the performance I had achieved a fairly large percentage of the alphabet. Yet for some strange reason nothing of what I imbibed had the slightest effect upon me, one poison probably acting as the antidote for another.

It was moonlight and, having nowhere in particular to go, I strolled down to the old Adam's House bar on lower Boylston Street, where for a time I continued my alphabetical career, to be presently interrupted by an ingratiating person who, introducing himself as "General D'Olier of Virginia," invited me to share a bottle of claret. During the consumption of the bottle, which was quickly followed by another, the general, who had instantly formed a pronounced attachment for me, confided not only most of his family history but the fact that he was considered the best shot south of Mason and Dixon's line. There was seemingly no reason why this should have aroused any spirit of emulation on my part, yet I remember very well that it did and that it led me in turn to speak boastfully of my own marksmanship.

Accordingly, the general and I, arm in arm, each carrying a partially emptied bottle, sallied forth shortly after midnight, seeking for a place to demonstrate the pre-eminence of our marksmanship. I was still feeling fit as a fiddle —a well-tuned fiddle—being now the better off for perhaps fifteen or sixteen assorted drinks largely constituted of alcohol. On Tremont Row we found an open-air shooting-gallery still obligingly open—rabbits whirling around the periphery of a circle, ducks swimming and suddenly disappearing, silver balls dancing upon jets of water. In spite of the fact that the general had shown a marked inclination to lean upon my shoulder when walking down Tremont Row, he now took off his coat and hat, selected a Flaubert rifle, and proceeded with a good deal of dexterity to knock the silver ball off the jet fourteen times in succession, missing only upon the fifteenth and last shot. It was now my turn.

Solemnly General D'Olier watched me bring the rifle to my shoulder.

"Pop!" Down went the ball!

"Hang it!" I muttered. "I *must* be sober! What is the use of going to all this trouble!" And that I was nowhere near the state which I desired to attain was demonstrated by the fact that, without the slightest expectation of doing so, I shot the ball down, not fourteen, but fifteen, times. I did not know whether to be disappointed at being so incontrovertibly sober or pleased at having won over so redoubtable a general, but on turning around to receive his congratulations I found that he had disappeared.

The event, however, that was to make the night epochal in the Train family had yet to come. Minus my general and also my hat I managed to catch the "last car" for Cambridge, which then left Scolley Square at 2 A. M., where I recall regaling my fellow passengers by appropriate selections from the "Siege of Lucknow," my prize rendition.

"Mine? Yes, a mine! Countermine!"

I crouched, an imaginary sapper listening for the invisible pick, then dug furiously with a phantom spade. I was possessed by the thrill of battle. Bullets fell upon and around me, cannons roared, bugles sounded, the wounded were carried off—"Millions of musket bullets, and thousands of cannon balls—" Hark! What was that? The cheers of the relieving column? Havelock!—Thank God! Thank God!

"Saved! We are saved!—Saved by the valor of Havelock! Saved by the blessing of Heaven!—And ever aloft on the palace roof the old banner of England blew!"

Sobbing, I was at last ejected by the conductor in Harvard Square, and still holding my own, worked my way across the deserted yard. A single lamp gleamed like a friendly beacon from one of the windows of Hollis Hall—my own, I concluded. My thoughtful roommate, having arrived home before me, must have placed it there. "A light in the window for me, Mother!"

I had some difficulty in crossing the yard owing to the tangle of wire fences which had unaccountably sprung up and which I had never before observed. As fast as I got my legs over one I found myself confronted by another! And the steps of Hollis were so obstructed that I was obliged to negotiate them upon my hands and knees. Crouching like my "sapper" I slowly ascended the stairs amid a furious hail of bullets and cannon balls, until I reached a door beneath which shone a crack of light.

"Saved! We are saved! Saved by the valor of Havelock! Saved by the blessing of Heaven!"

Still on all fours I butted my head against the door and pushed it open with my nose. To my bewilderment a fat man, in shirt sleeves and eye shade, was sitting at his desk, before a huge pile of blue books. He looked up good-naturedly and nodded.

"Good evening," he remarked in an ordinary conversational tone. "How do you do?"

It was Professor Byron Satterlee Hurlbut, later dean of

Harvard College. I recognized, although I did not know, him.

"Good evening, professor," I said. "I am very, very tired."

Professor Hurlbut regarded me searchingly.

"I should say that you were very, very drunk!" he replied. "Come in and lie down on my sofa for awhile."

Although I knew his diagnosis to be erroneous, I was not offended. The fat man seemed a good fellow, and I decided to accept his invitation.

"The sofa is over here—not there," explained the professor as he assisted me to adjust my legs. "Rather a rough night?"

"Millions of musket bullets and thousands of cannon balls!" I replied, and then passed out entirely.

I had a vague recollection of being later half carried across the yard to my own room and of being put to bed by the fat man, whom I insisted upon calling "Havelock" instead of Hurlbut. Subsequently we became intimate friends. Although I had upheld the Puritan tradition with respect to rum, I violated it in that curiously I had no consciousness of sin.

My four years at Harvard were years of frustration, embittered by my inability to achieve the social recognition from my classmates to which I felt entitled. Whether or no there be (or was) such a thing as Harvard indifference, I found Harvard almost wholly indifferent to my own existence, and this intensified all the characteristics engendered by my upbringing.

My mother never ceased to wear black for my father although she survived him over thirty years. In this economy, as well as respect, no doubt played a part. And since my dear mother was loath to buy any new apparel for herself, I felt that I should not allow her to do so for me. The result was that until my graduation from college I never knew what it was to have adequate or comfortable clothes. My trousers never matched my coats, the sleeves and legs were always too short, and everything was too tight. This made me abjectly miserable on all social occasions, but I managed to get a certain secret satisfaction out of it as a sort of penance. This, as I look back upon it, was entirely unnecessary. It would have been vastly preferable for me to go without a few books than to be forever on the point of bursting my waistband. But something told me that clothes were a frivolity. I resorted to every possible expedient to avoid buying a dress suit, and actually attended a certain number of dancing parties in Boston arrayed in a double-breasted blue jacket and gray trousers although all the other males present were in evening clothes.

I knew that somewhere in the club houses hidden away on the narrow side streets of Cambridge was going on a life of spontaneous good-fellowship, such as Owen Wister so delightfully describes in the story of his friendship with Theodore Roosevelt, but I did not share in it.

I still walked in the Puritan shadow apart from those, predestined by surname or birth upon Beacon Hill, to share in the joys of the social heaven. I was not of "the elect." It may have been, as so many of the disgruntled are apt to say of themselves, "the best thing that ever happened to me." But I am suspicious of false modesty in such statements, and I do not believe that, if it can be avoided, it does the young American any good to experience the torture of being "left out." That is by the mark, however. All I am seeking to show is that the Puritanism of New England, more or less focussed in Cambridge, was sympathetic to the aristocratic tradition, not only originally, when the students were listed in accordance with the supposed social rank of their parents and when "The Gentleman's Club" was founded, but also, with greatly diminished influence to be sure, throughout the last century. The fact, if true, is of no particular importance. Probably had that charmed circle, to which Roosevelt and Wister both belonged, been enlarged its vintage flavor would have been destroyed. Once at the very height of my jaundice, when he visited Cambridge as Secretary of War, I asked the future president if he thought there was such a thing as Harvard indifference and he replied: "No more than you could inherit something from a maiden aunt!" I do not blame him for taking that position, but I did not agree with him then and do not now. He was an irrepressible optimist. What is known as Harvard indifference is the direct offspring, not of any intellectual maiden aunt, but of the "stern daughter of the voice of God."

There is, or at least there was in my day, as much difference between the general atmosphere of Harvard and that of the ordinary fresh-water college as there would be between the Archbishop of Canterbury and a Methodist revivalist. It is a New England college, which, while it draws its students from all over the world and has Wall Street bankers among its overseers, is still essentially dominated by Puritan influences. This has both its good and its bad points.

That Harvard offers to its students in general less opportunity for what is commonly called "social life" in a narrow sense is obviously true. The hilarious mutual congratulation growing out of the coincidence that youths, seeking a classic education, buy soda water at the same drug store, and listen to the same lectures on fine arts or botany, is noticeably less obstreperous than elsewhere. So far as I am aware, there is little, if any, of the kind of college life typified by the guitar with the blue ribbon and the felt flag bearing the name of Alma Mater in large white letters. But neither is there any such at Oxford, Cambridge or the Sorbonne.

Students in preparatory schools, who are looking forward to four careless years of rollicking good fellowship with several hundred other youths based on the fact that they are approximately of the same age and let loose upon the town for the first time, should seek a college where the majority of undergraduates are sufficiently immature to want it.

There is no college where the unknown boy from the smaller town, who has no conspicuous or particularly attractive qualities of mind or body, can get more education in its best sense and less recognition of the kind called "social" than at Harvard. After all, the mere accident of boarding in Cambridge and being eighteen years old is small reason for a fictitious enthusiasm over one's personality on the part of one's classmates.

There are colleges where the fact that two undergraduates have names beginning with the same letter is regarded as enough upon which to found a beautiful friendship, but there is no bunk about this sort of thing at Harvard. The chances are against, rather than in favor of, the outsider getting inside,—as they are everywhere else. But that, in some cases, may be a valuable factor in the undergraduate's development. The "smart Aleck" may well be disappointed at the impression he creates or the enthusiasm he arouses, yet he may learn in consequence to behave more like the superior gentlemen in "The Gentleman's Club." Such persons may be prejudiced against Harvard before they come as well as afterwards, but it is an excellent reason for their going there.

On the other hand this congenital lack of enthusiasm may act as an unfortunate damper to youthful ideals of democracy. What is known as "Harvard indifference" is a genuine Puritan trait—the essence of the New England character. It may be socially impeccable, but it is not always ingratiating. The jokes about the Adamses, the Lowells and the Cabots, the cod, fishball and the bean are not for nothing. A Boston man is, or anyhow always used to be, different from a Kentuckian.

The New Englander is by nature more reserved and less responsive than the children of warmer parts of our country. And there is, too, a certain shyness and self-consciousness about us New Englanders that, taken with the conviction latent in our bones that gaiety and sin are somehow related, makes us advance slowly in friendship and embarrassed about our emotions even when these are entirely respectable.

Now this reluctance to give one's heart away, or, I perhaps should say, to let anybody know you have one, has its intellectual concomitant in a reserve of judgment and a detached impartiality that savors of coldness. It is neither snobbishness nor priggishness, although it may easily become either or both, in which event, it certainly is not endearing. Therefore, it seems to me that the Boston man who graduated from Harvard can afford to laugh good-naturedly at the allegation that he is "like an egg which has been laid twice—each time successfully," and acknowledge the corn.

We cannot add a cubit to our moral stature by yearning to be like those joyful sons of other institutions of learning who herald their democracy and mutual esteem by howling like wolves. Let us be content that the shades of the Puritan will always flit silently among us to temper our fervency and moderate our joy of living. Those sober men of the old time were not devoid of passion and numbered among them many of the "good and the great," of whom we are still able—on occasion—lustily to sing. But with all our pride of tradition, we might still attempt to cultivate a slightly more conciliatory manner, to simulate a greater geniality, to handle ourselves in such a way that when some barbarian calls one of us a snob, he can look him in the eye and say: "When you call me that,—smile!"

# CHAPTER XVI

## The Glass of Fashion

AT about the time that the grandfathers of the present generation were dying in the bloody cornfields of Maryland and Virginia, there emerged above the dull level of New York social life a remarkable young man, no less conspicuous in his own way than Commodore Vanderbilt, "Jubilee Jim" Fisk or Phineas T. Barnum, and for a period quite as much of a household word. This was the great Ward McAllister,—self-styled "Autocrat of Drawing-Rooms," creator of the "Four Hundred," and, later, of the "One Hundred and Fifty." "Ringmaster of the Social Circus" would have been a more apt title.

A quarter century after the Civil War he published his reminiscences, and exposed his spiritual and intellectual nakedness together with that of his coterie, in an equally remarkable book which he called "Society As I Have Found It," parodied by a jeering world into "Society As It Has Found Me Out."

Now, although McAllister was a silly fellow and fundamentally an ass, he took himself and his mission so seriously that there was something dignified and almost magnificent in his asininity. Yet the fact that this rather illiterate, vulgarly minded, and second-rate gentleman did for many years exert such an undoubted social influence is worthy of consideration. He was indeed a remarkable man and, now that he is dead, we should not be loath to acknowledge that he performed a great public service for which the American nation owes him a debt. That service was to make "Society" so ridiculous that it has never really recovered.

The photograph in the front of his book shows a tall, distinctly good-looking and intelligent man of fifty-five or sixty, with regular features, high forehead, moustache and

363

imperial. His was the era of Louis Napoleon. A rather impressive fellow, one would say, although the cutaway in which he is dressed appears to be not too well-fitting. Here I am told is exemplified a fact familiar in his lifetime, that this extraordinary *arbiter elegantorium* who dictated fashion and made and marred social careers at will, was noticeably defective in grammar and rarely had his trousers pressed. Aping the Parisian boulevardier, with his hat cocked slightly on one side and his cane thrust head-down in his coat pocket and standing rigidly in air, he strutted down Fifth Avenue and through life with a serene and imperturbable egotism that had a certain quality of greatness. He did not question his own title to social fame and power, and could conceive of no one else doing so, since he had that intense moral earnestness necessary for any leader in whatever cause, be it that of a Savonarola or in the cooking of hams.

For McAllister did know how to cook a ham, and for that esoteric knowledge, transmitted in his book, we also owe him gratitude—"a boiled Yorkshire ham, to cook which properly it must be simmered for six or seven hours until you can turn the bone; then lay it aside twelve hours to cool; then put it in an oven and constantly baste it with a pint of cider. It must be served hot, even after being cut. The oftener it is placed in the oven and heated the better it becomes. Thus cooked, they have been by one of my friends hermetically sealed in a tin case and sent to several distinguished men in England, who have found them a great delicacy." Thanks, Mr. McAllister!

McAllister, on his own statement, came of a distinguished Southern family of French-Huguenot extraction, his mother being the most beautiful woman he had ever seen, a descendant of Charlotte Corday, and the belle first of Charleston and afterwards of Savannah. Mr. McAllister himself drifted in early manhood to New York, where he resided in Tenth Street "with an old maiden lady, my relative and godmother, whom I always felt would endow me with all her worldly goods, but who, I regret to say, preferred the

Presbyterian Church and the Georgia Historical Society to myself." (Can we blame her?) "As the supposed heir of my saving godmother, the portals of New York society were easily open to me, and I well remember my first fancy ball, given by Mrs. John C. Stevens in her residence in College Place. A company of soldiers were called in to drill on the waxed floors to perfect them for dancing. A legacy of a thousand dollars I expended in a fancy dress, which I flattered myself was the handsomest and richest at the ball."

The next great social event which he recalls was another "great fancy ball" given by the Schermerhorns in their house on the corner of Great Jones Street and Lafayette Place. But the apostasy of his godmother left young Mr. McAllister without the wherewithal to buy further costumes, and, "disgusted with bookkeeping," he decided to take up law as an easy road to wealth and to join his brother in San Francisco. Since this was in the year 1850 during the real "Gold Rush," his decision may have been fundamentally sound, for his brother's motto was "Ten millions or nothing." Ward to his disgust found on his arrival that eggs (without which it was quite impossible for him to begin the day) cost $2 apiece, a fowl $8, a turkey $16. One week's mess bill for breakfast and dinner alone cost him $225. Nevertheless, fees were large! His first retainer was $4,000 in gold dust and looked good to him even with eggs at $24 per dozen. He resolved to go to work in earnest. "It struck me," he says with a naïve aptitude for simile, "that in that country it was root, pig, or die!"

After six months he felt sufficiently well-to-do to build himself a house. "My furniture, just from Paris, was acajou and white and blue horse-hair. My bed quilt cost me $250; it was a lovely Chinese floss silk shawl!" His law firm was soon making $100,000 a year and to him was delegated the duty of entertaining prospective clients, his father's injunction being "Be sure, my boy, that you always invite nice people." Modestly, Mr. McAllister confesses that "Such dinners as I then gave, I have never seen surpassed anywhere." Anyhow he paid—so he says, and let who can deny it!—his French cook $6,000 a year salary.

And yet, for some unexplained reason he stayed only two years in San Francisco! Was the family ambition to make ten millions or nothing so soon gratified? He does not say. Like Napoleon or Cæsar he merely remarks, "Two years was the length of my stay in San Francisco."

Thereafter he spent a winter in Washington, where he "was dining out all the time." "On these occasions there was always a room prepared to receive a guest who had indulged too freely in strong waters. Men then (1853) drank in good earnest, a striking contrast to the days in which we now live (1890) when really, at dinner, people only taste wine but do not drink it."

From Washington he passed over to London, where he hired a tout who "suggested that if I would defray the expense, he would show me London as no American had ever seen it"—or possibly want to, one might be constrained to add,—for his introduction to London society was a dinner and dog fight at the residence of a Regent Street dry-goods merchant, where he saw a contest between what seemed to him a myriad of rats and a bull terrier who easily killed them all, the drawing of a badger,—"a very amusing sight," —and fight after fight between bull terriers.

"Such drinking I never saw before or since; the host, calling for bumper after bumper, insisted on every one draining his glass. I skillfully threw my wine under the table. The host and all the company were soon intoxicated. The footmen in green and gold liveries never cracked a smile. The master, after a bumper, would fall forward on the table, smashing everything. His butler picked him up and replaced him in his chair. This was kept up until 3 a. m."

This rather rough party was compensated for by the inestimable privilege (procured for him by the tout who knew Her Majesty's chef) of seeing the royal table laid out for dinner. "Yes," he boasts, "I have seen Her Majesty's table at Windsor Castle all ready for her. I have heard her footmen, in green and gold, re-echo from hall to kitchen the note that 'dinner is served,' and then I was told to go; but I saw all I wanted to see." Alas, what anguish it must have caused McAllister as he scuttled down the back stairs to realize, as he confesses, that the table was laid only for "soup and fish."

Thrilled by his success McAllister frittered and flirted away a winter in Florence and Rome, where he learned to cook turkeys fed on walnuts and rejoiced in a cook to whom he paid twenty-four paulo ($2.40) a day, for which sum "he gave us breakfast and exquisite dinners."

Indeed, Mr. McAllister's mind seems always to dwell in and about his belly, where, if I remember my classics correctly, the Greeks supposed the soul to dwell, and his book might well have been sub-entitled "Genius and Gastric Juice." In order to be in condition to enjoy his victuals he hired an English doctor to visit him every day. "It was indeed a luxury," he declares, "his fee was two dollars." Now as two dollars a day was all that it cost McAllister for his meals, it must have seemed a great extravagance! But the secret is disclosed in the next line: "We became great friends, and as he was the court physician, he got me invitations to all the balls!"

At Florence, McAllister really learned "what a ball supper should be, and what were the proper mural decorations for a ball room and the halls opening into it." This was worth while, for it gave him that technical training necessary to his great social successes later on. Rome did well by him and he kept on wining and dining, following the hounds —he would "quietly take to the road when he met a formidable jump"—and also avoiding the American ambassador, because the latter was reputed to have said that, though his countrymen were an enterprising nation, "there was not a gentleman among them." It seems unnecessarily cruel on the part of McAllister to have deprived his country's representative of seeing an exception, even if it might have proved the rule.

He summered at Baden-Baden, dined daily within a table or two of the then Prince of Prussia, who appeared to be no judge of wine at all, but which defect McAllister forgave on account of the intense admiration he bore for him. "His habit of walking two hours under the trees on the Allee Lichtenthal was also mine, and it was with pleasure I bowed most respectfully to him day by day."

The sight of the Prince of Prussia gulping Rhine wine so affected his health that at Paris he hired an Irish doctor to travel with him for two months. "I agreed to give him a bottle of 1848 Latour for his dinner daily, pay his expenses, and to give him a medical fee such as I saw fit at the end of the trip. He was indeed a man among men. . . . This doctor made a new man of me. . . . Of water he had a holy horror. 'Drink what good wine you wish and let water alone.' "

And so after two winters at Paris, where he "dashed into society with a vim," and two summers at Baden-Baden, giving balls at both places, our hero at length returned to New York, full of fame and *fois gras*, resolved, with the impassioned zeal of a crusader, to make the social world a better and more appetizing place to live in.

In his chapter called "Home Again" he gives the account of the opening gun of his campaign, a dinner to Commodore Vanderbilt at the New York Hotel January 5, 1859. It was very French, but no doubt very good.

## CARTE DU DINER

Les huitres, salles
Le Potage du Consomme de Volaille, a la Royale
Le Basse payee, grillee, Sauce Remonlade
Les Pommes de Terre, a la Lyonnaise
La Mayonnaise de Homard, decoree a la gelee
Le Filet de Boeuf, pique, roti, aux champignons
Le Cailles, truffees, a la Financiere
Les Cotellettes d'Agne au, a la Soubise
Les Tomates, a la Americaine
Les Petits Pois, a la Française

Canvas-back Ducks, roasted
Le Celeri au jus
Les Huitres, grillees, a la Ste Augustine
Le Pouding de Cabinet
La Gilee, au rhum
Les Meringues, a la Chantilly
Les Glaces de Creme, a la Portugaise
Les Quatu Mendiants
Les Fruits
Etc.

The "Etc." probably refers to the liquid refreshment not otherwise noted, although how McAllister could have foregone the pleasure of advertising the variety and quality of his drinks is hard to understand. As a matter of general information it may be stated that this was the year in which Darwin published his "Origin of Species."

The dinner apparently squared him with the Commodore so far as stock-market tips were concerned, but at that early day the grand old man from Staten Island could hardly have been of much social assistance to the young Napoleon of the kitchens. Nothing further is said about New York at this point in the book, which, as a narrative, is to say the least "structurally weak," and, although we might not unnaturally expect some reference to the gastronomic hardships caused by the Civil War, the matter is slurred over and instead we are treated to a chapter (singularly malapropos) on "Merrymaking in the South," followed by another on "Life at Newport." One gathers, perhaps unjustifiably, that during the rebellion Mr. McAllister, perhaps because of family ties in the South and equivalent social bonds in the North, spent his time vibrating rather uncertainly between Newport and the Bahamas, for in a later chapter on "Cotillions In-doors and Out" he states quite casually: "One of the events of this winter was a grand domino ball, the largest ever given here. Our Civil War was then raging. . . . The following summer I invited my old friend, the governor of the Bahamas to pay me a visit at Newport."

But wherever he was, and whatever wars were raging, he

kept on giving dinners, luncheons, clam bakes, picnics and balls,—always balls. He was a clever dog, too! When he utilized his farm for a picnic he would hire "an entire flock of Southdown sheep, and two yoke of cattle, and several cows from the neighboring farm, for half a day, to be turned into my pasture lots, to give the place an animated look." A resourceful man, this McAllister! Scotch, certainly.

These picnics and clam bakes were wonderful affairs with an "army of skirmishers in the way of servants," a band, elaborate viands cooked by French chefs, and plenty of champagne. But they were not merely gastronomical engagements by any manner of means! Far from it! "Beauty was there to look upon, and wit to enliven the feast. The wittiest of men was then in his element, and I only wish I dared quote here his brilliant sallies." Why not? Was it that modesty forbade McAllister to quote himself?

"The beauty of the land was there," he continues, "and all, feeling that they were on a frolic, threw hauteur, ceremonial, and grand company manners aside, and, in place, assumed a spirit of simple enjoyment. . . . At these entertainments you formed lifetime intimacies with the most cultivated and charming men and women of this country. These little parties were then, and are now, the stepping stones to our best New York society. Men and women enjoyed a freedom that these rural surroundings permitted, and, like the lambs gambolling in the fields next them, they frisked about, and thus did away with much of the stiff conventionality pertaining to a city entertainment." How sweetly simple it all was! It is a pity that Mr. McAllister does not include a photograph of the frisking. But the long skirts and huge hats of the time may have made it difficult to frisk picturesquely.

"Now, do not for a moment imagine," he warns, "that all were indiscriminately asked to these little fetes." Rest assured, Mr. McAllister, we do not! "On the contrary, if you were not of the inner circle—" Quite so!

Yet even among these elect there were occasional little contretemps. Once when he was giving one of these simple little entertainments and had sent to New York for Delmonico with all his staff, all the coachmen and grooms "made a foray on the abundant supplies, tumbled Delmonico's French waiters in the cellar and locked them up; thus taking possession of the dining room, held high carnival. Every mouthful of solid food was eaten up, and all the champagne drunk. . . . Every coachman and groom was intoxicated, and as the whole party at once took flight to secure dinner at home, the scene on the road beggared description. The coachman swayed to and fro like the pendulum of a clock; the postilions of the demi d'Aumonts hung on by the manes of their horses, when they lost their equilibrium. The women, as usual, behaved admirably. As one said to me: 'My man is beastly intoxicated, but I shall appear not to notice it. The horses are gentle, they will go of themselves.' " The horses on sober thought appear to have had quite the best of it. Anyhow it is comforting to realize that somebody, at least, had a good time.

McAllister, conscious that this admitted "hauteur" on the part of his inwardly simple friends tended to exasperate the *hoi polloi*, loyally rallies to their defense. "The mistake made by the world at large is that fashionable people are selfish, frivolous, and indifferent to the welfare of their fellow creatures; all of which is a popular error, arising simply from a want of knowledge of the true state of things. *Progress* is fashion's watchword; it never stands still; it always advances; it values and appreciates beauty in women and genius and talent in men." (As so self-evidently in his own case.) "It is certainly always most charitable; it surrounds itself with the elegancies of life; it soars, it never crawls. I know the general belief is that all fashionable people are hollow and heartless. My experience is quite the contrary. I have found as warm, sympathetic loving hearts in the garb of fashion as out of it. Fashion selects its own votaries. You will see certain members of a family born to it, as it were, others of the same family with none of its attributes. You can give no explanation of this: 'One is taken the other left.' Such and such a man or woman are cited as having been always fashionable. The talent of and for society developes itself just as does the talent for art."

And now, having given us this charming sketch of the manners and customs of a by-gone era our author skips twenty years or so and tells us why he organized the Patriarchs' Balls.

"When you become very rich and powerful, and people pay you court, it follows in many cases that you become exacting and domineering. It soon became evident that people of moderate means, who had no social power to boast of, must needs be set aside and crowded out if the one-man power, or even the united power of two or three colossally rich men, controlled society. One reflected that it would not work. The homage we pay to a society leader must come from the esteem and admiration which is felt for him, but must not be exacted or forced. It occurred to me then, that if one in any way got out with the powers that be, his position might become critical, and be so forced out of the way as to really lose his social footing. Where then was the remedy for this?" Answer: The Patriarchs' Ball Committee where the odium for exclusions could be equally distributed. But instead of heading the list of twenty-five leaders of society Mr. McAllister cleverly contented himself with fourth place. "Social Unity" he called it, and the "patriarchs were chosen solely for their fitness."

I am informed by one in a position to know that McAllister did not himself organize the Patriarchs and that really, instead of being the leader of society, he was the servant of it. However that may be, his wardenship of the portcullis enabled him to let in and keep out whom he would. He had charge of the mailing lists, and invitations requested for people he did not like or approve of, never reached them.

This man McAllister was the greatest snob that ever lived. He divided those members of society worthy of his attention into two classes: (A) "nobs," (B) "swells." A "nob" was a person entitled by birth and breeding to an exclusive and exalted social position, and hence not required to make any social effort whatever to maintain it. He was what he was. While a "swell" was a person who paid for the privilege of knowing the nobs and had to keep on paying. As the swells did the work they were necessarily more in the public eye. But they couldn't fool McAllister! He knew who the gouty old Misses Whosisses were that pulled the wires.

Followed the "Golden Age of Feasting," the organization of the "Family Circle Dancing Class," etc. Mr. McAllister was now "The Autocrat." He was, he declares, "assailed on all sides, became in a sense a diplomat, committed himself to nothing, promised much, and did as little as possible." Indeed, he gave his entire mornings to the great work of keeping the wrong people out and letting the right people in.

One of these parties at Delmonico's described in verse in a daily chronicle, concluded:

> "And by whose magic wand is this
>   All conjured up, the height of bliss?
>   'Tis he who now before you looms
>   The Autocrat of Drawing Rooms."

One is inclined to suspect that the lines were perhaps composed by a certain gentleman there present for the edification of the company on the previous evening, but who unfortunately found no occasion to deliver them.

So there he was! He had achieved his ambition. "There is no power like the social power," he boasts; "it makes and unmakes." "Beauty in woman, genius in man," he admits, "happily I never fail to discover." He knew that the laurel crowning his brow belonged there. No one could dislodge or tear it away. He was undisputed emperor of society, with a faithful bodyguard of twenty-five impeccable gentlemen "chosen solely for their fitness." But nobody wanted to displace him! Society was glad to have a leader, to be relieved of responsibility, to let George do it. And George did do it.

He made himself genuinely useful to the sort of people he regarded as important and gave the world a good time laughing at them.

After nearly 200 pages of rumble-humble and balderdash, in which there is not a single wise or witty remark recorded, "Society As I Have Found It" peters out into a combination handbook of etiquette and cookery—"Entering Society," "Entertaining," "Madeiras," "Champagnes and Other Wines," "Dinners," "Cooks and Catering," "Balls," "Famous Newport Balls," "An Era of Extravagance," "Washington Dinners and New York Balls" and the latest fashions in visiting cards. He laid down the rule that "a dinner invitation, once accepted, is a sacred obligation. If you die before the dinner takes place your executor must attend the dinner." If he had only stopped there we should think more highly of him, but he spoils it by adding naïvely in parentheses: "(This is not to be taken literally, but to illustrate the obligation.)"

It all ends with a reproduction of a slipshod, but obviously highly cherished, invitation to a tea on board a yacht:

"Mr. ——

requests the pleasure of Mr. and Mrs. Ward McAllister's

Company on board the Yacht ——

on Thursday, August 15th,

from four until six o'clock

Boats at the N. Y. Yacht Club landing.    Newport, R. I."

and corrected in a scrawl so careless that the "August" might have started as "December."

Had he been an educated man he could have left behind him an invaluable collection of memoirs instead of merely a cook book. It would have been worth while had he recorded the stories he must have heard from old Mrs. Mason Jones, weighing 350 pounds and known as "Bloody Mary," about New York in the 30's and 40's. Alas! Instead he tells us what kind of gloves to wear at the opera and warns us in selecting a shin of beef to remember that "a fresh shin is always the best for soup."

Nevertheless, as we run through these pages of flatulent twaddle, we occasionally stumble upon an item of historic interest, such as the stupendous amount of drinking that went on as well as the tolerance with which it was regarded, the fact that at one time it was customary both in this country and in England to put a large square of red satin in the middle of the table in order that the silver placed upon it might show off to advantage, and that at this period (1863) "there were not more than one or two men in New York who spent in living and entertaining over sixty thousand dollars a year."

The horror with which mixed bathing was viewed sixty years ago is illustrated by an anecdote of what happened when the Governor of the Bahamas was visiting him at Newport. "On one occasion we visited the beach together when the surf was full of people. We saw an enormously tall, Rubens-like woman, clad in a clinging garment of calico, exhilarated by the bath, jumping up and down, and in her ecstacy throwing her arms up over her head.

" 'Who is the creature?' he exclaimed. 'Is this allowed here! My man, you should not tolerate it a moment!'

"I gave one look at the female and then, convulsed with laughter, seized his arm, exclaiming: 'It is your wife's English maid!' If I had given him an electric shock, he could not have sprung out of the wagon quicker. Rushing to the water's edge, he shouted: 'Down with you! Down with you this instant, you crazy jade! How dare you disgrace me in this way!' The poor girl, one could see, felt innocent of all wrong, but quitted the water at lightning speed when she saw the crowd the Governor had drawn around him."

It was not unusual for gentlemen who entertained to give valuable presents or "favors" to the ladies present. "At one dinner, on opening her napkin, each fair guest found a gold

bracelet with the monogram of Jerome Park in chased gold
in the center. Now it must be remembered that this habit of
giving ladies presents at dinner did not originate in this city.
Before my day the wealthy William Gaston, a bachelor, gave
superb dinners in Savannah, Georgia, and there always
placed at each lady's plate a beautiful Spanish fan of such
value that they are preserved by the grandchildren of those
ladies, and are proudly exhibited to this day."

W. E. D. Stokes to my own knowledge continued this
custom down into the present generation, to the embarrassment of some of his female guests—and to the great delight
of others.

Mr. McAllister deplored the increased cost of entertaining. In the good old days, on those informal Dutch-treat picnics where everybody rollicked in simplicity and "frisked,"
the cost was insignificant since each family took its own butler and carried out the wines and all the dishes. "We would
pay twenty-five dollars for the farm or grove to which we
went for the day. Twenty-five dollars for the county band,
as much for the hire of silver, linen, crockery, etc., and ten
dollars for a horse, wagon and man to take everything out,
making the entire outlay in money on each occasion eighty-
five to a hundred dollars." And he could give himself a picnic dinner and dance at his farm for sixty people for $300,
everything included. "What a difference to the present
time!" he mourns. "I got up one of these country dances and
luncheons summer before last at my farm (1889) where,
under a pretty grove of trees I had built a dancing platform
from which you can throw a biscuit into the beautiful waters
of Narragansett Bay. Lending the farm to the party, everyone bringing a dish, hiring the servants and music, cost us in
money eight hundred and six dollars and eighty-four cents."

"Society As I Have Found It" is a cheap and tawdry exposure of a vulgar man without a concept of anything finer
in life than terrapin and champagne, whose God was his
belly and whose idea of Heaven was to wallow in the flesh
pots. And yet he cannot be thus totally dismissed.

Ward McAllister, whether shoddy gentleman or jackass, illustrated two great truths—the inertia of the social mob and the power of an earnest fool consecrated to an idea. McAllister believed in the "nobs" and the "swells." To him they were the real people—the only people worth bothering about. He regarded himself as ordained by nature, if not by God, to lead them and to show them how to get the most out of life. That he imagined the only good things in life to be located south of the umbilicus does not greatly differentiate him from many other men. But that sensible, kindly, altruistic and educated people accepted his standards and suffered his control is something to give us pause.

It is not improbable that those to whom McAllister awarded the accolade of social knighthood were deserving of it. Among the twenty-five names are those of families who have and still do mean much in the life of New York City, —the Kanes, Warrens, Livingstons, Duncans, Sheldons, Phelpses, Posts, Kings, Schermerhorns, Riveses, Van Rensselaers, Goodhues,—and those who attended the Patriarchs' and constituted the so-called "Four Hundred" were neither foolish nor vulgar. There was a society in those days composed of refined old families, less ostentatious than it became in later years. Why then did they stand for this man and let him lead them by the nose? Why did they accept his standards even for a single evening? Unquestionably the answer must be sought in the willingness of the great mass of people to let others do the work for them, even if it costs them money or dignity, and permits the volunteer to acquire unworthy merit. We live in a world of one-man corporations, governments, and societies,—a world not of "controlling minorities" but of "controlling individuals."

Ward McAllister was no buffoon, but a social fanatic capering earnestly around ballrooms and determined that social honor should be bestowed only where social honor was due, —a second-rate fellow obsessed with a delusion that what was really brass was in fact gold. His conviction carried conviction with it. Besides, people of sense had other business to attend to. And so, because merrymakers are always more amusing to watch than those who mourn, and because most people are curious about the rich, the insignificant collection of people in the larger sense who centred about Mrs. Stevens, Mrs. Belmont, and Mrs. William Astor, of all of whom Ward McAllister was the Grand Vizier, became objects of interest and newspaper publicity. Certainly their doings were not of the slightest importance even as a study in social-economics. But McAllister drew public attention to them and, when he published his book, "Society" as such heard the first rumble of its doom in the laughter of the Gods.

Now there is "none so poor to do him reverence."

There is nothing peculiar, and there should be nothing to excite jealousy in others, in the prominence of the "nobs" and the "swells." The eye of the observer is naturally attracted by what is most conspicuous. He knows, or at least should know, that the Jungfrau is no more beautiful than a hundred of lesser practically unknown peaks, and that an eight-foot doorman in front of a theatre is no more of a chap than the rest of us, except in height. The fact that somebody lives in a marble palace or possesses $50,000,000 is a fact like any other fact. It may or may not interest us, depending on a variety of considerations, but generally speaking it is calculated to attract attention. There is no harm in that. It is only when it is assumed that because one dwells in marble halls or has a pot of money he must necessarily possess greater intelligence, ability, or charm than others who have not these material assets, that danger arises.

Time was when wealth, having been originally regarded as a sign of God's grace, begat arrogance in the possessor. To-day there are few purse-proud people left, and they are properly regarded as fools by most of their friends and by the world at large. The multimillionaire is no longer an object of great envy. The ultra rich are tolerated, rarely envied, and frequently pitied by their fellows, who know that they are no better and often less happy than the rest of the world. The trouble with McAllister was that he thought dia-

metrically otherwise. The "swells," in his opinion, were better, and certainly happier, than other people in direct ratio
to the size of their bank accounts. He sought rich people and
he got them, but he saw to it that the strain of millionaires
was properly blended with the blood of Old Father Knickerbocker. He called admission to Society "a badge of royalty"
and sought to make it more and more exclusive. The phrase
"The Four Hundred" became a slogan uttered, at first, as
much in awe as in jest. Later he reduced the sacred number
to a hundred and fifty. His penchant for lists led to his being
called Mr. "Make-a-lister." Yet he made them and they
were definitive. No aspirant for social honors could get by
his veto. This King of Snobs gave every "nob" and "swell"
due credit for his exact nobbery and swellishness.

"I well remember being asked by a member of my family:
'Why are you so eager to go to this leader's house?' My
reply always was: 'Because I enjoy such refined and cultivated entertainments. It improves and elevates one.' From
him I literally took my first lesson in the art of giving good
dinners."

Yet what sort of refinement and cultivation could have
been found in a society that catered to this shallow vulgarian
who misplaced his pronouns and, according to one who knew
him well and liked him well enough, "could not carry on
a conversation upon any matter of public interest since he
knew nothing about anything except eating, drinking, and
party giving." The "improvement" must have been purely
stomachic, the "elevation" alcoholic, a fact deducible from
his comment "from him I literally took my first lesson in
the art of giving good dinners."

No, McAllister in spite of being a gentleman of sorts,
well-intentioned and punctiliously polite, was *au fond* a very
second-rate person; and one is inclined to wonder whether
his social world may not have been pretty second-rate also.

But while it is distressing to one's national and civic pride
that women like Mrs. August Belmont should have accepted
this man, it is a satisfaction to learn that his book was greeted

with the derision it deserved. Said the New York *Evening Post* October 25, 1890:

"The book shows little more conception of what society is—or should be—than a polo pony has of ancient history. To assume to describe a 'Society' destitute of humour, of wit, of position or distinction, of kindly deeds and generous, unostentatious hospitality, is but to make the author and his subject alike ridiculous. . . . Had he confined his ambition to feeding The Three Hundred and Ninety-nine, and his empire to the kitchen, no complaint would have been possible but dyspepsia. . . . The difficulty with the book, if such a book can be treated at all seriously, is that it assumes to treat of the drawing-room, when it should have been confined to the kitchen and the servants' hall. Its atmosphere suggests that the master and mistress are out of town and that the servants have moved up to the drawing-room."

*The Times* in a lengthy review said:

"Mr. McAllister is emphatically a man of deeds, not words. When he is induced to become a man of words for the benefit and enjoyment of the public, it is not surprising that his words should not in all cases be such as writers of grammar and dictionaries can conscientiously sanction. . . . Sometimes the incertitude of his English makes his meaning difficult to arrive at, though it is but justice to him to say that the thought itself, when it is reached, is never abstruse or recondite. It is superfluous to add that with this weakness of his English he combines an admiration for French which is even less according to knowledge. . . . While he is thrice weak in his parts of speech, our leader of society is not weak at all points. The man seems really to know something about eating and drinking.

" 'When the demand for a social leader arises, the social leader appears. . . .' The first requisite for success, as in so many other things, is intense moral earnestness. No suspicion that he is making a continental laughing stock of himself must disturb his mind or interfere with the singleness of his devotion. . . . The degree of fervor that the author puts into undertakings that adults commonly leave to adolescents is really wonderful. . . . 'He who is serious about trifles is serious indeed.' . . . In writing this remarkable book, he has produced a social document of considerable interest, for he not only illuminates himself, but he sheds a somewhat garish light upon the 'society' whose leader he is."

*The World* said:

"That bright people will earnestly desire to get into society after reading Mr. McAllister's exposition of it is somewhat doubtful. They will come to the conclusion that they have something better to think about at this urgent hour. They certainly cannot form a very high conception of society if the author of this book is the result of its developing and refining processes. For the product is the most extraordinary example of trivial mindedness and pretentiousness that it is possible to conceive of. He is in every attitude and sentence the exemplar of authoritative puerility, giving dignity to emptiness and striving to make a blatant idiocy official. . . . It is not apparent that he knows anything about the elemental factors in this great seething and vital American life, with its pressing social issues. . . . But he knows how to cook a ham."

To an interviewer sent by the New York *Herald*, McAllister said:

"Society As I Have Found It" was written to make money. I see no reason why I should hesitate to acknowledge the fact. And it has been a success. . . . There has been a good deal of personal abuse and ridicule of me, but not much honest criticism of my book. . . . They will persist—everyone of 'em—in speaking of me as 'the autocrat of American drawing rooms,' 'the leader of New York society,' 'the head of the Four Hundred,' and so on. Now, I don't deserve any such exalted rank, and have never set up any such claim. The newspapers alone are responsible for dubbing me with these titles. . . . I wish the newspapers wouldn't make it appear that I pretend to be the leader of the Four Hundred. It's just about as true as that I ever limited New York society to four hundred. . . ."

To do McAllister full justice it is probable that he did not make the claim in the first instance. Others made it and he merely acquiesced. He would probably have been satisfied to plan dinners, engage servants, run social errands and do the dirty work for his friends. This gave him a strangle hold on society and he made use of it. He was responsible for "The Four Hundred"—perhaps not precisely as interpreted by the public and the press—but as a phrase, and it certainly represented his idea of the number of persons qualified for admission to the inner circle. Justly or unjustly it made him a butt. His ridiculous book finished him. From the date of its publication his influence steadily waned and he was no longer taken seriously even by the snobs, who once eager for the slightest of his favors now jeered at him. The book itself was not the success he claimed and he netted only $2,000 from it. His last years were spent in gossip, in walking about the town, in marketing and writing self-revelatory articles for the newspapers, which only detracted still further from his reputation. He died in 1897.

Ward McAllister has been dead over a quarter of a century;—why exhume him? Simply because his book is one point from which to estimate a possible social progress. He himself was unimportant. His treasure was laid up where moth and dust corrupt. What fame he had has vanished. He is almost totally forgotten. His name cannot be found in any biographical dictionary, roster of celebrities, or contemporary equivalent of "Who's Who." Yet he alone decided who was who for thirty odd years in fashionable New York life and this may fairly be taken as evidence of the latter's true importance.

Ward McAllister's great error was in confusing fashionable life with good society. We have progressed at least beyond the point where he would be possible to-day.

# CHAPTER XVII

## The "Gay Nineties"

OPPRESSED by a vague impression of original sin and still more by a sense of social inferiority, I made my début in New York during that period commonly referred to as the "gay nineties,"—when Ward McAllister, if no longer a name to conjure with, was still a vivid memory.

Just why the nineties were regarded as "gay,"—except by contrast to the drabness of the "Brownstone Era,"—I have never been able satisfactorily to find out. Other terms—quite as apposite—have been applied to them. In England they were called "the yellow" or "golden" nineties, the first adjective taking its color probably from Aubrey Beardsley's Yellow Book, or Oscar Wilde's chrysanthemum, the latter referring, perhaps, to the development of the South African gold mines, followed by the gold discoveries in the Klondike, or to the Jubilee period of the Queen's reign. In two other adjectives I have more interest, for each connotes the undoubted Puritanism of the decade,—"mauve" and "naughty." "Mauve" the nineties certainly were, for they had a prim and distinctly Puritan flavor of lavender and rose leaves.

It is in the phrase "naughty nineties"—so widely popular with my own generation—that I find most significance, since it so clearly connotes the rigidity of the Victorianism which enabled a young lady, who for the first time pedalled off on a safety bicycle, lobbed a ball over a tennis net, or surrendered herself to the sway of the "Boston" to regard herself as rather devilish, if not having taken the *premier pas* towards becoming a fallen woman. In point of fact, while the nineties may have been innocently "gay" they were anything but "naughty." On the contrary it was a romantic era in which everybody engaged in a conspiracy of pure-mindedness. We refused to look upon life save through rose-tinted glasses. Charles Dana Gibson and Richard Harding Davis had popularized, as national hero, a clean-shaven, square-shouldered young Galahad who, as drawn by Gibson, strangely resembled Davis; and as the ideal of American girlhood, a balloon-sleeved, wasp-waisted Venus in a rakish straw hat, easily recognizable as Irene Langhorne, shortly to become the artist's wife.

The social *status quo* seemed so firmly established that society encouraged so-called "parlor socialists" much as the French Court under Louis XVI applauded and even acted the plays of Beaumarchais. The word *decadent* was familiar as applied to the works of Aubrey Beardsley and Oscar Wilde, French novels were found only behind sofa cushions, Stevenson had yet to put into print the first "God damn," childbirth was spoken of, if at all, as a sort of veiled obscenity,—Queen Victoria had still to hold her Jubilee.

The rigors of chaperonage had steadily increased until by the 90's it had become a curse which tended to destroy the very object of its existence. Mrs. M. E. Sherwood, a New York lady of social position well qualified to speak, wrote in 1880:

"Little as we may care for the opinion of foreigners we do not wish our young ladies to appear in their eyes in a false attitude, and one of the first necessities of a proper attitude, one of the first demands of a polished society, is the presence of a chaperon. She should be a lady old enough to be the mother of her charge, and of unexceptionable manner. She must know society thoroughly herself, and respect its laws. She should be above the suspicion of reproach in character, and devoted to her work.

"The duties of a chaperon are very hard and unremitting, and sometimes very disagreeable. She must accompany her young lady everywhere; she must sit in the parlor when she receives gentlemen; she must go with her to the skating-rink, the ball, the party, the races, the dinners, and especially to theatre parties; she must preside at the table, and act the part of a mother, so far as she can; she must watch the characters of the men who approach her charge, and endeavor to save the inexperienced girl from the dangers of a bad marriage, if possible."

The custom was still on the up-grade, according to Miss Hall, in 1887:

"Society in America is growing more strict on this subject, however, than it used to be, and the chaperone is gradually assuming larger and larger powers, and taking more and more the position of an English or Continental matron."

D. Appleton & Co.'s "Social Etiquette of New York," published in 1897, said:

"Etiquette has made chaperonage in New York an established and even a rigid law, as also it is in most Eastern cities. The young unmarried woman neither enters society nor receives gentlemen visitors unattended by an elder or at least a married lady or a kinsman who is nearly related to her.

"The chaperon enters the drawing-room with her charge at her left, and slightly in advance of her. After she has exchanged the usual courtesies with the hostess the young lady is presented. As she moves on, her charge always accompanies her, and a gentleman will not ask the young girl to dance, to promenade, or go to supper, without first seeking permission of her chaperon, nor will he detain the young lady unreasonably long, if he is considerate and regardful of etiquette in such matters, and no well-bred man can be heedless of the proprieties.

"He cannot ask a young lady to accompany him to a theatre or other place of amusement without first asking her mother's or her chaperon's permission, and at the same time extending the same invitation to her also. If she consents for the young woman, she has a right, if she be engaged or indisposed, to ask permission to delegate the office of chaperon to some one else, and her request is likely to be granted."

One is inclined to wonder whether the danger to a young lady's virtue justified all this bother. Certainly the expense must have been discouraging if not well nigh prohibitive to most young men.

A bachelor might well be inclined to pause to-day before inviting a girl to the opera, if it involved anything such as outlined by D. Appleton & Co.

"Opera, and theatre parties are among the delights of the fortunate, and they are common with rich families, although they are more frequently given by bachelors, who have no well-equipped homes to which they can invite guests, and thus cancel some of their many social obligations.

"If one of these costly entertainments is to be given by an unmarried man, he first secures an acceptable *chaperon* for the young ladies of his proposed party. If she be his own kinswoman, all the better for the harmony of the affair. This selection spares him the unpleasant perplexity of choosing from among the mammas of his young lady guests. He proffers his invitations in person, or by note, soliciting first the consent of the mother that her daughter may be his guest for the evening, at the same time mentioning what married lady will accompany them, and also furnishing the names of the gentlemen who are invited to be present.

"The dinner hour is usually six o'clock for this style of party. Retiring from the table the party proceeds to the opera in carriages or a carry-all furnished by the host. Boxes have necessarily been secured, because the party is in full dress for the dinner.

"After the amusement, the guests return to the banqueting-room for slight refreshments, and then they separate, a gentleman accompanying each young lady, provided only her waiting-woman calls for her with her carriage. If her father or a kinsman comes for her, the gentleman who has been her attendant during the evening escorts her to her conveyance. He calls upon her within three days to inquire after her health, or he leaves his card, provided a visit be impossible to him.

"The bachelor host is compelled, by the laws of our best society, to pay his respects and return thanks to mother and daughter within a week, for the honor and pleasure he has received. The young ladies pay an early visit of thanks to the friend who so kindly chaperoned them."

I well remember all this rumble-bumble and fol-de-rol on first coming to New York in 1895, and a pretty penny it cost me too. Although I imagine that the Appleton book was probably a reprint and not a revision of its predecessor, it was a decade or so behind the times. However, I have paid for the carriage, if not for the "carry-all." And I called within the week.

In those days you might take a walk with a girl unaccompanied by a chaperon provided you got home before dark, but you were not allowed to ride with her unaccompanied by a groom, who must remain at all times within sight. On rare occasions "a party" of young people were allowed to go to some daylight form of entertainment by themselves— say the circus—but never in the evening. The chaperon was always within sight and hearing when a girl received a male caller unless she had announced their engagement. Even then the conduct of the affianced pair was strictly governed by convention. There is no etiquette more elaborate than that of matrimony and it has remained practically static, although the art of lovemaking has noticeably altered.

"The Gentleman—Simplex Munditis" tells us how one should have proposed in 1891: "Always plead your cause with eyes and speech only. When accepted it is left to the option of the suiter as to what mode of procedure will best express his delight and happiness. But perhaps for those of timid and bashful nature it is advisable to suggest a standard course of action, viz.: when the lady replies affirmatively, immediately clasp her in your arms; this is not, for true lovers, a very embarrassing position. Let the embrace be gentle, simply to signify and give strength and proof of your affectionate expressions prior to the acceptance.

"Always stand when proposing, as it lends dignity to the occasion and allows of more freedom in expressing the feelings; besides, it savors of very little earnestness to remain in any other attitude while making so important a confession."

But once engaged you had to mind your p's and q's and you still had the chaperon always at your heels—at least outside the house. A girl more or less retired from social intercourse until after her marriage. To be seen about too much would argue a lack of seriousness and hence was considered bad form. On her wedding day she must remain indoors and not see her husband before she met him at the altar. Miss Florence Howe notes that in Boston in 1887 "a young lady at the sea-shore greatly shocked public opinion by going down to the surf beach and bathing on the morning of her wedding day."

But a girl by no means got rid of the chaperon by marriage. After the honeymoon "a bride must on no account receive her visitors without a mother, or sister, or some friend being present, not even if her husband is at home. This is imperative. Young married ladies may visit their acquaintances alone; but they may not appear in any public places unattended. It is not considered *comme il faut* to ask a married lady to dance, when her husband is present, without previously ascertaining whether it be agreeable to him."

Attention, if carried too far even with the husband's consent, could seriously compromise any married lady; and that "what was sauce for the goose was sauce for the gander" is shown by the injunction that "when a man marries, it is understood that all former acquaintanceship *ends*, unless he intimate a desire to renew it, by sending you his own and his wife's card, if near, or by letter, if distant. If this be neglected, be sure no further intercourse is desired."

What killed the chaperon was the advent of the athletic era. The bicycle smashed her. Old ladies could not be persuaded to ride bicycles and the young ones couldn't be kept off them. Many a present-day grandmother remembers the unparalleled sense of freedom that was hers the first time she and a party of her friends enjoyed the experience of setting off on their "safeties" unaccompanied.

It was in the 90's that Mr. Eastman's Kodaks started an interest in amateur photography. The Kodak carried a universal focus lens, the shutter of which was released by pulling a short string. Each film took one hundred pictures and had to be sent to Rochester to be developed. Often, when the shutter was "on the blink" or there was a fly-speck on the lens, the whole hundred negatives turned out blanks, for there was no way of finding out whether or not the machine was in proper working order except by the results. The process of developing and printing sometimes took several weeks, which increased one's annoyance when all the pictures of one's best girl, Aunt Eliza, the new baby, Fido or the hired man, came back failures. When presently local dealers began to offer developing-and-printing service amateur photography became a national craze.

Very few people in 1895 had heard of an automobile in spite of the fact that Charles Duryea of Springfield, Mass., had won a fifty-four-mile motor race inaugurated by the Chicago *Times-Herald* from Chicago to Evanston and return. He did the 110 miles in 10 hours and 23 minutes.

During this decade small boys were driven frantic by being put into "Little Lord Fauntleroy" suits of sashed velvet by adoring mothers, who thought Frances Hodgson Burnett's saccharine herolet "such a perfect darling."

The popularity of "Looking Backward" as a "best seller" was followed by the tremendous vogue of DuMaurier's "Trilby," which captured the whole country. Its gay, "Bohemian" atmosphere exercised an irresistible lure upon the Puritan-Provincial mind, which could thus vicariously indulge in all the sins of the flesh without retribution in the hereafter, since of course the poor girl, being hypnotized, was not to blame. Its phrase "the altogether" (meaning, dear reader, "in the nude") appealed to the irked Victorians as a racy euphemism and probably played a large part in loosening up conventional discourse. It gave people a legitimate excuse to talk about demi-mondaines, grizettes, and—h'm! prostitutes.

The works of Marie Corelli, owing to the approval of Queen Victoria, were assiduously read by all "true women" on both sides of the Atlantic. Kipling and Stevenson were on the top of a literary heap, largely composed of Rider Haggard's "She" and "King Solomon's Mines," General Lew Wallace's "Ben Hur," Westcott's "David Harum," and novels by Paul Leicester Ford, Doctor Weir Mitchell, Ian Maclaren, Amelia Barr, Marion Crawford and Frank Stockton.

As I am now trespassing upon remote, yet jealously guarded, lands of memory it may be well to cite the authority of *The Century's* advertising pages as showing that roll collars were worn with evening clothes (Cluett advertised one calling it "the swellest of collars"), that porcelain bathtubs were just coming in, that "souvenir spoons" were all the rage, and—"believe it or not"—that moustache cups were considered well nigh indispensable, one firm advertising the "moustache spoon shield" for "neatness and comfort of moustache wearers—the neatest novelty of the age—can be immediately adjusted to any table spoon."

Victorian influence was still supreme in fashionable life and one of the Queen's later obsessions was reflected in all the drawing rooms of Fifth Avenue, the tables of which were crowded with photographs heavily framed in gold and silver filigree.

A new and distinct type of young man came into being—the cotillion leader—who acted as a manager at balls and as general social assistant to the hostess. Some of these attained a national, and sometimes not altogether agreeable, notoriety. The most famous was Harry Symes Lehr, court jester and grand vizier of the then leader of New York society, Mrs. William Astor, and afterwards of Mrs. Stuyvesant Fish. The son of an attaché of the German Consul at Baltimore, and a wine dealer by trade, he appeared in New York smooth, suave and impudent, documented with letters of introduction from the élite of Baltimore, and managed to secure through George Kessler the job of making Mumm's champagne popular. It was in this capacity that he first met the two ladies to whom he owed his great vogue.

He was blond and stocky, distinctly Teutonic, with a high-pitched voice and effeminate mannerisms which he skilfully used in female impersonations. His wit and audacity appealed to Mrs. Astor, and in spite of his being "in trade," she encouraged his ambition to become her friend. Installed as her social secretary, with quarters in her Fifth Avenue mansion and a good-sized expense account, in addition to his profits on the champagne business which he frankly continued while practising his avocation as a social entertainer, he became a fashionable Puck. Already the inner circle was getting rather bored by its long-drawn-out formal dinners, and Lehr, with his pranks, offered a much-needed diversion. His ingenuity in "putting on a show" for his various lady patronesses and friends would in these later days have earned him a magnificent salary from Dillingham or Ziegfeld. There was a touch of Noel Coward's bitter satire in some of his stunts, such as his famous "monkey dinner" at which he entertained a simian in full evening dress, who under the stimulus of some of Kessler's Mumm, hung from the chandelier and pelted the guests with nuts.

Lehr was outrageous in his effrontery but usually managed to make his victims feel that it would be a mistake for them to show offense even if they felt it. He initiated evening bathing parties in fountains; inaugurated the custom of drinking chorus girls' health out of their slippers; sent a bruised flower to a hospital by special ambulance; paraded with a large-sized doll on Bellevue Avenue, Newport, talking baby talk to Mrs. Fish; impersonated women at stag parties, and at others sang coloratura in a hermaphroditic soprano with appropriate oggles and flirtations of the bustle; designed frocks; gave "menagerie dinners" to Pomeranians waited on by social leaders; wore wrist bags, bangles, and attended, in a tweed suit and spotted necktie, a reception at the German Court, where his antics in the august presence of Emperor William are said to have led to the resignation of the American ambassador responsible for his appearance.

In three short years he sprang from obscurity to a celebrity that made his every word and gesture front-page news, had married a celebrated heiress, and had surpassed Ward McAllister both in his dictatorship of New York society and in making that society ridiculous. "Happy Harry" Lehr died a year or two ago, no longer happy but bitter and splenetic, neglected by his friends and almost forgotten by the circle whose tables he had once set upon a roar. "Alas! Poor Yorick!"

The reaction of Lehr's patronesses from the boredom of social functions was the first symptom of revolt against Victorian Puritanism. His antics, however, were by no means representative of society as a whole, which remained heavily conventional. The dinner party of the 90's—now happily almost extinct—was a formidable affair. "Favors" were still in fashion and from each luncheon or dinner every lady carried away some touching little memento such as a fan, a work basket, a statuette, or a muff.

"The familiar horseshoe," writes Mrs. Sherwood in 1897, "in silver or silver-gilt, holding up the menu-card, is another pretty favor, and a very nice one to carry home, as it becomes a penholder when it is put on the writing-table.

"Baskets in various styles are often seen. One tied with a broad ribbon at the side is very useful as a work-basket afterwards. Silvered and gilded beetles, or butterflies, fastened on the outside, have a fanciful effect.

"Wheelbarrows of tiny size for flowers are a favorite conceit. They are made of straw-work, entirely gilded, or painted black or brown, and picked out with gold; or perhaps pale green, with a bordering of brown. A very pretty one may be made of old cigar-box wood; on one side a monogram painted in red and gold, on the other a spray of autumn leaves.

"The designs for reticules and *chatelaines* are endless. At a very expensive luncheon, to which twenty-four ladies sat down, a silk reticule a foot square, filled with Maillard's confections and decorated with an exquisitely painted landscape effect, was presented to each guest. These lovely reticules may be any shape, and composed of almost any material. A very handsome style is an eight-sided, melon-shaped bag of black satin, with a decoration of bunches of scarlet flowers painted or embroidered. Silk braided with gold, brocade, and plush combined, and Turkish towelling with an *appliqué* of brilliant color, are all suitable and effective.

"In the winter a shaded satin muff, in which was hidden a *bonbonnière,* was the present that made glad the hearts of twenty-eight ladies. These are easily made in the house, and a plush muff with a bird's head is a favorite 'favor.'

"A very pretty set of favors, called 'fairies,' are little groups of children painted on muslin, with a background of ribbon. The muslin is so thin that the children seem floating on air. The lady's name is also painted on the ribbon.

"We find that favors for gentlemen, such as sunflowers, pin-cushions, small purses, scarf-pins, and sleeve-buttons, are more useful than those bestowed upon ladies, but not so ornamental.

"Little Leghorn hats trimmed with pompons of muslin, blue, pink, or white, are filled with natural flowers and hung on the arm. These are a lovely variation.

"Bags of plush and silk, embroidered with daisies, are very handsome and expensive favors; heavily trimmed with lace, they cost four dollars apiece, but are sold a little cheaper by the dozen. Blue sashes, with flowers painted on paper (and attached to the sash a paper on which may be written the menu), cost eighteen dollars a dozen. A dish of snails, fearfully realistic, can be bought for one dollar a plate, fruits for eighteen dollars a dozen, and fans anywhere from twelve up to a hundred dollars a dozen.

"A thousand dollars is not an unusual price for a luncheon, including flowers and favors, for eighteen to twenty-four guests. Indeed, it would be impossible to describe half of the fancies which minister to modern extravagance. The *bonbonnière* can cost anything, from five to five hundred dollars; fifty dollars for a satin box filled with candy is not an uncommon price. Sometimes, when the box is of oxidized sil-

ver—a quaint copy of the antique from Benvenuto Cellini—
this price is not too much; but when it is a thing which
tarnishes in a month, it seems ridiculously extravagant."

Mrs. Sherwood then describes for our delectation a typical
banquet in fashionable New York society:

"The open-work, white tablecloth lies on a red ground,
and above it rests a mat of red velvet, embroidered with peacock's feathers and gold lace. Above this stands a large silver
salver or oblong tray, lined with reflecting glass, on which
dresden swan and silver lilies seem floating in a veritable
lake. In the middle of this long tray stands a lofty vase of
silver or crystal, with flowers and fruit cunningly disposed
in it, and around it are placed tropical vines. At each of the
four corners of the table stand four ruby glass flagons set in
gold, standards of beautiful and rare designs. Cups or silver-
gilt vases, with centres of cut glass, hold the bonbons and
smaller fruits. Four candelabra hold up red wax-candles
with red shades, and flat, glass troughs, filled with flowers,
stand opposite each place, grouped in a floral pattern.

"At each place, as the servant draws back the chair, the
guest sees a bewildering number of glass goblets, wine and
champagne glasses, several forks, knives, and spoons, and a
majolica plate holding oysters on the half shell, with a bit of
lemon in the centre of the plate. After the oysters are eaten,
the plates are removed, and two kinds of soup are passed—
a white and a brown soup. Each lady has a bouquet, possibly
a painted reticule of silk filled with sugar-plums, and sometimes a pretty fan or ribbon with her name or monogram
painted on it.

"At his right hand each. guest finds a goblet of elegantly
engraved glass for water, two of the broad, flat, flaring shape
of the modern champagne glass (although some people are
using the long vase-like glass of the past for champagne), a
beautiful Bohemian green glass, apparently set with gems,
for the hock, a ruby-red glass for the claret, two other large
white claret or Burgundy glasses, and three wine-glasses of
cut or engraved glass.

"As the dinner goes on the guest revels in unexpected surprises in the beauty of the plates, some of which look as if made of solid gold; and when the Roman punch is served it comes in the heart of a red, red rose, or in the bosom of a swan.

"The modern married belle at a dinner is apt to be dressed in white, with much crystal trimming, with feathers in her hair, and with diamonds on her neck and arms, and a coronet on her head, which is not republican, and a pair of long, brown Swedish gloves drawn up to her shoulders; a feather fan of ostrich feathers hangs at her side by a ribbon or a chain of diamonds and pearls.

"The fine, stately fashion of wearing feathers in the hair has returned, and it is becoming to middle-aged women. It gives them a queenly air.

"Monstrous and inconvenient bouquets may be again the fashion, and a very ugly fashion it is. A lady does not know what to do with her two or three bouquets at a musicale or a dinner, so they are laid away on a table. Let us glance at the gentlemen at a modern, most modern, dinner. The vests are cut very low, and exhibit a plain shirt-front held by one stud, generally a cat's-eye; however, three studs are permissible. A few young men, sometimes called dudes—no one knows why—wear pink coral studs or pearls, generally black pearls. The old fob of our grandfathers is sometimes seen on very well-dressed men.

"Gentlemen now wear pearl-colored gloves embroidered in black to dinners, and do not remove them until they sit down to table. Seal rings for the third finger are replacing the sunken jewels in dead gold which have been so fashionable for several years for gentlemen, although this is a shifting fashion."

I have thought it worth while to include so exhaustive a quotation for the reason that, unless supported by printed evidence, my bare assertion that such horrible entertainments actually took place within living memory might not be believed. Alas, dear reader, I have been present at many of them, although I never retrieved any "sunflowers," "pin cushions" or "small purses." I do, however, recall attending a dinner of seventy given about 1899 by Mr. and Mrs. W. E. D. Stokes, at which each lady was presented with a gilt cage containing a pair of live love birds, emblematic of conjugal fidelity and happiness, and each gentleman received a basket of Indian grass from beneath the closed cover of which protruded a yellow ribbon attached to a golden safety pin.

Mrs. Stokes, later Mrs. Philip Lydig, arose at an appropriate moment and instructed the gentlemen to attach these ribbons to the table-cloth by means of the pins, and then gave the signal to open the baskets, from each of which instantly leaped a large bullfrog about whose middle was fastened the other end of the ribbon. The bullfrogs, ecstatic with delight at their release, sprang into the soup plates, the champagne glasses, the laps of the ladies or upon their bare necks and arms. As near to a riot as I have ever seen in high society followed, and when the last half-fainting female guest had been escorted out of the room, only a German count remained stealthily collecting the pins which, by biting, he had ascertained to be genuine 14-carat gold.

Such records of an evanescent phase of American life are not without value to the student of manners, who might otherwise be apt to question whether any former age could have been more ostentatious than our own. That the fag end of the Victorian era was socially pretentious and banal no one who accurately remembers it has any doubt. Because it was so conventional it was dull, which was the worst of its faults. Its repressions occasionally caused strange reactions, but on the whole, once athletics had come in, it produced a breed of women whose standards of personal conduct and dignity were probably as high as any in the history of the Commonwealth. On the other hand it led some, like the patronesses of Lehr, into extravagances which encouraged others to shake off Victoria's social yoke. To-day fashionable people, however foolish they may otherwise be, have sense enough not to feel obliged to be bored. They may waste their time as much as ever, but they no longer do so to the same extent sitting in their war paint around heavily laden dinner tables mumbling conversational platitudes and waited on by serfs in livery,—a custom derived in part from plethoric Teutonic feasts in the forests of the Elbe and in part from Puritan Thanksgivings.

Yet even in that era of orthodoxy, of Sabbatarianism, of propriety, and of what we now call excessive prudishness, those were not lacking who stigmatized it as meriting the fate of Sodom and Gomorrah.

Declared Bishop A. Cleveland Coxe in an article entitled "The Decay of Public Morals," in April, 1888: "As the result of much observation and inquiry I must own my fears that the elements which destroy great nations are powerfully at work toward our premature corruption and decay. . . . The home is a perishing institution. In a community tending to a dissolute condition, add the corrupting influences of the daily newspaper, stocked with reports of crime and garnished with crude pictorial illustrations of the details of murder, adultery, suicide, and scenes in courts of justice or about the gallows, I ask what is wanting to make boys experts in villainies, or to rob the young girl of the blush of innocence and the charm of maidenly modesty? The dime novel, and the petty theatre still more corrupting, are at hand to pander yet further to the destruction of domestic purity. Strolling companies of players infest the villages and defile their fences with full-length and highly colored pictures of naked women and licentious men. Sodom itself could not have presented such public allurements to vice as everywhere abound among us, even in country places; while in growing cities the unrebuked indecencies that are paraded before all eyes would disgrace a Gomorrah. . . .

"It must not be imagined that things are better among the more wealthy classes in our larger cities. Some of the most luxuriously furnished dwellings in New York or Philadelphia, in Chicago or New Orleans and San Francisco are notoriously the abodes of gilded misery. We hear not infrequently of 'fashionable' young women eloping with mere lads, their partners in the shameless waltz; if not with their fathers' coachmen who have been permitted to drive off with them unattended, or to follow them, as grooms, in their equestrian airings. In our great cities women are living in grandeur upon chief streets or park-sides, who are known to have enriched themselves by unmentionable crimes. Of late an idle class has developed in American cities, where until lately everybody was 'doing something' for self-support. We have a 'gilded youth,' who sport as 'dudes,' who live unmarried, come in and out as the habitués of club houses, show themselves, night after night, at the opera, give suppers to other people's wives, who *live*—nobody ventures to surmise just how! . . .

"The pitch of superlative degradation has been reached in the fact that women of the stage have been entertained in the homes of reputable citizens, though the fact was notorious that they were unmarried parents; nay, in one shocking instance the unwedded parent shameless produced and paraded her progeny in public, without rebuke."

When I first visited New York in the very year of the good bishop's diatribe against the gilded vice of the metropolis, I found a city little less Puritan in its outward aspects than my native Boston. Divorce—even in the American Babylon—still carried a social stigma. Mrs. John King Van Rensselaer writes of the 70's: "That domestic troubles should ever end in a divorce court was unthinkable; so families remained intact, whatever happened, and the most outrageous conduct by husbands and fathers was accorded no further publicity than the whisper of gossip . . . the much deplored, frequently assailed morals of current Society are no bit worse than they were in the prim and prudish half century ago. In that day the woman who obtained a divorce was a Pariah. There was no appeal. By her action she became a social outcast." A divorced woman though "utterly guiltless" was "socially dead."

Conversation in mixed company was still guarded, the

prejudice against novel-reading had not entirely died out, a woman who smoked would have been socially damned, and no youth could take a girl to see a Shakespearian tragedy, even if they were engaged to be married, unattended by a duenna. The hotels made it an iron-clad rule to receive no woman as a guest unless she was accompanied by her husband, and if I am not mistaken, it was as late as 1897 that Mrs. John Jacob Astor, finding herself stranded rather late one evening and seeking refuge at the Waldorf, only with great difficulty kept herself from being ejected, although she was the most prominent woman socially in the city.

Even in the "gay 90's," while there was much "liberal" preaching, Sunday in New York was still distinctly under the Puritan shadow. Every male, with any pretensions to a place in the social order, after a late breakfast put on his best double-breasted frock coat, steel-gray trousers, patent-leather shoes and Ascot tie, and in a tall silk hat costing some $18 and weighing nearly as many pounds, made expressly in London for a New York hatter, joined the church parade down Fifth Avenue, where, after attending divine service, he returned home to a heavy roast-beef dinner with Yorkshire pudding, accompanying vegetables and dessert. After sitting around for an hour or two in order to facilitate the digestive process, he might take his hat and go for another stroll, this time in Central Park. If enough of a hell rake, he might drop into his club on the way back to supper and stimulate his appetite with a sherry-and-bitters, a brandy-and-soda, or a glass of Scotch.

The evening meal was a "picked up" one, of cold meat and salad, for the servants were usually allowed the evening off. There was nothing to do thereafter but read, listen to the "Aeolian" or join in family hymns, for a game of cards would have been regarded as sacrilege. Great numbers of people attended evening church service. There were few concerts and no amusements on Broadway except "burlesques" given in street costume. There was no early morning exodus of golfers; indeed the word golf, "golluf" or "gollolluf" was known only in jest. How far we owe the introduction of the game to the then highly popular Scotch dialect story is matter for future sociologic investigation. Certainly the dialect story did not follow, but preceded, it. There was no general "week ending" in the country, no resort to country clubs, no motor trips, no dancing, practically no Sunday bridge or whist. The "gay" nineties in truth were not so "gay."

People had not yet learned to play, although the doctrine of open-air exercise, under the stimulus of the bicycle, was making rapid headway. The end of the nineteenth century still saw the average business man driving himself six days a week (including Saturday afternoons) to make "his pile" and to give his sons and daughters what were known as "social advantages." "Society" was still "society," eating elaborate course dinners of from twenty to forty covers off gold and silver plate surrounded by fleets of wine-glasses. But the dawn was about to break. Freedom of movement—first on the bicycle, then in the automobile—changed the whole complexion of existence. It brought the country to the city and the city to the country.

The New England town which, owing to physical limitation upon personal movement, in conjunction with the hypocrisies engendered by Puritan inhibitions, had festered for a century in its own moral grease, resulting in all sorts of abnormal sexual irregularities, including incest, suddenly ceased to be a prison for inbreeding. The new ease of communication transformed the whole country into a single neighborhood and made every county a neighbor to every other. Girls who did not wed across the road or in sight of their future husbands' chimneys no longer were obliged to look forward to a choice between spinsterhood and sin. They met and married young men from villages and cities at previously unheard of distances—even from other states—or, if they preferred, started out to make lives of their own in other parts of the country. The often lamented "standardization" of life since the coming of the telephone and the motor has, in the small town, usually been a standardization in the direction of a more normal and hygienic morality. The outlook of the inhabitants has become less introverted, more charitable toward one another, and more honest with themselves.

The "safety-" bicycle made its appearance in 1889, and before long all the world had taken to the wheel. It has been said that no invention for two hundred years had, from a physical point of view, done so much for the human family. In the year 1899 one American out of every seventy actually purchased a safety-bicycle. A quarter-century later only one in a thousand bought one, but the Ford had taken its place. Much of the college interest in athletics grew out of the popularity of the safety, and many successful men of the next quarter of a century acquired their vigor by their use of the wheel. The artisan and white-collar worker, as well as the young fashionable, discovered the easy accessibility of the country, and had it not been for the fact that the middle-aged woman refused at first to "make herself ridiculous," the country week-end, which did away with the Puritan Sabbath, would have come ten years sooner. As it was, we may fairly say that the Puritan shade, foreseeing what was to happen during the next quarter of a century, slid silently away astride the bicycle as the twentieth century came in.

# CHAPTER XVIII

## The Puritan and Prosperity

IT is not my purpose to prolong this sketch beyond the Victorian Era which terminated, generally speaking, with the Spanish-American War, the consequent emergence of America as a full-fledged world power, the South African War and the death of the Queen Empress in 1901. Politically, economically, scientifically, socially, "the turn of the century" marked the beginning of a new phase of American life.

Willy-nilly we became for the first time "socially minded." The invalidation by the Supreme Court of the Income-Tax Law of 1894 recalls, as Mark Sullivan points out in "Our Times," a state of mind which now seems curiously archaic. Joseph H. Choate had denounced the "communistic march" of events and prophesied the terrible possibility of a future day when incomes might be taxed even as high as 20 per cent! And Justice Field had declared in his opinion that the present assault upon capital . . . will be but the stepping stone to others larger and more sweeping till our political conditions will become a war of the poor against the rich; a war growing in intensity and bitterness."

The New York *Sun* said: "There is life left in the institutions which the founders of this republic devised and constructed. . . . The wave of socialistic revolution has gone far, but it breaks at the foot of the ultimate bulwark set up for protection of our liberties."

*The Tribune:* "Thanks to the court, our government is not to be dragged into communistic warfare against rights of property."

On the part of the plain people there had been for some time a growing and well-justified dissatisfaction with capital.

The phrase "corporate abuse" represented no imaginative idea. The root of the trouble lay in the fact that a corporation was not a human being, nobody being responsible for its actions (since responsibility was spread over a score of officers and directors and easily evaded) it had frequently no pride, shame, or sense of decency. There was no ethical restraint upon it and not much legal restraint either. One by one the railroads got into difficulties, and after the panic of 1893, most of them had to be reorganized,—a majority by J. P. Morgan & Co. Neither the Interstate Commerce Act of 1887 nor the Sherman Anti-Trust Law had as yet made serious trouble for big business, but the handwriting was on the wall.

The deluge of immigration during the nineties had brought many socialistic theories into the country along with it. The newcomers had none of the Puritan-Philistine regard for wealth or its owners. It was a period of gorgeous fancy-dress balls, of licentious and reckless rich men; "night life" began to be popular; and the uncurtained windows of Sherry's and Delmonico's were a continuing instigation to Socialism. Municipal politics had always been the most corrupt phase of American life, and the alleged relationship of the corruption to corporate privilege became a favorite subject of periodical literature. The "muckraker" appeared. A lot of what he said was bunkum, for at first glance inefficiency often resembles corruption, but whether "mauve" or "golden" the decade was a bad moment for millionaires. The reformers were in the saddle and the highways full of embryonic Jeremiahs who, pointing at all this ostentatious extravagance, cried out to the working men that "these riches came from your wages."

In 1901, in the midst of all this excitement about money, J. P. Morgan & Co. conceived and gave birth to the Steel Trust, for the successful delivery of which the attendant physician and his associates received a fee of $78,000,000, while Mr. Andrew Carnegie was observed hurrying from the bedside with a bag containing a quarter of a billion, which

he had received as his share of the payment made for the
Carnegie Iron Works,—up to that moment the largest
amount of money ever held in the hands of any single individual.

A period of disillusionment followed. We discovered
sinners in high office and corruption everywhere. Fortunes
were made in muck. The cities bowed their heads in shame,
and Miss Ida Tarbell, by her exposition of the iniquities of
Standard Oil, succeeded in driving John D. Rockefeller out
of the counting room and onto the golf course. The Sam-
son of Reform grasped the pillars of Faith and Reverence
in his strong young hands and shook the temple of National
Confidence. The "Victorian Era" was stigmatized as the
"Age of Bunk." The searchlight of iconoclasm flickered over
everything alike—exposing in turn the weaknesses and delinquencies of politics, society, big business, organized phi-
lanthrophy, marriage, theology and the Constitution. Principles were judged by personalities and crashed with those
who preached them. Nothing—no one—was secure. Even
the virtue of the Goddess of Liberty fell momentarily under
suspicion, while Capital cowered behind the threadbare protection of an economic system challenged as outworn.

This was the final phase of the antagonism to great wealth,
which crystallized during the Roosevelt administration
(1901–8), when the huge profit cleared by Carnegie and the
Morgan syndicate became generally known. The stock market boom of 1901, temporarily halted by the quarrel between
Harriman on the one hand and Morgan and Hill upon the
other, which resulted in the Northern Pacific panic and the
two hours' insolvency of Wall Street on May 9, 1901, was
followed by the Northern Securities suit in 1902, and the
decision of the Supreme Court in 1903 declaring that the
combination was in violation of the Anti-Trust Act of 1890.
Roosevelt went after the "wicked trusts" with a big stick;
and Charles Evans Hughes first appeared in the limelight
as counsel for the Armstrong Insurance Committee of Investigation in 1905–6, disclosing just enough of the iniquities

of the life insurance companies to shake the nation-wide popularity of District Attorney William Travers Jerome of New York County, because he could not find any punishments to fit their crimes.

Roosevelt threw his sombrero into the ring and in shrill but stentorian tones challenged the "malefactors of great wealth," leaving no doubt in the minds of the sons of toil that the "vested interests" were their enemies. It was quite true that some sort of transitional adjustment from an archaic economic and social condition to modern requirements was indispensable if not inevitable. There were serious labor troubles—a "general unrest among the masses of the people." The magazines after ten years still teemed with shameful stories of rich men whose lives were dedicated to lust and liquor. All corporations belonged to the "plunderbund." Millionaires—to say nothing of multi-millionaires—were no longer "generously good," but "highwaymen" and "crooks."

In 1907 occurred one of the worst panics in financial history. It was at its height in October and November of that year. The Knickerbocker Trust Company failed on October 22, and George Westinghouse's Electric and Manufacturing Company applied for receivers. Currency was quoted at a premium of 4½ per cent, and money on call, when obtainable, rose to 125 per cent. The nightly meetings in Mr. Morgan's library became the centre of interest and of hope. Under his calming influence the situation gradually readjusted itself, and by February, 1908, the panic was over.

In his special message to Congress on January 31, 1908, Roosevelt said: "Every one must feel the keenest sympathy for the large body of honest business men, of honest investors, of honest wage-earners, who suffer because involved in a crash for which they are in no way responsible. At such a time there is a natural tendency on the part of many men to feel gloomy and frightened at the outlook. . . . Our main quarrel is not with the representatives of the interests. They derive their chief power from the great sinister offenders who stand behind them. They are but puppets who move as

the strings are pulled. It is not the puppets, but the strong
cunning men and the mighty forces working for evil behind
and through the puppets, with whom we have to deal. We
seek to control law-defying wealth."

On that day public hostility to capital and to the possessors
of great fortunes reached its apex. The attitude of the American people as a whole had changed in less than a lifetime
from reverence toward wealth to distrust and hatred.

At about this time it first became known that the head of
the Standard Oil Company had accumulated a fortune of a
*billion* dollars.

Meanwhile Thorstein Veblen amiably explained the theory
of the leisure class; and the leisure class of Russian Poland
patronizingly accepted our invitation to come over and live
with us as the acknowledged arbiters of art, literature and
music. One could not be fashionable without being radical.
Wealth and socialism kissed each other and for a fleeting
moment the Have-nots and the Haves lay down together on
upper Fifth Avenue. The drama became all sicklied o'er
with a pale cast of Semiticism. Every social leader had her
pet Jew. Greenwich Village was restored by long-haired men
and short-haired women chattering of symbolism, cubes, and
planes. The honk of the motor drowned the sound of the
church bell; the choir boy turned caddy, and the children,
having eaten of the grapes of sophistication, set the parents'
teeth on edge by boldly questioning the sincerity of the Ten
Commandments and the marriage service.

New ideas—some of them iconoclastic and violent—had
become current. It was recognized in silk stocking circles that
labor had sometimes not been treated as equably as it might
have been in the past. The masses stirred and became articu-
late through a horde of professional uplifters, reformers,
sociologists, and labor leaders, many of whom were sincere
and some of whom were even sound in argument and conservative in statement. The leaders of big industry began to
take a sudden interest in "welfare" and "social service."

It became fashionable to talk about applying the "Golden

Rule in Industry." Business men all over the country hopped upon the tailboard of the philanthropic band wagon and shouted through their megaphones that they were going to apply the doctrines of the Sermon on the Mount, although half of them couldn't have told what the Golden Rule was.

The War revitalized the Constitution; it also forced a show-down on Sex. Pretense was no longer possible, there were no more inhibitions. The injunction to "be good, sweet maid, and let who will be clever" ceased to appeal to a younger generation fully aware that if one was clever it was quite un-necessary to be good; and who regarded with derision, if not with pity, fathers and mothers who must needs be virtuous when virtue was no longer a reward. The five years follow-ing the entry of the United States into the World War was the most uneasy period for Puritans in American history.

Russia, her "humanity uprooted," had gone Bolshevik, our own youth was running amuck, the "Ohio Gang" through the partial control of the National Government were sur-rendering the natural resources of the country in return for bribes carried in the same sort of black bags that had car-ried money to Albany fifty years before, the war millionaires were storming the ramparts of society in New York and Newport just as they had in the early 70's with the same crassness, the same vulgarity.

Then, from 1922 to 1929, coincident with the realization of the most amazing dreams of science and after a false start or two, came "the fifth great period of business prosperity in the history of the Republic." Lindbergh flew from Mineola to Paris; the movies burst into a pentecost of rasping speech and raucous song; we listened to "conferences" carried on simultaneously between speakers in London, San Francisco, Paris and Berlin; a lonely radio-man on a yacht lost in the forests of the upper Amazon tossed a random message across the jungle "If any one in Manhattan picks this up please call 4376 Plaza and ask how my wife is," and in less than six minutes got the reply: "Have called up as requested. Wife O. K. Sends love"; we set type by means of machinery that corrected its own mistakes; invented "robot" men who could automatically operate mines and factories; we telephoned from New York to Paris and Madrid; Byrd flew over the North Pole; photographs were transmitted through the air by radio; we discovered television and a new planet and an anti-serum for diphtheria and a cure for diabetes; convicted John T. Scopes at Dayton, Tenn., of the crime of teaching the doctrine of evolution, and hung Sacco and Vanzetti at Boston.

The "Billionaire Era" had arrived, the era of big, bigger and of "bigger business."

Individual income taxes for 1924 reached gigantic proportions. Fourteen men paid income taxes on over $5,000,000 each.

| NAME | TAX (not income) |
|---|---|
| John D. Rockefeller, Jr. | $6,278,000 |
| Henry Ford | 2,609,000 |
| Edsel Ford | 2,158,000 |
| Andrew W. Mellon | 1,883,000 |
| Payne Whitney | 1,677,000 |
| Edward S. Harkness | 1,532,000 |
| R. B. Mellon | 1,181,000 |
| Anna B. Harkness | 1,062,000 |
| Mrs. H. E. Dodge | 993,000 |
| F. W. Vanderbilt | 793,000 |
| George F. Baker | 792,000 |
| Thomas F. Ryan | 792,000 |
| Edward J. Berwind | 722,000 |
| Vincent Astor | 643,000 |

An inexhaustible flood of money poured into Wall Street. There was a tremendous expansion of industry throughout the country; "mergers" arose controlling entire industries. The "Coolidge Boom" was followed by the "Hoover Boom." New corporations appeared overnight and successfully floated billions of dollars' worth of new securities. There were 1,300 stocks listed on the New York Stock Exchange, and days when 6,000,000 shares changed hands. Banks and trust companies combined with one another until their capital transcended the grasp of the imagination; the United States was converted to "the gospel of common stocks" the phenomenal rise of which had made millionaires of many office boys; we loaned the very money to Europe with which it paid its debts to us; everybody was rich, everybody gambled, and a single seat upon the Exchange was sold for over half a million dollars.

Meanwhile 20,000,000 pleasure cars rolled and raced along the highways. The American family which did not own a house or apartment with overstuffed furniture, hardwood floors, imitation Persian or Chinese rugs, electric lamps and "torchiers," velour draperies, electric irons, a vacuum-cleaner, and a radio belonged in the pauper class. The former luxuries of life had become necessities. Every one seemed to be making money; nobody to lose. Every one had charge accounts at the big stores. Every one spent—and kept on spending. Yet savings bank deposits were at the largest volume in history! "O day of rest and gladness! O day of joy and light!"

And the earth surrendered its increase. Across the rippling fields, like army tanks along a thousand miles of Western Front, advanced the invisible line of reapers and binders; the air trembled to the clatter of thresher blades, the whir of knives, the snort of exhaust pipes, the chug and roar of engines, tall forests tottered and fell; into the stockyards crowded the bellowing, rearing herds; the afterglow of the southwest was dimmed by hanging smoke and the flare of the furnace paled the moonlight of the Alleghenies; men swarmed by hundreds of thousands into holes in the earth; factory chimneys were pillars of cloud by day and by night of fire; over the sleeping continent glowed the landing fields of commercial airways; towers of Babel rose toward heaven and frightened the wild geese with their clamor; the song of the saw, the hum of the dynamo, the rattle of the loom, the drone of the airplane, the rat-a-tat of the riveting machine filled the pulsating sky.

Already our automobiles, driven by hawk-faced men, were climbing the rocky passes of Tiflis and Albania; the Chinese, Hindoos and Berbers were sitting cross-legged before our gramophones; our chemicals were pouring into Germany, our fruit into France and England; our sewing machines, tractors, radios, pipes, pumps and faucets, cash registers and typewriters were flooding the foreign markets from Guatemala to Singapore.

And while the sky was etched with airplanes, and interminable lines of freight cars crept across the continent, and the mountains shook with blasting, stocks sold higher and higher. Prosperity had come! The public attitude towards wealth reversed itself again. If everyone was going to be rich, the millionaires were all right! Once more wealth came to be revered as evidence of the divine favor. Only now instead of Jehovah the descendants of the Puritans worshipped Pluto, the god of wealth—and of darkness.

§ 2

Mr. Stuart Chase in his recent thought-provoking series of articles in *The Nation* entitled "Prosperity—Fact or Myth" (now happily available in book form) argues that prosperity may be more apparent than real, and that in spite of telephones, radios and motors, increased wages and shorter working hours the worker may be no better off (he carefully avoids saying that he is not) than he was ten years ago. It is a brilliant and witty warning that we had best stop, look and listen before we commit ourselves to the theory that mass production will make in the end for prosperity. He takes his text from a full page advertisement, published in the New York papers on January 8, 1929, over the signature of Alfred P. Sloan, Jr., president of General Motors, who under the caption "What Is Real Progress?" answers the question from the viewpoint of the automobile manufacturer.

"This week the public is visiting the Automobile Show to see new models. Suppose you could drop a curtain over the

1929 show and raise it immediately upon the show of last year? How vividly the progressive changes would then appear! . . . in performance, in comfort, in beauty, in style. . . . The patronage of the public makes possible all this machinery of betterment; so the public is entitled to each improvement as promptly as it has been proved. . . . Such progress, born of the inherent ambition of an organization of active minds to do better and to give more, is of benefit to all. It offers you more for your money with each succeeding year. It gives you more value for your present car when you trade it in. This is real progress."

"Yes," mutters Mr. Chase, "in automobile making." We do make better and more brightly painted motor cars each year, a little better in some ways—usually minor ones—than last year's crop. But, he asks, how about "the man who buys one?" Is it "real progress" to have made him feel that he must have that glossy "betterment"? Wouldn't the old one —that 1928 model—perhaps serve his purposes practically as well? What real benefit is there to him in all these thousands of miles of new concrete and macadam, these hundreds of gasoline stations? Is he any better off because he can hop in his new bus after a hasty supper and run the family over to Centreville to see Gloria Swanson in the talkies?

Does the tremendous absorption of motor cars establish anything more than that by the application of high-powered salesmanship new wants have been temporarily created to fill which the machinery of mass production can be utilized for the time being? "But," he comments, "because a house has an electric washing machine does not mean that it is a prosperous one. It may only mean that the local washing machine salesman is an expert at his trade." It does not mean that the dwellers in it have less fear of sickness, accident, unemployment or dependency in old age, or that they have more leisure in which to rest or read or play or enjoy the beauties of nature. And to pay for all these new improvements over other new improvements the worker, and the business or professional man as well, must earn more and more money.

There is no progress and no prosperity in exchanging human time and energy for what we have no opportunity to use and perhaps really do not want.

On the other hand, Mr. Chase admits the United States has gained in the last ten years 30 per cent in physical productivity as against 15 per cent in population. The new science of management has not only increased output, but it has raised wages, reduced the length of the worker's week by at least five hours since 1904, increased his safety and lowered costs. Owing to the control of tuberculosis and various infectious diseases we have reduced American mortality *by half a million lives a year* since 1900. We have had in six years a 20 per cent increase per capita in the national income, a doubling of corporate profits, improvement in health and length of life, increase in savings, insurance, educational and housing facilities far in excess of the growth of population, and gradually rising wages against a scale of prices which has remained comparatively stationary. All this, as the saying is, "listens well,"—very well. It ought to spell prosperity, as it surely indicates a certain kind of progress, but, he asks, *does it?* The best that can be said, he thinks, is that whatever prosperity there may be is only comparative. Besides, it is not the whole picture.

Mr. Morris A. Copeland has calculated that in 1925 the average family income of 90 per cent of the population of the United States was only $2,200 per year, and that the average income per employee was but $1,384. This substantiates the estimate of the National Bureau of Economic Research for 1918 that 85 per cent of those employed earned less than $2,000, and 72 per cent less than $1,500. Mr. Chase wonders what this 20 per cent increase per capita of national income has done for these in the way of prosperity or progress.

The national income per capita has increased from $625 in 1922 to $742 in 1928. That is exactly $117. If it all went into more nutritive food, warmer clothing, and more airy dwellings it would mark a percentage of material progress in prosperity. But, he complains, it doesn't. It goes for a Ford, a radio, a telephone, a phonograph, silk stockings, imitation fur coats, movies, electric dew-dabs and gadgets, over-stuffed Davenports, electroliers, glossy oak furniture, lip sticks, "beauty shoppes," "hot dogs," gasoline, nut sundaes, tootsie rolls, chewing gum, cigarets, ice cream soda, safety razors, magazines.

In 1928 there had been distributed throughout this happy land of freedom:

| | |
|---:|---|
| 15,300,000 | electric flat irons |
| 6,828,000 | vacuum cleaners |
| 5,000,000 | washing machines |
| 4,900,000 | electric fans |
| 4,540,000 | electric toasters |
| 2,600,000 | electric heaters |
| 755,000 | electric refrigerators |
| 348,000 | ironing machines |
| | and |
| 21,630,000 | motor cars |

the last being regularly replaced at the rate of 4,000,000 per annum.

How are these things paid for? Over 60 per cent of all the motor cars are bought on the instalment plan. The American people have already mortgaged that per capita increased income to the tune of $6,000,000,000. The usual carrying charges on automobiles is 10 per cent; thus, if a man owes a balance of $1,000 on his new car, he must pay $100 additional for the privilege of paying off the debt in twelve monthly instalments. A family that is tied up to the extent of only $50 a month on instalment payments on automobiles, radios, washing machines, etc., must pay $5 a month interest, or $60 a year, for that "privilege." Most of the increase in per capita income must be absorbed by interest charges on deferred payments.

Therefore, says Mr. Chase, if the American has been forced into luxuries and supposed comforts at the expense of necessaries, all that has been accomplished has been a redistribution of income through a mistaken idea of what makes for prosperity under the influence of equally deluded neighbors and the insistence of the high pressure salesman. He has merely traded a mortgage for a motor car, his "over-time" for a Davenport which he has no leisure to use, shoes for gasoline, smaller living quarters for a radio. The world is doubtless a cleaner and certainly a noisier place to live in; but there is no more rest for the weary, no let up to the necessity of toil. We are still slaves to the machine—only the machine is grinning at us from the parlor mantelpiece, and from under its bill of sale in the doorway of the mortgaged garage. The question is whether all these millions of things have really got us anywhere from the point of view of a more full and satisfying life.

Wages, while tending to increase, are not keeping pace with the new almost compulsory standard of living which includes the radio, the telephone, the bath tub and the motor car, as is demonstrated by the fact that the workers have had to borrow to buy them. East side tenements are as unsavory to-day as they were before the installation of their myriads of radios or all of Rachael's daughters insisted on wearing silk stockings. There are thousands of families which combine the use of the old-fashioned backyard privy with that of the washing machine and the vacuum cleaner. We want the best even if we are willing to put up with the worst to have it. The development of American social life as briefly sketched in the foregoing chapters shows, ever since Revolutionary days, a consistent and constantly growing national ambition for wealth and what wealth will buy, to earn in order to spend. We spend even before we earn.

That, summarized, is Mr. Chase's general argument and (by obvious implication) his lament. How much better if our increased earnings went into necessaries rather than often merely showy luxuries! How much better if an actual cash surplus was tucked safely away to guarantee those necessities in sickness and old age, and the reduced working hours utilized for reading, thinking, enjoying nature, talking, playing, making friends, and savoring the simple joys of life which we are now too hurried to appreciate! It is a good brief for caution and possible readjustment.

But even in the face of the figures which seem to support the proposition that American prosperity may be an illusion and not an actuality, there lingers a feeling in the mind of at least one reader that there may exist for some, and eventually be evolved for the many, a technique of living whereby the illusion may become a fact rather than a myth. In the first place although he carefully qualifies even his inferential conclusions, Mr. Chase's underlying thought is strongly colored by the feeling that the telephone and the radio and the motor are not genuinely means to a more abundant life, or that if they are, or might become so, they are now paid for at a disproportionate or negationary cost. There is something, and perhaps a good deal, to be said upon the other side. The automobile has brought real happiness—one closely allied to what we call the spiritual—into millions of lives. Incidentally my farming neighbors down here in Maine don't buy the new models every year. They buy ten-year-old Fords for $15 and build 'em over; and when the "bus" is ready to scrap they salvage the engine and stick it in their fishing smacks.

On this general subject the New York *Times* recently said: "There can be no questioning the shift from 'necessities' to 'luxuries.' It is by no means to be deplored. The economists have always known that the proportion of income spent on food, shelter and clothing declines sharply as one moves up in the social scale. Among the poor housing and dress often have to wait upon food. The trend to luxury is not always to be measured in terms of automobiles and electric household conveniences and movies three times a week. It is luxury when the consumption of sugar rises as the consumption of rice, or rye, or potatoes declines. It is luxury when woolen clothing competes with cotton. Our modern age undoubtedly has its percentage of John Daws who sleep on grass to buy their wives a looking-glass. But in the main the drift to luxuries is the register of a rising level of well-being that is by no means confined, as is so often assumed in protests against the Machine Age, to mechanistic factors."

A steadily increasing demand for bath tubs, radio sets and automobiles by workingmen's families, whose incomes are well under $2,000 annually, is noted by the National Industrial Conference Board in the report of a comparison of a pre-war budget, used in its computation of changes in the cost of living, with a budget compiled by the Federal Bureau of Labor Statistics from a systematic investigation of 100 Detroit workingmen's families.

The average income, practically all derived from factory earnings, of these families was $1,711.87. This income under the pre-war budget would have been divided in the following percentages: food, 43.1; housing, 17.7; clothing, 13.2; fuel and light, 5.6 and sundries, 20.4. The Bureau of Labor investigation showed that the income is now divided according to these percentages: food, 32.3; housing, 22.6; clothing, 12.2; fuel and light, 6 and sundries, 26.9.

"The outstanding fact in this comparison," the Conference Board explains, "is the demonstration of a steady advance in living standards as indicated by the decreased proportion of the income required for food and the marked increase in sundry expenditures. There has been a slight decrease in expenditures for clothing and a material increase in the cost of housing.

"The latter item probably indicates that bath tubs, said to be a peculiar mark of American civilization, are not to be obtained without price and that new standards of comfort are demanded by the working classes. The percentage of expenditure attributed to miscellaneous purposes is considerably greater than that found in the characteristic workers' budgets of other countries. The nearest approach to it in foreign lands is found in Canada and Australia.

"It is interesting to note that 47, or nearly half, of the 100 families owned automobiles and that these automobiles were used in the main for pleasure purposes, since only eight of the workers used their machines regularly to carry them to work. Forty-three of the families reported telephone expenditures, mostly through pay stations, and thirty-six families owned radio sets. In one form or another, as many as eighty-seven families were carrying life insurance at an annual expenditure for all families of $59.16 or 3.4 per cent of the total living expenses.

"One who is in any degree familiar with the mode of living of the workers in European countries," the Conference Board concludes, "or indeed in our own country fifty years ago, must be deeply impressed by the contrast between the privations of those lands and of those times and the comparative degree of material comfort which at present the enterprising and energetic wage earner is able to attain in his family life."

Every man must manage his own life and make his own budget. If Shirley Higgins wants to work overtime in order to buy a radio on the instalment plan, I say good luck to him. When people can sit comfortably at home, and see as well as hear the best entertainments the country can offer, they will not be so much tempted to fare forth looking for amusement and diversion elsewhere. The radio has amplified the maximum Carnegie Hall concert audience about 4,000 times; that is to say, from 2,500 to 100,000,000 persons. About 340,000,000 persons listened to a series of thirty-four Saturday night concerts given over the air during the past winter. Already owing to the radio there has been a tremendous growth in "music consciousness" in America. The antennæ of culture rise towards the stars from chimney pot and roof tree all over the land. A "set" of some sort is within the reach of everyone, and that the radio has already become a permanent vehicle for culture of inestimable value is vouched for by Mr. Rockefeller's gigantic project for a $250,000,000 "radio centre" in New York City.

On the far-flung islands of this rocky coast where I am writing the lobsterman of a winter's evening "listens in" with his wife and children to music from across the seas he could never have afforded to hear on land before it was "put on the air." It is a reaching out in the right direction, even if it be for him perhaps something of an "over-extension."

Who is this nameless person who mortgages his safety, his old age, his better self under the misguided notion that he is happier in doing so? Is he "fact or myth"? Nothing is more elementary than that there is no such thing as "the average man." Where everybody is an exception to the rule, it does not leave much, if anything, of the rule itself. We all justly share in the general distrust of statistics and in deductions based upon them which deal in averages. We know that in a street corner huddle of ten people, consisting of nine Polaks who can't read and a university professor who owns a thousand volumes, we get by pursuing the statistical method "an average reader of one hundred books." Which simply isn't so. The nine ignoramuses remain ignoramuses. John D. Rockefeller's annual income of whatever it is—say, for fun, $10,000,000—does not increase the income of his ninety-nine nearest neighbors at Pocantico to $100,000 each, in spite of the law of averages. And if the Joneses' new baby happens to have six toes instead of five, the others in the family quartette will not acquire an extra fifth of a toe but will still be obliged to stagger around with five.

Now when we are told that the national income is $742 or whatever, we must remember that this figure is based to a large extent on the earnings or absence of earnings of ineffectuals whose income from age or incapacity is negligible. The shiftless, the indolent, the moron, the idiotic, the physically incapable, the congenital paupers, are myraid in number. They are mentally or physically as much disqualified as factors in the wage-earning national-income puzzle as the Jones dog or their new six-toed baby.

On the other hand there is an equally great, if not greater number of wage earners, who, in addition to their regular occupations, "do something on the side," even to the extent of carrying on a second trade, run a truck or gas station, rent out rooms or an overnight camp. This is apt to be true also of other members of the family who are not themselves actual employees.

In a word, while the "average" employee may earn only $1,300 per annum, and the "average" national income be but $742 per capita, and the "average" family have only $2,200, the earnings and income of most families are in fact considerably larger.

Moreover, as Mr. Chase frankly points out, the savings of the entire population increased from 8.4 billions in 1912 to 26.0 billions in 1927, while the number of depositors grew from 12.6 millions to 48.4 millions. There has also been a corresponding increase in life insurance. This does not look like over-extension. Mr. Chase wisely does not tell us whether he thinks prosperity a fact or a myth. He is, for a socialist, astonishingly optimistic. Testing prosperity by various definitions he finds we have not done so badly according to some of them, but that "the life more abundant" is a long way off yet. Nobody will, I think, in view of his conservatism be inclined to disagree with his general conclusions. If we take issue with anything in his book it will be upon his initial premises, the figures upon which his deductions as to prosperity, or the absence of it, are based, and to his hardly concealed opinion that motor cars, radios, telephones and bath tubs are not highly important factors in the more abundant life. I am among those who believe that they are. Nothing is easier than to decry materialism. Heaven knows I have done enough of it myself. But at just what point the "good" or the "abundant" life becomes hampered by material things is almost impossible to say. It is in the abuse and not the use of aids to leisure and comfort that the trouble lies.

As Herbert Hoover has said:

"The moral and intellectual progress of the Nation is not the offspring of poverty or low living standards. . . . The opportunity for education and the growth of understanding are the products of economic progress—not of economic degeneration. Devotion to economic improvement whether

in individual effort or in improved methods enlarges the
field of leadership; it is not a stimulant of idle or luxurious
living."

The recent discoveries of science have practically abolished
the old distinction between the material and the spiritual.
Einstein has finally reduced everything to mere "space."
Yet, at that, his latest pronouncement seems only to have
had the effect of putting science back to about where it started.
Did not Heraclitus say that all things came from fire, and
that stability was but an illusion in what was really a state
of flux? The distinctions remain, however, if the differences
do not. In practice Beethoven remains Beethoven, and beefsteak is still beefsteak, even if both are but illusions reducible
to a single basic principle. Assuming music to be a higher
good than food, nevertheless we must eat to live; further,
assuming that we have eaten, we cannot enjoy music without
the leisure to do so. Hence the most spiritual of us must start
by having his beefsteak before he can enjoy his Beethoven,
—only he must not spend so much time on the steak that he
has none left for the music.

Professor Commons in defending the utilitarianism of
the University of Wisconsin, sometimes referred to as the
"Butter-Fat University," says a *Times* editorial, once alleged
that he did not see why there could not be as much idealism in
breeding a perfect animal or growing a "Wisconsin No. 7"
ear of corn, or in devising an absolutely exact instrument for
measuring the amount of butter-fat in milk, as in carving a
Venus de Milo. There may be a closer relationship between
butter-fat and the Venus than we think.

I am enough of an optimist to believe that, by a process
of cost reductions and comparatively simple readjustments
—in spite of stock market crashes, unemployment, the per-
plexities of the Farm Board and international complications
arising out of the tariff,—the situation of the common man
will continue to improve as it has constantly in the past and
that a way will be found whereby the comforts, conveniences
and even the luxuries of modern invention—whether they

be regarded as "material" or "cultural"—will be assured to him, even if they are not already.

The present system of buying these things upon the instalment plan is by no means unsound, as Prof. Seligman has taken the pains to demonstrate in two large volumes. At worst the American people have but reduced their 26 billions of savings to 20 billions, and if they prefer to keep their surplus in the bank and pay on the instalment plan as an incentive to thrift, so much the better.

Is it not possible that we have merely succeeded in obscuring the subject with all this talk about "average national income" and the ratio of the increase of population to that of production? I wonder if the problem is really as complicated as it is made to appear; and whether it can be solved any more readily by statistics than it can by past experience. There are unexpected factors which inevitably enter into all social-economic questions, and these unbidden guests are as apt to wear a smile as a frown. Above all it should not be forgotten that not only is necessity the mother of invention, but that invention has always proven to be a very lusty infant. Let us drop the statistical method of approach for a moment and adopt that merely of the ordinary reasonably optimistic observer.

If, as we are out riding, we come upon a freshly painted farmhouse and outbuildings, its fences neatly white-washed, its hedgerows trimmed, its garden carefully tended, with a motor in the front yard and the smoke rising from the kitchen chimney, the first thing that occurs to us is not to wonder whether there is a mortgage on the farm, what the ratio of production is to cost of operation, or whether the radio is paid for. We merely say, "That chap is doing well! Wish I could live on a farm!"

We know that, if the owner were really running behind, the farm would not have a fresh coat of paint, and that no farmer ever mortgaged a barn in order to make it a different color. The same thing would be true of the care of the fences and the garden. We would feel quite sure that

until the ploughing had been done the farmer would not
have wasted any time on appearances. It may well be that
after he has paid for his motor and his radio he will have no
cash surplus and no more leisure than before. He may even
from time to time slip a little behind. A "cash surplus" is
not everything. In the meanwhile he is living more comfortably than he ever did, educating his children, and having a
wider contact with human activities, whether "cultural" or
otherwise. By and large, if he couldn't afford to paint his
barn, he wouldn't. So with the radio. But he will have his
motor no matter what, using his ingenuity to pinch the cost
off somewhere else.

Who shall say that the farmer is not more prosperous than
he was without these things, even though he is putting less
aside or temporarily pledging his credit in order to possess
them? You cannot reduce everything to mere dollars and
cents. My great-grandfather, that prosperous Poohbah of
Weston in Revolutionary times, with all his fees for "running
paupers out of town," calling town meetings, and wood selling, probably did not see a hundred dollars in hard cash
from one year's end to the other. The frontiersman lives
crudely, but well, without any money at all. So, practically,
do many of my country neighbors in Maine who raise their
own truck, build their own houses, catch their own fish, breed
their own poultry, pigs and cattle, and lay in their winter's
supply of meat at the point of their rifles. There is more than
one way to kill a cat or pay for a second-hand car, particularly if the ownership of that car means an extra hour for
work or play as it usually does.

My gardener lives two miles away. Last year he covered
the distance on foot morning and night and ate his lunch
under a nearby tree. This year he bought an old motor for
$20, drives home for his lunch and saves at least an hour a
day merely in going to and from his work. It is idle to discuss whether his car is a "prime essential" or not. He is not
going to walk any longer when everybody else can ride.
Willy-nilly he will have his car,—and a radio, too. Economy

has very little to do with it. It may be that he will end in the poor farm some day, but meantime he has got them and along with his entire family is getting the benefit of them. All these inventions which minister to the physical well being and happiness of mankind have come to stay. You can demonstrate on paper as much as you will that the workman cannot afford to buy them, but he will get them somehow, and gradually they will become so much a part of the background of everyday existence that they will be assumed to be necessary as a matter of course and included as factors in an ever-increasing minimum wage for an ever-decreasing working day.

The same sort of figures that tend to prove that the worker cannot remain economically safe and possess automobiles, radios, electric washing machines, flat irons, vacuum cleaners and electric fans, and the same argument that is used to prove that these do not contribute towards a more abundant life, could have been invoked with equal effectiveness against the bicycle, the sewing machine, the aeolian, the player piano, the phonograph, and at a more remote period the mangle, the carpet, the carpet sweeper, the bath tub, the water closet, the coal stove, the gas and electric light, none of which strictly speaking are any more "prime necessities" than the motor car. The luxuries of one decade are the necessities of the next. The scale of living improves from generation to generation, and with the increase in comfort and convenience come increased health and leisure for cultural things.

If my friend Jones has another ten-pound baby, I do not rush over and inquire anxiously as to the ratio of the doctor's bill to his general overhead or the average cost of the five other Jones children with relation to the increase of his annual earnings. Instead, I pound him on the back and exclaim heartily: "Good work, Jonesy, old man! Congratulations to the missus!"—remembering no more the anguish and travail of Mrs. Jones, out of joy that another man child has been born into the world.

## § 3

Our mechanical and scientific development has, quite naturally, affected our mode of living, and has tended to weaken the tie of the family, which is no longer a self-sufficient and self-supporting unit involving close co-opera-tion. In fact it might be said that no co-operation is needed at all. In the old days everything was made in the house or raised on the farm. There were no "servants," only "help," and everyone really had to help, or the shirts were not made, the bread was not baked, the linen not washed, the hay not got in, or the sick nursed, to mention only three or four obvious illustrations. We have come a long way on the co-operative road, are much more socialistic than most of us imagine. To-day a family of the same class as my grand-father's buys practically everything, including services which, a few years ago, it would have performed itself as a matter of course.

To-day nothing whatever is made at home, not even candy. The bread comes from the bakery, the butter by parcel post, the janitor cleans the sidewalk, John doesn't play the fiddle because it's easier to turn on the radio and listen to Rudy Vallee's jazz orchestra; doctors and nurses take the place of grandma with her herbs, simples and poultices, her doses of sulphur and molasses and camomile tea; father and mother have no time to teach the children anything—(what would be the use with such excellent public schools?)—discipline for any but the youngest children is viewed as cruel (besides, the others wouldn't stand for it); nobody stays at home any more, for the movie house, the theatre, the ball game or at least the drug store is always calling; there are no family parties (probably a blessing owing to the constantly shrink-ing size of the house or apartment), friends are "all over the lot," church-going is limited to the mother and younger children, there are fewer family "pow wows" over politics, books or domestic policies,—housekeeping is reduced to a minimum. The reader can carry on for himself ad infinitum.

In a word the members of the family have ceased to be dependent on one another, have individual interests and are prone to scatter as never before, while family life—and perhaps affection—constantly tends to diminish in amount and intensity. This makes for individualism and specialization. It may be that the old loyalties are replaced by larger ones. I do not know. I rather suspect that they are not. But the family is growing less and less important.

As against this the individual unquestionably has a chance for a fuller, if not happier, existence. Specialization makes for progress, even if the specialist is a less well rounded person. The wife is no longer economically dependent upon the husband, the daughters can "step out" and live their own lives. There are no more "old maid aunts" to be looked after, for there are no more old maids.

There is nothing new about this lament over the destruction of family life. Over twenty years ago Louise Creighton, the celebrated English writer, in her "Art of Living," said:

"The old quiet home-life, with its limitations, its little duties, its monotonous occupations, has been swept away, and with it the quiet demure maiden, who blushed and fainted, and was not supposed to have an opinion of her own. In her place has come the modern young woman on her bicycle, who looks as if she thoroughly knew how to take care of herself, and meant to go her own way."

Now she is doing "solos" in her private airplane!

The limitations and defects of our so-called "business civilization" are so obvious that there is a natural temptation to relate whatever displeases us in American life to the fact that monetary profit seems to be the immediate object of most of our activities, not excluding the artistic. We are told that in America a man's success is usually judged by his accumulations, and that even his usefulness to the community, his "service," is measured by the amount of his salary or the extent of his profits. Granted that apparently there is some justification for the first part of this sweeping generality, it carries no opprobrium with it. It is merely saying that in the game of money getting the one who gets most is accounted best. But the last part seems to me to be wholly unfounded. Merit and ability are as much revered and admired in America as in England, irrespective of their monetary return. It is ridiculous to assert or imply that, as Americans, we judge greatness in the arts or professions merely in terms of earning capacity.

No more than in past centuries do we judge the value of the scientist, the artist, the preacher, the author or the philosopher by what he earns. To the business man wealth may be the concrete symbol of his power and achievement, but men do not live by bread alone in present America any more than they did in the first year of the Republic. Had affluence been his incentive my grandfather would never have been a clergyman, and the same thing is true of the thousands of young men to-day who, regardless of financial return, elect laborious and inconspicuous lives as ministers, teachers, musicians, painters, editorial writers, or research workers in the laboratories of biology and science which make possible our stupendous and inspiring modern civilization. Were material prosperity the only incentive to American endeavor we should never have had an Edison, a Burbank, a Loeb, an Osler, a Roosevelt, a Wilson or a Lindbergh.

I do not for an instant subscribe to Mr. Chase's depressing generality that "above all else, the owners (of production) have entrenched themselves as the dictators of American life and habit. They have ousted the philosopher, teacher, statesman, editor and preacher, as the spiritual leaders of the mass of men. They dominate government, press, university, church, the arts. They sit secure on the apex of a pecuniary economy. To them men's eyes turn as once they turned to high altars, the man on horseback, and the porticoes of the Academy. The gods have taken up their quarters in the market place, an abode magnificent in gilt and marble, but hitherto untried. . . ."

It seems to me that in this resounding paragraph the author of "Prosperity" has let his eloquence run away with him. If Mr. James W. Gerard's list of the sixty-four men who, he says, "rule the United States" is in the least accurate I, for one, am not worrying about their "ousting" all the philosophers, preachers, professors, artists and editors as leaders of the masses. A roster that includes the younger Rockefeller, George F. Baker, Henry Ford, Tom Lamont, and Owen Young—to mention only a few names that catch the eye—does not exactly threaten the independence of religion, education, the press, or all the arts. And how about the enthusiasm with which the public regards the achievements of Byrd and Lindbergh?

To assume that business men have no common sense outside of business is to assert that they are fools. They know their own limitations as well as anyone else does. They are quite ready to believe that Galsworthy is a better novelist than Edgar Wallace even if they prefer the latter and want "to be shown" why. If they employ an architect to squeeze all the space possible out of a new building, who is (as one is said to have called himself) "a manufacturer of a commodity known as building space," they don't do so imagining that they are to get a monument of art. And if they want a work of art, as they frequently do, they go to an artist and not to a contractor. The very nature of their own calling leads them to respect experts and specialists in other lines. They admire a contemporary who pulls off a big financial deal for his ability to play the game they are themselves engaged in, but this does not cause them to regard him as a prophet any more than the collegian expects his hero half-back to possess a knowledge of incunabula.

We have changed from a 90 per cent to a 29 per cent agricultural people. We are at present in a mechanical and commercial era, using the same brains and the same energy as heretofore in attacking a different frontier, that of manufactured commodities. When we have conquered the economic wilderness of mass production we shall undoubtedly turn with equal enthusiasm in some entirely different direction, possibly that of the arts.

"Wealth" in its economic sense—either goods or money sufficient to give reasonable security and afford a certain amount of leisure—is indispensable to both artistic creation and the full development of the spiritual side of human life. A hardscrabble existence pinches the soul as well as the body. The eras in which the arts have flourished most followed affluent periods when men had time to enjoy life. The flower of the Italian renaissance had its roots in the expanding commercialism of Florence; the Medici were business men.

Anyhow our "business civilization" seems to be teeming with artists, writers, and musicians. The air is full of music. There has never been such an age for reading. There has never been so much first class writing. Education has become a national industry and the growth of its facilities is increasing at a rate surpassing that of the population. The machine age has also done a good deal to broaden our definition of culture. Fifty years ago university education was practically all either literary or politico-economic. To take engineering courses at college was to invite a polite lift to the social eyebrow; to admit frankly that one expected to earn one's living by dealing with machinery or mechanics was to ally oneself with the servant class. Students from the Massachusetts Institute of Technology did not attend Papanti's select dancing classes in Boston in my youth. I can perfectly remember the scorn tinging the accent of the socially damning indictment "O, *he's* at *Tech!*" In those days gentlemen were gentlemen;—"Beggars, pedlers, musicians, tradesmen and manufacturers go to the back door." Now the engineer ranks with the lawyer and the physician. The management of industry has become a science—if not almost an art. The physical strength and capacity of the worker are carefully studied, his "fatigue-curve" plotted, and his "accident-rate," together with his hours of work, are reduced coincident with an increase in his wages.

All aristocracies—including those of our purely business civilization—have to justify themselves. We are told that in England "the broad lands of the feudal lord, unlike the stocks and bonds of the modern business magnate, were not his solely for pleasure. Just as his men owed service to him, so he owed physical protection to them; and he was not likely to retain his lands and castles long if he could not give it. A considerable part of the wealth and power of England is still in the hands of these landowners, large and small, who still perform in more modern ways the duties that go with wealth."

Well, have the overlords of American business failed to perform the duties that go with wealth? Have any class of men who ever lived treated their accumulations more as a public trust than those of the present era? Can any country boast a more genuinely socially minded type of men than that represented by a Carnegie, a Rockefeller, a Harkness, or a Rosenwald? American philanthropy since the World War has reached the colossal amount of $20,000,000,000— almost the total cost of the War to the United States. Neither is it a mere buying of masses or indulgences. It does not take Ralph Waldo Emerson to satisfy a hard-headed business man that "a millionaire cannot wear 10,000 pairs of $10 shoes" or eat more than four or five meals per diem.

The tyranny of mere things is being largely done away with. The era of great country estates is past. The rich man wants leisure in which "to live." Everyone is trying to simplify existence in order to gain time for what he wants to do. In this simplification our mechanical progress has been of the greatest aid. The enormous popularity of athletic sports, of camp and open air life of every kind, for both old and young, is the best evidence that Americans have not lost their sense of values. I can remember distinctly when my contemporaries spent their off time hanging around the clubs setting each other up to drinks; now the clubs are empty and the same fellows are on the golf course. Ten million fishing licenses were issued in the United States last year. In point of fact, whether or not we are going in for any higher thinking, most of us are reverting as much as we can to the simple life.

Men *au fond* are like all other animals. They know what is

good for them, even if they are rather perverse at times. We are not the fools that we look and frequently act. The number of men who "die in harness" is becoming less and less. The "age of retirement" is no longer a phrase but an actuality, yet now it only means retirement from business, not from activity. I know bankers who have become painters, lawyers who have become philosophers, stockbrokers who write history and surgeons who have turned archæologists. These men were not materialists while engaged in the occupations at which they made their money. Their interests were large and so were their sympathies. They had not forfeited their sense of adventure even if they were born in the twentieth century. There was still "something lost behind the ranges" waiting for them—an "everlasting whisper" that called them beyond "the edge of cultivation," beyond the frontier of present material progress.

§

The future of American civilization is becoming an object of concern to an ever-increasing number of writers most of whom, even when they are not entirely pessimistic, are distinctly apprehensive about it. As one of the brotherhood I know how much easier it is to get a hearing—and incidentally to earn a living—by being a "knocker" rather than a "booster." One can always sell a story that "exposes" the rottenness of society. Such writing is a profitable business. Most people are disgruntled over something and are inclined to listen to anybody who voices a grievance. The school of pessimistic writers is constantly growing in accordance with the law of supply and demand.

The world needs pessimists, "muck-rakers," "crape-hangers," busybodies and "active minorities" to keep us guessing, sting us into action, and prevent the crooks from stealing the court house. Dissatisfaction of some kind is essential to progress. But that is no reason why we should listen only to the "calamity chorus" or believe all that they tell us, even when they believe it themselves. As Dwight Morrow once said in my hearing at a dinner to H. G. Wells, when the latter was in a particularly depressed state of mind, "Hope is better than history." To which I might now add that after giving our history the once-over it does not look so bad.

The fact is that nobody knows, and that nobody can guess, what is going to happen within the next ten, fifty or a hundred years. The unknown factor is as important here as elsewhere. But we can at least comfort ourselves with this, that in every decade in our national history there have been precisely the same diatribes against the materialism of American life.

We have always been objects of interest to ourselves and others. The flow of volumes on the workings of American democracy has not ceased from De Tocqueville's day to the present. One attitude of mind is exemplified by the following excerpts from a brilliant writer upon Western Civilization:

"Our only foe," says Frederick Jessup Stimson, "is not machinery, nor saved and reproductive capital, but class selfishness and narrowness, standardization at the lowest level, poverty of thought and taste and feeling, levelling all men's desire to the lowest common denominator. . . . To the Divine eye, the spectacle of millions of humans consuming the stored energy of the earth in whirling aimlessly about in motor cars—now for the most part closed even to natural beauty—must only resemble the purposeless evolutions of a swarm of flies in a beam of light. . . . We Americans are still jostling one another for the barest materialities, in danger perhaps of losing, or never attaining, the joy of life."

A more tempered criticism is that made by Professor C. Deslisle Burns, of Glasgow University, at the tenth session of the Institute of Politics held this year at Williamstown, Massachusetts. The problem as he saw it was whether "the increased efficiency for wealth and power, which American influence in Europe produces, will not corrode or corrupt the magnificent tradition of Western culture that still survives there.

"A farmer in a Ford car may be better off than one who drives a horse-cart, but he may lack that inner quality which alone makes a man civilized. . . . Industrialization tends to concentrate men's minds upon ways and means, and to weaken their interest in the purposes for which alone such ways and means can be used. But men who are satisfied with themselves do not stop to ask why they do what they are accustomed to do; and Americanization, which has certainly increased our power to live, has not yet revealed any good reason of its own for living at all."

As against these sombre warnings we may set the more optimistic opinions of such philosophers as Charles Beard, who believes, not only that our political experiment in democracy has more than justified itself, but that "America in this age offers material subsistence for the life of the mind more varied and more lucrative than any nation that has flourished since the beginnings of civilization in the Nile Valley."

We are at the beginning, not the end. This "business civilization" of ours is still young. But if this were the end, and we were to appraise the development of mankind, not only from the dawn of civilization but during the last one hundred and fifty years of American life, should we not say that it had progressed?

# CHAPTER XIX

## Puritan's Progress

NOW that the time has come to draw together the loose threads of fact and fancy from which this book is woven, I find myself somewhat at a loss to defend its pattern. If its faint thread of biography on the one hand, its reflections upon the influence of Puritanism and its apparently happy-go-lucky assemblage of heterogeneous historical and economic data on the other, seem to the reader to justify neither its title nor its existence, I have nothing to say. Possibly my explanation may, after all, be only a natural and perhaps pardonable attempt to rationalize and excuse what began as a literary holiday and ended after an unexpectedly lengthy period as a laborious, although enjoyable and, so far as I personally am concerned, an intellectually profitable undertaking.

I had started on an impulse from New York in 1930 and I had found myself back in the Massachusetts of John Hancock and Samuel Adams of 1783. I had learned very little about the Train family but, while floundering around Greatgran'ther Train's wood lot, I had picked up, along with the burdocks, much interesting historical gossip, some of it accurate, some of it, no doubt, apocryphal. Now one cannot spend nearly a year browsing through histories, biographies and diaries without gaining certain impressions, if not opinions. I had become pretty well "fed up" with New York City life at the time I made my bolt for Framingham that Sunday morning and I may as well confess, here and now, that I was quite prepared, and indeed expected, to reach the conclusion that modern life was all a mistake and that men were better off and truly happier in the days of my grandfather than they are now when, supposedly, "wealth accumulates and men decay." I was ready to scrap almost all the comforts, conveniences and benefits to which I was accustomed in favor of the simpler living and, presumably, higher thinking of former days.

Yet it was not long before I realized that the difference between my grandfather's life in 1783 and my own in 1930 was to all intents and purposes the same existing to-day between that in one of the smaller hamlets of Vermont or Maine and in any large city in the United States, and that, if I wanted to live the simple life, there was nothing to prevent my doing so except the fact that I was used to something so utterly different. Mark you, I do not say something "better," but something "different." I knew perfectly well that with all due respect to the salubrious climate, the romantic scenery, and stimulating local society of such delightful places, nothing could hire me to live in Pugwash or Pottsville Corners.

There has been from earliest times a universal inclination on the part of the human race to assume that mankind has degenerated from a golden age; that the precious apples were all in the Garden of Hesperides; that there has been no subsequent crop; and that Adam having fallen, his descendants are still falling.

The first scholar to question this theory, as Professor Preserved Smith (obviously another of us Puritans) points out in his "History of Modern Culture," was Jean Bodin in 1566, who presented, in a work entitled "A Method for Easily Understanding History," the novel idea that the golden age lay not in the past, but in the future. As Prof. Smith says: "The great importance of the idea of progress in the history of culture is that its adoption marked a complete volte-face in the attitude of the race. . . . The race, once backward-looking, has become forward looking." Bacon had already hinted at something of the sort before. "These be the ancient times," said he, "when the world is growing old; our own age is more truly antiquity than is the time which is computed backward, beginning with our age." Pascal also: "Those whom we call the ancients were really new to everything; whereas it is in ourselves, who have added to their knowledge the experience of other ages, that we must look for the antiquity which we revere in them."

Sentiment and patriotism inevitably gild with a tender light the lives of our ancestors. Poets and philosophers stress the homely virtue of the olden time. But, in spite of the opportunity for target practice afforded my great-grandfather by the retreating Britishers at Lexington, I have no real reason to suppose that he lived a better life, or was given to any higher thinking, than those of his descendants who can now avail themselves of modern sanitary conveniences, electric lighting, the telephone, schools, libraries, colleges, skilled surgery, and yes—I will say it!—of the opportunities for amusement and education afforded by the radio and the movies.

Glancing back over this manuscript to the date of my grandfather's birth in 1783, that is to say, over a period at utmost but one twenty-five-thousandth part of the lifetime of the human family and possibly only one six-hundred-thousandth part of it, I do not find that human nature has changed in the last century and a half. If, of course, we compare the countryman of the Revolution with the urbanite of to-day, one will bear no more resemblance to the other than does the gentle reader to old Mr. Homo Heidelbergeasis of B. C. 260,000, but, if, on the other hand, we compare him with the present day frontier-farmer of New Brunswick we will find little outward difference between them and none whatever inside.

Heredity is the unseen wireless that directs and controls our lives. We struggle to adjust ourselves to the successive stages of our environment and evolve shells, wings, feathers, and fur. We walk, ride, drive, are dragged along by "puffing Billies," straddle bicycles, whirl off in motor cars or roar into the ether above the clouds; we develop different manners and slightly new morals; but fundamentally we remain the same. As I re-read these pages for misplaced commas and all the other typographical ills that the galley slave is heir to, I find myself chuckling again and again at the way that "history repeats itself." Indeed, this melange of biography, historical record and amateur philosophy will have sufficiently served its purpose if it has but demonstrated how the good people of each generation under comparatively similar circumstances have done and said precisely the same things as ourselves; how in each decade since 1783 they have honestly believed not only that their young folk were all on their way to perdition, but have been convinced that what was then the "modern" world was going rapidly to the dogs; how, in short, there is "nothing new under the sun."

We have seen how the most vital changes in our civilization have been brought about by mere mechanical discoveries, such as the railroad and the motor car; how our manners, and even our moral ideas, may be likewise altered, as shown in our change of attitude towards the independence of women, wrought by the typewriter and the bicycle; and how every new invention of value has been greeted with distrust, if not with jeers, until gradually it proved indispensable.

We have observed extravagance and demoralization after every war, usually followed in due course by a financial panic and, shortly thereafter, by a religious revival.

We have perceived how "Society," perenially ridiculous, has always inevitably surrendered to the onslaughts of the persistent and vulgar rich who have used it as a means to their own advancement.

We have found political corruption omnipresent throughout the history of the Republic, no less in "the nobler, ampler, purer days of our fathers" than in those of the "Black Horse Cavalry" and of the "Ohio Gang," concurrently with immense advances in state and national government, both in efficiency and in general standards of public honor.

We have—ever since women and children worked thirteen hours a day in the mills owned by New England Puritans over a century ago—been constantly warned that the demands of the machine age would reduce the worker to the status and condition of a slave, despite the fact that there has been in all respects a steady improvement in the condition of the common man.

We have listened to the crescendo of foreign and native critics who have accused American civilization of materialism in every decade since the Revolution, until we are almost persuaded that our cultural future is well nigh hopeless.

It will do us no harm to be made aware of our danger. It is true that the majority of us are concerned with the production of material things which are intended to make man's lot on earth easier, if not happier,—but that has always been so. It has been true of all countries in every age. While man cannot live by bread alone, he cannot get along without the bread.

Finally, we have seen that our forefathers, whether Pilgrims, Puritans, Revolutionary heroes, saints or statesmen, were very much like other men, that the intensity of their political or religious beliefs was by no means their only trait, that, simply because people lived what seems to us a long time ago and had few of the conveniences of modern life, it did not follow that they were, in consequence, any happier, healthier, or more useful than those who came after them, that plain living and high thinking are by no means dependent upon discomfort, and that Puritanism was conducive to material prosperity, and is characteristic of it in America today, in the sense of obligation which wealth almost inevitably confers.

I am, as must be fully apparent to the most casual of readers, neither a student nor a philosopher. I am versed in neither science nor metaphysics. I pretend to be no more than an ignoramus writing for others like myself. But in the words of a late well-known financier I am not inclined "to go short" of the United States or of the Universe either. Although I have spent most of my active life in the prosecution of so-called criminals, including both paupers and millionaires, I have nevertheless a profound belief in the essential kindliness and decency of human nature as well as faith in the future of mankind.

Progress in human society is no more orderly, regular and uniform than has been the development of man itself. The evolutionary curve is not constant, but rises, dips and rises again, gradually, over immense periods of time, ascending to higher and higher levels. The history of the human race shows "dark ages" analogous to the "ice ages" which have from time to time existed upon the globe; yet contemporaneously with the glaciers of the "ice age" there remained elsewhere on the earth tropical swamps teeming with animal life, just as, during the so-called "dark ages," there lived races that had attained a high degree of culture which were unaffected by the blight that had settled upon Europe. Even to speak of "ages" at all is apt to create a false impression. We must not forget that, while for purposes of convenience we designate certain eras according to significant factors in the development of society, even these aspects of human life were to a large extent local, and that the age of bronze in one place could be, and was, contemporaneous with that of stone in another, as for example in Rome and Britain when trading first began between them.

This is as true to-day as it was in the time of the woolly rhinoceros and the sabre-toothed tiger. The old and the new coexist side by side. You do not have to go far to find peoples who are even now practically in the "iron," "bronze" or even the "stone age," who frequently remain happily in their status quo even after being introduced to the marvels of modern civilization. The Berber women of Morocco still follow their men to battle and hack up wounded prisoners with their daggers, while French airplanes buzz overhead transmitting the news of what is going on to regional headquarters by wireless. It may well be that in a civilization which has only reached that of "stone," the radio and the talking machine do not much disturb the complacency that continues below the auditory nerve.

It is only by surveying mankind in the large and over

great periods of time that we can declare positively that he
has progressed. Even the civilized races are not entirely
civilized by any means. You will find islands of barbarism in
every country, and pockets of savagery in every town. In some
of our largest cities gangsters will be riddling each other
with machine gun bullets within earshot of a prayer meeting.
So, too, the individual fluctuates from year to year, from
moment to moment. He is more civilized at one time than
another,—in January, perhaps, than in June. He is Socrates
to-day and a cave man to-morrow, if he be not essentially a
cave man all the time. It would depend entirely upon the
spot where a visitor from Mars happened to land how far
he would regard the "Earth" as a civilized place of abode.
It is always a question of which side of the shield you are
looking at, where you are standing, what facts you select.
You can make any person, any place, any era astounding or
ridiculous by choosing the requisite data. Indeed, for a long
time I had it in mind to write a concluding chapter for this
book to be entitled "In Those Days," in which I purposed to
trick the reader into supposing that he was reading an account
of the middle ages, whereas it was but a plain statement of
facts culled from the pages of contemporary newspapers.

In studying this vast welter which we call civilization with
its inconsistencies, its overlappings, its fantastic contradic-
tions, the shorter the span of our inquiry the more difficult it
naturally becomes to form any opinion as to progress, the
harder it is to tell whether we are in the recession of a wave
in a rising tide or on the crest of a roller in a falling one.
Of course we have progressed since animal life emerged
from the slime, as well as since that later date when Homo
Sapiens crept up behind his Uncle Pithecanthropus Erectus
and cracked his skull in order to usurp his place as Old Man
of the Tribe. What we mean by progress is progress from a
definite and, from the evolutionary aspect, a comparatively
recent date. Are we on the down or the up jog of the curve?
From an evolutionary point of view all United States history
might be said to be but a wave-length in the televisional

drama of human life. The advance of civilization during 5,000 years necessarily makes that during any shorter period seem infinitesimal.

Let us at any rate disabuse ourselves of the misconception that the value of a civilization can be appraised only by its famous men, its monuments or its scientific discoveries. You cannot assess the value of Roman civilization merely by Marcus Aurelius, of that of Greece by Plato, any more than you can test the prosperity of the United States by the wealth of John D. Rockefeller. Preeminence in any one art or science, or even in all the arts and sciences, does not necessarily mean progress. The Taj Mahal and the pyramid of Cheops are not so much the funeral monuments of those in whose memory they were erected as of the thousands of miserable human beings who died under the lash in the course of their construction. The highest degree of artistic achievement has not proven incompatible with the extremest cruelty. The dagger and poison cup flourished side by side with Raphael's angels. Mountains do not mark the level of a country above the sea, although they attract the eye. You cannot judge the progress of civilization by its peaks; it is the plateau that counts.

Great artists and great geniuses, like giants, are usually accidents, and like other biologic "sports" do not breed true. The real test of progress is to be found in the well being of the common, not in the existence of the uncommon, man. A modern sewage disposal plant may be a better indication of human progress than the Parthenon.

If we take scientific invention as a test of progress we are in no better case. The discovery in itself, however "epoch making," is no final measure of progress, apart from its effect upon mankind. And here we find ourselves in another dilemma. For the direct results of many striking discoveries are apparently by no means beneficial to the race in the first instance. The invention of gunpowder is commonly referred to as one of the great monuments of human progress, yet gunpowder enormously intensified the horrors of war. The answer would seem to be that such inventions are inevitable in the march of scientific progress towards that universal knowledge which is the ultimate end of all human endeavor. The most momentous discoveries are apt to be accidental by-products of a search for something else. They are neither bad nor good in themselves. Any one of them may be, according as it is used, a curse or a blessing.

The fact that the motor car seems at present to be a prolific cause of roadside lechery is no more an argument against it as a factor in economic progress than the equal opportunity afforded by steamboats, camp meetings, and the family buggy for like purposes was an argument against them, and it might be only fair, before reaching a final conclusion as to its undesirability, to inquire whether the former total of "sex crimes" in haymows and coal cellars has not been correspondingly reduced. In spite of the millions of persons who have been killed in railroad accidents, and of the thousands who have met death in airplanes, who shall say that the railroad and the flying machine do not mark immense advances in the development of civilization? What could possibly typify man's progress more than the ability to lift himself out of his earthly environment into the clear air of Heaven?

The past century has been the age of marvels so far as science is concerned, and we are still but on the marge of the sea of discovery. We have achieved a wholly preposterous material prosperity. We have, moreover, markedly increased the span of human life and otherwise biologically done ourselves proud. The "new woman" is really a new woman, for college girls to-day are two inches taller, ten pounds heavier, and have larger feet than their sisters of the last generation.

Even my son shares apparently in the general dilation. A letter just received from the "Statistical Study of Old Americans, Division of Anthropology, Harvard University," states that it may interest me to know "that the results to date show an increase in physical measurements, on the part of the sons, of 8.15 pounds in weight and 3.55 cms. or 1½ inches in height. Similar increases are noted in all other measurements thus far compared." I am glad to learn that, in spite of the psalmist's denial of our ability to do so, we have, so to speak, by taking thought, added even a part of a cubit to our stature, but I am even more pleased to have the assurance of the Division of Anthropology that I am of "the Old White American stock," disgusting as the phrase may sound. I had been getting rather nervous while writing this book as to the genuineness of my own claims; but now I do not have to worry any longer; everything is all right; I am an "Old White American," much as I dislike the descriptio generis. Why couldn't the Division of Anthropology have called me a "son of the Puritans"? Do they want to take all the romance out of life? "Old White American"! "Old Rose-combed White Leghorn"!

Anyhow my son is bigger than I am, as indeed I always knew him to be, and he will probably live longer, work less, and participate in a greatly augmented per capita share of national income.

As to our scientific and material progress during the last 150 years there is, and can be, of course no question. The globe has shrunk to a mere nothing; we telephone to London and Madrid; the Arab, his burnoose flying, whirls through the desert atop an autobus, covering the equivalent of a month's caravan trip by camel in a single day; we ride from Cairo to the Cape in Pullmans and motors de luxe; the Congo savage has his talking machine, and the Albanian bandit reads *The Saturday Evening Post* and *Ladies' Home Journal*; the airplane zooms over the ice caps of both Poles, while prehistoric dragons in the swamps of New Guinea raise their horny snouts in fear of a hitherto unknown death-dealing pterodactyl; we are as at home in the Fayyum and the Gobi as we are on Broadway; there are no more terrestrial frontiers, no more waste places.

Do you recall when you were a child how the wood lot beyond the meadow seemed a vast forest in the shadows of which you were fearful of being lost? Now it is only a wood lot, and Tom Smith lives just across it. When I was a little boy visiting my uncle he offered as a great treat, provided I was very, very good, to take me fishing. What preparations I went through! For days I dug strenuously for worms, bought hooks, cut poles—thought of nothing else. The morning came and, with my paraphernalia, I climbed up beside him into an old chaise drawn by an even older white horse and we started out at dawn. So impatient was I that it seemed as if we drove for hours into the country, until at last we came to a deep broad river, where all day long I fished up and down the banks while my guardian dozed under an elm tree. It was a great adventure, like searching for the source of the Zambesi and involving for me almost as great a sense of hardship and danger.

Twenty years later I was driving along the same road with my uncle, then a nonogenarian.

"Where was that river you took me fishing when I was a kid?" I asked him.

We were at the moment crossing a culvert through which trickled a tiny brook so diminutive as to be hardly discernible amid the grass. There was a farm house within fifty yards; the city itself less than half a mile away.

"There it is!" he said, pointing to the brook.

"What!—But it took hours to get to it!—It was a great river—ten or fifteen miles away!"

He smiled.

"That is your river. It took us about ten minutes to get here that day. Nothing is changed a particle since then—except yourself."

As a boy I used to go camping every summer in Northern Maine. For days and weeks I would paddle down solitary hidden streams and silent forest lakes, through the heart of an almost trackless wilderness. To-day those same rivers are lined with motor highways, and the scream of the klaxon has replaced the call of the blue jay and the laughter of the loon.

We are growing up; everything is getting nearer; but it

is by no means clear that we gain anything by a mere change of tempo, or by being able to fly from place to place instead of by riding or walking. Suppose we could simply close our eyes and say, "Timbuktu, please!" to find ourselves instantly on the main square surrounded by snake charmers and dancers, would we be any better off than we are to-day? Had my poor old grandfather been told that, before his grandson would be fifty years old, men would transport themselves by steam and gas combustion over the land, through the air and under the sea, communicate with one another at will throughout the globe, capture and record the tones of the human voice, and see through solids—he would have shuddered. The fate of Adam would be ours! Men would have become as gods—knowing good and evil! There's the rub! Has all this enabled us to know good from evil, even if it has made us as gods? As gods? More than gods? What Hermes, Posidon or even Zeus could do what we do? Why, Olympus was a broken down car barn compared to the Grand Central Terminal in New York, a travelling circus beside one of our broadcasting stations! Yet the question remains whether having, like Adam, eaten of the tree of knowledge, we know that we are naked.

The annihilation of space and time, the extension of our sight, hearing and other senses, the ability to transport ourselves to the bottom of the sea or to the centre of the earth, to escape disease and even conquer death through the reduction of infant mortality and our mastery of smallpox, yellow fever, diphtheria and diabetes, might only result in the development of a race of soulless demigods,—considerably "lower than the angels,"—who had nothing left to do but loaf stupidly around like the gods and goddesses of a very dull and highly electrified Olympus. Such a vision cannot arouse the slightest enthusiasm in any of us. We know that progress means something besides parachutes and plumbing fixtures; and a curious thing about it all is the matter-of-fact way in which we accept, almost as a matter of course, the facilities placed at our disposal by the enormous advance of science. When I told my step-son, aged twelve, that Lindbergh had flown across the Atlantic, he remarked merely: "Why not?"

The truth is that the ordinary human being, apart from his increased comfort, is about where he was before. He does not bother his head over any of it. He concerns himself, as William James said, with his own house, his own affairs, his own ache and his own religion, whatever it may be. The airplane, the radio and the motor are just like any other facts in his existence, and he no more wonders about them than does the Kurdish herdsman who accepts the machine that soars over his head as merely a new sort of bird. It really makes little difference to us whether we telegraph or write letters, fly through the air or go afoot,—we are still occupied for the most part in earning a living. It is all pretty much the same whether we move at six, sixty or a hundred and sixty miles per hour. The human brain is limited in its capacity. The scientist finds equal absorption in the intricacies of a butterfly's wing and the problems of television. Either "fill his mind." My world, and your world, is still the same size, quite large enough for our activities even if the actual earth itself has lost something of its mystery.

I am willing to concede that "something," although, except for people like Byrd or Lindbergh, there is still enough wilderness available to satisfy the sporting instincts of most of us. But, by and large, I incline to believe that scientific achievement has less bearing upon the other aspects of progress than one might easily assume.

The important question is not whether we have bath tubs or electric fans, but whether we have forfeited something spiritually in consequence. Are we softer and less admirable than we were before we had all these comforts and conveniences? Have we paid for them in courage, honesty, fortitude, in appreciation for, and creative power in, the arts, in mercy, kindliness, loyalty, charity and sympathy? Have we lost, as Professor William James alleged, "the power of even imagining what the ancient idealization of poverty could have meant—liberation from material attachments; the unbribed soul; the manlier indifference; the paying our way by what we are or do, and not by what we have; the right to fling away our life at any moment irresponsibly—the more athletic trim, in short the moral fighting shape"?

This inquiry regarding the health of our souls is not only a natural but an easy one. Abbots, brahmins, lamas and gooroos had been regularly asking it since long before the Crucifixion. It would of course be rather presumptuous for any of us to claim that every day we were getting, spiritually, better and better; it is not only expected of us, but it is probably more seemly, to bow our heads and admit that we are miserable and also retrograding sinners. I think that what my altogether charming and brilliant preceptor William James had in mind, when he penned the paragraph just quoted, was the truly "ancient idealization of poverty" represented by the ascetics, who were themselves heirs at law, if not next of kin, to the philosophers of the East.

I concede that we are a long way from the idealization of poverty as personified in the beggars of Benares and of Mecca with their bowls, the "marabouts" of Morocco (who are incidentally the most rapacious of all the "holy"), the mendicant friars, and the members of all those ancient and modern sects who not only starve the flesh but mortify it. But I may, perhaps, be allowed to call attention to the fact that this ancient "idealization of poverty" flourished and still flourishes chiefly in those countries where the climate requires only a minimum of food and clothing, and where the devotee of poverty can sit under the shade of a banyan or palm and meditate upon infinity without physical inconvenience or the need of earning a living. Once the temperature falls below zero he has to get up and hustle to buy a coat and pants. Peoples among whom beggars are viewed as having an attribute of sanctity are apt to be not only unsanitary, but singularly lacking in honesty, tenderness and other qualities usually termed spiritual. Spirituality, like materialism, can possibly be overdone.

With respect to those periods in European history to which many writers turn with eyes of yearning, let them remember that slavery existed in Greece at the time of Pericles, that men were thrown to the beasts of Ephesus, that trickery and guile were held in high esteem, that cruelty was universal, and love, in our meaning of the word, practically unknown; while in those mediæval towns, where the arts flourished and cathedrals rose, more pigs rooted in the gutters than did in New York in the 1840's, and that the great bulk of mankind lived about as the pigs did. Indeed, in one of the ancient chronicles of France it may be read how the King, standing at his palace window, fainted at the stench which rose from below. Epidemics yearly killed off vast numbers of the population, and the survivors were as ready to cut each other's throats as they were to kneel before their beautifully carven altars. They lived in a world of ghosts, witches, and devils whose evil influences they spent a large part of their time trying to counteract. They were undernourished, diseased, suffered constantly from festering wounds received in brawl and battle, were overworked, abused, maltreated, tortured, killed or died young, usually without regret. They did not value their lives greatly and no wonder.

I agree with Professor James that "we" (meaning a considerable proportion of those of the American people who can read, write, and pay for theatre tickets) tend at the present time to regard as necessary many things that were unknown even at the date when he wrote; that those same people also spend a great deal of their leisure unprofitably and that many of them, so far from having unbribed souls, perhaps have no souls at all. But—and that "but" is a very large one so far as I am personally concerned—"the right to fling away our life at any moment irresponsibly" never existed for any of us, and when it comes to liberation from material attachments, the "manlier indifference" (to wealth, I suppose he means) and "the paying our way by what we are or do, not by what we have," I think that my former teacher is accusing "us" of losing something which our ancestors had to no greater de-

gree than ourselves. The number of people in proportion
to the whole population who have "unbribed souls" is no
smaller than it was in the Greece of Plato, the Rome of Augustus, the Germany of Luther, the England of Wycliff, or
the America of Cotton Mather. Some, for religious reasons,
were readier than others to "fling away their lives irresponsibly," and were eager to suffer the rack, the wheel, and the
stake because they believed that death would bring them in-
effable happiness and relieve them from a rather miserable
existence. It was a practical choice. "We" would do the same
thing had we their faith and provided it were necessary. But
—thank Heaven—it is not!

There are as many ready to go hungry for the sake of Art
as ever. But does a readiness to go hungry for the sake of
art—and incidentally to compel your wife and family to go
hungry with you—bespeak a higher spiritual aspiration than
the willingness of an artist to forsake his art and to drive a
taxi that he may give his children an education? That is a
finely flung phrase of Professor James, but flung, perhaps,
a bit irresponsibly.

There is no reason to assume that as a race, or as a nation,
we have retrograded in these or most other respects in the
last one hundred and fifty years. We are still able to render
unto Cæsar the things that are Cæsar's and to God the things
that are God's! Men and women show no less fortitude in
suffering to-day than in earlier and hardier times. Human
nature rises to the occasion when an operation must be performed without an anæsthetic. Bravery, fortunately, is a
common attribute. The record of our "comfort softened"
boys in the World War proves that quite well enough. Sport
and athletics neutralize what might otherwise be the ener-
vating effects, both physical and moral, of easy living; while
courage and endurance seem to depend less upon physical
qualities than upon those of the mind and spirit. The white
legionnaire, under the scorching sun of the Soudan, out-
marches the black, who collapses first. College men from
homes of refinement, and even of luxury, habitually show

more pluck than physically perfect specimens of the navvy type.

The number of entries in the Women's Air Derby does not indicate that the "weaker sex" has become any less intrepid. The race of Puritans has not lost its sense of adventure when one's ninety-five-year-old uncle casually flies from Vienna to Budapest. We have transferred our sphere of daring from the earth to the sky. No, there is as much courage in the world as there ever was and as much romance.

On the other hand, we have enormously increased our regard for the value of human life, health and happiness. We give generously "out of our abundance," often not wisely but too well. There is no longer any use for orphan asylums so great is the demand for children for adoption. The cue of would-be foster parents is constantly augmented. A hundred and fifty years ago war was chronic in human society, a world without war would have seemed utterly inconceivable, almost, perhaps, undesirable. To-day we have gone a long way on the road to its elimination and have definitely discredited it as a means of settling disputes. Let fire, pestilence or famine play havoc in any quarter of the globe and before twenty-four hours have passed succor has started on the way. If some foreign city is destroyed by an earthquake, plans are afoot to rebuild it almost before the flames among its ruins have been extinguished. And this vast alleviation of human suffering has been made possible only through our improvements in communication and transport.

It would be hard to find a better test for spiritual progress than the words of Francis Bacon: "The nobler a soul is, the more objects of compassion it hath." Infinite opportunity to make that compassion effective has been brought about by what, at first glance, would seem to be purely material progress. All mankind is now its object.

"That is all very well," I can hear some one say, "but it relates merely to the technique of giving. That I send my dollar to a starving Chinaman, rather than give it to a Bowery bum, does not prove me to have a more noble soul. What about the inner life?"

For one who deals not in ghostly matters the only answer is to point to the nearest hospice.

"Thou shalt love the Lord thy God with all thy heart and with all thy mind and with all thy strength. This is the first and great commandment and the second is like unto it. *Thou shalt love thy neighbor as thy self.*"

Let the reader apply these tests for himself and then, if he be not satisfied, retire to a monastery.

But monks and Puritans make poor bedfellows and as yet I have no intention of joining any brotherhood. I have too much regard for the memory of my good old grandfather with his hatred of all things idolatrous including the keeping of Christmas. Has not the "Anthropological Division" placed me definitely among the Puritans? I had almost forgotten those semi-mythical souls who nevertheless walk unseen at our elbows and whisper in our ears.

We cannot escape them. They are always there beside us although their shadows are now so faint as to be imperceptible. But we can hear their voice—the "still, small voice" of the Puritan conscience—bidding us to beware the lure of Satan and to improve the hour!

Whatever the original Puritans and their earlier descendants may have been really like we may of one thing be fully certain—their seriousness of purpose. Salvation was the sole preoccupation of their minds. Life, to the Puritan, was "a lottery with the winning numbers already drawn. Was he a winner or not? He could never know on this earth; he could only hope that he had been foreordained as one of the elect. That hope he buttressed upon what he regarded as the evidences of God's favor and his ability to live in accordance with His will, although he knew, to be sure, that he might be utterly deceived." Among the chief evidences of God's favor was wordly prosperity,—a prosperity which under the circumstances must naturally be entirely divorced from worldliness of mind,—one of those peculiar paradoxes offered by the development of a religion theoretically self-abnegatory but essentially egotistic.

The German sociologist Max Weber asserts that Protestantism is the main root of the capitalistic spirit, and that Puritanism is the phase of Protestantism which has been most stimulating to business enterprise; while Rheinhold Niebuhr has similarly pointed out that the new spirit in modern business is the direct result of the doctrine of the Reformation that all work was sacred. Originally trade was considered as beneath any one but a slave, and Plato rated the artisan and the shopkeeper among the lowest in an ideal social hierarchy. This was the general viewpoint until the rise of the mediæval Italian city-states where commerce obtained a certain amount of recognition. It required the Reformation, however, to establish the doctrine that all work was not only respectable, but holy. This resulted almost immediately in a higher type of business honesty than had existed theretofore and also made profit seeking respectable, reinstating, by its emphasis upon Old Testament doctrine, the old Hebraic theory that prosperity was an indubitable proof of sanctity.

"Completely emancipated from the ancient scruples against business enterprise," says Niebuhr, "we have been able to give ourselves to commercial and industrial tasks with a passion unknown to Europe. That is the real secret of our financial success. The sanctification of secular tasks is certainly not wrong in itself; the moral limitations of our American civilization are due to the complete sanctification of secular motives as well as secular tasks. . . . Puritanism is in a sense a religious sublimation of the traditional virtues of the middle class—virtues of sobriety, honesty, and thrift."

Henry Seidel Canby calls attention to the emphasis placed by the Puritans upon a constant striving for improvement. The qualities of will and self-discipline have, he says in "Quakers and Puritans," remained fast in the subconsciousness of the descendants of the latter and shows itself as a mental habit of "moral strenuosity."

The legacy of the Puritans was not their ethical formula for making everybody good, nor their fear of the passions, nor their anti-æstheticism, so much as a certain mental habit, —the mental habit of willing to achieve and to accomplish which New England gave to the United States. This will to achieve and accomplish, which among the early Calvinists was the means of distinguishing the elect from the damned, became, as America grew away from the rigidity of Calvinism, the will to succeed in any fashion, expressed in that form of American energy which would not permit them ever to lie down and take their ease, or to be content with what they had or were, or never to cease trying to rise in the scale. Though the original aim was lost the transmuted will and the habit of energy remain.

This "in both its ethical and unethical forms," he goes on to say, "whether in the reforming clergyman or the tireless organizer of business, or the American undergraduate, strenuous beyond compare in the pursuit of their ideals,—it is essentially Puritan, and specifically in America owes its strength and immediate origin to the leaders of New England thought who were the strongest intellectual and moral forces in our early history. We have lost or denied the ends they sought, we have substituted the control of Nature or of other men for the will of God as they interpreted it, but . . . the mind has kept the direction they gave. . . ."

This seriousness of purpose, now largely diverted from religion to business, still characterizes the American people, who are apt to regard any expenditure of time which does not show concrete results as pure waste, and to treat social life as an opportunity for business contacts. Friendships, which might otherwise be disinterested, become means to an end. "Big deals," often as not, are "put over" upon the golf course. That is why we take our pleasures so seriously, if not fiercely. Golf is not golf unless there is a bet on every hole. Every sport becomes a "contest."

This will to win—"the will to power"—is featured in our advertising pages. Note the fierce determination of the clean-shaven young man with the bulldog chin, the glint of his steely eye, the dominating strength portrayed in his broad shoulders and folded arms. You are assured that you can be

like him, if you will, merely by using a certain sort of safety
razor, taking a correspondence course, or smoking a certain
brand of cigaret. "Knowledge is power"—either to land a
knockout or make a million. So knowledge becomes a duty,
—that is, enough knowledge to make the million.

We don't do the things we like so much as the things we
think we ought to do. That is the reason we spoil a fine afternoon by lunching with the Joneses and go to so many "entertainments" that do not entertain. We make, as the saying is,
"a business" of everything—including our amusements. We
frequent the theatre not so much to enjoy the play as to be
able to say that we have been. "Have you seen 'Piffling
Polly'?" asks our hostess. Now we do not care tuppence for
"Piffling Polly," nevertheless, instead of frankly saying so,
we hastily and earnestly reply: "No, not yet! But we have
tickets for next week!"

At the risk of the charge of light-mindedness I give it as
my opinion that the features of early Puritan life and character most detrimental to human happiness were the consciousness of sin, absence of divorce, imprisonment for debt,
and indigestion. Now imprisonment for debt and the absence
of divorce were not peculiar to New England, but a dyspeptic
attitude of mind and manner undoubtedly was. The irrita-
tion of the Puritan gastro-intestinal tract by unwholesome,
poorly cooked, insufficient and inadequately masticated food
might account for many things, such as lack of tenderness
towards children, harshness towards evildoers, and an acid
outlook on life. Especially would it tend to accentuate an
individual sense of sin. There is a close causal connection
between "something in the mind" and "something on the
stomach." Will not some one of our many Foundations in-
augurate a survey to determine whether the Puritans were
Puritans because they had indigestion or had indigestion because they were Puritans? It is at any rate worth noting, perhaps, that with the general improvement in cooking and
comfort the acerbity of their descendants has tended to disappear, while remaining unabated in primitive localities.

The chief item in Puritan progress is the extent to which

we have freed ourselves from the consciousness of sin. But, while we have dumped that Old Man of the Sea from our shoulders once and for all, his ghost revisits the glimpses of the moon (the honeymoon as well as every other) in the form of the "New England conscience," forever stressing the moral aspect of everything and viewing with innate distrust whatever makes for joy and gladness.

This feeling that pleasure must somehow connote evil, and conversely that what is unpleasant must be good, was not only rooted in the general Christian doctrine that sufferers in this life would be rewarded in the hereafter and, hence, that suffering was in itself creditable, but it gave people an excuse for being disagreeable in order to reduce pride in others. Thus the biting tongue of the New England spinster had the support both of its own malice and of a religious theory,—a curious kind of charity with a "reverse English" on it, which, even if it made people squirm, nevertheless, did them good.

Although, happily, we have to a great extent outgrown the individual habit of disciplining others for quasi-missionary purposes,—a habit which tended strikingly to react upon the would-be missionary,—collectively we have the passion as strongly ingrained in us as ever. Through our organizations for the prevention of vice, our official and voluntary censorships, and our prohibitory legislation, we insist upon making our contemporaries not only law-abiding but good as well. It is, as some one has said, an easy step from the resolution to do God's will—that is, God's will as interpreted by us—to a belief that one's own will is God's, thus giving our personal views a Divine sanction. This shows itself in the fact that as Americans we are convinced of our overwhelming moral superiority to any other nation upon the face of the globe. One of the keenest distinctions ever made as between the British and ourselves is that "the American finds as much difficulty in admitting an Englishman to moral equality as the Englishman in admitting an American to social equality."

We Puritans have a keen scent for the fumes of hell which deprives our pleasures of spontaneity and of the care-free quality of the Continental. We are in the main good-natured and generous. There is plenty of raucous hilarity and back-slapping, but, while we have a sense of humor, we are not really gay. And gaiety, if we but recognize it, is the most comprehensive of all virtues, for it signifies faith, hope, charity and courage.

That eccentric old connection of mine, George Francis Train, after he had gone somewhat "ga-ga," used in Union Square to hold Sunday morning services of what he called the "Church of the Laughing Jackass." Whether George Francis intended to refer to himself by the term I know not, but, dotty as he undoubtedly was, I am inclined to suspect that there was method in his madness. I never heard one of his sermons. Probably, if I had, I should have been griev-ously disappointed, but of one thing I am quite sure, that the more the gospel of laughter is preached in this weary world the better. After all, it is the gospel of kindness and of forti-tude, and what two things are better?

I for one have never been able to understand the intense preoccupation over human ethics generally attributed to an all-powerful and exceedingly busy Deity. To-day most of us have a higher opinion of God than that He can particularly concern Himself over technical decisions made by hair-split-ting theologians or the delegates to church conventions.

The idea that one can profitably reason about matters of religious belief constantly diminishes. I do not mean that we are less religious, but merely that we have become less dogmatic. Most of us no longer think that before God "formed us in the belly" he predestined us to either eternal rapture or the gnawing of the worm. We are in that happily paradoxical state where, although most of us have ceased to be-lieve in witches, we agree that nothing is impossible. Science, metaphysics, and religion are genuinely nearer to-day than ever before. Nobody any longer accepts Jacques Loeb's mechanistic conception of the universe, and the electro-chemist is ready to admit the possibility "that, if by huge magnifications and delicate measurements he can attain a physical perception of things undreamed of, he may by a similar spiritual perception gain knowledge now unsuspected which may harmonize both worlds."

Science is beginning to recognize that there may be a "reflection of an underlying reality" in man's mystical illusions, which are basically no more illusory than his conceptions of matter. Without entering upon the domain of metaphysics one need but to turn to such books as Eddington's "Nature of the Physical World" to find this thought repeatedly and significantly expressed. "Substance," he says, "is one of the greatest illusions"; the true relation of the world to man is one "not hinted at in a purely scientific analysis of its content. . . . The physicist now regards his own external world in a way which I can only describe as more mystical, though not less exact and practical, than that which was prescribed some years ago, when it was taken for granted that nothing could be true unless an engineer could make a model of it. . . . That overweening phase, when it was almost necessary to ask the permission of physics to call one's soul one's own, is past."

Our present enjoyment of the achievements of science does not necessarily mean that we are any more "materialistic" than we were before, or that we shall become in the future less and less concerned with spiritual things.

I believe that there is more sympathy, more tenderness, more compassion in the world than ever before,—although, God knows, there is not nearly enough.

None of us can hope to escape his inheritance. It is easier for us Puritans to be just than to be generous, to be brave than to be tolerant, to be (as the Chinese have it) "useful and tense" than "useful and carefree." I am and shall remain a psalm-singing old deacon at heart. So, as my homing instinct led me back to Framingham, I come back to the Puritans again, back with a genuinely increased respect for their many sterling qualities, but with no envy of their manner of life.

I am content to live in 1931. I am glad that I was born in 1875 and not in 1783.

The old white meeting-house still stands unperturbed upon its quiet knoll. Above the noise of the radio and the honk of the motor its bell still calls to prayer, while from the towers of Manhattan the pale shaft of the searchlight rakes the stars—for what?

"And here will I make an end. And if I have done well, and as is fitting the story, it is that which I desired; but if slenderly and meanly, it is that which I could attain unto. And here shall be an end."

·   ·   ·   ·   ·   ·   ·   ·   ·   ·

*"Say not thou, What is the cause that the former days were better than these? For thou dost not inquire wisely concerning this."*

# Index

Abinakis, war with, 33
Abolition movement, 147–48, 193
Abortionists' advertisements, 275
Academy of Music, New York, 211
Adams, Charles Francis, 256
Adams, Henry, condescension of, 8; cited, 182
Adams, James Truslow, cited, 188, 274, 294
Adams, John, 52, 136; newspaper account of his election to Vice-Presidency, 60; not a democrat, 73
Adams, John Quincy, age in 1783, 52; use of flint and steel, 144; second President from Massachusetts, 146; on the slavery question, 147; and petition for separation of the Union, 255
Adams Family, the, by J. T. Adams, 274
Advantage and Necessity of the Christian Religion, by Leland, 98
Advertisements, army deserters, 63–4; abortionists', 275; newspapers and magazines, 308–10, 328, 390
Advertising circulars, 329–30
Age of Reason, influence of, 76
Aiken, Dr., 89
Ainsworth, William Harrison, writings, 231
Alarm clock, 156
Alarm men, 33, 39
Albert of Saxe-Coburg, 215
Alcoholic beverages, see Drinking
Allen, Hepzibah, 78
America As I Found It, by Mrs. M. L. Duncan, 202
American Anti-Slavery Society, 148
American Baptist Magazine and Missionary Intelligencer, 149
American Bible Society, and abolition movement, 148
American Federation of Labor, 300
American Gentlemen's Guide, 222
American Mind in Action, by H. O'Higgins and E. H. Reede, 286
American Museum, The, poem on Connecticut Sabbath, 116–17
American Preceptor, 87
Ames, Fisher, quoted, 72
Anabaptists, see Baptists
Analogy of Religion to the Constitution and the Course of Nature, by Butler, 98

Anderson's Scotch Pills, 82
Anglomania, 315, 318
Animal exhibitions, 54
Annabel Lee, by Poe, 211
Anthony, Susan B., 193, 283
Anthony Comstock—Roundsman of the Lord, by Heywood Broun and Margaret Leech, 284
Anti-bilious cordials, patented, 156
Anti-Catholicism, 188–89, 326–27
Anti-slavery movement, see Abolition movement
Anti-snoring devices, patented, 157
Anti-Trust Act, 404
Appleton, D., & Company, Social Etiquette of New York, 385, 386–87
Appleton's Annual Cyclopædia, 304
Architecture, in the 1850's, 197; in the seventies, 277
Armstrong Insurance Committee of Investigation, 404
Arnold, Benedict, treason of, 136
Asbury, Francis, cited, 109
Astor, Mrs. John Jacob, 399
Astor, Vincent, income tax, 408
Astor, William B., 278
Astor, Mrs. William, 311; and Ward McAllister, 378; and Harry Lehr, 390–91
Astor House, New York City, 197–99
Astrology, belief in, 46
Atheism in the revolutionary period, 76
Atlantic Monthly, The, 211; and Bret Harte, 231; article on H. A. Coit, 340
At the Sign of the Buckthorn, 278
Autocrat of the Breakfast Table, by Holmes, 154
Automobiles, first race, 389; modern use of, 409, 410; value of yearly models questioned, 410–11; distribution and replacement figures, 413; instalment buying, 413; second hand, 415; owned by workingmen, 416–17, 422–23
Azdel, Kenneth, smoking, 207

Baby doctors, 311
Babyhood, first magazine dealing with care of pregnancy, 311
Bacon, Dr. Leonard, installation, 128
Bacon, Francis, 434, 449
Baker, George F., 408, 427
Balls, at Saratoga, 168; Patriarchs' balls, 372, 377